THE MAKING OF A
SCOTTISH
LANDSCAPE

THE MAKING OF A
SCOTTISH LANDSCAPE

MORAY'S REGULAR REVOLUTION

1760–1840

JOHN R. BARRETT

FONTHILL

To uncomplaining friend

Fonthill Media Limited
www.fonthillmedia.com
office@fonthillmedia.com

First published in the United Kingdom 2015

British Library Cataloguing in Publication Data:
A catalogue record for this book is available from the British Library

Typeset in 10pt on 13.5pt Minion Pro
Printed and bound by CPI Group (UK) Ltd, Croydon, CR0 4YY

CONTENTS

ACKNOWLEDGEMENTS

Research into Moray's regular revolution could not have been completed without financial assistance from The Catherine Mackichan Bursary Trust in 2009, a bursary from Aberdeen University in 2010, and a generous Donald Withrington Scholarship in 2010–11. I am heartily grateful for these material affirmations of the value of my research. I also thank my academic supervisors at Aberdeen University—Professor Marjory Harper, Dr Andrew Newby, Dr Elizabeth Macknight, and Dr Michael Brown, who have been generous with advice, constructive criticism and encouragement—steering my research past the shoals of antiquarianism.

I am grateful for the professionalism of archivists, librarians and search room staff, wherever I have found it, nationally and locally. Particular thanks are due to Alexandra Mackenzie-Kopp and Christine Smithers for allowing access to Brodie muniments, and for supporting my studies at Brodie Castle with good humour, tea and sandwiches. And very special thanks are due to my near neighbour, Clare Russell, lady-laird of Ballindalloch and lord lieutenant of Banffshire, for allowing me into her home to consult her family muniments; and also to Mr Oliver Russell at Ballindalloch Castle for his courteous interest in my work, and for the coffee, cake and puddings that sustained it.

I am delighted to acknowledge the inspiration, oral advice and historical insights I have received from staff at the Royal Commission on the Ancient and Historical Monuments of Scotland. I am especially indebted to Tertia Barnet, Ishbel McKinnon, Danny Dutton, Brian Wilkinson, Eve Boyle and Piers Dixon, and to others involved in the Scotland's Rural Past project: for practical instruction imparted with unfailing cheerfulness; and for the camaraderie of a shared enthusiasm for the study of historical landscapes. I thank members of the Strathavon Survey ('The Other SAS')—Archie Bain, Christine Clerk and Alastair Mitchell—who have kindly allowed me to plunder their survey data, and to join them in their exploration of settlements and farmscapes in Inveravon, Kirkmichael, Strathspey and beyond.

I am grateful too to Dave Anderson, Elizabeth Beaton, Alan Braby, Strat Halliday, Fraser Hunter, Richard Oram, Peter Quelch, Tanja Romankiewicz, Sinclair Ross and Jonathan Wordsworth who have generously shared with me their diverse historical and archaeological expertise, and who have offered advice on countless aspects of historical interpretation and fieldwork.

I owe a special debt of gratitude to my colleague, Dr David Iredale, who mentored me in the arcane ways of archives, who first taught me how to be a historian, and who never doubted that I could bring this research to a conclusion. Finally, I thank Christine Clerk for relentless encouragement, wise insights, and maps—and also for patient support in all matters technological.

1

INTRODUCTION

A regular revolution

Moray folk are rural folk, and fiercely proud of the deep-rooted agricultural traditions of their timeless countryside. Moray is a land of fertile arable and lush pasture, where the ploughman's straight furrow is celebrated in bothy ballads as the sublime apogee of the farmer's art. Moray's farmscapes offer vistas of neat fenced fields, hedgerows, stately trees and drystane dykes. Rich grassland feeds fat cattle and heavy-fleeced sheep. Rippling barley ripens for the ever-thirsty stills of Speyside's famous whisky industry. Agricultural landscapes are studded with stone-built cottages and steadings, the rugged complexion of their rubble walls moderated by a pleasing symmetry of aspect. Bleak moors frame and fringe this green idyll: dourly brown for eleven months of the year; blushing purple in August. Long into the Summer, snow clings to the corries and high tops of the distant mountains, making a clean contrast with the dark blocks of pine plantation that clothe the lower hills, and the forests of larch that phase from green to gold to bare sticks with the change of seasons.

This is, of course, a man-made countryside; and Moray is just one modest patch in the runkled quilt of Scotland's many-textured environment. The rural revolution of the later eighteenth century is just one chapter in the unfolding story of the making of the Scottish landscape. Moray's regular revolution is just one of many local variations on a theme that was played in all the regions of Scotland. Moray folk—some of whom may trace their roots in the north-east soil through ten generations—are not unique among Scots in being scarcely able say how or when or why their familiar farmscapes came into being. This lapse of popular memory perhaps testifies to the enormity of the revolution that transformed Moray during the generations around 1800.

In 1746, while the last, doomed, spasm of militant Jacobitism was being crushed at Culloden, a small stream of modernism was already trickling through Moray. From the 1760s onwards a torrent of Improvement engulfed Moray. And all classes of Moray folk were swept up in the flood, swimming together in the current of the regular revolution. Change came through cooperation. Without conflict, distress or dissent, Moray folk embraced an Enlightenment vision of order. Moray farmscapes were rigorously replanned. The countryside was transformed, and so too were hearts and minds. New fieldscapes obliterated all but a shadowy vestige of predecessor countrysides; and the new farming practices that Moray folk enthusiastically embraced became admired traditions, while all that had gone before faded from memory.

Moray defined

The country of Moray perches on the hunched north-east shoulder of Scotland, hunkered between the Cairngorm mountains and the cold North Sea. Moray shrinks demurely from the intrusions of Scotland's summer tourists, who pass quickly through—leaving behind the castle country of Aberdeenshire and looking forward to the romance of the highlands. And Moray coyly evades the notice of historians, who prefer to seek Scotland's story in the more intense experiences and the more accessible or picturesque landscapes of the north and west and south.

The country of Moray is not readily defined—though doubtless the men of Moray always knew (and know) the bounds of their patrimony. Greater Moray—the Province of Moravia—extended from Easter Ross to the River Spey, and traced descent from the Pictish kingdoms of Fiddich and (perhaps) Fortriu. Lesser Moray is found in Elginshire—a shrivelled administrative vestige in the Moravian heartland; a minor county ashamed even to bear the ancient name.

Moray's regular revolution is explored in a wedge of Moravia: defined by the rivers Spey, Findhorn and Avon; extending from the lowlands of the Moray Firth (the laich of Moray) to the Cairngorm plateau. This region forms a core of the political entities (province, earldom, bishopric, sheriffdom, synod, presbytery, county, district) that have been known as Moray.

The twenty-one parishes of the study segment comprise eighteen in Elginshire and three in Banffshire, which, for convenience, are referred to simply as Moray.

The twenty-one parishes come in a range of sizes. Smaller parishes predominate in the laich: the burghal parish of Forres contains just 5,440 acres; though most lowland parishes cover between 6,000 and 10,000 acres, with Urquhart covering 13,661 acres, and Dyke & Moy 15,464 acres. Upland parishes extend from 20,134 acres (Rothes—including part of Dundurcus) to 32,904 acres (Edinkillie). The highland district comprises Aberlour (14,781 acres), Inveravon (49,259 acres) and Kirkmichael (57,558 acres).[1]

The topography of Moray is determined, of course, by geology, which in turn has influenced agricultural practices and economic possibilities. The laich is suited to arable husbandry. Uplands and highlands rising to the south are more suited to pastoral farming, though arable crops will flourish in sheltered locations. Trees will grow throughout the region—except, perhaps, on the thinnest soils of the most exposed tops.

In the laich, postglacial deposits of sand and gravel underlie light soils that are well-drained and easily-worked: sandy in the east, loamy in the west with clay-soil in some areas of Alves, Duffus and Spynie.[2] Modern analysis deems the best laichland soils 'capable of producing a wide range of crops', and soils generally in the laich 'capable of producing consistently high yields of ... cereals and grass ... and/or moderate yields of potatoes, field beans and other vegetables and root crops'.[3] These 'fruitful and rich' soils made lowland Moray 'a pleasant country' even before the improvers set to work.[4] Peat bog and standing water filled several poorly-drained

Location map: Moray in Scotland. (*C. Clerk*)

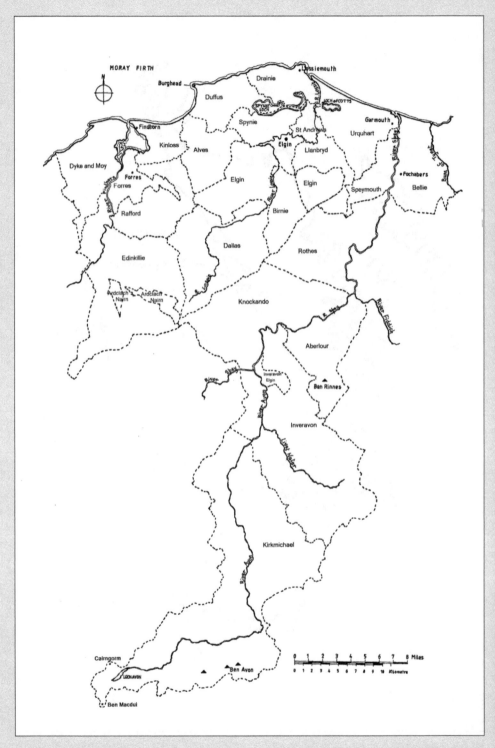

Moray: parish boundaries (*C. Clerk*)

low-lying areas, for example the Mosstowie basin, which was a particular resource during the early-modern period, supplying fuel and grazing for the burgh of Elgin. Loch Spynie formed a significant feature within the laich, with several smaller lochs lying to the east.[5] Drainage and reclamation of these lochs was a signal achievement of Moray improvers.

The Moray coastline is characterised by extensive dune systems in the west. Eastward movement of windblown sand hampered agriculture in coastal parishes throughout the early-modern period. This phenomenon, perhaps exacerbated by turf-cutting and the pulling of bent for thatch, was reported during the later sixteenth century;[6] it overwhelmed the barony of Culbin during the seventeenth century.[7] Further sand blow overspread fertile areas of Duffus parish in the mid-eighteenth century.[8] Reclamation in Duffus was effected on William Young's Inverugie estate and also on Gordonstoun lands from before 1790, continuing to the 1830s—by means of deep trenching,[9] laboriously 'bringing the soil above the sand by the spade'.[10] Moving sands isolated the Roseisle embayment allowing eventual reclamation and improvement of the residual Outlet Loch in Duffus. Shifting sands also periodically obstructed the mouth of the Findhorn, while clogging the harbours of Burghead, Hopeman and Lossiemouth. In the eastern laich, the coast between the Lossie and Speybay is characterised by sterile shingle banks which, from time to time, hamper navigation at the mouth of the Spey. Large areas of Moray's dune and shingle remained relatively unproductive until the close of the nineteenth century.[11] In the parishes of Duffus, Drainie, Alves and Elgin, Permian and Triassic strata provided lime-rich cornstones that could be burned for agricultural use, and high-quality freestone that determined the character of a great rebuilding in the laich.[12]

The laich of Moray was temperate, fertile and intensively cropped during the early-modern period:

> second to none in its healthy climate, in tenderness and goodness of the earth it far exceeds all other of our northern provinces. Such is the temperateness of the air here that, when all surrounding places are stiff with the cruelty of winter, snow does not persist here nor ice cause any great problem for crops or trees ... Nothing grown anywhere in the kingdom, which does not abundantly flourish here ... crops ... in amazing and consistent plenty ... fruits of every kind of tree, grasses, flowers, or vegetables ... winter is scarcely felt ... this whole region is given over to crop and cultivation.[13]

This habit of intensive grain production, and various natural advantages, provided a basis upon which improvers might easily impose their rigorous regimes. The dry climate of the laich was a consequence of its east-coast location in the rain-shadow of the Cairngorms. Modern data show mean average temperatures, sunshine duration and rainfall, in the laich comparable with those in Lothian—with the bonus of longer day-length in the growing season.[14] Historically, the mild laichland climate was the subject of frequent encomiums. Within a general pattern of cool wet weather that reached its nadir between 1570 and 1740— and which did not improve until the mid-nineteenth century—Moray's weather was notably mild.[15] Arthur Johnstoun celebrated the agricultural abundance of the laich in 1642.

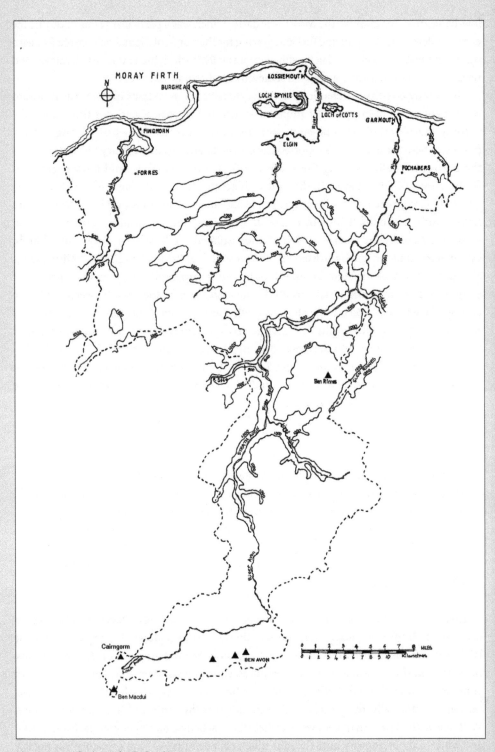

Moray: simplified relief. (*C. Clerk*)

TO ELGIN'S Praise the Ancient BAJAE yields
HESPERIAN-Gardens, and brave TEMPE'S-Fields:
Both Sea and Land doth still Thy needs supplie,
That Fishes, This Cornes doth afford to Thee.
CORCYRA. Aples unto Thee hath sent,
DAMASCUS, Pruns, CERASUS, Cherries lent.
The Bees seem to have left their ATTICK-hyve,
And come to Thee, their Honey-trade to dryve[16]

And a couple of years later Robert Gordon of Straloch particularly mentioned Moray's early harvests:

When autumn has scarcely begun elsewhere, here everything is ripe, cut and conveyed to open threshing areas[17]

Daniel Defoe especially noted:

the harvest in this country ... is not only forward and early, as well as rich and strong; but 'tis more early than Northumberland ... Darbyshire, and even ... the east of Kent ... I have seen the wheat of this country ... brought to market to Edinburgh, before the wheat of Edinburgh is fit to reap.[18]

These writers were, perhaps, observing a particularly benign local manifestation of climatic amelioration, following the late-medieval cold snap. Improving weather may have encouraged landowners in their sanguine expectations regarding the benefits of agricultural improvement. There were setbacks, notably when King William's 'ill years' spread famine across Scotland during the 1690s. This decade of poor weather was a final spasm of a climatic downturn that lasted for two generations from around 1650. The poor weather of this 'little Ice Age' was probably the result of minimal sunspot activity—a recurrent feature of the 300-year solar activity cycle, during which a reduction in ultra-violet radiation resulted in diversion of the jet stream allowing cold easterly airflows to affect British weather.[19] The extent of distress in Scotland during the 1690s was perhaps exacerbated and prolonged by weather effects attributable to volcanic eruptions in Iceland during 1695. There were further Scottish crop failures in 1740, 1756, 1766, 1778 and 1782–3. It has been suggested that the impact of the 1782 harvest failure was also magnified by subsequent poor weather, caused by the eruption of the Laki volcano in Iceland during 1783 and 1784[20]—though no exceptional weather events were reported in Moray at that time. Nor did occasional poor harvests seriously undermine a general belief in the unusual balminess of the laichland climate. Indeed, the laich of Moray perhaps suffered less hardship than other regions when harvests failed. William Leslie asserted (in 1798) that lowland Moray escaped the worst effects even of the 'ill years':

in the famine which prevailed over Scotland for 7 years in the end of the last century ... the
land in Moray was all that time so productive, as to spare considerable quantities of grain;
and ... people came from the county of Aberdeen to buy oat-meal.[21]

The earliness of the Moray harvest was noted by James Donaldson in 1794: the season
began as early as 27 August in 1784; between 1788 and 1792 harvest was gathered consistently
during the first week in September.[22] In 1807 laichland harvest began on 20 August.[23] The
balmy climate was advertised in Moray's first published guidebook, which encouraged
tourists with 'A very old and common saying ... that Moray has 15, and according to others,
that it has 40 days more of summer than most other parts of Scotland'.[24] In the twentieth
century local patriotism took hyperbole a stage further, marketing the western laich as the
'Riviera of the north'.[25] Modern historians have also recognised the mild laichland climate as
a factor in the agricultural prosperity that made the region 'the granary of Scotland'.[26]
    Upland and highland parishes of Moray receive similar sunshine but slightly higher
precipitation to that experienced in the laich. Higher altitude and diminished maritime
influence bring lower temperatures, late frosts and long-lying snow which reduce the
possibilities for arable husbandry.[27] William Leslie noted in 1811:

In the hilly part ... the harvests are generally late, always precarious, and often interrupted:
what remains beyond the end of October is for the most part damaged by rains.[28]

Upland Moray rises from 500–750 feet in Birnie, Rothes, Dallas, to over 900 feet in
Knockando, with hilltops at around 1,500 feet. Underlying geology consists of schists,
overlain with glacial clays, topped off with peat and thin, poorly-drained acidic soils. This
region is now deemed 'suited to rotations which, although primarily based on ley grassland,
include forage crops and cereals ... [though] yields are very variable'.[29] Nonetheless, arable
husbandry flourished in upland parishes during the eighteenth century, particularly on
alluvial sandy-loam or clayey-loam soils on terraces in the river valleys of the Spey, Avon
and Lossie.[30] Moorland in the upland zone was a valuable resource under cooperative
agricultural regimes. This untilled pasturage—redefined as waste—offered a challenge that
progressive landowners found hard to resist; and energetic improvers pushed new settlement
and plantations ever higher onto marginal upland in the second half of the eighteenth
century.
    The highland parishes of Aberlour, Inveravon and Kirkmichael all belonged to Banffshire
(except for the Ballindalloch pocket of Inveravon, which fell into Elginshire)—until
engrossed into the District of Moray in 1975. The three Banffshire parishes consist of land
generally over 1,250 feet, though cut down to below 800 feet in the valleys of the Spey, Livet
and Avon. Summits in Aberlour and Inveravon stand at over 2,000 feet, with Ben Rinnes a
conspicuous mountain at 2,755 feet. In Kirkmichael the foot of Moray rests upon Ben Avon
at 3,843 feet, and extends a toe to the top of Scotland's second-highest peak—Ben Macdui at
4,296 feet.[31] The predominant highland rocks are schists. Quartzites form the Cromdale hills.
Country rocks around Tomintoul include sandstones and Delnabo conglomerate. Intrusive

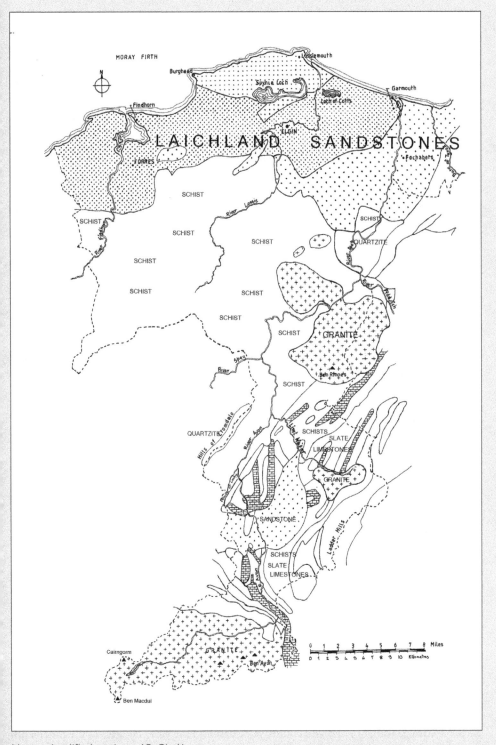

Moray: simplified geology. (*C. Clerk*)

granites erupt as Ben Rinnes, the Convals, and the main Cairngorm plateau, which Moray meets in the south of Kirmichael.[32] Highland geology afforded rubble for building purposes, the supply continually renewed as new land was cleared for pasture, or boulder clays trenched to drain new arable. Glacial clays also provided mortar for mason work as a new vernacular building style emerged around 1760. However, Highland bedrock—especially granite—is both more difficult to work and heavier to carry than laichland sandstone. It was quarried for building only later in the improvement period, and the great rebuilding in highland parishes lagged behind the laich. Slates of several qualities from upland and highland parishes supplied both roofing and flooring, and were also exported into the laich, until the mid-eighteenth century when fashion swung in favour of imported grey slate.[33]

Moray's highland rocks weathered to produce thin, poor, acidic soils. Extensive areas are blanketed with peat. High moorland, however, provided valuable grazing, which, if poor in quality, was generous in extent. Much of this region is now deemed to have only 'limited potential' for arable husbandry.[34] During the eighteenth century, however, there was significant settlement and arable farming in highland parishes, chiefly concentrated on terraces that the rivers Avon and Spey sculpted from the boulder clays that fill their glacially-enlarged valleys. The natural acidity of soils—increased by centuries of intensive cropping—might be ameliorated by application of lime, which occurs in extensive bands in Glenlivet, Glenrinnes, and upper Strathavon.[35] William Leslie, a zealot for the cause of agricultural innovation, writing in 1811 with an improver's optimism, regarded highland peat-soil as offering a challenge that could be overcome by determined intervention:

> its sponginess is corrected by sand, and when manured it is moderately productive ... [though] neither pease nor red clover will vegetate there but on land to which lime has been previously applied.[36]

Highland Moray and the laich were closely connected—even mutually dependent. Lowland cattle grazed Kirkmichael shielings in summer.[37] Highlanders bought grain from arable parishes to supplement their own harvests;[38] processing barley into whisky, which was sold to the laich or southwards out of Moray. Highland timber supplied laichland wrights. Highlanders also travelled frequently into the lowlands: in the performance of long carriages for their masters; to attend courts and burgh markets on their own accounts; or to pay rents at their landlords' girnels. When agrarian change came, it was applied across Moray, by landowners who owned property in both highland and lowland areas.

In common with other lowland regions of Scotland, the English tongue predominated in the laich by the 1680s: the traveller James Allan rarely met a monoglot Gael in journeys between his usual base in Kinloss in the laich and his Munro patrons in Easter Ross.[39] In 1773, Johnson and Boswell did not hear Gaelic until they reached Nairn.[40] Highland Moray lagged behind the laich in adopting English: the Gaelic had died out in Inveravon by 1750, but it clung on in the 'upper part' of Edinkillie; in Kirkmichael it was in terminal decline by 1790.[41] A strong strain of Highland culture persisted into the early decades of the nineteenth century in Kirkmichael, where Roman Catholicism retained its vitality in a society that depended heavily upon cattle and distilling. Upper Strathavon lagged somewhat behind other districts in some aspects of improvement, though this was a consequence of climate and topography rather than cultural or religious predispositions.

Moray enjoyed easy communications with centres of power and learning, readily receiving information and new ideas from the south throughout the early-modern period. Letters were carried and Moray folk moved freely southward by sea and land. During the later seventeenth century Aberdeen was just two day's ride from Elgin—even in January snows.[42] Edinburgh could be reached in a week by road; or by ship from Cromarty, Inverness, Findhorn and Speymouth.

Moray was securely connected to national cultural currents. Around 1690 the newest female fashions were troubling Presbyterian ministers in Inverness within five years of their appearance at court.[43] In the eighteenth century, Moray landowners swam happily in the Enlightenment mainstream. They maintained connections with wider Scottish (and British) society through family networks and in the course of political, religious and legal concerns that drew individuals routinely to Edinburgh and London. Military and commercial adventures, and the grand tour, carried Moray folk of all classes to Europe and the colonies, further broadening provincial horizons.

Movement within the region was seldom a difficulty. Lairds travelled the laich by coach in the 1720s.[44] Droving routes through Strathavon linked highland Moray with Deeside and southern counties. The Great Road pushed through the laich during the 1760s connected Moray firmly to the military road network that focused upon Inverness and Fort George. Thus in 1773 Johnson and Boswell made their whole journey from Edinburgh to Inverness in a chaise. They travelled the forty-five miles from Banff to Forres in a single day, with time to spare for meal breaks, for admiring Elgin cathedral, and for a ten-mile side trip, crossing and recrossing the Findhorn in order to relish Macbeth's blasted heath.[45]

Throughout Moray's varied landscapes, landowners pursued policies of improvement and rationalisation that were in step with national trends. Connections among the leaders of Moray society ensured that there was no delay in the transmission of the latest fashions, including fads for estate rationalisation. Although Moray was geographically detached from central-belt economic and cultural centres, this had never prevented magnates such as the earls of Moray and Huntly from occupying a place at the heart of Scottish politics. Moray folk in general, and laichlanders in particular, had long looked southwards to the Scottish lowlands (rather than north and west to the Gaelic highlands) for political and cultural soul mates. For example, Moray gentlemen, including Brodie, Ballindalloch and Innes, had stiffened the parliamentary cause in the 1640s and preserved Presbyterianism in the 1680s.

Far from being a backwater, Moray was a significant vector in the transmission of improvement ideas. The earl of Findlater, a leading Moray landowner, was a national hero of the improvement movement, closely connected to its source in Lothian. The master of Ballindalloch was intimate with the marquis of Stafford (owner of Sutherland estates); Ballindalloch introduced the marquis to Patrick Sellar and William Young—minor landowners in the laich, but major Moray improvers, whom Stafford employed to improve his Sutherland property.[46] Eric Richards, the modern historian of the Highland Clearances, noticed the laich as the nursery in which Sellar learned the improving catechism; observing that this region of the 'remote north-east shoulder of the Scottish mainland' was 'a favoured land for agricultural experiment ... an outlier of the improvement movement ... more progressive than the rest of Scotland'.[47] The remoteness of Moray is, though, arguably a matter of perspective, and too easily overstated. Meanwhile mobile craftsmen exported Moray's regular rebuilding nationwide. Rothes was a notable dormitory for masons, who 'in the spring set out ... to Glasgow, Edinburgh, Perth, Aberdeen, and sometimes near a hundred of them, to the Hebrides'.[48] The number of masons reported, must be extravagantly inflated, though a significant number of masons was notable among the Rothes population into the 1840s.[49]

The language of improvement

Academic discussion of the improvement era has been hampered by value-laden vocabulary.[50] From the fourteenth century onwards (and perhaps from even earlier) English writers used the word 'improvement' in a specific agricultural sense to describe 'turning land to better account by reclamation of waste or unoccupied land by inclosing and bringing it into cultivation'.[51] From the mid-seventeenth century, however, the word was loaded with increasing burdens of positivity; meanwhile landowners gentrified improvement by embracing the title 'improver' as they began to introduce agricultural innovations on their estates. Thus Walter Blith titled his 1649 agricultural tract *The English Improver*; and in its 1652 sequel, *The English Improver Improved*, Blith asserted: 'all sorts of lands ... will admit of very large improvement'.[52] Meanwhile, improvements (areas of unoccupied and underutilised land or uncultivated pasture, shieling glens, sand-dune, and muir—defined as 'waste'—broken in for arable cultivation) were a commonplace of early-modern Scottish husbandry. The dunged ground where cattle were folded overnight on upland grazings was typically ploughed for a crop of oats, and these shieling improvements might, in due course be colonised as permanent farmsteads or townships. In the lexicon of eighteenth-century innovators, the word 'improvement' expanded its meaning to encompass a sweeping package of agricultural, tenural and social change. At the same time the title 'improver' invested its holder with an aura of impeccable modernity and moral virtue.

By contrast, though, various aspects of improvement acquired negative connotations in popular perception, despite their positive value within the improvers' ethos. 'Enclosure' was sullied by association with the legal enclosure of common field landscapes in England, which led to dispossession and distress among smaller husbandmen. Similarly, the Scottish procedure for 'removal of tenants'—a commonplace aspect of the relationship between heritor and husbandman—acquired a crushing burden of negativity when rebranded as 'clearance' and woven into a mythology of couthy crofters, incendiary factors and invasion by alien *caoraich mora*.

But these linguistic mires can be sidestepped. A more value-neutral terminology is available. The word 'cooperative' happily encompass pre-improvement agriculture and township life. The landscapes and agricultural practices of improvement are more appropriately described as 'regular', in various senses, to suggest both the symmetries of landscapes and buildings, and the rules that governed land tenure and farming.[53] The men who effected the regular revolution may, though, be permitted to retain their assumed distinction as 'improvers'.

Actors and agents

The regular revolution in Moray was inspired and driven forward by the same cast of characters and agents of change that effected both the agricultural transformation of the lowlands and the clearance of the highlands. At the heart of the drama was the land itself and its living inhabitants—'the plants, the animals and the men'.[54] And it was the men of Moray (and a leaven of outsiders) who were the chief agents of change.

In highlands, islands, lowlands—and in Moray too—the leading role was taken by landowners. Proprietors inspired with a spirit of scientific rationalism—the product of Enlightenment thought—embraced the title 'improver'. The improver ethos was manifested as a compulsion to subdue nature: to tame the land and make it work for the proprietor's profit and for the common good. Enlightened gentlemen, unable to thole wilderness or waste, improved and enclosed common grazings, pushed settlement high onto marginal moorland, or clad the offensive nakedness of uncultivated countryside with trees. They regularised farming landscapes, agricultural practice and farming tenure; and they classicised the built environment. These reforms, funded by the landowner from his own resources, in the expectation of handsome returns, ran many estates into serious debt; and some landowners were bankrupted by the expenses of their improving enthusiasm.

The landowner's practical role might be fussily hands-on or distantly strategic. The proprietor might be permanently resident or periodically absent. On estates with resident lairds, the farming landscape that formed the setting for his mansion was also the everyday view from his drawing room window. This might give added zest to improving inclinations: revealed as a tender care for the welfare of the families that populated the vista; or an urge to remove distasteful irregularities that spoiled the prospect. The residence or absence of the proprietor—his physical closeness, patriarchal concern or social distance from his people—might be potent factors affecting the direction and implementation, success or failure, of improvement. Non-residence did not necessarily remove the proprietor from day-to-day affairs. Continual correspondence with servants on the estate allowed the laird to keep firm control of developments at home. Occasionally, the proprietor's absence from the estate might actually accelerate improvement by freeing determined managers on the ground from the interference of capricious, ignorant or over-cautious masters.

Networking among landowners was a key vector in the transmission of regularising ideas, emerging as a notable feature of the Moray model: also, arguably, promoting a competitive spirit among proprietors who each sought to out-improve their fellow improvers. Political and legal business, family connections and social interaction knitted improvers together in a dense web of personal contact and written communication. Networking created opportunities for individual landowners to assimilate practical advice from their peers, and to observe in the field the experiments and achievements of fellow improvers. Personal communications among landowners were supported by wider networks. A burgeoning trade in published tracts gave the authority of the printed word to a gentleman's improving inclinations. Agricultural societies brought likeminded landowners into convivial contact with one another—and also in a neutral social context with the more prosperous and genteel of their tenants farmers. Mobile professionals further knitted the improver network: factors, land surveyors, architects, ploughmen and grieves spread the improvement gospel within the farmer clubs and in their flittings from estate to estate.[55]

Behind every improving laird was a lady, who might be an under-appreciated spur to improvement or a unseen moderating influence; or, indeed, the gentlewoman's experience of household management and domestic accounting might prove valuable transferable skills that could be applied to the wider estate. Occasionally a gentlewoman was pushed to the fore by particular circumstances. Thus Mary Sleigh, the lady of Brodie, managed the estate and effected major reorganisations before 1750—during the minority of the heir.[56] Marital alliances expanded improver networks, and a new wife might contribute new ideas on estate management: for example Henrietta Morduant, daughter of the duke of Peterborough, who introduced English improvement to Moray following her marriage to Alexander Gordon, the Gordon heir, in 1706.[57] At lower social levels too, women exerted significant influence—urging their husbands to embrace new methods, or counselling caution over the pursuit of innovation and the outlay of capital on the farm. Unfortunately, women seldom figure in the documentary record of the regular revolution. Nonetheless, women were a significant element in the agricultural labour force, and might, on occasion engage in sturdy collective bargaining on their own account.[58]

Moray's clergymen exerted only minor influence over the progress of the regular revolution. The general tone of *Statistical Accounts* (written by incumbent clergy during the 1790s, and again in the 1830s and 1840s) show that parish ministers were firmly in the improvers' camp, though only one Moray minister seems to have been especially active as an improving evangelist. William Leslie, the incumbent at St Andrews-Lhanbryd, was both an improving landowner and a professional commentator: author of a *General View of the Agriculture in the Counties of Nairn and Moray* (London, 1811), and of a complement to the *Statistical Account* in his *Survey of the Province of Moray* (Aberdeen, 1798). In general, though, clergymen did not take centre stage in the drama of the regular revolution; and only rarely did a minister deliver a line. The most significant contribution of the kirk and clergy was architectural and self-interested, urging the rebuilding of kirks and manses in the latest regular styles. George Gordon, the Roman Catholic parish priest at Tombae in Kirkmichael, took a uniquely hands-on approach by designing his own chapel: a 'delicate box with ... pretty gothic windows and finials'.[59]

Parish schoolmasters, who were closely linked to the established church, were also usually silent. The schoolmaster of Urquhart was a rare exception, in urging the improvement of husbandmen's housing in 1766.[60]

Tenant farmers were the cast-of-thousands spear-carriers of improvement. And, though regularisation was imposed from above, the tenant farmer was the key to the success or failure of each particular scheme. Tenants might be foot-dragging conservative clogs upon progress, or the heroic foot soldiers of the revolution. The land hungry tenants and sub-tenants of Moray's cooperative townships were willing recruits to the revolutionary cause, finding that their own ambitions could be realised through their lairds' self-interested enthusiasm.

The Moray model—cooperation and consent

It is appropriate here to set the tone for the following chapters, by sketching, with broad strokes, an impression of the regular revolution in Moray. Contrasting before-and-after simplifications of landscape and land use will demonstrate the comprehensive nature of the changes wrought by Moray's improvers during the generations either side of 1800. The gross simplifications of these snapshots are enlarged and resolved into fine detail in the substantive chapters, which discuss Moray's cooperative countryside (chapter 2); and which focus upon the key aspects of its transformation (chapters 3–9).

During the early eighteenth century, almost all of the land of Moray was owned by some thirty or forty major proprietors, including four aristocratic magnates and two royal burghs. The estates of Moray consisted of blocks of territory, partly intermingled with one another in a patchwork of possessions. The landscape of the cooperative countryside within each estate was shaped by the agricultural operations of husbandmen dwelling in hundreds of townships, peppered across the laich and beading the glens and the cultivable terraces of major river valleys in highland parishes.

Each township was an irregular cluster of buxomly-rounded, thatched, turf-and-cruck buildings comprising the dwelling houses and farmsteads of perhaps a dozen families. Around each township lay the arable fields, cultivated with staple crops of pease, barley and oats, that provided a subsistence for township families—and a surplus for sale. The irregular areas of arable were not effectively fenced, though they might be defined by turf-and-stone walls. Arable fields were divided internally into strips: each measuring perhaps an acre in extent, and separated one from another by untilled baulks. Each curving strip was cultivated as, perhaps, half-a-dozen humpbacked ridges. Strips, baulks and ridges gave the countryside the appearance of a candlewick bedspread draped over the lumpy topography of the cultivated landscape.

The strips were allocated among the township's several husbandmen. Each possessor in each of the township's common fields was obliged to cooperate with neighbours: planting and harvesting the same crops at the same time; sharing the work of ploughing and harrowing. Each husbandman, however, reaped his own harvest and prospered or starved by the produce of his possession. After harvest, township cattle were allowed to graze promiscuously on the arable, feeding on the stubble and the green herbage that grew on the baulks and germinated below the grain crop. Cooperation also extended to communal resources such as mills: thus tenants were obliged by estate custom to have their grain ground at a particular mill (thirlage)—and to pay for the service. Thus the township community contributed to the upkeep of the machinery.

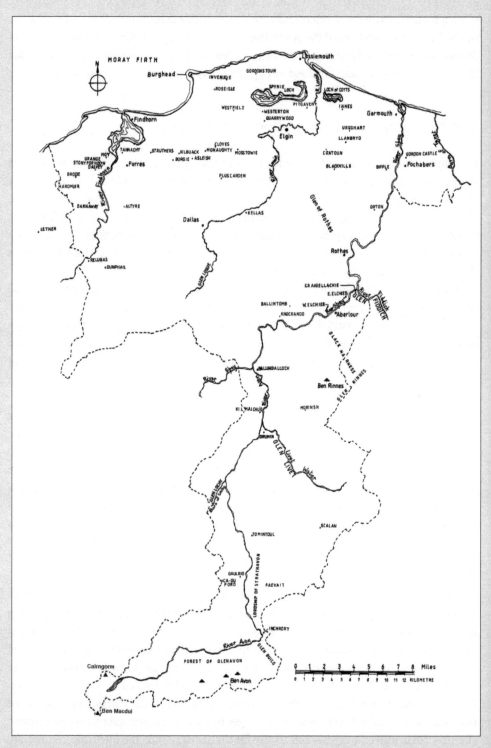

Moray: principal estates and districts. (*C. Clerk*)

A turf head-dyke separated arable from common pasture. This untilled land was a communal resource, perhaps shared without division by several adjacent townships. Pasture ground provided heather and bent for thatch, turf for building work, and peat for fuel. Especially, though, land beyond the head-dyke provided grazing for sheep, goats, horses and cattle. The beasts were, typically driven out and herded by day, then brought home to be folded or housed at night.

The landowner cultivated a small proportion of the estate as a home farm (mains) for his own subsistence and profit. The remainder of the estate was farmed out by the laird to tenants. Each township was possessed by, perhaps, two or three tenants who paid rent to the landowner. Tenancies were granted and continued at the will of the laird; written leases and secure tenure was not usual. Rents were largely paid in kind—chiefly in barley and oatmeal. Grain paid as rent was gathered into the laird's girnel (rent-house) from where it was sold, usually for export to cities in the south of Scotland, to England, or even to the continent of Europe. A small number of tenants paid money rents. All tenants also owed lesser dues, including labour on the laird's land and a hen for each smoking chimney in the township.

Each tenant cultivated a proportion of his farm on his own account, and sublet the remainder to sub-tenants who paid for their holdings in money, in kind and in labour. Landless cottars in the township—occupying just a house and yard—paid for their possessions by working for tenants and sub-tenants, or with money earned by following a trade. Township folk earned money from sales of surplus produce to neighbours or in burgh markets; also from sales of cattle to drovers, and from rural manufactures including textiles (woollens and linen), wright work, smith work and whisky.

All timber on the estate belonged to the laird, though this semi-natural woodland was managed as a communal resource, protected from over-exploitation by legislation, local customs and vigilant foresters. Township folk might be allowed to graze their horses and cattle among mature trees; also to gather fallen wood and cut leafy branches for fodder. Large timber for building work had to be purchased. Otherwise structural timbers were supplied by the laird on the understanding that they might be repossessed (or value claimed) when the husbandman died moved away.

The regular revolution of the period 1760–1840 replaced the communality and sustainability of the township economy with regulation, individualism and capitalistic exploitation; redesigning the countryside to accommodate the reformed ethic of 'improvement'. Within each estate, townships were removed and the land reallocated as discrete farms in a range of sizes. Each farm was designed to be a self-supporting commercial enterprise, without sub-tenants and without sharing resources with neighbours. The farm was possessed and worked by a single tenant farmer—assisted, perhaps, by paid labourers. The farmer paid a money rent, and was secure in his tenancy under a written, nineteen-year lease. The farmer was solely responsible for the cultivation of his arable fields, the care of his cattle, and the marketing of the produce of the farm.

There was an expansion in arable acreage as under-utilised land was brought into cultivation. Upland moor was colonised and common pasture broken in as small possessions by 'settlers'. Sand-covered land in the laich of Moray was reclaimed for arable cropping. Bogs and lochs were drained. Land-hungry husbandmen, displaced by the removal of townships, clamoured for tenancy of the new farms, bidding up rents. Those who did not become farmers found work as agricultural labourers, employed under the labour-intensive regimes of the new agriculture; perhaps inhabiting cottages on the new farms.

Each improved farm was an independent unit, separated from its neighbours by walls and fences. Within the farm, rectangular fields were planned out and enclosed by straight stock proof walls, fences and hedgerows; accessed by straight new roads. This regular fieldscape was ploughed in straight ridges. Cultivation regimes were specified in leases that obliged farmers to adopt regular rotations of grain crops, sown grasses, and roots. New and heavier breeds of cattle and sheep grazed the enclosed fields. The beasts were kept on the farm all day long and all year round; the loss of common grazings was made up for with hay and turnips grown on the farm. A new range of farm machinery was introduced using technologies of the wider industrial revolution. The equipment included iron ploughs and harrows; carts with iron axles; and threshing machines driven by water-wheels or horses. Large workhorses were bred to provide power to work the new equipment.

Moray's landowners were swept up in the national mania for forestry, planting uncultivated land with hardwood trees, and especially with blocks of Scots pine and larch. The new forests were the lairds' own private commercial enterprises. Plantation timber was sold to farmers for fencing their enclosed fields, and also harvested for ship-building and for export. Straight sawn softwood also supplied the rafters, joists and deals required for new styles of domestic, agricultural and public buildings.

The regular revolution involved a great rebuilding in both town and country. Turf-and-cruck township architecture was replaced by new farmhouses with masonry walls, sharply-square corners, gable-end flues and symmetrical façades beneath rafter roofs covered with slate or thatch. Classical symmetry also replaced irregular vernacular in burgh dwellings. Farm buildings were arranged in rigid rectangular patterns, with the farm square as the ideal plan. Gentlemen's tower houses were replaced with convenient, symmetrical neoclassical mansions. Kirks were rebuilt—and other public buildings designed—in a regular neoclassical style. Landowners erected new villages to rehouse displaced township families, and to serve as commercial and industrial centres that would retain population and increase economic activity within their estates. These new settlements too were designed to a neoclassical template with straight streets and central squares and rigid building regulations.

This, in short, was Moray's regular revolution. It was a bloodless revolution—a consensual revolution—achieved without significant distress. Social dislocation was managed so that there was no popular protest or resistance.

Consent and discontent

Several sub-plots in the drama of Moray's regular revolution focus upon human responses to change. Resistance to innovation was insignificant in the story of improvement in Moray. This contrasts with the determined opposition to improvement in other regions, for example in Easter Ross and Sutherland. While the land might sulkily resist improvement, there was no large body of conservative Moray peasants obstructing the course of change—though the regular revolution was said to be hampered by 'want of education' among smaller tenants in Banffshire.[61] Human resistance to change, implemented under different templates in different regions of Scotland, is discussed below. In the north-east tenants, on the whole, embraced innovation, and their progressive spirit was recognised as early as 1794:

> however slow the progress of improvements may be ... it is not to be attributed to the ignorance or obstinacy of the people, nor to the bigoted prejudices in favour of old customs ... I know of no bigotry so great as that of those, who ... still ... exclaim against the obstinacy of country people.[62]

Moray tenants and sub-tenants, meanwhile, actively cooperated with—or passively consented to—sweeping changes in agricultural practice and rural settlement patterns; and many were enthusiastically willing to share with their landlords the title 'improver'. The *Statistical Accounts* confirm this, characterising Moray husbandmen as 'cheerful, though poor', 'satisfied with their condition', 'peaceable', 'not querulous, but peaceable and well disposed', and 'well affected to the present king and constitution'.[63] When protests did arise, they were not driven by political principle or deep social trends.[64] Small-scale resistance to change that did occur from time to time, stemmed rather from particular circumstances, exacerbated by the ordinary resentments, suspicions and jealousies that might be endemic in any close-knit community, whether among township tenants or between neighbouring heritors.

The absence of popular resistance does not mean that the lower orders in Moray were supine or voiceless. Several historians have demonstrated that Scottish rural communities in general were both willing and able to riot when provoked.[65] In Galloway, innovators such as Viscount Kenmuir reorganised farms and enclosed grazings in a process that involved eviction of township husbandmen. Enterprising individuals recognised this as an opportunity, and emigrated to America. Those who remained resisted the improvements by demolishing the dykes that divided their common grazings. These 'Levellers', actuated in part by the rebellious quasi-democratic Covenanting tradition, were suppressed (like their Cameronian forebears) by the military, and many were transported.[66] The Galloway enclosures, however, were a particular and local development of extensive parks (covering two or three square miles each) for fattening cattle destined for the English market. The Levellers' revolt was also unique to Galloway, and the only coherent popular resistance to improvement in lowland Scotland.[67] Taken as a whole, there was little in the lowland Scottish experience that could be regarded as a rural rebellion equivalent to the machine-breaking, cattle-maiming and Captain Swing riots that accompanied agrarian change in England.[68] Moray's labouring folk, of course, might riot periodically. Drunken brawls spilled out into the streets of the burghs. Contentious elections sparked partisan violence. Food shortages and high prices were loudly protested—sometimes with the support of cudgels. The men of Moray did not, however, rise up against the march of improvement.

A notable sub-theme in *A Regular Revolution* is the role of tenant farmers in forcing the pace of change. Land-hunger drove husbandmen into the improvers' camp. In their eagerness for farms, prospective tenants accepted whatever improving clauses the proprietor might insert into leases; meanwhile, aggressive bidding for farms pushed up rents. New possessions on marginal land—reclaimed from bog or moor—were enthusiastically taken up, as sub-tenants seized opportunities to join the farmer class.[69] The tenant class, before, during and after the regular revolution, was far from a docile pawn in the landowners' schemes. Tenants exhibited considerable spirit, and were not backward in expressing opinions to the factor, if not to the laird.

A significant consequence of the improvement process, in Moray as elsewhere, was the erasure of sub-tenants from the social landscape. Technically this was a clearance; but, arguably, when the dust settled, little real change had occurred. The several varieties of sub-tenants, servants and cottars re-emerged, converted into new classes of settler, village craftsman and agricultural labourer. This was accomplished by means that ensured the retention of population in the parish, while the individuals concerned did not object or, indeed, may scarcely have noticed the change.

It is possible, in Moray at least, to advance a revisionist view—of a consensual revolution that contrasts with the gloomy conventional commonplace of clearance as a dismal draconian dispossession of powerless peasants.[70] Arguably, the conversion of cottars into agricultural labourers liberated the rural poor from the tyrannies of township life. As feed servants working for money wages the rural labourer was freed from dependence upon the goodwill of tenant farmers for access to land and to work that might be remunerated only with a dole of oatmeal. Improvement might, furthermore, give the dispossessed cottar a regularly-built house in a new village, where his tenancy was guaranteed by a written lease; meanwhile access to lotted land provided a subsistence, or even a stepping-stone to the farmer class. The condition of Moray's displaced cottars may, indeed, have been enhanced by their transformation into wage labourers. Improvers' grand schemes for transforming Moray landscapes—especially by tree-planting, drainage and reclamation—demanded sizeable gangs of labourers working for money wages. The large number of simultaneous schemes may have resulted in periodic labour shortages, driving up wages which rose ahead of prices during the period 1760–1840.[71] Meanwhile, workers might pick and choose from among the various projects and employment opportunities on offer. Some deserted Moray's agricultural improvements for more lucrative work elsewhere: for example, large-scale infrastructure projects such as road-building for turnpike trusts or navvying on the Caledonian canal.[72] As large numbers of workers came together, especially on time-sensitive projects such as tree-planting, they spontaneously—without wider social or political agendas or outside agitation—embraced opportunities for collective bargaining and industrial action. Only a few episodes are explicitly documented in estate archives, though the handful of recorded strikes and negotiations may be representative of a very significant, if under-documented, strand in the improvement narrative.[73]

Rising money wages were expended on personal comforts, stimulating further economic activity. Labouring people and tenant farmers in Dyke & Moy in the 1790s were said to be 'better fed and clothed, and have greater variety of convenient furniture, than they had 40 years ago ... the use of tea makes rather an alarming progress'.[74] In Speymouth, although men still wore the traditional bonnet, it was said: 'A watch is no uncommon thing among the servants'.[75] In 1798 William Leslie lamented the rising cost and decreasing deference of labour—trends exacerbated by the falling value of money and stagnating corn prices:

> About 40 years ago, the average price of a boll of grain was 12s. and the yearly wages of a ploughman about L.2: at present, though less industrious and more expensively maintained, his wages have risen about 300 per cent. and the value of grain not quite 30 ... Besides the excess in the expence of farm servants, another evil almost universally complained of, is their insolence, idleness, and wastefulness.[76]

Highland variations on this theme were developed by the minister of Kirkmichael:

> [farmers] feel ... the condition of servants, is more eligible than that of their masters ... wages immoderately high, inspire ... pride, insolence and indifference ... Nice in their choice of food ... They must sleep in the morning as long, and go to bed at night as soon, as their pleasure dictates. Expostulations are opposed by rudeness.[77]

Regularisation transformed the relationship between the husbandman and his land. Rectilinear fieldscapes were imposed upon the irregularities of the landscape as farmers learned to dominate the inconveniences of the natural world with which they had formerly cooperated and compromised. Instead of valuing the natural resources offered by uncultivated land (peat for fuel, feal for building, bent for thatch) all land was regarded as improvable, even when that involved the expense of clearing rocks, draining bogs, and trenching dunes. Cooperative townships, that grew naturally from the landscape, built with sustainable natural materials, were replaced with starkly angular dwellings and farmsteads whose lime-harling, terracotta chimneys and ironwork announced that rural life had been embraced into the industrialising economy. Relationships between landlords and tenants, and between tenants and labourers, came to be represented solely by cash transactions. The produce of farms, which had provided a subsistence for those who occupied the land (with a surplus for rent and sale) became simply a commodity for the market. Money earned through the sale of the crop was used to purchase exotic and industrial products such as the coal, tea, sugar, cotton cloth, ironmongery and bone meal, that supplanted locally-produced peat, ale, whisky, linen, plaiding, wright work, seaware and dung.

The exact boundaries of the region within which the consensual Moray model applied are not clearly established. Probably, uncontested regularisation was achieved throughout the Moray Firth lowlands, in areas with climates and topographies similar to those of the Moray heartland. The consensual region certainly extends west into Nairnshire and east of the Spey into Banffshire, and perhaps also into Aberdeenshire. These are territories into which key Moray improvers—including the earls of Moray, Fife and Findlater, and the dukes of Gordon and their numerous Gordon relatives—also extended their influence. Elsewhere in Scotland, by contrast, regularisation was a vexatious process. Some schemes ended in failure.[78] Nor did proximity to Moray, or the accident of falling under the ownership or influence of a Moray landlord, mean that regularisation would necessarily be accomplished in a peaceable consensual manner.

Highland, island and lowland templates—clearance and distress

The quiet consensuality of Moray's regular revolution contrasts with notorious episodes of improvement in the highlands and islands—which resulted in widespread hardship and legacies of bitter resentment. The irony of several highland improvements is that they were pushed through with brutal insouciance by the very men whose improving activities were (and are) applauded in Moray.

The improvement of Barra was effected by the same Colonel John Gordon of Cluny who is honoured as a modernising benefactor for his improvements in Rathven in western Banffshire. In the Hebrides, though, Cluny is even today despised for implementing an improvement scheme that 'had all the appearance of an atrocity arising ... from the wanton cruelty of a millionaire landlord'.[79]

In Barra—as elsewhere in the Hebrides—improvement blended a response to increasing population with a desire to increase rental income. Improvement schemes dismantled communal townships by relocating township husbandmen to discrete crofts, typically near the coast, where each crofter supplemented the bare subsistence won from a small enclosed arable field (and some grazing and peat cutting on nearby moorland) with industrial activities such as fishing and kelp burning.[80] However, the land allocated as crofts was not always suitable for cultivating grain, nor sufficient to provide a subsistence—and crofters increasingly depended on potatoes. Then, after 1815, kelping collapsed, and the limited produce of the croft proved insufficient to support the crofter families and pay rents. Nonetheless, the Barra factor, Alexander Stewart, continued transplanting inland township folk to coastal crofts, in a scheme subsequently discussed with another villain of the clearance legend—Patrick Sellar. By the 1830s Barra was under such stress, that its Macneill laird, teetering on the brink of bankruptcy, contemplated transporting the surplus two-thirds of Barra families to Canada to resolve the twin problems of poverty and over-population.[81]

Gordon of Cluny bought Barra in 1841. He invested many thousands of pounds in his island estates, while continuing his predecessor's policy of creating commercial farms in the interior and crofting communities on the coast. In 1847 the potato crop failed and famine followed. Gordon's reputation for miserliness was confirmed as he failed to provide the food relief that his starving tenants believed should have been forthcoming. Gordon, indeed, declared his opinion that the tenants' distress was the result of their own indolence. Gordon's final solution for Barra was eviction and forced emigration. The brutality with which this policy was implemented, and the misery that resulted were the subject of lurid press reports and national outcry as destitute and starving Barra emigrants were stranded on the quaysides or wandered begging through the streets of Glasgow, Edinburgh, Inverness and Quebec.[82]

Mainland improvement schemes in the highlands have left similar legacies of resentment; and partisan commentators coined the disparaging new usage 'clearance'—particularly to characterise Sutherland estate improvements of the early nineteenth century.[83] In part, popular prejudice was (and indeed still is) fuelled by eloquent descriptions and denunciations by Donald Macleod and Alexander Mackenzie, who, writing a generation after the event, compared the marquis of Stafford's improvements with the Cawnpore massacre and the worst horrors of slavery; though, conversely, Harriet Beecher Stowe (who knew a thing or two about real slavery) regarded the Sutherland clearances as 'an almost sublime instance of the benevolent employment of superior wealth and power in shortening the struggles of civilisation'.[84] Polarisation of opinion continues in the twenty-first century: the Sutherland clearances were recently described as 'the most emotive episode in modern Highland history, indeed in the whole of modern Scottish history'.[85]

Key players in the Sutherland drama were a native landowner, the countess of Sutherland, and her husband, the marquis of Stafford, an English industrialist. To implement their improving schemes these aristocratic proprietors employed two exemplary improvers from the laich of Moray: a lawyer and experienced factor, Patrick Sellar of Westfield; and his neighbour William Young of Inverugie—with whom the countess was unashamedly entranced. Writing in 1810 she declared:

> Mr Young, a grave intelligent young man ... I wish you could see the farms he has reclaimed from Deserts—the fishing village [Hopeman] in which he has settled the Inhabitants ... the admirable neatness of the Cottages and of his own house.[86]

Even before this cast of characters was assembled, the main plot lines had been established. The improving template for highland estates required removal of cooperative townships and relocation of their inhabitants to make room for large-scale sheep farms. This model was inaugurated in the 1760s in Easter Ross, spreading thence into Sutherland. It seems that township folk in the highlands were more deeply rooted in their land—and more set in their ways—than their socially and geographically mobile contemporaries in Moray. In 1792, *Bliadhna Nan Caorach* ('the year of the sheep') Easter Ross township folk rose up in protest and drove the invading flocks of Cheviot sheep from Strath Oykel, Strathcarron and Strath Rusdale. This action established a tradition of resistance to change.

The marquis of Stafford arrived in Sutherland as an explorer in a foreign land. To the English capitalist Sutherland seemed 'quite a wild corner inhabited by an infinite multitude roaming at large ... despising all barriers and all regulations, and firmly believing in witchcraft'.[87] Sellar and Young, Stafford's improving apparatchiks also arrived in Sutherland as immigrants and colonial innovators. They regarded Sutherland husbandmen with 'the same impatient contempt their grandsons were later to feel toward African and Indian'.[88] It is a measure, perhaps, of the extent to which the regular revolution had progressed in Moray, that Sellar could, in 1809, regard Sutherland—which was just a short boat ride from Burghead—as a '*terra incognita*', inhabited by a 'barely civilised' primitive people[89] bogged down in a culture that was a century behind that of his native Morayshire.[90] Other contemporaries offered a more kindly view of the highlanders:

> Never were there a happier or more contented people, or a people more strongly attached to the soil ... nor one who does not look back on this period of comfort and enjoyment with sad and hopeless regret.

Furthermore:

> These people, blameless in every respect, save their poverty and ignorance of modern agriculture, could not believe that such harsh measures proceeded from their honoured superiors ... The whole was attributed to their acting agents.[91]

The plan for Sutherland required the extinction of cooperative townships; the relocation of township families to new possessions, usually planned as crofts, chiefly on the coast; the creation of large sheep farms in the interior; and the erection of new towns (including Helmsdale and Brora) where displaced people would find employment in new industries including fishing. The intention was laudable enough: to remedy periodic famine (caused, it was thought, by inefficient agriculture and overpopulation) while also preventing loss of human resources through emigration; and to promote economic development, which would ultimately benefit every inhabitant of the estate.

In the event, improvement was pushed through with unsympathetic determination and at breakneck speed as the proprietors sought to catch up with the rest of the nation's improvers. The result was 'muddle and confusion'.[92] Schemes to resettle people were botched, with families ordered to flit from communal townships before the new lots were ready for their resettlement.[93] Patrick Sellar in particular acted with imperious insouciance when evicting and relocating populations—most notoriously in Strathnaver where he had a personal interest in the clearance of land upon which he had taken a lease for a sheep farm. He subsequently admitted to:

> too much keenness of temper to be so useful in my office as I ought ... A man less anxious might better suit the situation and temper of the people.[94]

Furthermore, Sellar failed to appreciate or accommodate the key cultural differences that distinguished Sutherland from Moray. Sutherlanders did not have the mobile habits of Moray husbandmen. Sutherlanders indeed, seem to have had no appreciation of the meaning of a summons of removal. When served with the writ they simply ignored it and stayed put, naively trusting that their matriarchal landlady would never allow eviction of her people. But the age of the patriarchal landlord was already over; and Sellar, as the agent of the new capitalist proprietor—and as the incoming capitalist tenant—saw no alternative but to remove impediments to progress by force. The Strathnaver townships had been decerned to remove by Whitsun 1814. The people were still in occupation a month later when Sellar arrived with four officers and twenty men. Those people who did not willingly vacate their dwellings were physically expelled. To prevent the people returning their houses were burned. A woman died. Sellar was indicted. And though he was exonerated by a jury of his peers, Patrick Sellar was condemned by popular opinion in Sutherland, and his name was written indelibly into the annals of turpitude.[95]

At almost every stage the Sutherland improvements were bedevilled by inept implementation. This exacerbated a sense of injustice among native husbandmen, who resented and resisted the 'English devils' acting for the proprietors—under the erroneous belief that they enjoyed an inalienable tenure of the land they cultivated. A key difference between the Sutherland clearances and the consensual Moray model was the intrusion of outsiders—including Stafford, Sellar, Young, and the Cheviot sheep. Indeed, significant racial prejudice (on both sides) coloured interactions between Gaelic natives and immigrant improvers. Furthermore, the Sutherland improvements were pushed through in a single decade while Moray's regular revolution spread in many different schemes, tailored to local circumstances by resident landowners, and implemented over the extended period of two generations. Moray's improvement was a success. Sutherland's, by contrast, 'failed as a permanent solution to the problems of the county'. Later in the nineteenth century Sutherland experienced the very things that the clearances had been intended to prevent: famine swept the county in the 1840s, followed by mass emigration.[96]

The modern historian of the highland clearances concedes also that 'Clearances of a sort occurred in the Lowlands'.[97] Professor Tom Devine has assumed a leading role in the study of rural change in the lowlands, with a particular study of the counties of Lanark, Ayr, Fife and Angus;[98] modestly declaring 'the Lowland Clearances still await their historian'.[99] The term 'lowland clearances' was adopted as the seductive title for an assemblage of academic opinion collected by P. Aitchison and A. Cassell, which, however, only occasionally strays into Moray.[100] Some years before these studies were published, the regular revolution in Moray was described as 'lowland clearances';[101] though this rashly emotive characterisation is now abandoned. The term 'lowland clearances', however, is gaining currency, if only as a convenient shorthand to describe developments in southern and central Scotland that might have been positively characterised in a previous generation as 'the agricultural revolution'.

Moray shared in the general lowland experience of improvement observable in central Scotland and in Fife, Angus and lowland Perthshire. The central lowlands, however, differ from Moray insofar as 'lowland lairds had already distanced themselves from common folk by 1760 ... For many great lords Scotland became less of a home than a holiday spot'.[102] Many Moray landowners also were absent for long periods—entrusting the day-to-day running of their estates to factors; nonetheless, most maintained a close connection with their properties, who took some care to remain personally accessible to their people.

The distance between proprietors and people on estates in the Scottish lowlands was exacerbated as landowners came 'to regard their lands as sources of income rather than as the basis of personal authority and power'[103]—as 'commercial criteria became supreme'.[104] To maximise the productivity of their estates, landowners formalised relations with husbandmen, and replanned agricultural landscapes. Cooperative townships were replaced with single-tenant farms: large farms, covering several hundred acres were preferred wherever feasible. The new farms were possessed under written leases that specified regular rotations involving fallowing and new-fangled crops such as turnips and clover. Meanwhile under-utilised land, comprising the communal grazings and other resources of the township economy were improved for arable cropping or forestry. Much of the cost of improvement was borne by the landowner, who might (or might not) manage the pace of change to avoid unduly alienating resident populations.[105] Thus far, improvement in lowland Scotland mirrors Moray's regular revolution as 'peasant society ... was replaced by a new capitalist order'—in which the sometime peasant became the new commercial farmer.[106]

Debate among historians concerns the social impacts of these changes: whether they can bear characterisation as 'lowland clearances'; whether change caused social dislocation, distress and/or depopulation; and whether there was popular resistance to change. It has been argued that rural changes 'were more fundamental and thorough in the south and east' than in the highlands—with lowland small tenants experiencing 'considerable loss of land'.[107] Indeed, the cottar and sub-tenant class that was dispossessed by lowland improvement may have formed the most numerous social group in the lowland cooperative countryside.[108] Clearance of cottars and small sub-tenants from estates in south and central Scotland resulted in a 'catastrophic haemorrhage of population'.[109] In Ayrshire, Lanarkshire and Angus 'the clearance of cottars represented a remarkable change in the very structure of rural society' leading to 'the emergence of a predominantly landless labour force', while migration and settlement removal extinguished an 'entire tier of the social order'.[110] This was, though, a slow-motion disaster, its impact softened because it took place over a protracted timescale of up to 150 years.[111] Nonetheless, T. C. Smout uncovered evidence of 'tremendous suffering and problems and resentments' among dispossessed cottars and sub-tenants.[112] The minister of Kilmany, Fife, referred to the 'annihilation of the little cottagers'; and his colleague at Marrikie, Angus, described how cottagers there had been 'exterminated'.[113] However, despite this strong language, describing a significant social change, rural lowlanders did not nurture any lasting memory of lost rights or a persistent resentment of the kind that is associated with much highland and island improvement; nor is there any focused demonization of the lowland improvers.

Professor Tom Devine observed that 'protest in the Lowlands was muted and rare'. However he also identified notable resistance to the division of commonties: at Smailhome, Roxburghshire in the 1730s; and at Aberlady, East Lothian in 1786; and elsewhere, passive resistance obstructed or temporarily thwarted some improvement plans.[114] C. Whatley also identified widespread discontent among common folk, bubbling up as threats against the persons and property of improving gentlemen. Lowland landlords appreciated the risks, and so were careful to manage change and 'not to allow boils to fester let alone erupt'.[115] This, after all, was the age of the American and French revolutions. Landowners provided housing in new villages for dispossessed cottagers. And they exploited the calming and coercive power of education, the kirk, charity and paternalism to prevent dispossession from resulting in distress that might fuel disaffection.[116] Estate improvement opened up employment opportunities both on the new farms and in new rural villages. Meanwhile, 'by 1800 ... Scotland had already become one of the five most urbanised societies in Western Europe';[117] and the proximity of Edinburgh and growing manufacturing towns to the improved lowlands, meant that the landless and the workless had alternative options and opportunities when their township world was dismantled.[118]

Outward migration was the safety-valve that relieved social pressures, ensuring there was no significant unemployed rural underclass that might become radicalised into violent rebellion. However, landowners could not prevent low-level discontent from boiling over during periods of food shortage, or when a rise in prices was feared. Thus there were significant episodes during the improvement period when lowland Scotland was 'on fire with meal rioting'.[119] And it is arguable—though by no means proven—that disaffection engendered by lowland clearances underlies subsequent urban radicalism. The personal disaffection of dispossessed cottars, and the inherited discontent of their children may have erupted at last in radical agitation for political reform, Chartism and trade unionism. This, though, is mere speculation. As regards the question of whether there was vigorous opposition to the lowland clearances in southern and eastern Scotland, C. Whatley declared 'the changes brought about by the extraordinarily rapid process of modernisation of Scottish society ... were received much less calmly than has been suggested hitherto'[120]—though subsequently moderating his opinion to an equivocal, 'not proven'.[121] But even this stands in sharp contrast with the Moray experience of revolution by general consent and popular complicity.

2

A COOPERATIVE COUNTRYSIDE

A system so atrocious

Scottish society was predominantly rural until the nineteenth century. The twenty-one parishes of Moray comprised something less than 30,000 souls in the mid-eighteenth century.[1] At least eighty per cent of these Moray folk dwelt in rural townships where most were employed in cultivating the soil. The lives and livelihoods of those who were not husbandmen (including rural craftsmen) were nonetheless closely connected to the agricultural activities of their neighbours. Most of the several hundred inhabitants of the towns of Garmouth and Fochabers were involved in agriculture. And even the 5,000 or 6,000 folk who lived in Moray's two royal burghs, cultivated some land, or depended upon those who did. For example, Elgin's textile manufacturers and leather-workers processed raw materials supplied by rural husbandmen; while seventy wrights supplied ploughs and carts across a broad hinterland. Forres entrepreneurs employed 'a considerable number' of women in rural townships to spin flax (either grown in Moray or imported from the Netherlands) in a domestic industry that brought a cash income to township families, and linked rural folk to the wider Scottish economy.[2] Only the maritime families (perhaps 200 households) of Burghead and Findhorn—with a further handful of fishermen at Stotfield, Maviston, Garmouth and Lossiemouth—had no immediate connection with agriculture.[3]

Henry Grey Graham, writing in the 1890s, voiced, with scarcely a qualification—and certainly without irony—a bleak impression pre-improvement agriculture. Graham characterised the cooperative countryside as the product of a 'system so atrocious' that the benighted Scottish people were reduced to helpless superstition within a system that 'seemed rather to dignify dirt and to consecrate laziness'.[4] This view, taken from the far end of the regular revolution, was observed through the distorting lens of standards set by several generations of improvers. From this perspective, whatever had preceded the regular revolution could never seem anything but barbarous, inefficient, and ignorant, without even the redeeming gloss of couthy tradition.

Modern analysis moderates Graham's censorious invective, adopting a more 'sympathetic and positive' understanding, liberated from the inherited opinions of 'improving writers ...

[who] had a vested interest in demonstrating the weaknesses of the old order and praising the excellence of the new'.[5] However, a worthy attempt to 'rehabilitate the rural economy in the era before improvement ... to understand the old system within its own terms' remained encumbered with value-heavy linguistic baggage, for example contrasting 'the old order' with 'dynamic improvement'.

The subtle complexity of cooperative agriculture was recognised in the 1880s, by the duke of Argyll, who as the descendant of a leading improver, was probably no less unbiased than other commentators:

> It was a system of which all the parts so hung together, and which as a whole was so rooted in all the routine habits of daily and yearly life, that not one stone of it could be touched without the whole structure tumbling. Any change involved a total change in the prospects and in the life of every family concerned.[6]

However, cooperation, communality and self-sufficiency were old-fashioned virtues underpinned by tradition, which clashed with the ethos of scientific capitalistic individuality that germinated in the Enlightenment and blossomed in the Victorian age.[7] The complexities of the cooperative countryside were managed through compromises and negotiations, local regulations and a slew of legislation.[8] Land use and land tenure under cooperative regimes involved constant accommodations: with the inconvenient irregularities and capriciously distributed resources of the physical environment; and also with the interests of the many individuals who depended upon the land for a living. From an improver's perspective this was a Bad Thing:

> the quarrels and the misunderstandings ... were violent and incessant ... no operation could begin without mutual help with horses, oxen, and men, and common arrangements as to crops, they were all required to be agreed.[9]

From another viewpoint, communality and cooperation underpinned a virtuous close-knit society in which, 'All the intercourse of life was carried on by a kind of tacit agreement and interchange of good offices'.[10] Paul Vinogradoff identified in common field agriculture a system that:

> considered every man's rights and property as interwoven with other people's rights and property ... a system particularly adapted to bring home the superior right of the community as a whole and the inferior, derivative character of individual rights.[11]

Agricultural practices in Moray were local adaptations that shared general characteristics with patterns of husbandry followed throughout Scotland.[12] The basic division of the estate was the farm, though the word farmer was seldom used. The land of the farm was divided, typically, into infield and outfield. Infield land received all the available dung, which allowed continuous cropping; though some regimes included fallow breaks. The dunged land was sown with rotations of barley (bear/bere) and oats. These were dietary staples, consumed as bannocks, ale, whisky and porridge. Whisky distilling added value to surplus barley; sales of the spirit earned significant cash income for highland husbandmen. Modest amounts of rye were cultivated; and, because hens did not relish this crop, it might be sown strategically to screen the oats and barley from depredations by poultry.[13] Straw from the white crops fed cattle during the winter. Flax was grown for home spinning, for sacking, ropes, and (supplemented with imported Netherland flax) to supply township linen weavers involved in this major Scottish industry.[14] The value of legumes in restoring fertility—'improving and fatning the ground'—was widely recognised.[15] However, legislation that obliged farmers to sow peas and beans, could not force the seed to grow on acid soils, and the acts were never rigorously enforced.[16] Nonetheless pease were significant in laichland common field crop rotations, with bountiful crops documented at Gordonstoun around 1740.[17] I. Whyte regarded the cultivation of legumes in four-course rotations at Innes as a precursor to improvement.[18] Though, arguably, it rather epitomised the conservative roots of cooperative husbandry—originating in the medieval countryside where pulses were an ordinary white crop and pease pudding a dietary staple. After harvest, the arable became a pasture: cattle grazed promiscuously across the ridges, dunging the plough land as they cropped the stubble and green herbage that had germinated with the corn. Wheat was sown in relatively small quantities. It was grown as a cash crop; otherwise it did not suit the township regime. Wheat straw had little feeding value for cattle; and township houses did not have ovens in which wheaten bread could be baked. Furthermore, because the seed was sown in November–December, cattle on the arable required constant herding to protect the wheat shott over the winter.

Beyond the permanent arable was the outfield, divided from infield by a feal dyke. Outfield was kept largely under natural grass, upon which township cattle and sheep grazed. Nutrient transfer, from pasture to infield was a key element in the sustainability of township agriculture.[19] Estate regulations (and baron courts) governed this grazing, especially ensuring that cattle were herded to prevent a 'start and o'er loup' across the head-dyke into growing crops. In 1552 the Elgin burgh court book recorded:

> ye baillies ... statut and ordainit [tha]t every horss ox cow or stirk [tha]t beis fundin in ye corin heruest sall pay for ane start [th]e hird being p[re]sent sall pay ilk best Id and ye hird beand absent iiijd[20]

Portions of outfield were cropped in rotation, usually with oats: 'in dry fields it was usual to leave the ground lea for six years, and then to take up to three crops of oats'.[21] Before ploughing, the designated portion was enclosed with a turf dyke or fenced with flakes 'for confining the cattle during the night time, and for two or three hours each day at noon. It thus gets a tolerably full dunging'.[22] Turf might be stripped, dried and burned to fertilise outfield land.[23] To prevent damage to the outfield, muirburn was closely regulated by local custom and parliamentary legislation.[24] When the fertility of the dunged outfield or 'bruntland' became exhausted, the ground was allowed to revert to grass and a new patch of outfield broken in.[25]

Cropping in Moray varied this general pattern, according to location and soil quality. In fertile lowland districts there was little or no outfield: several laichland parishes presented vistas of uninterrupted tillage resembling the common field countryside of the English midlands.[26] The sweep of Roseisle arable was punctuated only by insignificant untilled patches 'fit only for sheep'; and even the fringe of dunes was dotted with arable improvements.[27] The 1771 survey of Coxtown reported:

> there is no such thing here as Infield or Outfield, every Tennant dunging and labouring as much as he can only reserving some alternately for Pasturage to horses &ca.[28]

This rotation—alternating white crops and pasture—refreshed soil on the fallowed rigs, which were dunged by grazing beasts. Some grass seed was deliberately sown, though usually communal fallowing relied upon the natural germination of grass seeds along with the grain crop. However, this might produce poor pasture, dominated by couch grass, dockens, stinking willie and creeping buttercup. These latter two weeds merited special notice in Dyke & Moy where, under an improved regime, the minister observed 'crops are not nearly so choked as formerly by the gool or yellow gowan'.[29] Some fallow grass was harvested as hay for winter feed. Duff estate vouchers for 1724–25 recorded payments to labourers cutting and winning hay, and 'for a load of stra for lying beneath the hay [stacks]'.[30] Grange estate comprisings in 1723 noted the 'Grass hows', built by a tenant named Alexander Alands (for storing hay);[31] with another recorded in 1741 among buildings occupied by William Collie.[32]

In upland Moray, arable was ploughed as islands of cultivation within landscapes of mountain, moorland, woodland and bog. Arable was concentrated along river valleys, and in the highlands on terraces above the Spey and Avon.[33] The extent of ploughed land on highland farms might be very restricted, as farmers accepted the limitation imposed by weather and soil. The whole davoch of Inverourie in Strathavon contained only 165 acres of arable divided among eleven townships. Bellenellan tilled just twenty acres; Milton ploughed sixteen acres; Tomnacroich and Belon fourteen acres each; Easter Lyn five acres and Lagavatich just three acres. Records do not reveal how (or whether) this arable land was divided into infield and outfield. However, beyond the head-dyke, upland communities enjoyed very extensive moorland grazing, and in these districts townships, if poor in arable, were rich in cattle.[34] At lower elevations, sheltered grazing was available within semi-natural woodland that covered slopes below arable terraces.[35] Above the head-dykes extensive moorland grazing was available, which, though poor in quality, was generous in extent. At Inverourie, this extended to the watershed on the Hills of Cromdale. Soil on the quartzite was thin—'Generally hard & stony'; nonetheless tathings on this unpromising mountainside supplemented infield arable. The vast extent of shared moorland (some half-a-dozen square miles—over 3,000 acres—for Inverourie) raised the tenants of the davoch above mere subsistence.[36] Moorland pasture provided grazing for the cattle that were the basis of highland prosperity. Peat bogs provided township fuel. Hill land also yielded sustainable supplies of building materials. The glens and clear streams of highland parishes offered ample water supplies and seclusion for distilling, which added value to the barley harvest, and provided cash income over and above the subsistence provided by cattle and crops.

Arable land was allocated to one or more tenants who enjoyed the farm from the laird, and who were responsible for paying the rent. A tenant usually cultivated only a portion of the farm on his (or her) own account. The remainder—even the majority—of the farm was subset to a variety of sub-tenants who comprised the township population—but who are usually not noticed in rentals. The leading sub-tenants were husbandmen (and women too) who won a subsistence from their portions, (perhaps sub-letting to lesser husbandmen (mailanders), as well as producing a surplus that was paid to the tenant as rent and/or sold for cash in burgh markets. The humblest sub-tenants were cottars who cultivated no arable strips, but enjoyed a house with kailyard attached, and the right to graze a cow or a few goats with the township herds. The cottar class included rural craftsmen—smiths, wrights, shoemakers, weavers, tailors—whose main living was earned from their trade. Unskilled cottars worked for wages (paid in cash or oatmeal) on tenants' and sub-tenants' possessions, and also on the laird's land—enjoying, it has been said, a standard of living more miserable than those of slaves working on the sugar plantations of Grenada.[37]

The allocation of plough land among tenants and sub-tenants within the farm both shaped rural landscapes and governed arable husbandry. Arable was unfenced. A turf-and-stone head-dyke defined the boundary between cultivable ground and common pasture, though only symbolically separating crops from cattle, which would readily cross the march if not supervised by herds. Within the head-dyke, the arable was divided into strips which might extend twenty yards in width and a furlong in length—notionally one acre in area, which was as much as a plough team might manage in a day. In practice, sub-division, amalgamation, soil type and topography all combined to ensure wide variations in both the width and length of strips; though the strip area was generally between one rood and a couple of acres.[38] On multiple-tenant farms the possessions of several tenants were mingled within the arable, perhaps also alternating with the laird's in-hand land; though more usually proprietors worked discrete home farms free of the accommodations inherent in cooperative agriculture. Strips were divided one from another by baulks or mearings of untilled ground upon which weeds flourished and stones were dumped.[39] Arable was divided into several shotts, equivalent to the furlongs and brakes of English common field landscapes, bounded by untilled baulks, access tracks and headlands. Each division was dignified with its own name. Irregular corners of cultivable land were tilled as short butts, occasionally, identified by place-names on estate plans as 'new land'; sometimes aligned across the grain of the principal arable.

Each husbandman (tenants and sub-tenants) cultivated a number of strips dispersed across the arable.[40] There is some slender evidence that, during the middle ages, strips were distributed among township folk on a *solskifte* pattern: with allocations made according to the pattern of houses in the township in a sunwise (clockwise) rotation.[41] Some writers have insisted that the allocation of land in strips was contrived to ensure fair shares of good bad and indifferent land.[42] It is, furthermore, suggested that in some farming districts, strips were periodically reallocated to ensure a fair distribution.[43] Though there is little evidence for this in Moray, strips were occasionally redefined and reallocated. For example, Grange baron court responded, in 1711, to the petition of thirteen Hempriggs tenants who complained: 'Lands are ... unequallie divided some of them haveing as they alleage Less Land Conforme to their pay'. The reallocation was, though, only 'For Divideing of the S[ai]ds Lands Conforme to ther rexive payes ... for a Standard to them in tyme Comeing'—for regularising the rent charged per acre, and for avoiding 'Clamore & debate'. It had nothing to do with equalising possessions.[44] Furthermore, the redistribution affected only tenants' possessions: the baron court had no interest in how allocation among sub-tenants was managed. Estate maps, routinely depict remarkably unequal possessions and no evident patterns of distribution. Nor is it likely that even the most draconian baron court could oblige a tenant to relinquish a strip of good land or accept a strip of bad, simply to ensure fairness in periodic redivisions. Cooperation was not communism, and there were clear social and economic divisions among tenants and among the various classes of sub-tenant. The inconvenience of dispersed strips would be cited by improvers as one of the many defects in cooperative agriculture that required remedy: 'proprietors ... have only small pieces of land belonging to them ... most improperly separated, and detached'.[45] The acres of Elgin common fields occupied by Charles Burges, feuar in Garmouth, are typical:

> Four Riggs and a head rigg ... lying east and west in ... the Holmes ...two riggs and a Tongue of the aughteen part land lying South and North at the East end of ... the Holmes ... two Butts and a tongue of land ... lying East and west above the Marywell Brae ... And Two Riggs ... in that parcel of the Lands called the Linthaugh ... Together with a proportional part of the common pasturage.[46]

Plough land was drained by ridging. Within each strip were some half-a-dozen longitudinal ridges and furrows: the crown of the ridge rising to a height of perhaps three or four feet above the gutter of the furrow. Ridging was achieved by ploughing so that the soil was continually turned inwards and raised towards the centre of the ridge.[47] The landscape of arable agriculture thus took on a corrugated aspect: 'like a piece of striped cloth with banks full of weeds and ridges of corn in constant succession'.[48] Strips and ridges were seldom straight: 'the ridges crooked in the shape of an S, and very high, and full of noxious weeds'.[49] The grain of medieval and early-modern arable curved in a reversed-C or reversed-S, generally explained in terms of the manoeuvre required to turn a plough team of up to twelve oxen on the untilled headland at the end of the strip.[50] However, regardless of practical considerations, the sinuous curve of plough land perhaps reflected a medieval aesthetic that inevitably jarred the regularly classical sensitivities of Enlightenment improvers.[51] Discrete crofts within the arable might be farmed with some degree of independence of the cooperative regime. These small acres were frequently named for their possessor; or identified as the perquisite of a township tradesman: for example, Brewhouse Croft, Miln Croft, Smiddy Croft—or near Forres, Hangman's Well Croft. The features of this arable landscape, including head-dykes and traces of ridging survive today only in a few upland localities; laichland landscapes have been comprehensively improved and ridges levelled. However cooperative countrysides throughout Moray are depicted on estate plans and described at length in estate surveys.

'Ane Accompt of ... Waster Moy possesed be William Dunbar and Subbtenants' preserves a verbal depiction of communal arable of exemplary clarity. Some sixty 'ackers' were listed in nine divisions. These divisions, equivalent to the shotts, brakes and furlongs of English common field arable, formed the basic divisions for crop rotation. The strips each comprised from four to nine rigs. Irregular 'ackers', composed of short 'butts' filled in the uneven margins of each arable division; the Midelshot was almost entirely composed of butts, suggesting a shott improved from a patch of waste after the main arable field was set out. The 'ackers' were probably not statute acres, precisely measured by a land surveyor; they were, however, nicely contrived to contain the amount of land that might be ploughed by a regular team in a day on the local soil.

I[te]mo ther is twal ackers of land begening att Comisars Gardeing and eindeing at mores Croft the fors[ai]d acker being on of the twall In the first acker Six Riges 2 ackers five riges 3 acker th[e]r is four riges 4 the same 5 the same 6 the same 7 the same 8 the same 9 the same 10 acker ther six for the acker 11 acker the same 12 acker Called mores Croft ther is teen buts and ane head Rige ...

In the Midelshot ther is five ackers and ane half the eight buts nixt the rod the first acker 2 acker six buts 3 acker the five butts 4 acker the same the fyft acker and ane half ther is 9 riges ...

In the Kirkland ther is 14 ackers and ane half the first acker ther is five riges 2 acker ther teen butts 3 acker five riges 4 acker six rig 5 acker the same the 6 Acker ther is seven butts 7 acker ther is eight buts 8 acker the same 9 acker ther seven butts 10 acker the same 11 acker ther is eight butts 12 acker the same 13 acker the same 14 acker seven butts (*damage*) the half acker more ane bolls pay.[52]

Arable was tilled with the 'old Scotch plough'.[53] The ploughs were made of local timber, typically birch or alder, the parts pegged together. Ironmongery including the sock and coulter, were manufactured by rural smiths. The harness was also locally manufactured: of rawhide, leather, hair rope and twisted birch- or pine-root. The old ploughs were damned by reformers as 'enormous unwieldy constructions',[54] though weight and bulk both contributed to effectiveness in shifting soil.

Maintaining the plough was a communal responsibility, in which the whole township community shared interest and obligation. However, the particular arrangements governing the use, ownership and maintenance of the plough are not recorded; nor are the negotiations that ensued when a husbandman died or moved away or changed his status in the hierarchy of tenants and sub-tenants. This may perhaps evidence the willingness of township folk to compromise and accommodate to ensure that cooperative agriculture was not hampered by internecine squabbles. Similarly, every husbandman had an interest (and presumably a voice in proportion to his holding) when ploughing was planned, though discussions of township parliaments were never minuted.

Further cooperation was required in assembling the plough team, which was conscripted from among the beasts of several husbandmen. The team comprised from four to twelve oxen (or a mixed yoking of oxen and horses) according to the stiffness of the soil. Even on light laichland soils 'the land was tilled by 6, 8, or 10 oxen ... and sometimes by 2 or 4 oxen, with 1 or 2 horses'.[55] Ploughing required a gang of three or four workers. A ploughman steered the plough from the stilts; a gadsman goaded and encouraged the oxen; a driver (sometimes a woman) guided the ploughman, watching for obstacles; a fourth man kept the point of the beam in the furrow. Clods were broken with mallets or spades in the wake of the team. To the accompaniment of 'a hideous Irish noise'[56]—blending encouragements to the oxen, instructions to the workers, Gaelic work songs and miscellaneous banter—the cavalcade ploughed perhaps an acre a day. Lord Kames wrote of the Scotch plough:

> When well-made it is very proper for breaking up ... uncultivated grounds ... the mouldboard lays the furrow-like slice regularly over, and its long stilts ... give the ploughman great command.[57]

This commendation may be extended to embrace the sustainability and economy of an implement constructed of locally-available materials, to a practical design that was readily manufactured by a township wright and maintained by a handy husbandman using ordinary hand-tools—and costing around 5*s*.[58]

Kames found nothing to applaud in the township harrows which were 'more fit to raise laughter than raise soil'.[59] Harrows were also of wood with readily replaceable teeth of fire-hardened whin-root. (There was a popular belief that iron teeth would poison the ground). The implement was dragged by horses, or occasionally by township women—and sometimes attached to the tails of young horses as a means of breaking them in.[60] Sustainable practicality also governed the design of wooden sledges and solid-wheeled kellocks, which were typically adapted to carry creels of dung, turf, peat or grain as a species of practical containerisation. Murray carts added high railed sides to a basic tumbril for the transport of sheaves of corn.[61] Every *Statistical Account* for Moray indicated that, despite the disparagements of improvers, these township implements remained in use until the close of the eighteenth century.

Beyond the outfield, unfenced moorland was exploited as a communal resource. Moorland peat cuttings provided fuel for township heating, cooking and kilns—with a bonus of bogwood, which was dried for firing and might even come in sizes suitable for house-building.[62] Dallas folk earned significant income from peat sales to Elgin and Forres.[63] Similar traffic was reported at Grange, where peat was cut for sale to Findhorn and Burghead. The trade, notionally a breach of the barony's custom, was, however, permitted to continue, the estate profiting from a mulct of half-a-merk on each load sold.[64] Upland mosses on the Fife estate of Kellas were the subject of industrial-scale exploitation: bog wood was processed into charcoal for parochial smithies; and peat supplied the burghs of Elgin and Forres with fuel:

> Robert Fraser Smith in Newtown & George Jenkin in Pittenrich ... work their smidy Caole in the heart of the best Mosses extracting great firs for manufacturing the same ... the mosses of Kellas ... there is moss sufficient there to serve the whole of Lord Fife Estate in Murray .. to the End of time ... the Mosses are so valuable and Extensive fite to serve the whole Country in fire ... the Tennents of Kellas ... leading peats to Elgin ... dispose of more in that way than double their rent.[65]

Moorland plants yielded vegetable dyes: gorse (yellow), crottle lichen (russet), bedstraw (red), heather (grey/green), blaeberry (purple)—in tones suitable for the rustic tartans of country plaiding.[66]

The sustainable harvesting of building materials effected nutrient transfer from muir to arable. Township building materials, including stone, feal and divot, with heather, bents, bracken and broom for thatching were won from the muir. Turf was also cut for flooring sheep cotts, and for mixing with township dung to fertilise the infield.[67] Local rights and regulations enforced in baron courts, prevented destruction of pasture through over exploitation.[68] The court of Grange noted on 22 April 1742, 'the great hurt & damage of John Dunbar ... to Cast Foggage feale & divott ... in a most irregular & disorderly way ... And To Sell & dispose of Feal & divot to ... Strangers', before making new regulations to prevent the inhabitants casting further feal 'till the Sward [the]rof be again grown Strong'.[69] Turf-cutting for local use continued into the 1830s, even on some laichland farms.[70]

Sustainability and cooperation governed grazing regimes that supported, in every parish, a sizeable population of black cattle, goats and white- or dun-faced sheep.

> A man who pays £3 sterling of annual rent will perhaps have 20 black cattle, 3 or 4 horses, 20 sheep and 10 goats. During summer and autumn the pastures could maintain thrice the number, but they would perish during the winter or spring.[71]

Township cattle were kept for their milk, as draught animals, and fattened for sale to burgh fleshers or export through the droving trade. Sheep too were bred for sale to fleshers and kept also for their milk and wool. The sweetness of whiteface mutton was probably the result of the mixed herbage upon which the native sheep fed. Whiteface wool was 'of a very fine staple ... approached in quality that of Shetland' suitable for hand spinning and township weavers.[72]

Considerable numbers of goats also fed on township grazings. The herds were probably folded or housed in winter, leaving a spoor of 'Goatcott' place-names, for example at Kilbuiack in the laich[73] and at Ballindalloch.[74] Elgin was a centre for glovemaking during the seventeenth century (processing goatskins);[75] and Scotland exported up to 100,000 goatskins in 1698.[76] However, goats are sparsely documented and rarely involved in rentals.[77] Certainly, the Strathavon forester kept up to a hundred goats in the 1770s;[78] though only 310 grazed the whole of Kirkmichael around 1790.[79] Some goats may have survived in the laich into the nineteenth century, until banished by emphatic prohibitions in improving leases.[80] Feral descendants of township goats survive as small isolated herds in the Cairngorms.[81]

Cattle performed the fundamental function of processing outfield herbage into dung thus transferring nutrients from pasture to arable. Typically, beasts were driven out each morning and returned home at night to be folded or housed in byres, where their dung accumulated. Sheep too were grazed by day and housed or folded at night; the dung from their cots being considered particularly valuable as manure.[82] Seaweed was gathered 'near the firth' to enrich the dung heap.[83] The kelp that storms threw up was harvested, in a communal effort, whenever it was available—sometimes at the cost of abandoning other farm work, and even on Sunday:

Whenever sea-weed is washed up on the shore, every other operation on the farms in its vicinity is suspended, and men, women, and horses are day and night employed in one great exertion, to secure the whole quantity which may be deposited.[84]

Tenants in upper Strathavon especially engaged in a considerable cattle trade, developed from earlier rieving habits. Cattle-fattening increased dung production, thus enhancing the fertility of poor highland soils. Cattle fattened on Kirkmichael pastures were sold to drovers who took them by Loch Bulig to Deeside and thence southwards, eventually to England. The imperious forester, Robert Willox MacGregor, used his local power to overstock the forest, galling other tenants who complained: 'How soon one drove are fatt he sells them off and buys more'.[85]

Moorland beyond township head-dykes was common to the adjacent communities, whose cattle grazed promiscuously under the supervision of herds. Thus, for example, the ring of townships (Milntown, Torvanich, Tombreckachie, Ackbrake, Shenwell) skirting conical Tomdow, grazed the hill without boundaries.[86] The Coxtown muir was grazed by all tenants of the barony.[87] The Cromdale hills were grazed without division by the string of Strathavon townships that beaded a terrace above the river: including Lyne, Altnaha, Tomnacroik and Belon, Inverourie, Balnallan, Balrianach and Milton. To prevent over-grazing, local customs and interventions by the factor determined the number of beasts that each possessor might pasture on the muir. These 'soams' might be written into tacks.[88] Conflicts arose on the marches between estates. Thus William Grant in Easter Gaulrig (Strathavon) pursued an exemplary case in the sheriff court against several Abernethy farmers in 1766 for damage done to corn on his shieling improvement by cattle that had been allowed to cross the Ailnach onto Gordon land.[89] Disputes between Grant and Gordon on the debatable Caplich frontier were finally settled by arbitration in the 1770s.[90]

These disputes might be defused where grazings were defined as commonties. Elginshire commonties (which seem to have medieval origins) comprised: Alves, Carden, Monaughty (Alves parish); Munlundy (Dallas); Broadhills, Elgin burgh (Elgin); Mundole, Pilmuir (Forres); Muirton (Kinloss); Blackhills/Coxtoun (St Andrews-Lhanbryd); Garmouth (Speymouth & Urquhart); Spindle Muir (Spynie).[91] Tenants of the several estates adjacent to commonties enjoyed the usual moorland rights: to graze cattle and sheep; also to gather fieldstones, quarry freestone, and to cut peat, feal, turf and divot.[92] The busy shieling ground of Faevait, where the Don rises above Inchrory in Strathavon, was a source of discord between Gordon and Mar. From the late seventeenth century onwards, factors of the rival lordships periodically drove Faevait, poinding cattle and making legal interruption by demolishing herdsmens' houses. The multiple interests included the duke of Gordon (as lord of Strathavon), the lairds of Dun and Grange (whose Corgarff tenants grazed Faevait), Grant of Carron (who had held Culquoich under a wadset—and whose tenants claimed shieling rights), and William Forbes of Skellater. Difficulties were compounded by confiscation of the earl of Mar's estate following the 1715 rising, and their subsequent division between Mar's son and Duff of Braco, first lord Fife. Further tension arose from the suspect loyalties of Gordon's principal bailie, Gordon of Glenbucket. In 1728 an agreement was reached, that 'the Faevait be a Commonty for ... people of Strathae [Strathavon] and the people of Corgarff'. Nonetheless, neighbouring proprietors continued to regard parts of Faevait as exclusive possessions: legal interruptions and poindings of *gall* (stranger) cattle continued into the 1760s.[93]

Nutrient transfer from moorland to arable was effected across wider cooperative networks as lowland cattle were sent into highland parishes for summer 'grassing'.[94] Throughout the eighteenth century, cattle from the western laich were sent into Edinkillie—where children deserted schools in summer to assist with the herding.[95] Cattle from the Fife estates in coastal Banffshire were sent to Glass and Cabrach.[96] Cattle from the eastern laich, and also from Nairnshire and the lower Spey valley, were grassed in Inveravon and Kirkmichael.[97] In a mutual exchange, Corgarff tenants grassed Moray cattle on the Faevait in summer, and wintered their own cattle in Moray.[98] Summer grassing relieved pressure on limited lowland pasture—allowing grass to recover, or to be cut as hay for winter feed. Summer grassing also ensured that the cattle (which were no longer required for ploughing) were unable to stray into ripening laichland corn. Highland communities, which could not always produce enough grain for subsistence, meanwhile benefited from the money they were paid for grassing lowland cattle, and from the fertility that the stranger cattle contributed to grazing grounds as they processed rough grass into dung. Subsequently, highland nutrients were transferred back to the laich as fat and flesh on cattle that returned home, refreshed by their summer vacation. This was a lucrative business for highland husbandmen; and greed occasionally led to abuse of the pasture:

> Robert Willox Taxman of Gaulrig ... takes in a great Many Grasing Catle from the low Countrie eats up all the pasture that poor men pays for & keeps ther own Catle and horses in the forrest & these Grasing Catle by which means the forrest is Eaten up like sheep pasture[99]

The annual flitting of cattle is recorded when accounting for money payments for grassing, and disputes over cattle that were not returned.[100] In general grassing arrangements are undocumented and details must be inferred. Presumably the cattle moved on well-defined drove ways, favouring upland routes that avoided arable land: for example the Mannoch Road linking the eastern laich, through Birnie to the Spey at Knockando. The drovers' passage through grazings pertaining to townships along the way was presumably accompanied by negotiation, conflict, conviviality, and cash payments for access to water and overnight accommodation. Thus the grassing season knitted extended social and economic networks—perhaps also contributing to genetic diversity—even among those who were only incidentally involved.

Highland townships (and some lowland communities) enjoyed grazing rights at a distance from the settlement. Grass in remote glens was exploited as shielings, when, during summer months, cattle, and a proportion of the township population, decamped to an upland 'summer town'. Most Moray shielings lay within ten miles of their townships; some glens were only a couple of miles away; though some Strathavon glens were up to eighteen miles distant.[101] However, it was worthwhile to move the cattle to feed on grass that was not usually accessible. During the shieling season lower pastures rested and recovered. The flitting also reduced the risk of beasts straying into arable crops. Meanwhile, empty township byres could be cleaned and renovated ready for the cattle's return in autumn.[102] In some districts of Scotland, shieling dwellings were substantial buildings up to eight bays long and built with substantial timbers.[103] In Moray, most shieling dwellings were small temporary shelters— turf bothies and creelwork thatched huts—inhabited by herds who were well accustomed to open-air living. Shieling places surveyed above the Avon remain as green places, close to sources of water, with the remains of turf- and boulder-walled enclosures, and the founds of dwellings that were rebuilt each year as diminutive versions of turf-walled township houses.[104] Dunged ground where cattle were folded on the shieling might be further fertilised by muirburn, then ploughed as moorland 'improvements', and sown with a crop of oats. Shieling improvements that proved fertile were colonised as new farms or townships. Thus the grazing place of Oldshields on the Coxtoun muir became a discrete farm before 1770, its arable land tilled as irregular patches, with new rigs probing fingers of reclamation into the muir.[105] A shieling improvement at Lynemore on the border of Ballindalloch's Knockando estate was occupied as an arable farm ('new land' before 1759).[106] At about the same date, Torbain, a shieling of Auchnakyle, and Ballintuim, a Gaulrig shieling, also became new possessions: Balintuim occupied by three husbandmen, and several cottars.[107]

Rents and tenants

The landowner's principal concern was, naturally, to extract an income from his estate. After a flirtation with feuing in the sixteenth century—and with wadsetting early in the seventeenth[108]—proprietors embraced simple customary tenancy as yielding the most assured income from land. Tenant husbandmen enjoyed their possessions at the will of the laird, and in return paid a rent, usually in kind. The bulk of rent was paid in bolls of threshed barley and oatmeal. Tenants were obliged to deliver their 'ferm bear' to the estate rent-house or girnel. This substantial stone structure might dominate the largest township of the barony, rivalled for size only by the parish kirk and laird's house. A five-bay slated granary dominated Oldtown of Roseisle.[109] Another stood at Monaughty.[110] Fife's Moray estates were served by granaries at Netherbyre (Pluscarden), Reidhall (Mosstodloch), Quarrywood and Morristown.[111] Granaries were also built at the ports from which estate grain rents were exported. Lethen required rents to be delivered to Nairn or Findhorn. Fife rents were paid at Speybay or Garmouth and Portsoy. Grain exports were landowners' chief source of money income, binding Moray into wider economic networks. Most Moray grain went to southern Scotland or to London, in a trade dominated by Perth merchants named Richardson and/or Roberston.[112] During the 1750s Fife grain was exported to Ireland, though most, probably, was shipped south.[113] Stoneyforenoon grain was exported to Norway (via Inverness and Queensferry) during the decades around 1720, with ships bringing return cargoes of salt, tobacco, brandy and timber.[114] Ballindalloch grain (also handled by Robertson) was exported to Holland in the 1770s.[115]

A significant list of produce other than grain might also be due as rent. The abstract rental of Tarras, near Forres, comprised: 12 chalders 5½ bolls of bear; £33 cash in great customs; and small customs consisting of 144 capons, seventy-eight poultry, eight geese and twelve leet (720 loads) of peat. [116] On Brodie's Cloves estate tenants paid specified numbers of cuts of linen yarn.[117] Gordon rentals during the 1750s included small but significant payments of butter, tallow, eggs, sheep, poultry, and more rarely a goat, swine or steer.[118] Rents always included reek hens, each bird notionally representing a payment for the reeking lum of one firehouse. Rents were paid in kind on most Moray estates into the early decades of the nineteenth century.

Some rents were paid in money. Several Strathavon tacksmen paid money rents (£56 for Tomnalinen and Croftbain; £24 for Over Downan) in 1680—sums equivalent to those paid by neighbouring possessors under feu charters and wadsets.[119] By 1708, it seems that most Strathavon and Glenlivet farms paid money rents.[120] Thus the inhabitants of cooperative townships—far from being benighted peasants operating at a level of mere subsistence— were involved in the wider money economy. Money was earned from grassing; from grain and cattle sales; from spinning lint; knitting stockings; weaving linen and plaiding.[121] In some districts industrial-scale peat extraction earned tenants more than double the value of their rents.[122] Meanwhile whisky distilling, which added value to the grain crop, knitted Moray's highland townships into the commercial fabric of the nation. In Inveravon there were 'smuggling houses ... on almost every streamlet';[123] and, in 1828, Gordon's factor reported:

> there are few names indeed in the rental who, are not concerned directly or indirectly in the traffic except the gentlemen who occupy farms in the lower ends of Glenlivet and Strathavon.[124]

These commercial enterprises enabled even sub-tenants in Strathavon to pay rents for their possessions largely in cash, though with additional customary payments in kind and services. These common burdens—properly owed by tenants, but cascaded downward to sub-tenants—included mucking and harvest work on the proprietor's land, cutting and carrying peats to the proprietor's house; long and short carriages on the landowner's business; and carrying building materials to the proprietor's house, the mill and the parish kirk. Sub-tenants included both husbandmen who held land from a principal tenant and mailanders, who held land from a sub-tenant.

A one-off payment, known as a grassum secured occupancy for a specified term—usually between three and ten years—the receipt recording the payment providing evidence of the agreement in case of dispute. In the absence of a receipt the tenant might petition for access to the laird's own records.[125] Sub-tenants too paid grassums—often worth more than a year's rent—to the principal tenant. For example, Robert Mckandy, mailander to James Gordon, tacksman of Cruichly, paid £16 13s 4d in rent annually for half an oxgate, with £37 16s as grassum for seven years' possession; also six fowls, one reek hen, a dozen eggs, a quarter of butter, with two days work harrowing, mucking and harvesting, three hands casting and leading peat. Occasionally the grassum was paid entirely in kind, for example, William Robertson, mailander, paid eight wedders and a hog for a ten-year possession.[126]

Cooperation did not preclude exploitation.

> Most of the farmers ... did not think themselves '*well set down*' unless they could sublet as much as paid the greater part of their rent, and yet leave themselves a comfortable holding.[127]

This ethos was widespread in Moray. For example, on the Ballindalloch farm of Corshellach in 1819, 'the [six] sub-tenants pays about £32 ... which leaves £10 to the principal tenant to pay for 31 or 32 Bolls sowing.'[128] The earl of Fife's factor, William Rose, experienced difficulty in discovering what rents tenants received from sub-tenants, observing 'few countrey men are willing to tell these things especially when they grow suspicious of one another'; though one tenant, John Roy, received 'of clear profite on his possession ... near about £49 or £50'.[129] Exploitation by tenants so concerned the earl that he directly instructed Dougal Robertson, tacksman of Hillside, 'not to oppress the Subtennents', while taking 'some nine optional years of the nineteen' of Robertson's lease 'to be a check upon him'.[130] On Gordon lands in Strathavon and Glenlivet, profitable subsetting was general and unrestrained:

Tombrackachies—rent £40; paid by sub-tenants—£174 6s 8d

East & West Deskie—rent £42 14s 5d; paid by sub-tenants—£86

Nether Achnarrow—rent £8 1s 1⁴/₁₂d; paid by sub-tenants—£28

Blairfindy & Tammoir—rent £33 6s 8d; paid by sub-tenants—£141 6s 8d

Cruckley—rent £41 13s 4d; paid by sub-tenants—£76 12s 0d

Tombae—rent £40; paid by sub-tenants—£150 6s 8d

Lyn of Inverourie—rent £66 13s 4d; paid by sub-tenants—£88 6s 8d[131]

These profits, of course, were additional to the tenant's income from sales of surplus livestock and corn from his own arable.

The cavalcade of tenants' packhorses and kellocks progressing with sacks of bear and meal to the girnel at Whitsun and Martinmas, was an event too commonplace to attract the notice of writers or painters. A glimpse of the spectacle was preserved, however, when, in 1714, a dozen or more tenants of William Duff of Braco employed Thomas Duff, merchant in Banff, to pursue their laird for compensation in respect of losses sustained through delays at the girnel:

> for detaining us with one hundred and seventie six horses ... the most pairt of a day which Keept us from home at night at the harbour of Speymouth To deliver the said William Duffs ferms ... because there was no weights to take the said meal of our hands ... occasioned us in The neglect of our labour and our harvest at home by all which wee sustained the loss of five hundred merks amongst us.[132]

On the Grange estate farm bear was paid in 'small parcels' that complicated record-keeping.[133] Indeed, tenants on many estates paid their ferms in dribs and drabs, and most estate chamberlains maintained involved records of 'deficient bolls', with arrears of rent stretching back several years. Alexander Dunbar of Stoneyforenoon was driven to fury by his tenants' insouciant unconcern for their arrears:

> I desire that the Kentesackers be acquainted [tha]t if they don't pay up their Arrears either in Bear Oats or Meall ... I promise them they will suffer if they don't now pay up ... they will pay att least 8 pounds Scots p[e]r Boll.[134]

As farm bear was brought in, every sackful required careful examination in case tenants tried to deceive the girnel keeper. Details of the process emerge when difficulties arose, such as the 'passionat and furious' row that ensued when:

> James Bremner presented a sack of his Corns at Granges Grannary ... the same was Insufficiently dressed upon which James Bremner alleaged it was owing to the Corns being put in a New Sack ... Emptying the whole sack upon the floor of the Loft and taking a handful of it ... it was Fowler at the Bottom than at the top ... he made tryall of it but found he Could not Clean it with the hasp.[135]

Tenants' rent obligations included specified numbers of days' work (of men and horses) labouring for the proprietor. Most tenants also owed long and short carriages, which might involve transporting goods or carrying messages. Tenants were also obliged to contribute labour, materials and carriages for upholding the laird's mansion place and communal facilities including the parish kirk, manse, school, schoolmaster's house and mill. These duties were typically cascaded downwards by tenants to sub-tenants and cottars.[136] Thus seventeen sub-tenants of Gordon Stuart in Lyn of Inverourie owed a total of fifty-four days (with men and horses) at harvest work and mucking; thirty-seven days at peat cutting; thirty further specified days of unspecified labour; and other undefined additional work, notably carrying shares of the master's peat proportionate to the size of possessions.[137]

To preserve a full range of services to the community, tenants (and their dependants) were obliged to use specified craftsmen within the barony. Thus the Grange baron court statuted:

> Ilk tennent and possessor of the Lands of Burgie ... To work all [thei]r Smith wark with William Smith present smith in Burgie and his successors smiths.[138]

Indeed, there was a considerable amount of ironmongery among township equipment. The Grange smith shoed horses; crafted locks and other door furniture; forged picks, forks and axes; made oxen thrammels and harness fittings; and manufactured iron parts for ploughs and carts and harrows.[139] Thirlage ensured the upkeep of the mill, by obliging husbandmen to send their grain only to specified mills for grinding. The miller retained a portion of the grain or meal as payment. The miller's monopoly was rigorously protected even to the extent of forbidding the use of hand querns.[140] Millers were sometimes preferred as estate factors, for example William Gairns at Miln of Moy for the Stoneyforenoon estate during the 1720s. The miller was a sound choice as factor because he was a significant businessman, who also had a finger on the pulse of local agriculture and grain markets, while being distanced from other tenants by popular resentment, fuelled by a reputation for cupidity.

A significant minority of township husbandmen enjoyed their possessions under a written tack rather than by custom, as Moray landowners caught up with a trend that had been growing since the early seventeenth century.[141] Gordon tenants enjoyed their possessions under written tacks during the first decade of the eighteenth century. In 1708, among twenty-seven Strathavon possessions, at least ten were held under written tacks.[142] Most of these were for only a handful of years, such as the five-year tack on Easter Lettock (1709); and none affected the cooperative management of the possessions.[143]

In a half-way stage between customary tenure and written tack, Ballindalloch granted four oxgates of Easter Drimgrain for fifteen years, from 1733, for one hundred merks (with services and four reek hens), 'by a Verball paction' recorded in the baron court book.[144] This tenure saved the cost of registering tacks, while creating a legal record of the agreement; though the tenant depended upon the proprietor's goodwill for access to the record. The arrangement was never widespread and did not develop into secure copyhold tenure. Ballindalloch granted tacks from the 1730s, though there was little consistency in the terms agreed. Mains of Kirdells with Baildow were farmed out in 1731 for a bare 'three or seven years', which gave little security or certainty. Ballinluig was leased for seven years (1729); Delrachie for eleven years (1733); Upper Kirdelbeg and two oxgates of Nether Kirdellbeg for fifteen years (1748); Croft Konochie for seventeen years (1743); and four oxgates of Delchirach also for seventeen years (1735). The tacks did not affect cooperative arrangements. Five tacks secured the tenancies of five possessors at Struthers in Kinloss for nine years: the arable was allocated as runrig strips; and the five tenants enjoyed rights to 'Common pasturages casting and winning peats turfs firr and Foggage' on the Drum of Pluscarden.[145] Joseph Dunbar of Grange, similarly, was granting short tacks from the 1720s—for example, for nine years possession of Craighead and Inchdemmy in 1724.[146] Nine years remained usual for a generation at Grange.[147]

Long tacks relieved the proprietor from the burdensome business of pursuing many possessors for small sums of rent. Previous habits of wadsetting had, perhaps accustomed landowners to losing control over property for long periods; and at least a tack did not affect the proprietor's title. Ballindalloch farmed out the towns and lands of Tormore, Lynriach, Boaldow and Knockshalg, with one oxgate of Tombreck under a tack for three-nineteen years in 1738; and Delnapot, Cloddach and Achimine were leased as a single holding for two-nineteen years from 1743. The several farms in these extensive possessions remained separate cooperative townships.[148] Those who had previously enjoyed their land as tenants were now, perforce, demoted. As sub-tenants they paid rents to the tacksman rather than to Ballindalloch's chamberlain. The tacksman, meanwhile, might increase rents arbitrarily, knowing that his sub-tenants had little scope for redress through the appeals to custom in the baron court. Brodie granted similarly extensive tacks: for example Alleesk/Dykeside (1750), Drum (1748), Penick and Inshoch (1750), though typically for nineteen years. Brodie also granted tacks for individual runrig possessions within cooperative townships, usually for nineteen-year terms: for example a 'Room and Possession' in Corrage (1739), and another in Dyke (1748).[149]

With or without tacks and grassums, there was a significant turnover of tenants. This hampered Brodie's attempts in 1769 to collect arrears of rent dating back some ten years: among twenty-eight defaulters cited as defendants in a sheriff court process, one had died and eleven had moved away (though most went to other possessions on Brodie's scattered estates).[150] On Brodie's Kinneddar estate, of seventeen tenants listed in the 1751 rental, only six were named among the thirteen tenants listed in 1756. There was a similar turnover at Grieshop where only five (possibly six) of the seventeen 1751 tenants were still in possession in 1756.[151] Altyre rentals document a complete replacement of tenants every couple of decades, as individuals and families rose to notice or sank to obscurity in the hierarchy of tenants and sub-tenants. Twenty-one tenants possessed fifteen farms in the 1638 rental. In 1738 these farms were possessed by forty tenants. Among these just one shared a surname with a 1638 tenant: Alexander Naughty at Newtyle alone may have preserved the tenant status of his ancestor James Naughtie. Only eleven (possibly twelve) of the 1738 tenants were still in possession (including those with the same surname—possibly near relations) in 1748. Only thirteen tenants listed in 1751 survived from the 1748 rental (with two more whose surnames suggest near relationship to 1748 tenants). Just twelve of the 1748 tenants were still in possession among thirty-one named in 1756. Only three of the 1756 tenants were among thirty-four in possession in 1775.[152] Tenant turnover, representing a dynamic element within the cooperative system, was evident among the twenty-two farms of the Gordon lordship of Strathavon. All but one were held by single tenants. Only five tenants in 1748 shared a name with the tenant in 1737, though a further six shared a surname with the predecessor tenant. Nine tenant names changed completely between 1737 and 1748. Only seven of the 1748 tenants survived to appear in the 1752–54 rental (with a further two tenants sharing surnames). Amalgamations and divisions of farms, together with different criteria in compiling rentals, resulted in a list of thirty-two farms in 1764. Only seven tenants survived from the 1752–54 rental; ten of the 1764 tenants were certainly different men from those in possession a decade before.

Mobility within the tenantry was too commonplace to merit mention by early commentators. Indeed, it was long-surviving tenants who attracted attention. The minister of Alves declared in 1793 that many farms in his parish 'have been continued in the possession of the same families for several generations'. He amplified his report with an example: 'a family of the name of ANDERSON, have occupied a farm ... for upwards of 400 years ... a circumstance that deserves particular notice'—as evidence of the patriarchal care of the earls of Moray.[153] The report may be the origin of a subsequent sentimental anecdote concerning a 'grey-haired old man of plain but decent appearance', who deferentially responded to an enquiry from the earl of Moray by declaring 'that he had paid his Lordship and his forebe'ers "twa and fifty rents"', before cannily extracting the promise of a vacant tenancy for his son.[154]

Woodland

Military surveyors mapped trees covering perhaps three per cent of Scottish lowland landscapes and at least seven per cent of highland parishes around 1750.[155] The accuracy of this overview is confirmed, in Moray, by estate plans drawn from the 1760s onwards; and in Strathavon by the traveller James Robertson who reported in the 1770s: 'the hills on each side are covered with hazle, birch, alder, quaking asp, willow, bird's cherry, roses and honeysuckle'.[156] In the western laich of Moray, military surveyors indicated notable swathes of semi-natural woodland in Kinloss, and on the lands of Brodie and Earnhill, with Darnaway forest to the south. In upland Moray trees extended along the Lossie into Dallas; lined burns in the Glen of Rothes and Knockando; and flourished in uninterrupted masses along both sides of the Spey valley between Elchies and Rothes. In highland parishes there was extensive tree cover below arable terraces along the Findhorn, Spey and Avon, and on the burnsides in Glenlivet, Glenrinnes and Glenconglass.[157] Sir John Sinclair reckoned there was 21,000 acres of natural woodland in Elginshire, and 6,000 acres in Banffshire, in 1814.[158] Lauchlan Shaw, the historian of the province of Moray, thought 'no Country in Scotland is more plentifully served' (with timber) in 1775; and he observed in 'Almost all the Glens ... Birch, Hasle, Alar, Aspine, Saugh or Sallow, Holly, Willow, Haws, Service-tree, &c.' with 'large Oaks' in Inveravon.[159] Sarah Murray, who travelled an unusual route in 1796, along the new carriage road from Aviemore to Dulsie Bridge, admired 'tall ash trees ... with huge trunks ... likewise the hazel, the alder, and the crooked maple, with all sorts of shrubs' along the Findhorn.[160] Estate plans add further evidence for woodland 'fit for common use', for example clothing steep slopes below the cultivated terraces in upper Strathavon.[161] This semi-natural woodland consisted of birch, alder, hazel, gean, willow, ash, oak and rowan, growing in places unsuitable for arable cultivation. The trees which, strictly, all belonged to the landowners, were protected by a broad sweep of legislation,[162] to prevent improvident exploitation. Meanwhile, woodland was sustainably managed by coppicing and pollarding to supply the requirements of the cooperative countryside; and grass beneath mature trees provided grazing for township cattle and horses.[163] Indeed, cattle dung and the trampling of hooves that disturbed the ground and worked fallen leaves and seeds into the soil, assisted the regeneration of semi-natural woodland.[164] Some woods were surrounded with banks and ditches or stone and feal dykes.[165] In practice, though, these enclosures were intended to define the extent of woodland; beasts were prevented from straying into woodland by herds rather than fences.

Factors and foresters exercised close supervision of woodland, protecting the resource from overexploitation and abuse. A jobsworth forester, indeed, knew and accounted for every tree in his wood: trees left standing after extraction of timber from Burghenerich in Strathavon were counted and appreciated on 21 April 1734—and the wood found to contain 3,900 trees worth £443.[166] In practice local folk routinely cut growing timber in defiance of the law, the forester and the baron court.[167] This was tolerated by landowners; and, provided the culprits confessed and the depredation was not heinous, the cutting of 'green wood' was punished only by nominal fines, often levied as an additional mulct in the offender's rent.[168]

Early tacks for Brodie farms were used to enhance the estate's timber resources, by requiring tenants to plant barren (native deciduous) trees around their yard-dykes. It is likely that the planting of yard-dyke trees was an old customary obligation codified only at a late date when tacks became fashionable. The requirement may hark back to a statute of 1475 that obliged tenants to fence their yards with 'living wood' rather than palings;[169] though the intention of this act was to create hedged yards while yard-dyke trees were grown as standards. Yard-dyke trees may also be rooted in the 1535 statute which required tenants to plant one tree for every merkland.[170] Be that as it may, the yard-dykes of Moray's cooperative townships (and early improved farms too) sprouted flourishing growths of standard timber trees. Around 1740, from eighteen to seventy-six saplings were supplied to each of twenty-two Monaughty tenants, who were obliged to 'nurse and uphold' the growing trees.[171] At Asleesk the new tenant was obliged to plant barren trees around corn and kailyard dykes, and to 'nurse & Conserve [the same] to the utmost of his Power' during his nineteen-year tack. The earl of Fife followed the trend. The 1735 tack for Lynemore in Mortlach required the tenant to plant eighteen barren trees; the Whitefield tack of 1749 specified eleven trees.[172] The obligation to plant yard-dyke trees became commonplace in Fife tacks, enshrined in improving regulations of 1776;[173] saplings for tenants to plant were supplied by the Duff House gardener.[174]

Estate records seldom specify species, beyond 'barren' trees. Exceptionally, the 1746 lease on Newton of Cairnborrow specified 'plains or ashes'.[175] Yard-dyke trees remain a notable feature of Strathavon and Glenlivet townships,[176] though this planting was not an obligation in Gordon tacks. Arguably, the handful of trees that flourished around each tenant's yard represented at least the crucks and rooftree of the possessor's next house. As such the tenant shared his laird's interest in the welfare of the yard-dyke trees. The total number of yard-dyke trees was not inconsiderable. A survey of township timber in Rothiemay during 1760 counted a dozen or so trees in the yards of each of forty-six tenants:[177] some five hundred mature trees represented a valuable resource.

Subsequently, changing architectural fashion and the availability of softwood from large-scale plantations and from industrial exploitation of highland pinewoods, meant that yard-dyke trees were not always harvested. In upland parishes especially, township yard-dyke trees survive, in magnificent maturity or terminal decrepitude, as significant landscape features, and key markers of deserted and destroyed settlements. Surviving yard-dyke trees show evidence of coppicing and pollarding: management and exploitation extending the life of the plantings. In the corners of a square enclosure at Tomnacroik of Belon in Kirkmichael, there is a stupendous larch and an impressive ash. There are solitary old Scots pines at the neighbouring townships of Lyne and Altnaha. A sprawling Scots pine in a yard-dyke at Delnapot in Knockando, stands out among the mature pinewood of a later plantation. At Ladderfoot in Glenlivet, the yard-dyke of a farmstead occupying an improvement on the margins of cultivation supports a row of gnarled birch. At Craighead and Quirn on Allt a Choire below Carn Daimh (also Glenlivet) craggily contorted ancient rowans survive, perhaps from the beginnings of settlement on this upland improvement. The yard-dyke of Tervieside on Ballindalloch's Morinsh estate supports a variety of spectacularly twisted dead or dying trees. At the Morinsh commonty improvement of Badeach the yard-dyke supports four sycamores and a beech. There are remarkable old rowans at Lynemore (new land in 1759) above Inveravon. At Altyoun there are old hollies and gean in the yard dykes. At Delavorar towering larch and ash shade the rick stands. In Glack Harness on the Aberlour-Mortlach frontier, trees were planted around the yards of settler farms, preserving a township practice into an early stage of improvement. The Glack trees were in flourishing maturity when mapped by Ordnance Surveyors around 1870; and several of these individually-planned Scots pine and larch trees survive today, rooted among the stones of the yard-dyke.[178]

Townships

The cooperative township epitomised the sustainability, self-sufficiency and cooperative nature of early-modern rural life. The term 'fermtoun' is sometimes adopted for these rural settlements, though their inhabitants usually preferred the Anglo-Saxon word *tun* or the Gaelic *baile*. Modern researchers prefer the term 'township'. Few traces of cooperative townships survive in the improved fieldscapes of the laich, though many were planned by land surveyors as a preliminary to improvement. In upland parishes the founds of township buildings survive in the field.[179]

A township was usually built at each local social or economic focus. However, apart from the dignity of being named castletown, kirktown or milton (*baile mullich*) most enjoyed no special status. The majority of townships were located conveniently for access to the arable and pasture of the farm. Where feasible, the settlement occupied a dry level stance, with access to water (either in wells or burns), and on land that was not suitable for arable cultivation. Thus the townships of Strathavon stand above cultivable terraces, on rocky sloping moorland, where earth fast boulders supported the quoins of buildings.

Edward Burt described 'A Highland town' as 'a few huts for dwellings with barns, stables ... all irregularly placed, some one way, some another'.[180] Nonetheless, most townships were planned with deliberation to accommodate the agricultural operations of several husbandmen, as well as to defuse the inevitable animosities of close-knit (and sometimes also closely-related) communities. The layout was usually irregular but, arguably, never haphazard. Large laichland townships, such as Oldtown of Roseisle, Urquhart, Lhanbryd and Easter Alves were planned so that principal buildings stood around an open area— perhaps planted end-on to the green so that neighbours overlooked neither each other, nor the communal space.[181] Similar planning considerations preserved privacy and good neighbourhood in smaller townships.

Laichland hamlets contained the farmsteads of a dozen or more tenants or major sub-tenants, as well as several families of cottars.[182] More typical townships contained the farmsteads of a handful of husbandmen with several cottars—perhaps half-a-dozen families. A typical suite of farmstead buildings comprised a dwellinghouse, one or more byres, kiln, barn, stable, sheepcote and henhouse.[183] These buildings were arranged to suit agricultural requirements rather than according to standard plans or abstract ideals of taste and symmetry.

Several constructional techniques are evident among rural buildings. Secure tenure under feu charter, encouraged durable building in the burghal style: with clay-mortared stone walls, lime harling and thatched or slated roofs. The house of John Gray, squarewright in Fochabers, appraised in 1735, was built in this manner, with three windows and a 'hearth and Chimney being brick'.[184] A score of Fochabers houses were similarly valued in 1753 for 'Mud and Stone Work' prior to removal 'for Gaving way to the Avenue' and 'Falling within the New Park' at Gordon Castle.[185] In Garmouth, houses of two full storeys, were built of cob (a clay-straw mix raised in courses on a stone found).[186] Quoins and dressings at the doors and windows were of quarried freestone. The cob walls were protected (and concealed)

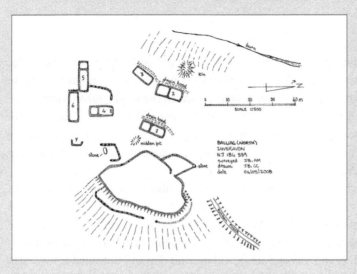

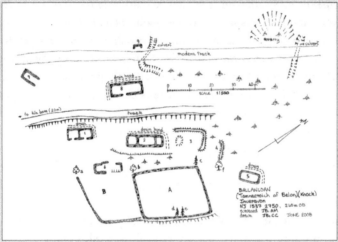

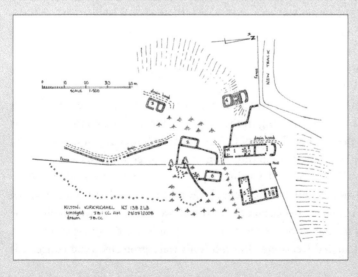

Township plans.
(C. Clerk, SAS)

by lime harling. With regularised façades, Speymouth cob survived the improvers' great rebuilding.[187] Elsewhere cob was rare.[188] Clay-and-bool (Auchinhalrig work) was a durable walling built with cobbles bedded in clay and protected with lime harling, used for houses in Garmouth. Auchinhalrig work survived the architectural revolution to build the new village of Kingston and settler farms in Bellie and St Andrews-Lhanbryd; and to be considered for a regular farm steading at Edom in Pluscarden, under a contract advertised in 1820.[189]

Cruck-framing was the usual vernacular style for dwellings and farm buildings throughout the laich and highland Moray. The A-frame couples of structural crucks and lesser timbers were cut in estate woodland.[190] The principal timbers in township buildings belonged to the landowner, though an outgoing tenant might claim ownership (or the value) of any timber he had added at his own cost. Canny husbandmen maintained written records to support claims for reimbursement of the cost of improvements (meliorations). When James Melton was removed in 1768 from the Mosstowie possession that had been held previously by his father and grandfather, he produced a document dated 1738, valuing his firehouse timber at £2 13s 4d, and claimed the cost of meliorations through three generations asserting 'I have greatly Repaired and Augmented said House have putt up a kiln a Stable a Byre & a Coat'.[191] Valuations of house-timber are thus a principal source documenting buildings in the laich.

Couples were of the species usual in managed semi-natural woodland: oak, birch and pine are documented, though ash, alder, gean and willow were widely available and presumably employed. Mismatched timbers in houses at Grange suggest replacement of decayed elements in buildings that were otherwise substantial and permanent structures, renovated and repaired, perhaps through several decades or generations: 'in the hall tuo sufficient couples on [where] roft oake and another firre ... in the meikle barn six s[ufficient] firnished couples all oak and birk'.[192] The longevity of turf-and-cruck dwellings is further confirmed by map evidence, showing houses certainly occupying the same site for generations—with a possibility that they endured for a century or longer.[193] This contradicts opinions that houses were 'poor and flimsy', with 'only a short lifetime'; though it is possible that walls (if not crucks) might be renewed every half-dozen years.[194] Cruck frames were jointed and pegged, supporting the rafters and purlins of hipped roofs, covered with a layer of divot and a thatch of heather, bracken, or bents. Exact details of the structure are undetermined. Valuations of timber do not include end-crucks that experiment suggests are necessary to support the hips; nonetheless it is generally supposed that roofs were usually hipped.[195] Gabled houses are shown on estate plans in Glenlivet and Strathavon, though the depiction of townships is largely schematic and unreliable.[196]

Indeed, many aspects of township architecture are only imperfectly understood. The wave of architectural regularisation that swept away township vernacular building (and the townships too), within a century erased also all memory of turf-and-cruck construction techniques. Even the vocabulary of turf-and-cruck has been forgotten: nobody now remembers the meaning of such words as 'grip', 'side', and 'miduell'; and experimental reconstructions of cruck-framed structures are, for want of surviving models, bedevilled by debate and hedged with questions and caveats.[197]

An alternative timber framing (mud-and-stud or stake-and-rice) employed vertical posts to support roof trusses in gable-ended houses with timber lums.[198] The light timber framing was infilled with thick mud-daub supported by wattle panels, weatherproofed with lime wash or harl. Gabled mud-and-stud dwellings were occupied by labourers' families until the 1820s—demolished at Broom of Moy by the muckle spate of 1829;[199] meanwhile 'stake and rise' was specified in 1811, for tollhouses on Moray's turnpike roads.[200]

Because the walls of a cruck-framed structure were not loadbearing, it was possible in most districts to build with turf. The wall was raised upon a stone found, on which the feet of couples also rested.[201] These stone founds, recorded by surface survey in Strathavon, Strathspey and Glenlivet, comprise, typically, a course or two of large stones less than a metre high and some seventy centimetres thick.[202] The quoins of turf walls were buxomly rounded to match the seamless curve of heather-thatched roofs. Feal was readily gathered from beyond the head-dyke; light to transport; and could be built by ordinary township labour.[203] If not over-exploited, turf would replenish indefinitely. Furthermore, when houses were replaced or renovated, old turf walling could be mixed with the farm dung, effecting a nutrient transfer from muir to arable.[204]

Township buildings were all single-pile structures.[205] The husbandman's dwelling was typically a longhouse (byre house): the family inhabited the upper end, and cattle were stalled at the lower. Upland byre houses might extend up to 40 feet in length, though a length of around 30 feet (or less) was more usual. The size of available timber determined the breadth of township buildings: about twelve feet was the maximum that could be spanned by upland crucks, giving an interior floor space around eight feet broad.[206] Larger timbers allowed higher and broader buildings: a six-bay cruck-framed barn at Corrimony, Inverness-shire, stands 65 feet long and 18 feet broad, which may represent the footprint of larger laichland dwellings and small-lairds' houses.[207]

The byre house had a single centrally-placed doorway, used by both the family and its beasts; though some examples were elaborated with separate doors to house and byre. Window openings were few and small. The door was a sturdy enough to merit valuation, and was fitted with a lock to preserve privacy and possessions from neighbours.[208] The living space (firehouse) was heated by a hearth, placed centrally on the floor or against an end wall, which was protected from the heat of the peats by a stone fireback. Smoke was carried away by a timber 'hanging lum', in which flitches of bacon might be hung.[209] Smoke that evaded the chimney drifted among the heads of the couples impregnating the divot and thatch with soot that enhanced its value as compost when stripped and put on the dung heap. Laichland tenants might enjoy commodious dwellings, sometimes without the inconvenience of a byre-end. Most of the houses appraised on the estate of Stoneyforenoon in 1724 consisted of just two or three couples, but probably were attached in longhouse style to their byres. James Piterkin's house extended to five bays, and Alexander Lie's to six.[210] With a byre attached this made a significant range of building. The most opulent laichland farmhouses, divided by partition walls and box beds, contained a three-bay firehouse, with an unheated spence or benner house of similar size, a smaller chamber, and perhaps also a pantry.[211] The house of Hierom Tulloch, a leading tenant at Grange, comprised a three-bay hall; a pantry of similar size 'on the northwest end'; with a kitchen, and 'outer chamber' both also three bays long.[212] Domestic convenience was occasionally enhanced further with a detached privy or 'litell howse'—recorded among Alexander Aland's buildings in 1723; and worth £4 6s 8d on John Roan's possession in 1724.[213] Domestic interiors were lined with creelwork in the manner noted by Boswell in Glenmorriston:

> The house here was built of thick turfs and thatched with thinner turfs and heath. It had three rooms in length, and a little room which projected. Where we sat, the side walls were wainscotted ... with wicker.[214]

In the byre, creelwork and timber partitions divided the space into stalls.[215] Cruck-framed dwellings were unceiled, though in some homes a tent of canvas pinned to the roof timbers prevented dirt falling from the thatch.[216] In large houses a loft floor (of deals or turf-covered cabers) might be supported by the collars of the cruck frames.[217] Externally, many houses were dignified with a stone-kerbed and cobbled terrace along the front. A stone drain led urine from the byre, perhaps to be collected in a barrel, where it fermented for use in grain preparation,[218] laundry and washing fleeces,[219] or as a mordant in dyeing.[220] Otherwise the byre drained into a dung pit, conveniently located before the husbandman's door so that manure from the byre and domestic waste could be shovelled directly in from the house.

Cottars' houses, were simpler structures, without a byre, consisting of just two or three bays (around 24 feet in length) and perhaps located on the township margin.[221] A house of this kind might be erected within a couple of weeks, the largest part of the process being the cutting and transporting of turf.[222] Cottar-house style was embraced by moorland improvers (who were often aspirational cottars). The fragility of this vernacular was evidenced at Greenside of Coxtoun, where Robert Taylor's house was 'thrown down' without difficulty by 'evil minded people ... [who] broke & Destroyed the Whole Timber and other Matterials'. The house was almost as easily rebuilt as destroyed, with the help of £3 (Scots) from Taylor's landlord, the earl of Fife.[223]

A yard, defined by turf-and-stone walling, was usually attached at the rear of each byre house and cottar's dwelling. This kailyard supplied vegetables for the table. Additional yards contained stacks of grain and pease on stone bases. The yard might be roughly rectangular or irregularly oval, perhaps planned to incorporate earth fast boulders as founds for the walls.

Township kilns were fired periodically throughout the year: to dry corn in the sheaf after harvest, and again before threshing; to dry grain periodically during storage, and especially before milling; and in malting ale or whisky.[224] At Ballintuim (Strathavon) three principal husbandmen each operated a kiln; though at Belon, Bailecnoic and Ballinluig a single kiln served the whole township. The kiln comprised a circular stone-lined bowl, some six feet deep and eight feet in diameter at the top. A peat fire in a stone hearth supplied heat, which was drawn along a flue into the kilnbowl, and through the grain which was spread on a timber floor laid across the top of the bowl. As a fire precaution, kilns were usually located at a distance from other buildings, sited to catch a breeze and perhaps excavated into sloping ground, for example in the gully of a burn at Ballinluig (Strathavon) and Quirn (Glenlivet), or on a steep brae at Milton and Stocktown (Glenlochy).[225] The kiln might be housed in a discrete building, roofed with a single cruck frame; or, more usually, integrated with a barn.[226] The waste of fuel involved in multiple kilns was tackled (ineffectually) by the earl of Fife who yearned to 'mak a' these lums reek through ae lum'. The single lum envisaged was at the lofty masonry kiln-barn erected at Rothiemay around 1745. In practice no estate monopolies were established; grain-drying and malting continued in township kilns on most Moray farms.[227]

Barns (with or without kilns) were freestanding structures extending some 20 feet to 30 feet in length. Typically, the barn had two (opposed) doorways, and the building was oriented so that the prevailing wind gave a through-draught for winnowing. Other farm buildings including a stable, were built close to the house: occasionally added as a wing at right-angles; more often in a straggling line, perhaps under a continuous roof—extending some 80 feet at Bailecnoic, and 114 feet at Torbain. Sheepcotes (and some barns) were built cruck-framed with thatched roofs, but with walls of un-daubed wattle to allow a free flow of air to the interior.[228]

Township architecture attracted considerable criticism from improvers: 'mean squalid dark hovels',[229] 'low and feeble ... so ordered that it does not cost more time to erect such a cottage than to pull it down';[230] 'very poor and mean'.[231] The muted visual impact of buildings that grew organically from the soil was not appreciated by improvers. Nor was the sustainable nature of turf-and-cruck especially valued—even though the thermal properties of turf walls and divot-and-thatch roofs were superior to those of stone walls and slate-and-sarking roofs that improvers approved.[232] Perhaps it was these characteristics that encouraged some husbandmen to resist pressure for architectural change. Turf-walled dwellings were roofed and inhabited, in the laich until the 1830s, and beyond 1860 in Strathavon.[233] Their survival, in defiance of improvers—to be planned by the first Ordnance Survey, and recorded as curiosities by pioneer photographers[234]—is a testimony to the substantial utility of an organic vernacular architecture within an economy and society based upon cooperation, localism and self-sufficient sustainability.

Cooperative husbandry was productive and resilient; and might have survived indefinitely—adapting to changing circumstances, expanding settlement onto uplands. However, the complex interdependencies that strengthened township life proved a fatal weakness; and as improvers began to pick at threads in the fabric—reforming particular aspects of land use and tenure—the web was weakened, and within a short time irretrievably unravelled. Cooperative agriculture was neither a conservative bulwark against change nor a springboard for improvement. There was, certainly, no inherent inclination among husbandmen to abandon their way of life; but neither was there any inherent weakness in the system that might have prevented the continuation of cooperative agriculture in Scotland. However, as Sir John Sinclair observed: 'In no country in Europe are the rights of proprietors so well defined and so carefully protected';[235] and these rights, exercised in the implementation of improvement, proved an irresistible force. Prescient husbandmen recognised the potential benefits of improvement. Wise husbandmen recognised the futility of resistance. Most husbandmen were content to abandon tradition and ride the wave of improvement, if only to please their laird.

3

REVOLUTIONARY THEORY

An enormous advance

When sheriff-substitute Charles Rampini wrote his history of Moray and Nairn during the closing decade of the nineteenth century, he had no doubt that landscape and agriculture had been transformed in a momentous episode; at its heart was an 'enormous advance ... in the cultivation of the soil ... almost a revolution'. Although Rampini lacked the moderating perspective of distance, he benefited from the close-up impression of his own observation. Rampini, writing in the 1890s dated these changes as 'the growth of the last sixty or seventy years only'. Arguably, though, the growth that Rampini recognised was a second, industrialised, phase representing the fruition of processes that were seeded around 1760 and which were in flourishing growth by the 1820s.[1] This rural revolution progressed patchily as improving policies were implemented with different emphases and at different rates by different innovators—and even at different rates among the several estates of a single landowner.

The uneven progress and extended timescale of change in Scotland has fuelled debates about whether there was a Scottish Agricultural Revolution at all, rather than an evolution, accelerating from slow beginnings in the seventeenth century or even earlier. A flurry of discussion followed G. Wittington's provocative question: 'Was there a Scottish agricultural revolution?', though that debate, if not stillborn, failed to thrive and was soon knocked on the head. The majority of academic debate focuses upon the nature and rate of change and matters of local detail within a process that bears broad description as an agricultural revolution.[2] I. H. Adams was 'convinced that an economic event of such a description did occur in Scotland', and amplified the sentiment: 'The evidence seems overwhelming that Scotland experienced an Agricultural Revolution ... it started in the aftermath of the 1745 Rebellion'.[3] I. Whyte identified a comprehensive 'Agricultural Revolution [that] obliterated most traces of the pre-existing agricultural landscape'.[4] A. Fenton was 'in no doubt that the speed and range of change in Scotland amounted to an agricultural revolution'.[5] J. S. Smith recognised a revolution that progressed in a 'series of surges of landscape change ... in the period from 1750 to 1830'.[6] J. E. Handley, meanwhile, had embraced the expression without qualification as the title for his broad study of the period.[7]

The effects of this revolution are writ large upon Moray landscapes. Today there survives scarcely a vestige of any activity not associated with new agricultural practices introduced from the later eighteenth century onwards; and where a vestige survives—chiefly in highland parishes—the faintness and fragmentary condition of the remains are slight enough to confirm that a juggernaut of change did indeed pass this way, crushing the pre-existing culture and landscape beneath its wheels. Indeed, little of the landscape travelled by General William Roy's military surveyors in the 1740s survived to be planned by the Ordnance Surveyors in the 1860s: what did remain were the decaying dykes of redundant fieldscapes, and buildings either roofless or in the final stages of terminal decay.

T. Devine characterised the improvement phenomenon as 'almost a craze'.[8] Other historians agreed: W. Ferguson described improvement in England as a 'passion', whilst 'in Scotland it became almost a mania'.[9] So comprehensive was the rural revolution, that the memory of cooperative agriculture and its associated landscape has been wiped from popular consciousness. In Moray today, no folk memory survives of any tradition other than improvement culture. Rectilinear fieldscapes and drystane dykes are regarded as timeless. Symmetrical stone-built cottages are admired as hoary vernacular. The nineteenth-century ploughman's straight furrow, the horsegin and the bothy ballad are the subject of romantic veneration.

The *Statistical Accounts* help to pin down dates for the regular revolution in Moray. The first *Accounts* indicate significant, but patchy, regularisation of agriculture and landscape by the 1790s. An improving zeal had certainly infected gentleman-farmers and agricultural aristocrats. Green shoots of improvement were germinating in every parish, with especially vigorous growth in the laich; but the improvement craze had not reached epidemic proportions among ordinary tenants and husbandmen.[10]

Statistical Accounts may be used to track the progress of improvement—from a low base in the 1790s to a more general implementation in the 1830s—by noting the mention (or omission) of key indicators of improvement in each parish report. These indicators comprise specific references to: improvement, enclosure, division/amalgamation of farms, turnips, potatoes, clover and sown grasses, improved ploughs and use of horses in ploughing, lime, new villages, improved sheep breeds, new houses, and long leases.

Among the twenty-one Moray parishes, only eight were specifically stated to be undergoing improvement in the 1790s. However, turnips (a key marker for improved agriculture) were grown in fourteen parishes; potatoes in thirteen. Notably, 'a considerable quantity' of both exotic roots was raised in highland Kirkmichael.[11] Clover and/or sown grass was cultivated in ten. Plantations of trees were established in twelve parishes. Enclosure was mentioned in seven parishes; lime in only five. Just three laichland ministers reported the reorganisation of farms through amalgamation or division. Laichland parishes took the lead in adopting regular practices. Spynie ticks ten boxes; Alves and Birnie each tick eight. The average for eleven laichland parishes is 6.2 hits.[12] There seems to be little difference between the six upland and three highland parishes. The average for these nine parishes is only 3.8 hits. Among these, however, Dallas and Rafford each tick six boxes and Inveravon ticks five, showing them to be no less improved (by this measure) than Drainie, St Andrews-Lhanbryd,

Speymouth and Urquhart in the laich. This may reflect the influence of improving landlords such as Ballindalloch in Inveravon and Gordonstoun in Dallas.

In the *New Statistical Accounts* of 1834–45, most reporters confirmed the key markers of improved agriculture. In Edinkillie, Reverend Peter Farries identified the introduction of improved practices with notable precision. The agriculture of his parish had been raised since 1792 from 'a very wretched state ... Although the great benefit of green crops, and a proper rotation, has been shewn by some of the gentlemen',[13] to a commendably improved condition

> since the beginning of the present century when Mr Alexander Wilson, late tenant at Gervally, was brought from Berwickshire by Mr Cumin of Relugas ... His merits as an agriculturist have been recognized ... by five extensive and most respectable proprietors, who erected a marble tablet to his memory .... to mark the sense they entertain of his zeal and fidelity in the management and Improvement of the estates in this neighbourhood.[14]

The *New Statistical Accounts* recorded a wide range of improvement practices in every parish. Turnips and clover or sown grasses were noted everywhere except Forres. Liming was widespread. Dwellings and farm buildings were improved in thirteen parishes, and formal long leases were reported in nine.

The *General Views of Agriculture*, broadly agree with the *Statistical Accounts* in describing a relatively low level of agricultural innovation before 1794. James Donaldson asserted that change in Elginshire had been under way from 1746 onwards, though 'making little progress, until about the year 1768', when improvement was boosted by the earl of Fife.[15] In Banffshire, Donaldson dated the beginnings of change to the year 1748 and credited the innovation to the efforts of the earl of Findlater.[16] The second round of *General Views* (published 1811 and 1812) suggested steady progress in the tide of improvement. However, regularisation still had far to go. The revolution was hampered by 'want of education' among smaller tenants in Banffshire.[17] Even in the fertile laich, progress was patchy and contrasts striking. William Leslie observed in 1811: 'in Alves and Kinloss ... the grounds much resemble the landscape between Cambridge and Ware'; though in other laichland parishes 'pretty extensive plots of waste are everywhere intermingled ... covered with whin bushes, broom, or the most stunted and useless kind of heath'.[18]

The improvement ethos

The practical and ideological package labelled 'improvement' was embraced by Scottish landowners as a patriotic duty: a manifestation of virtuous and enlightened modernity that contrasted with a recent past of clannish conflict, domestic inconvenience and cooperative agriculture punctuated by periodic famine. Thus an early agricultural treatise could be advertised as *An essay on the Husbandry of Scotland ... by a Lover of His* Country;[19] and even the unrepentant Jacobite, William Mackintosh of Borlum, promoted his *Essay* on improvement as the work of 'a LOVER of his COUNTRY'[20]—demonstrating, perhaps that the improving ethos transcended political allegiance.

Improvement was seized upon as a way forward for prescient landowners who recognised that the Union of 1707 and the collapse of Jacobitism had drawn a line under the past. Perceptive Scottish landowners recognised too the relative backwardness of North Britain. The Union had extinguished the political role of ordinary landowners; heritors found an outlet for their energies in the cultivation of their own gardens—and the vigorous improvement of their estates, inspired by English example, and loyalty to the king 'farmer George'.[21]

The improvement ethos was built upon a foundation of Enlightenment thought and cross-border contact. Thus the regular revolution was broadly cultural rather than narrowly agricultural. Improvers introduced reason and order to agriculture, landscape, and to relationships between those who owned and those who cultivated the soil. Regarding nature as tameable, the improvers changed the nature of the relationship between man and the environment: the rational, systematic and quasi-scientific systems of the improvers contrasting with cooperative practices based upon disorderly tradition, habit, and the untutored folk knowledge of peasant husbandmen.

Landowners who had experienced classical culture—during a grand tour or a university education—brought a classicising influence to bear upon their own domains. Landscape was reordered into rectilinear patterns. Buildings were reconstructed in geometrical arrangements behind symmetrical façades. Printed regulations governed tenancies and systematised the cultivation of the soil.[22] Settlements were planned as straight streets and squares.

Rational principles underpinned Lord Kames' seminal tract on agriculture, significantly subtitled: 'An Attempt to improve AGRICULTURE By subjecting it to the Test of RATIONAL PRINCIPLES'.[23] Furthermore, Kames invoked both 'Des Cartes' and 'Dr Black, professor of chymistry in the college of Edinburgh' in support of his rational and improving treatise.[24] And in a deferential nod towards the agricultural enthusiasm of George III, Kames noted, 'In every well-governed state, agriculture had been duly honoured'.[25]

The shift in emphasis, which assigned to landowners (rather than township husbandmen) a role as arbiters of correct agricultural practice, had been gaining currency since the 1730s. Sir John Dalrymple, 'a lover of his country', noted with disapproval: 'Husbandry, till of late, was intirely managed in Scotland by the Vulgar, who, like Moles, blindly ran on in the Tract their Fathers had made'.[26]

Kames chose the curious oxymoron, *The Gentleman Farmer*, as title for his treatise. The revolutionary implications of this usage can hardly be underestimated. It was not Kames' own coining, but it was a recent colloquialism with a gloss of newness still upon it.[27] The shockingly contradictory notion of a gentleman-farmer was made acceptable to ordinary Scottish landowners through its promotion by a leading Enlightenment thinker and senior member of the legal establishment. Kames took pains to emphasise that agriculture was an appropriate interest—even a hands-on activity—for a gentleman.[28] This was radical stuff: a gentleman, by definition, did not work, but lived on the income provided by tenants who farmed (that is, paid rent for—and by extension, also worked) the land. To suggest that a gentleman might get his hands dirty (or at least be interested in day-to-day activities of those who did) might seem a dangerously democratic assault upon the fabric of society. Samuel Johnson, who liked to posture as a conservative Tory, regarded the gentleman-farmer as an absurd chimera. He lampooned the agricultural enthusiasm of James Burnett, Lord Monboddo, who was one of Kames' Court of Session colleagues. Burnett greeted Johnson and Boswell in the character of '*Farmer Burnet*' dressed in 'a rustick suit, and ... a little round hat' before treating his guests to 'his family dinner, a farmer's dinner'. Johnson was unimpressed.

> he did not approve of a judge's calling himself *Farmer* Burnett, and going about with a little round hat ... He laughed heartily at his lordship's saying he was an *enthusiastical* farmer; 'for, (said he,) what can he do in farming by his *enthusiasm?*'[29]

Nonetheless, Kames recommended gentleman-farming as a profitable and healthful lifestyle in which the landowner's self-interest also served the greater good. He declared, 'Every gentleman-farmer must of course be a patriot'.[30] In this he echoed sentiments already current, and which an educated gentleman might be expected to recognise:

> God and Nature fix'd the general frame,
> And bade self-love and social be the same.[31]

Sir Archibald Grant, the famous improver of Monymusk in Aberdeenshire, had already embraced the sentiment that Kames articulated, in advice to his son in 1754:

> Next to our duety to God ... attention to health is our second duety, and our next is to qualify ourselves to be useful in the world.'[32]

Perhaps Monymusk had read William Mackintosh's improving *Essay* which urged landowners to embrace modern husbandry by declaring, 'It is just, it is human, and what Religion requires of us'.[33]

Thus agriculture under the improvers was elevated into a virtuous pursuit for visionary gentlemen. A lecture programme at Edinburgh University incorporated agriculture within the family of natural philosophy as a noble science. Writing in 1770, Matthew Peters asserted that agriculture was 'next in kindred to philosophy'.[34] David Souter emphasised the scientific aspects of manurance as a gentlemanly pursuit, identifying as the key drivers of improvement:

> investigations and experiments in chemistry ... the institution of an agricultural class in one of the Scottish universities ... treatises and periodical publications written by men of eminent abilities ...the institution of numerous agricultural societies, composed of farmers, and of gentlemen of superior intelligence.

These 'gentlemen', of course, included Souter's patrons on the Board of Agriculture.[35] Souter asserted furthermore, that the cultivation of the soil might confer a status equal to that of a physician or lawyer—insofar as the improving farmer required to be 'trained with as much care, and must pass through as regular a course of preparatory discipline, as is required in almost any other profession'.[36] This elevation of the status of the husbandman was generally accepted among theoreticians, appearing also in the *General View of Stirlingshire*, whose author declared, 'agricultural improvements ... have had the happy effect of giving dignity to the profession of a farmer'.[37] However, respect for the farmer's profession did not necessarily extend to the person of the practical farmers cultivating land beyond the fence of the proprietor's own back yard. Thus, even though John Gray offered £200 (£5 above valuation) for a lease on the farm of Viewfield or Barnyards on the Fife estate, the factor noted:

> From its immediate vicinity to Innes, one of the principal Mansion Houses of the Family, it is however necessary to select a Tenant of character and respectability, and who is likely to be personally agreeable to the ... occupier of that residence.[38]

Gray, a sub-tenant aspiring to the status of farmer, did not fit the profile, and his offer was rejected.

Beneath the gloss of noble purpose—in the earlier stages of the improvement craze at least—it is probable that agricultural activity was, for some landowners, little more than a current fad embraced as part of a dilettante's portfolio of pastimes. The improvement of the home farm or of a landowner's place and its policies might be simply conspicuous consumption—a demonstration of a heritor's wealth and fashionable modernity. That certainly was the poet Southey's view of improvements wrought just across the Firth from Moray, at Novar, where Sir Hector Munro

> expended [on his estate] the whole wealth which he acquired in India, so that he was obliged to go to India again and make a second fortune for the purpose of enabling him to live on it.[39]

Improvement evangelism

Practical improvement was accompanied by a growing body of theoretical advice in print. This new literary genre seems to have originated during the late seventeenth century. The generation 1680–1720 saw a cautious handful of publications on agriculture. Among the earliest was John Donaldson's practical manual of 1697, whose title advertised the economic benefits of improvement: *Husbandry Anatomised, or an Enquiry into the Present Manner of Teiling and Manuring the Ground in Scotland for the most part; and Several Rules and Measures Laid Down for the Better Improvement Thereof, in so much that One Third Part of the Expense of the Present Way of Labouring Thereof May be Saved*. Donaldson's treatise devoted ample space to improvement of the soil through application of dung, lime, marl and sea-ware; subsequent chapters discussed 'The great Profit of Hedging and Inclosures', with guidance also on sheep husbandry, dairying, fallowing of outfield, and turnips, which, he declared, 'were rare in Scotland at this time'.[40] Lord Belhaven's *The Country-Man's Rudiments* (1699) was produced as an accessible pamphlet rather than a weighty tome, with advice for farmers in East Lothian on ploughing, harrowing, farm buildings, liming, potatoes and turnips, rents and ridging.

From small beginnings publishers created a thriving market. Output increased with approximately one new title a year published during the generation down to 1760. Among the tracts that appeared during this preliminary phase was William Mackintosh's *Essay on ... Inclosing, Fallowing, Planting, &c.* Mackintosh applauded the modernising efforts of contemporary landowners, giving equal notice to Mr Scot of Scotstarbat in Fife and to Sir Robert Gordon of Gordonstoun and Mr Dunbar [of Thunderton] in Duffus in the laich of Moray.[41] However, improving landowners did not universally applaud Mackintosh: a copy of 'An Essay upon improving all Scotland by Borlum McKintosh' was purchased for the Gordon Castle library; but, perhaps because improvement theory had developed beyond Mackintosh's vision, his treatise was disparaged as 'a foolish Book' in the 1754 catalogue.[42]

Production of improvement texts increased three- or four-fold during the period 1790–1820. The vitality of the improvement literature industry was noted by Lord Kames in the 1770s as a natural matter of supply and demand. He puffed his *Gentleman Farmer* and disparaged competitors in a preface that declared sarcastically 'hold out your purse and wares will never be wanting'.[43] The output of improving tracts developed most strongly, however, during decades when improvement was already well under way: agricultural publications followed rather than led the craze.

In north-east Scotland, Sir Archibald Grant of Monymusk was ahead of the trend. J. Glass asserted that Grant was 'very well read in the means of agricultural improvement'.[44] In fact Grant's enthusiasm and his practical efforts originated before 1720, thus antedating the surge in agricultural tracts. Other improving landowners too managed quite well without written instructions. For example, Gordonstoun was under improvement before 1740 (anticipating the wave of publications), and even in 1816 its library contained only four agricultural titles of which the only improvement tract was *A Treatise Concerning the Manner of Fallowing*, published by the Society for Improving the Knowledge of Agriculture (Edinburgh, 1724).[45] The swarm of publications also failed to settle at Ballindalloch. Around 1797 General Grant's library contained a range of classical and popular literature, history, divinity and natural philosophy, but only nine volumes on husbandry and none of the most modern treatises. Records of loans from Ballindalloch's library, however, demonstrate the wide circulation that books might achieve.[46] Monymusk too was a generous lender of books.[47] So was Brodie, whose borrowers included Altyre, Pitgavenie Burgie, Kilravock and Dalvey.[48] However, Brodie possessed a bare handful of agricultural titles.[49] Gordon Castle library catalogues include some thirty titles that might be classed as improvement tracts. Most, though, were published before 1730. Among the more modern of Gordon's acquisitions were Lord Kames' *Gentleman Farmer*, Sir John Sinclair's *Systems of Husbandry in Scotland* and William Leslie's *Survey of the Province of Moray*; and pamphlets on ploughs, flax, fruit trees and the cultivation of moss-earth. Gordon possessed Shaw's *History of the Province of Moray*; Adam Smith's *Wealth of Nations*; a *General View of the Agriculture of* Kincardineshire (though none of the *Views* of Moray and Banffshire); and a copy of *The Grampians Desolate*. Few of Gordon's loans are recorded, though several volumes of popular literature—including Defoe's *Roxana* and Dryden's *poetry* were borrowed 'By Lady Lyon at Brodie House'; 'an old copy of Littleton's Dictionary & the Grammatical Exercises' were loaned to James Brown, schoolmaster; and a score of law texts were 'In John Gordon of Cluny's custody'.[50] It seems likely, therefore, that the dukes of Gordon learned how to be improvers primarily by word-of-mouth advice and by observation of practical examples; or perhaps the dukes borrowed books from fellow enthusiasts. Improving tracts were disseminated by subscription libraries, including one founded in 1789 by Isaac Forsyth, bookseller and improver in Elgin.[51] On the whole, though, improvement ideas were circulated among proprietors by personal communication and practical example rather than in print.

The flood of agricultural publications was a manifestation of a more general craze as Enlightenment intellectuals sought out the patterns and laws that governed the world of nature; and as a natural concomitant they sought to regulate, by rational rules, the affairs of men.

> THE EIGHTEENTH CENTURY was seized by a rage for order ... The vogue was for organizing, structuring and methodizing. Works of reference became both fashionable and necessary.[52]

A major contribution to—and manifestation of—this process was a growing body of reference books: from Samuel Johnson's *Dictionary of the English Language* (1755) to Hume's six-volume *History of England* (1754–62) and the *Encyclopaedia Britannica* (1768–71). Sitting comfortably within this information revolution was the plethora of agricultural treatises.

The appetite for agricultural tracts evidences a more general cultural change underpinning agricultural improvement. It might have seemed unthinkable before the mid-eighteenth century for texts on such an earthy subject as practical agriculture to rub shoulders in the book room of the big house with the usual library of theology, law, classics and philosophy. However, by the second half of the century such juxtaposition was commonplace; and Lord Kames, a celebrity polymath spanning agriculture, law and philosophy, was a living exemplar of this cultural phenomenon. Even so, many improving tracts were destined 'to grace shelves, to honour past actions', as artefacts to be possessed—included in a gentleman's library as evidence of the landowner's improving credentials—rather than as practical guides for everyday use in the fields.[53] The sixth earl of Findlater assembled, 'In Cullen House ... one of the richest collections to be found in Scotland of works on agriculture published in the eighteenth century' which, regardless of any practical improvements, was itself deemed worthy of applause.[54] Naturally, few of the agricultural experts were likely to admit that their books remained unread on library shelves. Indeed, David Souter was confident that tenants of larger farms 'whose possessions are of sufficient extent to relieve them from the drudgery of common labour ... will ... seek information from books'. He also thought that farmers might have leisure to study and apply lessons from works such as the *General Views* and *Statistical Accounts*, 'taking comparative views of the state of farming in other places with its state at home'.[55]

Sir Archibald Grant of Monymusk enthusiastically embraced the honourable name of farmer in *The Farmers' New-Year's Gift to his Countrymen* (1757), which concentrated on the virtues of different manures. The sequel (1760) was a *Dissertation on the Chief Obstacles to the Improvement of Land, and Introducing Better Methods of Agriculture throughout Scotland*. Grant's 1766 booklet *The Practical Farmer's Pocket-Companion ... In a Letter from a Gentleman in the South of Scotland, who has had long experience of the rules he prescribes*, offered ordinary husbandmen an accessible outline of best practice on most aspects of improved agriculture including manures, inclosing, fallowing, crop rotation, sown grasses, turnips, tree-planting, livestock and ploughing. The *Pocket-Companion* was sold at a discounted price:

> tho' it contains matter enough to have made an eighteen pence pamphlet it is sold at threepence, that Gentlemen ... may put numbers of them in the hands of their tenants. They who order fifty copies, will have them at the rate of one Guinea per Hundred.[56]

Notwithstanding such efforts, it seems unlikely that most husbandmen ever saw—far less used—published manuals and theoretical tracts in the field. Indeed, even Monymusk might on occasion admit that 'common farmers do not read'[57] Tenants who signed leases in the eighteenth century could manage, in many instances, only a scratchy initial: and even if such tenants could read but not write, they were certainly not men of bookish habits likely to seek guidance in print—beyond their biblical ordinary. The price of books also placed agricultural treatises beyond the reach of most ordinary farmers. William Lorrimer, the factor at Castle Grant was one of many who complained that agricultural books were 'too expensive'. Improvement treatises might cost from three shillings upwards (a week's wages for a labouring man); and the price of Charles Varlo's *Modern Farmer's Guide* (1768), though advertised for the use of farmers and country gentlemen and the simple and unlearned, was a swingeing twelve shillings.[58] But this hardly mattered. A landowner who had absorbed improvement ideas could mediate the substance of his reading to his tenants; and, as Scottish landowners enjoyed almost unlimited power over the management of their estates, the tenant had little choice but to comply with his master's diktat—however eccentric or counter-intuitive it might appear. New practices might be communicated or imposed through the factor or in the terms of a lease, while the prescient husbandman, seeing which way his laird's enthusiasm lay, could be expected to turn improver without overt prompting, to secure a tenancy or simply to curry favour with laird or factor.

Serial publications perhaps came closer to the ordinary husbandman's orbit, though stamp duties and high cover prices probably kept even these beyond the reach of many. At sixpence, the monthly *The Scots Farmer*, represented a significant expenditure. For those who could afford them, periodicals offered a distillation of sturdier agricultural literature. For example, in its very first year the *Scots Magazine* contained 'A treatise on horse-hoeing husbandry'.[59]

The Farmer's Magazine (1776–80) offered a 'useful family companion, Consisting of practical essays ... on the different branches of husbandry ... A miscellaneous collection of valuable family receipts ... Useful hints and curious observations'. The magazine was available in Isaac Forsyth's library, and especially recommended by the proprietor, who urged subscribers to submit articles describing their own schemes for publication in its pages.[60] Successors included a *Farmer's Magazine* (Edinburgh, 1800–25), 'devoted to agriculture and rural affairs', and *The British Farmer's Magazine* (1826–79), which carried agriculture through the final stages of improvement and into thorough regularity.

Arthur Young—pamphleteer, novelist, parliamentary reporter, estate steward, secretary to the Board of Agriculture, and (failed) farmer—published *Annals of Agriculture* (1784–1815). The *Annals* offered a forum for progressive news, views and descriptions of agricultural innovations; and an arena in which theoreticians might ride their improving hobby horses. The circulation was only 350 copies and it unclear how far the *Annals* penetrated Scotland to preach among the already-converted improvers of Moray.[61] Young's literary output also included agricultural monographs, such as *Essays on the Management of Hogs* (London, 1769), and *A Course of Experimental Agriculture* (London, 1773). The epitaph Young contrived for his wife, Martha, who died in 1815, reflected the all-consuming nature of an improver's agricultural obsession: Martha was immortalised as 'the great-grand-daughter of John Allen, esq., of Lyng House in the county of Norfolk, the first person ... who there used marl'.[62]

Practical improvers provided examples of best practice and regular agriculture that were more instructive than the most eloquent treatise. Thus improvement spread contagiously through personal contacts among gentlemen and farmers. In general, Scottish agricultural innovation began in southern counties, applying lessons learned from English agriculturalists. Shortly after the union of 1707, Thomas Hamilton, sixth earl of Haddington (1680–1735), began reorganising his estate of Tyninghame, East Lothian, by seeding the land with progressive tenants, whom he recruited from more advanced agricultural environments. The earl declared:

> I now took pleasure in planting, and inclosing ... I got some farmers from Dorsetshire ...
> From these Englishmen, we came to the knowledge of sowing and management of grass
> seeds.[63]

For the illumination of those who might wish to follow his example, the earl published (1735) *A Short Treatise on Forest Trees, Acquaticks, Ever-greens, Fences and Grass-Seeds*. Scottish landowners actively sought out advice and example, initially from England, and subsequently from one another. Dr Hutton of Slighshouses, Berwickshire, imported Norfolk ploughmen (with their Norfolk ploughs) to work his estate from 1754 onwards. William Dawson, farmer at Frogden near Kelso, worked on farms in Yorkshire, Essex and Leicestershire, returning to the Borders with a portmanteau of improved practices including: drainage of bogs, the use of lime, turnip husbandry, and ploughing with horses in straight furrows. Dawson trained Scottish ploughmen in the new style of working, and his pupils spread the word by practical example into East Lothian and Angus.[64] Landowners beyond the Moray Firth followed suit, introducing English-trained factors and grieves from Lothian, or recruiting directly from England managers who would improve their estates: by 1792 all the gentlemen's farms in Kiltearn were managed by southerners.[65]

Before mid-century, improvement spread through southern counties of Scotland, embraced by aristocratic innovators such as John, earl of Stair (1673–1747) who introduced clover and turnips on his west Lothian estate.[66] Meanwhile ordinary gentlemen too made exemplary experiments in improvement. For example, William Craig of Arbigland (1703–98) introduced horse-hoeing and turnip cultivation to Kirkcudbright during the first half of the eighteenth century.[67] John Cockburn of Ormiston (1679–1758) abolished runrig on his East Lothian estate, reallocating the land as discrete farms of enclosed fields, which were tenanted under written leases for specified terms of years. Cockburn planted trees on poorer land, and under his management the rental of Ormiston doubled.[68] This 'patriotic zeal' earned Cockburn high praise from Lord Kames.[69]

North-east landowners did not lag very far behind, even though I. Whyte asserted that 'significant change did not affect the North-East until the end of the century'.[70] During the first generation of the eighteenth century improvement was leap-frogged from England to north-east Scotland by Henrietta Morduant, daughter of the duke of Peterborough—married in 1706 to Alexander Gordon, heir to the Gordon dukedom. Henrietta brought to Bog of Gight on the Spey a trousseau of progressive agricultural practice including hay-making, fallowing, tree-planting and English ploughs—with English ploughmen—which attracted the applause of the notable improver, Mackintosh of Borlum.[71] However, Henrietta's improvements were not entirely innovatory. Already there was enclosure and rational management of grazing parks for cattle in the vicinity of Gordon Castle—established during the closing years of the seventeenth century.[72] There were significant enclosed landscapes in western Moray by around 1750, notably in Forres and Dyke & Moy, where military surveyors recorded the landscape legacy of Mary Sleigh, wife of Lord Lyon Alexander Brodie of Brodie.[73]

> This excellent Lady ... had acquired liberal views of the benefit and mutual relations of agriculture, manufactures, and commerce ... she knew the value of people on an estate ... The men she employed in levelling, trenching, draining, and raising fences ... She enclosed and subdivided the extensive mains ... trained up hedges ... made new roads; straightened old ones ... put trees in the gardens of every farm-stead.[74]

Mary Sleigh's example influenced her neighbours, the earl of Moray, and Grant of Moy. Military surveyors mapped further improved landscapes in east Moray around Innes; and at Gordonstoun. In Inveravon they surveyed fields, bounded by hedgerows and standard trees, near Ballindalloch Castle, as well as extensive rectilinear enclosures dividing uncultivated moorland.[75] On Speyside, meanwhile, Patrick Grant of Elchies had been sowing grasses and enclosing fields since 1726.[76]

Sir Archibald Grant of Monymusk, one of the most brilliant luminaries of Scottish agricultural improvement, was also a Moray landowner, with a small property in Knockando, though his principal estate was in Aberdeenshire. Monymusk's achievement has been magnified by the happy survival of estate papers, and by Archibald's own vigorous self-promotion. Monymusk improvements from 1716 onwards offered an early example of what might be achieved in the north-east countryside.[77] Always his own best publicist, Sir Archibald wrote a seminal tract titled 'A description of the present state of Monymusk and what hath been done to make it what it is'.[78] More modestly Cumin of Auchray, also in Aberdeenshire, was encouraging cultivation of flax, turnips and sown grasses, and the use of lime, from the 1730s. The *Statistical Account* for Monquhitter depicted him as the model of a hands-on improving landlord—as 'he frequently walked or rode through his estates, freely conversing with his tenants, rousing them to industry'.[79]

From the 1740s Lord Deskford (1716–70)—later sixth earl of Findlater—was determinedly improving his Banffshire estates.[80] A landscape of strictly rectangular enclosed, hedged fields and straight access roads, was created in the vicinity of Cullen House by the 1750s;[81] while William Leslie credited Findlater with introducing Norfolk turnips to north-east farmers around 1760.[82] The earl was happy to be taught by others—even by others of lower rank. He employed English overseers to manage his model farm at Colleonard and introduce the 'improved methods of the Lothians and England': planting grass, turnips and potatoes, and making enclosures. In the spirit of the age Findlater 'put the best theory and practice to the test of actual experiment'.[83] From 1760 onwards Findlater's home farm cash book documented the distribution among tenants of key articles of improved husbandry, including lime, turnip and kale seed, seed potatoes, and tree seedlings.[84] Findlater sent his own tenants' sons to Berwickshire to learn Lord Kames's methods for application in Banffshire.[85] The earl also proudly showed off his experimental improvements to visiting 'gentlemen of the neighbourhood ... and several of the farmers ... [who] were, of course, led to see and consider the example thus set before them'.[86] Findlater was credited with

> the exclusive merit of introducing into the north of Scotland those improvements in agriculture ... which in the space of a few years raised his country from a state of barbarism to a degree of civilisation equal to that of the most improved districts of the south.[87]

This deferential adulation probably overstated the influence of the earl, who was just one among several who seeded the craze in the north-east. Indeed, Alexander Boswell, lord Auchinleck, advanced the duke of Gordon to equal billing with Findlater as 'the only Improvers I know who carry thro' the whole Plan with equal care and attention'.[88] Be that as it may, aristocratic improvers presumably expected their exemplary agricultural innovations to be admired and imitated by tenants; and, though few tenants would recognise the quotation, most would self-interestedly follow Quintilian's maxim: 'What a prince does seems like a command'.

The traveller Thomas Newte, after paying the usual homage to Lord Findlater, admired the exemplary improvements of the gentleman-farmer of Cantray on the Nairn:

> a gentleman ... who has done more towards the improvement of the country than any individual, perhaps in the North of Scotland ... A fortune fairly acquired in business is

expended by Mr. Davidson, with equal taste and patriotism, in converting bleak and barren moors into lively and fertile enclosures ... The blowing up of rocks, the burning of lime, the making of ditches and drains, the trenching of ground, &c. has doubtless been attended with great expense. But, though Mr, Davidson may not, his son will reap, and that in an ample manner, the fruits of his labour ... Were every land-holder to follow ... the example of Mr. Davidson of Cantray, the face of the country, in thirty years would be materially changed.[89]

Moray's own agricultural revolution was exported into Inverness-shire, reaching Stratherrick in 1800—where, however, improvement had already taken hold.[90] More famous (because more notorious) was the transmission of Moray's improvement into Sutherland. The vector here was a pair of minor landowners who became famous as improvers (or notorious as clearers): William Young of Inverugie, and Patrick Sellar of Westfield, who had previously worked as a surveyor for Altyre and Gordonstoun.[91]

Improvement was also promoted as government policy from the 1750s onwards by the Annexed Estates Commissioners, a 'powerhouse of ideas and example', who proved a 'vital catalyst that set alight the spirit of improvement that was to sweep through Scotland for the next generation'.[92] The Commissioners (among whom were Lord Kames, Lord Deskford, and William Grant, lord Prestongrange, a brother of Sir Archibald of Monymusk) were tasked with the administration of estates forfeited by Jacobite landowners and subsequently annexed by the crown: on the west coast (Barrisdale and Kinlochmoidart); in Perthshire, Aberdeenshire and in Cromartyshire. They sought to embrace the tenantry of rebellious lairds into the Hanoverian commonwealth: civilizing township folk by promoting amongst them 'the Protestant Religion, good Government, Industry and Manufactures'.[93] The Commissioners intruded southern-trained grieves to manage home farms, and so improvement leap-frogged from Lothian to the forfeited estates of Cromarty, a day's ride (or a short boat trip) from the laich of Moray. Underpinning the Commissioners' work was the sanguine expectation that (with the support of the disarming acts and other proscriptions) the commercialisation of agriculture would wean highlanders from the allurements of Jacobitism, while rural prosperity would allow rebellious highlanders to be embraced into the political and cultural mainstream.

The Commissioners were prone to believe their own propaganda, and their moral influence was not always translated into practical improvement. In the north-east, four decades of commissioners' influence in Easter Ross proved of 'questionable significance'. The earl of Cromarty, had followed the fashion and joined the Society of Improvers, but his estate remained 'largely unimproved' when forfeited in 1746. The commissioners sponsored significant industrial growth, but 'their impact on agricultural development was, all in all, slight'.[94]

As the improving ethos was established in a number of foci throughout Scotland, the rapid spread of the cult was assured. Among the missionaries who carried the good news of improvement were mobile farm managers, whom gentleman-farmers recruited from a national grieve-pool. Few could match the exemplary busyness of the idealised laichland farm manager,

Mr Jamieson [who] shines conspicuously. His mind seems stored with resources for every emergency ... He shapes his conduct to the circumstances ... constantly preserving the greatest order and regularity.[95]

However, when George Vintner, a Northumbrian grieve, found himself between jobs in Portsoy in May 1774, he advertised his services in the *Aberdeen Journal*, emphasising both geographical breadth and practical ability:

This man was born in Northumberland and has been his whole lifetime employed in managing large Farms and improving Ground both in England and Scotland and has a thorough Knowledge in breeding Horses and Cattle and likewise in fattening cattle.[96]

Practical workmen, such as dykers, masons and ploughmen, who flitted from fee to fee, formed a significant, if poorly-documented, regiment of revolutionary foot-soldiers. Their achievement is, however writ large upon the landscape: in the regular houses they built, the double-drystone dykes that section up improved farmscapes; and in the tradition of the horseman's straight furrow. The emergent profession of the land surveyor, is strikingly well documented. Land surveyors formed a regiment of mobile enthusiasts. In moving from contract to contract they disseminated the still-accumulating experience of their improving employers, to strengthen the fabric of the regular revolution.

On the whole, Moray's improvers occupied a small world in which social occasions and contract work continually threw modern-minded men together. Thus, for instance, the administrative task of compiling the Elgin parish rental for 1825 was undertaken by three professional improvers: George McWilliam, land surveyor of choice for the earl of Fife; John Skirving, factor to the earl of Moray; and William Robertson, Moray's leading architect.[97]

Probably, though, Moray's landowners were the most powerful conduit for improvement ideas. The craze was spread, without forcing, through the easy communication that existed among improving proprietors themselves, rather than by the evangelical writings of remote theoreticians. Family connections, legal business, financial transactions and political activities linked landowners in networks within which ideas were readily transmitted, and practical applications demonstrated.

The ramifications of the lairds of Brodie suggest how extensive the network of contacts might be. The Brodie heartland was in the western laich, in Dyke & Moy. Across the border in Nairnshire, Brodie lands at Penick and Lochloy marched with those of cousins, the Brodies of Lethen.[98] In the heart of the laich, Brodie lands of Asleisk and Monaughty, again marched with Lethen (at Kilbuaick). On the coast, Brodie estates included Kinneddar and Spynie. James Brodie of Brodie (1637–1708) fathered at least nine daughters, whom he married off to neighbouring improvers including Lord Forbes; Robert Dunbar of Grangehill; Alexander Cumming of Altyre; Robert Dunbar of Dunphail; George Brodie of Asleisk and James Brodie of Whitehill. James's heir, Alexander Brodie (1697–1754) was MP for Elginshire (subsequently for the Inverness burghs). Alexander owned property in Caithness; and he was uncle to George Sinclair of Ulbster, whose son, Sir John Sinclair, heads the pantheon of

Scottish improvers. Alexander was also a senior Hanoverian politician, enjoying the office of Lord Lyon. He was intimately associated with social, political and cultural life of London and Edinburgh—where he discovered a taste for luxurious excess. While Brodie wasted the estate, his wife, Mary Sleigh, attended to its improvement. She landscaped the policies of Brodie castle, with extensive tree planting, decorative walks and an artificial lake. Alexander's heir, a second cousin, James Brodie of Spynie, eloped with lady Margaret Duff, daughter of William, first earl of Fife. And when the debts of the estate (now swelled to £31,500) finally brought Brodie to bankruptcy in 1774, James Duff, second earl of Fife, came to the rescue by purchasing the whole estate, clearing the debt, and reconveying to Brodie (under a stringent entail) a rump of lands in west Moray . The Lethen relations, meanwhile, were reconnected with Moray through the marriage of Sophia Brodie of Coulmony to her cousin, Lewis Dunbar of Grange, who had returned from the West Indies with a fortune to invest in his ancestral estate. Lewis and Sophie moved to Burgie, which became thereafter the seat of the Brodie-Dunbars. The details of these Brodie interrelationships are perhaps unimportant; but the existence of such a web (and similar webs exist for most landed families) suggests that the infection of improvement could hardly fail to insinuate itself throughout the landed class—without further urging by proselytising enthusiasts and printed tracts.[99]

A craze for clubs

Improving landowners naturally fell into like-minded company, and they affirmed their various enthusiasms by forming clubs. Clubbable gentlemen in Edinburgh could chose among a number of convivial societies. The Select Society (Founded 1759) was formed around an intellectual elite of the Edinburgh Enlightenment, including the painter Allan Ramsay, philosopher David Hume, economist Adam Smith and Lord Kames. The Poker Club (1762) was dedicated to stirring up political questions. The Pious Club met to eat pies and to drink. The clubs met ostensibly for conversation and exchange of ideas—even if that did degenerate into bawdy banter as the claret kicked in. The company might involve a mingling of social classes, with even quite humble folk admitted (for example Robert Burns to the Crochallan Fencibles) if they could contribute to the conversation.[100]

Clubbable landowners convened in agricultural societies. Among the earliest was Honourable Society of Improvers in the Knowledge of Agriculture in Scotland (founded 1723). The club attracted over 300 members (including the earl of Findlater);[101] and they accepted a challenge to 'mark down their thoughts', to correspond throughout the nation, and to form 'small societies of gentlemen and farmers in their several counties'. The Honourable Society perished in the 'Forty-five, but a successor emerged in 1755 in the Edinburgh Society for Encouraging the Arts, Sciences, Manufactures and Agriculture. The Edinburgh Society offered premiums for agricultural essays and prizes for planting trees, making manure, butter and cheese, for cultivation of potatoes, and for breeding calves and stallions. This became a pattern for farmer's clubs, which cascaded the improving craze downwards by the lure of prizes.[102]

Provincials—often under aristocratic encouragement—followed the clubbing trend. Archibald Grant emphasised the value of communication and debate in promoting improvement:

> A man even of knowledge in any science or business, improves much by converse on the subject, altho' with persons of much inferior knowledge ... and therefore, clubs of farmers, would be extremely useful; and at least in moonlights and long nights would be easy and no expense.[103]

A Society of Farmers in Buchan was formed, perhaps in 1735;[104] and a north-east society 'of Honest Farmers residing in the counties of Banff and Aberdeen' convened at Backlaw to discuss 'the proper method to cultivate and improve Grounds of different Sorts' in 1749.[105] In 1758, a club was established under Archibald Grant's encouragement, at Gordon's Mill, Aberdeenshire. It lasted barely seven years but during that time it considered a full range of agricultural topics. For example, a 1760 report itemised some fifteen 'errors and neglects' of the common farmer, including want of enclosures and 'the preposterous method they follow in gathering dunghills'. The club also published an exemplary form of improving lease which specified cropping regimes and other improvements, but omitted mention of compensation to the tenant for the cost of these innovations.[106]

The Royal Highland and Agricultural Society of Scotland, though based in Edinburgh, spread its net widely. Members received reports and recommendations on villages, communications, agriculture and fisheries. In contrast with its modernising outlook, the society also demonstrated a romantic affection for Gaelic culture, employing its own piper and debating the Ossian poems. Prizes were awarded for improved ploughs, and farm machinery, for dairy produce, cattle and sheep breeding, enclosing, and field crops. Ploughing matches began in 1801 at Hoddam, Annandale, establishing a rural tradition that continues after two centuries. The Society also published transactions and essays by members.[107] The first collection of prize essays included contributions on gooseberries, wool, coal and salt duties, kelp and potatoes. The sixth volume included 'Comparative experiments in the sowing of wheat', by the earl of Fife's Moray factor, miller and farmer, John Lawson at Oldmills, Elgin.[108]

It was a little while before the clubbing craze crossed the Spey. Moray was, however, connected with the farmers' club club: through the networks that connected landowners nationwide. Meanwhile Moray tenants received practical training from established agricultural societies, including the club founded in 1736 by John Cockburn of Ormiston.[109] An Elgin Farmer Society existed during 1784–85, though nothing of its business is recorded beyond a correspondence concerning the unfairness of the horse tax.[110] This society laid a foundation for the Morayshire Farmer Club, created in 1799. The club met under the direction of Isaac Forsyth, bookseller in Elgin.[111] Forsyth travelled widely to observe agricultural practice. He was entranced by the hedgerows defining enclosed fieldscapes around Ipswich. He approved of oak plantations by Loch Lomond and the cotton mills of New Lanark. He especially admired Mr Coke's estate at Holkham, Norfolk with its Southdown and Leicester sheep, Devon and Galloway cattle, and modern machinery. Forsyth was also the publisher of William Leslie's (1798) *Survey of the Province of Moray*, which was venerated locally as 'the muckle Isaac'.[112] Leslie applauded the Morayshire Farmer Club for its encouragement of the Newmill woollen manufactory; for importing 'the most celebrated new implements of agriculture to serve as models to the artisans of the country'; for peculiar attention to the improvement of the breed of horses; and for making available a library of improving volumes including Board of Agriculture reports and a set of the *Farmer's Magazine*.[113] The Moray historian, H. B. Mackintosh, regarded the Morayshire Farmer Club as:

> the first child to the Highland Agricultural Society, which is the parent of all the agricultural societies in the north. It has been the means of turning an art into a science and of practically showing landlords and tenants what other minds can do and are doing towards the development of farming—the first and great civilizer of mankind.[114]

The Morayshire club membership included both landowners and their factors. The club admitted the earl of Fife in November 1813, recognising that 'His Lordship appears to give universal Satisfaction to his Tennantry Indeed his condicension is extraordinary'. The earl, thus flattered, gave 20 guineas as a premium for cattle breeding.[115]

A Forres club existed in the first decade of the nineteenth century, though its activities are sketchy. It managed 'an importation of coal, for the supply of members'; and was also concerned in an enterprise, pursued jointly with the Elgin club and also involving Patrick Sellar, to cure pork at Burghead for export to London.[116] A Banffshire Farming Society predated the Morayshire Farmer Club, but is documented only in a memorandum, dated 2 February 1798, protesting to the earl of Fife about the Excise Act of 1784 and the advantage this gave Dutch gin over Scotch whisky with consequent impact upon Banffshire farmers and the drinking habits of the lower orders.[117]

A Badenoch and Strathspey Farming Society was founded in 1803 by duchess Jane Maxwell and patronised by the duke of Gordon. Founding members included the lairds of Grant, Rothiemurchus and Cluny, though the cost of membership (one guinea subscription and 5s yearly) was beyond the means of ordinary tenants. The diversity of the club's interests epitomises the complexity of improvement, as an ethos spun from numerous, agricultural, economic and cultural strands. A Strathspey farmer might win premiums for the best bull (8 guineas); best tup (5 guineas); and best acre of turnips (5 guineas). His wife might win a medal (worth 2 guineas) for the best spindle of linen yarn; and his son or daughter might compete for a one guinea prize, inaugurated by the duchess of Gordon, for the best reading in Gaelic and translation into English.[118]

4

PRACTICAL REVOLUTIONARIES & STATUTORY REGULATION

Funding improvement

Agricultural improvement could prove an expensive hobby. A key factor in the progress of the regular revolution was the ability of landowners to underwrite the initial costs. John Sinclair—the national hero of improvement—reformed his estates on credit and was bankrupted with debts of £50,000.[1] John Cockburn too embraced the fad with more enthusiasm than financial acumen and the cost of reforming agriculture at Ormiston ruined him.[2] These difficulties were less evident among Moray lairds, many of whom were able to apply money accumulated from wider business networks to agricultural improvement. Elchies could draw upon the profits of his Edinburgh legal business. Thomas Sellar of Westfield (father of Patrick) too earned a comfortable income as 'Trusty Tom', the lawyer and man of business preferred by several north-east landowners.[3] Other Moray lairds held government positions (for example James Brodie as Lord Lyon and James Grant of Ballindalloch as a senior army officer) and drew handsome incomes from the perquisites and peculations of public office. If not squandered on luxurious living, money so acquired might be patriotically invested in estate improvement.[4]

The Monymusk estate offers an object lesson in how money earned in business might be applied—and also of the value of networking among landowners. Monymusk was acquired originally by Sir Francis Grant, in 1713, as an investment for the profits of his legal business. Grant's son, Archibald, found capital for a rolling programme of estate improvement by marrying a succession of wealthy widows, and from a portfolio of business interests that included mining, textiles and shipping. However, when not being applauded as a patriotic agriculturist, Sir Archibald was 'widely regarded as a scheming rogue' for his dodgy financial dealings. A crisis arose from the collapse of the Charitable Corporation which, in 1731, brought Monymusk to the brink of ruin. Sir Archibald asked his cousin, Alexander Grant of Dalvey (in Dyke & Moy) to find him 'something in the Jamaica way' to recoup his losses. The something that Dalvey found was a fourth wife, Elizabeth Clark, a widow, who came with £30,000, chiefly in the form of a Jamaica sugar plantation. Monymusk shrewdly kept the plantation in the family by marrying his son, Captain Archibald, to Elizabeth's daughter; and ultimately, Monymusk controlled 2,269 acres in Jamaica, earning (in a good year) a clear profit of over £300. Dalvey, meanwhile, was 'one of the most successful colonial entrepreneurs in Scotland'. His own Jamaican estates produced 190,785 lb of sugar and 2,090 gallons of rum (worth £4,497) in 1752.[5]

In partnership with a Caithness entrepreneur, Richard Oswald, Dalvey also established a major factory on the Sierra Leone River, trading guns, alcohol, iron and cloth for slaves. Some 12,000 slaves were sold from Dalvey's fort between 1749 and 1784, chiefly for shipment to American plantations. Profits from this enterprise came to Scotland, and a significant proportion was invested in improvements in west Moray.[6]

Francis Grant of Grant also had interests in Jamaican plantations. Similarly, plantations (in Florida) provided a cash cushion during improvement of Ballindalloch in Inveravon. Nearer to home, commercial exploitation of fisheries (such as the Spey salmon by Gordon and Fife) or natural forest (Glenmore by Gordon, Glenfeshie by Ballindalloch, Mar by Fife) also provided cash income to support agricultural improvement.

Estate management

Regularisation was a dramatic change, requiring more than the mere application of capital. The creation of a new world—farmed under new forms of tenure and husbandry, within new boundaries on the ground—required a sternly determined kind of manager. The role of the estate factor expanded to meet the need. The factor had long been a key figure in Scottish estate administration. He was the interface between the proprietor and the possessors of the land; relieving his master from the burden of day-to-day concern with the quarrels of township folk and the collection of rents. Under improving regimes, the factor was loaded with the unenviable task of converting the philosophical vision of intellectual theorists and the impractical idealism of improving proprietors, into a real structure of tenancy, and a regularised landscape on the ground of his master's estate.

During the early years of the improvement craze, good reforming factors were hard to find. James Stuart Mackenzie, a Scottish improver educated in England, complained to the earl of Findlater that 'there is hardly such a thing [in Scotland] as what they call in England a land steward'.[7] The role of the factor was revitalised under the influence of best practice in England, where the equivalent office of land steward had already been reinvigorated in the service of agricultural change. A trustworthy steward was the English landowner's man on the ground. He was well paid. Indeed, he might have a contractual interest in his master's prosperity. For example, the duke of Chandos offered his steward 18*d* in the pound for the first £200 of rent collected, rising to 2*s* 6*d* in the pound on rent collected above £300. Some stewards received a fee (say one per cent) for negotiating a valuable lease. Others enjoyed free accommodation, perhaps in the landowner's mansion. All discovered—and many took advantage of—opportunities for peculation, so that 'the arts of stewards' became synonymous with dishonesty.[8] For Nathaniel Kent, employment as a land steward was a first step on the ladder to success. He earned wide respect with his book *Hints to Gentlemen* *of Landed Property* (1775), and his reputation among improving gentlemen earned him a role at the heart of the improvement movement, compiling county surveys for the Board of Agriculture.[9]

There was no formal training or apprenticeship for Scottish estate factors—other than, perhaps, serving and observing a predecessor. However, most would-be factors could draw upon transferable skills acquired in the practice of other professions. The factor might be variously a farmer, lawyer or merchant. William Marshall (1748–1833) climbed the ladder of indoor service at Gordon Castle, from houseboy to house steward. His administrative ability (and his genius as a fiddler) attracted the attention of the duke, who encouraged his servant to improve himself. Marshall attended lectures on mechanics, electricity, magnetism and astronomy at Aberdeen University; and he learned how to make clocks, sundials and violins. After a falling-out with the duke, following the loss of £100 17s 11d of Gordon's money (allegedly) stolen from Marshall while in London—Marshall settled as a farmer, firstly at Burnside of Tynet, then at Keithmore. Marshall's energetic approach attracted plaudits and he was admired as 'a most complete and attentive farmer, up every morning at five o'clock'. He was rehabilitated in 1794 and appointed the duke's factor for the 'Lands of Cabrach and Glen Rinnes and the Lordships of Achindoun, Strathaven and Glenlivet'.[10]

Several minor landowners served as factors for greater estates. The laird of Brightmony had acted for Burgie during the first half of the eighteenth century. Lesmurdie was the earl of Fife's factor at Balvenie during the 1720s; Tannachy (until his bankruptcy in 1761–62) was Fife's factor in the laich. There might be advantages in employing a near relative. Thus John Gordon of Cluny acted as factor for the duke of Gordon in Urquhart and Duffus.

Guidance for factors constituted a sub-genre within improvement literature. Edward Laurence set the tone with his book *The Duty of a Steward to his Lord* (London, 1727). The book went through several editions: the second 'shewing the way to plenty'; the third giving guidance on 'several Methods likely to IMPROVE their Lords Estates'with 'Directions for the Management and Improvement of a FARM' and methods for encouraging tenants, raising turnips, managing woodland, planting hedgerows and making dung. Laurence's ideal steward was multi-competent hands-on manager, encouraged to:

> *ride over the whole Estate at least once a month*, in order to view both the Lands and Stock of the Tenants carefully and distinctly, taking MEMORANDUMS of the same.[11]

The genre was carried into the following century on the wave of improvement, with, for example John Lawrence's book, *The Modern Land Steward* (London, 1801), which offered practical advice on timber measuring and accountancy.

The professionalisation of estate factors went hand-in-hand with the progress of the regularising craze in Moray. The tenth earl of Moray employed, from 1823, a professional factor: 'Mr John Skirving, a famous agriculturist in the Lothians and of a high reputation throughout Scotland'. Skirving was the author of an improving tract titled *Hints for the Consideration of Farmers on Taking Land in the North of Scotland* (Elgin, 1832). It seems that despite the tree-planting mania of the ninth earl, Moray's western estates were largely unimproved until Skirving set to work. A popular anecdote—conceived to compliment the earl of Moray on his modernising zeal and his wise choice of factor—placed Skirving in a shared carriage with a neighbour laird. As they passed through a landscape of the factor's own recent improvements, the laird, unaware of the identity of his travelling companion, exclaimed, 'What a fool of a man is this new factor of Lord Moray, with his ridiculous notion of things!' Skirving held his tongue until the carriage reached the laird's own estate, upon which he cried, 'What a fool of a man is this Laird, building such a big house on so small a property!'[12] This impertinence was possible because Skirving enjoyed the backing of the earl of Moray; and the anecdote underlines the status and arrogance that a powerful factor might assume.

On the extensive estates of great magnates, numerous factors were employed, each responsible for a particular district, barony or lordship. The job sometimes descended through several generations of the same family. The earl of Findlater, who 'chose his factors and men of business with great discrimination', employed John Wilson for fifty years on his Banffshire estates; and thereafter Findlater employed Wilson's nephew and grand-nephew. In Moray, Findlater employed Peter May, land surveyor, and afterwards May's nephew, George Brown (also a land surveyor), and Brown's son Peter.[13]

Within the province of Moray, on the Grant estates in Strathspey that marched with Gordon and Ballindalloch in Inveravon and Kirkmichael, an impetuous rush to improvement, driven by an over-enthusiastic factor, proved ill-judged: a precipitate expansion of population and arable husbandry proved unsustainable, ending in evictions and depopulation.[14]

The traditional basis of prosperity for the Grants of Freuchie, and their Strathspey tenants, had been cattle—in an economy that depended upon upland grazings and shielings. This regime flourished during the eighteenth century while Grant lairds were absent for most of the year. However, in 1762 Sir Ludovick Grant handed control of the estate to his son James.

James Grant took personal control of the estate under the guidance of William Lorimer, his 'well read and well travelled' former tutor. Lorimer was a self-taught improver. He had studied improvement literature; and he had observed agricultural practice and estate reorganisation in England (where he had particularly studied the 'Norfolk Method' of farming), in Scotland and also in America. Lorrimer was, furthermore, the son of a small landowner, William Lorimer of Dyttach, who had served as chamberlain to the earl of Findlater who was admired (among improvers) as exemplary modernising landowner.[15] Thus family connections knitted networks among landowners and their closest advisers. Lorimer's self-instruction was also, of course, education for his master, the young laird of Grant. Lorimer sought information from 'a surveyor ... from the South of Scotland who understands ... farming and country improvements'; 'about planting in Argyllshire and Banff'; and miscellaneous information on methods of inclosing ground and improving soil, on wages, prices, cattle breeding, linen manufacture and distilling.[16] He corresponded with Lord Kames who warmly approved the plans that he and James Grant drew up for improvements in Strathspey as an 'example of good sense as well of benevolence ... a blissing to your country'. Kames advised Lorimer's pupil to heed the example of his 'uncle Lord Deskford who for publick spirit has justly acquired the esteem of all good men'.[17]

The young laird enthusiastically embraced the role of a hands-on improver. Lorimer directed Grant's attention to the exemplary enterprise of the laird of Macleod whose improvements raised his annual rental income by £800 and of Sir James Macdonald on Skye, who envisaged schemes that would increase his annual income by £1,000.[18] Lorimer persuaded Grant that he would be recognised as 'one of the greatest patriots of the Kingdom', by adventurous improvement schemes that would settle some 200 additional tenants on the estate and raise annual rental income by up to £300.[19]

Lorimer's plan was inspired by a colonial zeal. He regarded the transhumance practiced in Strathspey as uncivilised and slothful; lands used only as pasture (and the pastoralists who used it) were failing to fulfill their productive potential. Lorimer's big idea was to attract settlers into Strathspey, to colonise pasture and improve it into productive arable. In 1763 there were 102 conversions of shielings or waste into arable, many of them involving the enclosure of grazing land enjoyed by pre-existing tenants.[20] The settlers included both immigrants and native Strathspey sub-tenants and tenants. Settlement was followed by a generation of sporadic conflict, trespass, complaint, and 'Luddite activities' as pre-existing tenants tried to access traditional upland grazings cut off or colonised by new settler farms.[21]

Grant's decision to interrupt the estate's cattle trade in favour of arable, destroyed a profitable element of the local economy. Meanwhile, poor weather spoiled successive crops on the new—and marginal—settler farms. Rent arrears accumulated; and Grant debts reached £123,438 in the 1780s.[22] Following Lorimer's death, Grant began to reverse the policy he had embraced in the white heat of a youthful improving zeal. Some of the settler farms were amalgamated to form larger units; and many of these flourished until the end of the nineteenth century. Most of the recent arable improvements, though, were converted back into pasture through mass eviction of their occupants. In 1793 hundreds of settler tenants were legally removed; and the evictions continued until 1809, by which time almost all of the settlers had been cleared and their improvements reconnected with the estate's older townships and farms—to be enjoyed again as shieling ground and pasture for cattle.[23]

Elsewhere improving landowners adopted the safer strategy of recruiting progressive farmers and land surveyors as factors. These practical improvers might eventually buy into the gentry, thus blurring class boundaries between the landowner and his staff. For example, Peter Brown, land surveyor, was proprietor of Linkwood, while also acting as factor for the Dunbar Brodies of Lethen in the early nineteenth century. Fife's principal factor in Moray down to the end of the 1840s, was a gentleman-farmer, Alexander Forteath of Newton—a vigorous improver who gave 'long and faithful services ... during a period of nearly half a century'.[24] Subordinate to Forteath was John Lawson, tenant of Oldmills, an improving farmer who acted both as enforcer and exemplar in cascading the improvement craze down to small tenants in the Elgin district. As a miller, Lawson was closely associated with the agricultural operations of the estate; as a businessman he was a safe pair of hands for the significant sums of money that passed through his books. Perhaps a miller was driven into the proprietor's camp by the general contempt of tenants who were thirled to their mills. Perhaps too the miller's reputation for grasping cupidity was a positive recommendation for landowners who sought an active manager who would maximise receipts from rents. In practical terms, Lawson dealt with the minutiae of everyday administration and also major financial transactions, including an involvement in loans (from £300 to £10,000) raised by the earl. In 1800 a representative selection of Lawson's activities included: repairing thatch and a broken window for the Urquhart schoolmaster; setting small possessions in Moss of Meft 'for industrious people to settle and improve'; managing crop rotation in the parks at Innes; advising on the purchase of Leuchars to 'improve the Innes estate'; considering offers for farms; resisting encroachments by neighbours; selling grain and buying cattle.[25] This range of activity was usual. Gordon's Strathavon factor, William Marshall, was responsible, during 1795, for selling wood and wattling in Glenlivet; providing lime for building purposes; receiving interest on loans (£500 to Charles Grant at Deskie, £800 to James Gordon at Croughly) to finance improvement; accounting for hens and wedders received as rent; paying for meliorations on the houses of outgoing tenants; remunerating minor officials (£1 *per annum* to a moss grieve); converting services into money rents; poinding cattle for rent arrears.[26]

Moray factors worked within a supportive network of fellow professionals and improvement enthusiasts. They dined with improving farmers and landowners as members of the Morayshire Farmers' Club, meetings which provided a forum for mutual encouragement and the exchange of practical advice.[27] Donald Smith, factor for Gordonstoun and Altyre until 1810, included among his correspondents William Young of Inverugie, the co-improver of the Sutherland estates. Smith was naturally acquainted with Thomas Sellar, proprietor of Westfield, who served as Gordonstoun's lawyer. Sellar also worked as factor for the duke of Gordon's laichland estates of Earnside, Alves and Kirktown. Thomas Sellar's son Patrick worked as a surveyor for the Gordon Cummings of Altyre and Gordonstoun before joining William Young in Sutherland.

The factor's portfolio typically included the appointment and supervision of lesser functionaries, including moss grieves who supervised peat cuttings, and foresters who protected growing timber in plantations and who patrolled hunting reserves. At least ten foresters received yearly allowances (of from £1 to four guineas, with additional allowances of meal) for Fife's plantations in Moray, stretching from Alves to Urquhart. The duke of Gordon's Strathavon forester, Robert Willox, seems to have been appointed on the set-a-thief-to-catch-a-thief principle. Willox (a Macgregor) was tenant of Gaulrig, a holding that comprised four populous townships. Willox was the trusted agent of John Ross, Gordon Castle factor from 1769 onwards: Ross confided to Willox, 'the Duke has much dependance on your attachment and activity'. With this backing—and because the duke's agent for Strathavon was himself an absentee, residing at Braehead, in Keith—Willox was able to operate with considerable autonomy. Willox involved himself in distributing the duke's charitable meal to paupers; appointing schoolmasters; considering offers for tenancies; and recording submissions in the Faevait arbitration.[28] He recommended his friends when tenancies fell vacant, for example, giving a glowing testimonial to support Peter Grant's candidature for the possession of Tambreck in 1771:

> the Hights offer Inclosed for Tambreck I got yet; and the best tenant this man is worth monie ... there is no better payer of his rent ... he is not the petter Grant that is principall tacksman of Delvrogat but a fare better tennant.[29]

In defending his master's Strathavon forest Willox was constantly 'at war in three Countries': poinding strayed cattle and collecting fines for their redemption—which profited both the estate and himself. Meanwhile, Willox pastured his own cattle, sheep, goats and horses in the forest (according to complaints by the wood forester, John Stewart). Furthermore Willox (allegedly) killed many more deer than were ever sent to the duke's table at Bog o' Gight. Robert's natural son, Grigor, followed his father's example, reinforcing Willox tyranny over Strathavon folk with supernatural powers embodied in a magic crystal and a kelpie's bridle.[30] A Gaulrig sub-tenant, John McHardy, 'who had the misfortune to be a subtennant of Robert Willox', bravely submitted a petition against the Willox regime of 'unparralleld managment; oppression, & crueltie ... experimentally felt by a great Many poor in this Contrie'—even though the forester was 'such a favourit with the familie of Gordon that poor people are afraid to mention his opresion'.[31]

Landowners relied heavily upon their factors during absences—for the social season or when fulfilling military and political duties. Regular mails maintained contact, but considerable latitude might be allowed (or assumed) by the factor. The Ballindalloch factor, John Duff, wrote at least once a month to his master, Major William Grant, during absences in Edinburgh. Duff's letters—never fewer than two closely-written pages of local gossip and estate business—were supported by further letters from Alexander Christie, Ballindalloch's gardener and nurseryman.[32]

A crucial phase in the improvement of Altyre and Gordonstoun occurred under the factory of Donald Smith from 1795 onwards—while Sir William Penrose Cumming ordinarily wintered in Edinburgh. The laird was absent after 1812 on a grand tour that lasted three years. He returned briefly in 1815, before leaving for a three-year tour of northern Europe. Improvement at home proceeded apace while the laird was abroad.[33]

In the absence of professional qualifications to guide the landowner, his choice of factor depended upon intuitive judgment of a candidate's character—and on luck. William Mitchell, the Gordon factor for Glenlivet in 1823, admitted to 'embarrassment' arising from his mismanagement of his own farm of Drumin. When loans from friends dried up, Mitchell borrowed money from other tenants. Finally,

> his credit having ultimately become suspected—his friends and Country acquaintance became clamorous for payment ... and he was therefore from time to time obliged to apply the Dukes money to relieve him ... [and] render fictitious statements.

Furthermore, he issued receipts to tenants who had not paid their rents, 'but which he supposed would pay'. On a farm rented at £128 a year, Mitchell racked up debts of £4,037. He also misappropriated some £3,700 of the duke of Gordon's rents, while carefully muddying the waters by ensuring that no account books or vouchers were available. Mitchell's wife, Jane Smith, 'consoled herself ... with the hope that the proceeds of the roups would have been sufficient for clearing all his debts' which had arisen from 'the carelessness of her husband and the state in which he frequently was by too free an indulgence in ardent spirits'. In the event Mitchell's assets amounted only to some £300 and a feu in Huntly. The duke paid a high price for a poor choice of factor.[34]

Determined improvers took the hand-on approach appropriate to a gentleman-farmer, which also allowed them to exercise a check upon the possible dishonesty or incompetence of factors. Ludovick Dunbar of Grange settled in his seat at Burgie through necessity rather than choice. The estate was burdened by debt, and Ludovick's presence was required to protect it from his eccentric mother whose 'humour and way of life has always been distasteful and disagreeable to me But of late She appeared like one deprived of reason'. Ludovick resolved to 'manage my affairs myself'. He admitted to being 'quite a stranger to Country business, but I design to apply myself ... in which Ile very much want the assistance of my friends'.[35] In managing the estate personally, Ludovick followed his predecessor's example. A generation earlier James Dunbar had taken on a wide range of administrative duties. He supplied trees to Sir Harie Innes of Innes; supervised the conditions of tenants' tacks; sold malt to Forres brewsters; and negotiated with David Dunbar, the Kirkcaldie merchant who received his shiploads of bear and sent return cargoes of salt for sale in west Moray.[36]

Mary Sleigh, the mistress of Brodie, pushed through vigorous schemes for landscaping the castle policies and initiating extensive timber plantations on behalf of her infant son. She also began the conversion of Brodie rents in kind into cash: accounts for 1756 included 'Peats which Lady Brodie got the Tennants to pay in cash ... Carriage Money which she also prevail'd with them to pay in cash'.[37]

The inception of improvement in Banff was said to date from the time when the future earl of Findlater (then Lord Deskford) 'came to reside in the neighbourhood'. Personal residence meant he could personally oversee the 'introduction of improvements in agriculture'. James Donaldson, reporting on the agriculture of Banff, thought that such personal presence was part of the 'proper connection' between landlord and tenant; and furthermore that such a 'proper attention to their own interests' would secure to landowners the introduction of a 'general spirit of improvement' among the tenantry. Donaldson demurely deplored absentee proprietors whose other employments prevented their taking so active a role in the improvement of their estates, 'which the importance of the object so justly merits'.[38]

The earl of Fife, who was often absent for significant periods, might nonetheless attempt to exert close control upon his factors in Moray. For a time he micromanaged James George, factor at Innes: demanding monthly reports so that he could 'Direct what work is to be carried on'. When demanding a state of expense of 'Incloseing the moor at Stony briggs', the earl insisted that 'no trees to be planted but when James George is present'. He requested lists of day labourers so he could personally 'direct who are to be employed again'. And he ordered 'The Cow just now feeding should be sold ... and as she is gone in the feet any tolerable price should not be refused'.[39] The earl took a close interest in the offers received for vacant tenancies.[40] Writing to John Lawson in 1817, he reminded his factor of repairs needed at Pluscarden, including planting the hill behind the abbey ruins, and dressing the abbey gardens with grass and fruit trees; also giving instructions on finding proper places for settlers in the district.[41] Fife also personally intervened to preserve the amenity and aesthetic appearance of the replanned village of Lhanbryd where, he thought, a proposed wall would 'have a 'formal and hurtfull effect—Hedge rows are more in harmony with the locality'.[42] Micromanagement could never be successful in an estate as extensive as the Fife domain;

and it would always be intermittent because the earl was frequently away from home pursuing other interests in London and Edinburgh. In general, the earls of Fife—and other Moray landowners—learned to trust the growing professionalism of factors who shared their masters' zeal for improving, and maximising returns from, the land.

Legalities of improvement

Sweeping changes to landscape, agricultural practice and tenure were effected with relatively little recourse to law. Despite abolition of heritable jurisdictions following the 'forty-five, Scottish landowners enjoyed almost unrestricted power over the management of their estates, and proprietors needed no specific legal empowerment for most aspects of estate regularisation. However, legislation developed to support cooperative regimes might be applied to legitimise improvement. For example, laws devised to preserve managed woodland for common use in the cooperative countryside were used to privatise plantations on improved estates, and exclude township folk from time-honoured moorland resources.[43] William Leslie was scathing regarding the effect of anachronistic, 'impolitic and oppressive' woodland legislation upon improving tenants' enterprise insofar as, when 'strictly executed ... the tenant is prohibited from planting ... unproductive ground'.[44]

An act of 1695 identified runrig as 'highly prejudicial to the Policy and Improvement of the Nation by planting and inclosing'. The act was concerned only with proprietorial runrig, but it allowed any one of the heritors concerned to apply to the sheriff or JPs for a reallocation of the lands in discrete blocks.[45] Division and reallocation of runrig might take years to accomplish. However, good will, a shared purpose and wise arbitration could overcome obstacles, and quibbles of self-interest might be set aside in the worthy pursuit of improvement. Almost a century elapsed before the act was invoked in Moray, where prorietorial runrig was neither widespread nor problematical. In the 1780s, the lands of Roseisle, in Duffus, were mapped by Alexander Taylor, land surveyor, with an intention of sorting out the complications of ownership as a preliminary to improvement. The resulting plan shows arable and pasture, townships, houses, yards and waste, with annotations describing the quality and improvability of the ground—all within a striking stripy landscape, the ownership (chiefly by the duke of Gordon and Gordonstoun) of alternating arable strips shown in contrasting colours.[46] However, the estates remained intermingled until 1795, when Penrose-Cumming of Altyre succeeded as Gordonstoun heir, determined to tackle the Roseisle question in earnest. Gordonstoun's interest in Roseisle was complicated by a rival claim to the estate. This claim was dismissed by the House of Lords in 1800, opening the way to a separation of Gordon and Gordonstoun in Roseisle, with an excambion, approved in Parliament in 1810.[47] Even then, of course, tenant runrig continued. At Roseisle, as probably elsewhere, separation of proprietorial runrig might be a preliminary to change, but it did not immediately affect either the cultivation of the land or the general appearance of the landscape.

The runrig burgh arable of Elgin feuholders (known as the Aughteen Parts or Grieshop Lands) were reorganised between 1781 and 1800, in a manner that closely resembled an

English enclosure award. The 'intricate job' of surveying the district, occupying a meander of the River Lossie, was undertaken by George Brown, land surveyor, who mapped dispersed holdings composed of some 1,200 scattered strips, butts and pendicles, evolved from a medieval allocation of common field strips among an original sixty-four burgesses.[48] It was noted that among this complex, if commonplace, runrig 'some rigs of one auchteen part are near two English miles asunder'.[49] The final allocation divided the area into twenty-five lots divided by straight marches contrived in most cases to give each lot access to an existing road. The largest lot, belonging to Lord Findlater and representing fourteen aughteen parts, extended to ninety-eight acres; Provost Brander's five parts extended to twenty-one acres; Joseph King's four parts to fifteen acres. Dr Thomas Stephen's nine parts (lot 10) included a mix of arable and waste ground including three acres of 'High Ground covered with whins', and approximately eight acres of 'Uneven Sand & Gravel'. The smallest lots consisted of just two or three acres.[50]

Elsewhere, regularisation passed over properties held as feus. The duke of Gordon's Garmouth and Fochabers folk enjoyed their tofts in town and their arable commonfield strips as heritable feus. When the duke sought to remove and regularise Fochabers, he was obliged to buy out the feuholders in a protracted series of individual negotiations.[51] At Garmouth, the village did not undergo radical replanning, and vestigial remains of Garmouth's arable strips remained as an anachronistic interruption to the regular rectilinear fieldscape for more than fifty years after improvement elsewhere in Speymouth.[52]

The division of a commonty (facilitated by legislation of 1647, repealed at the Restoration, revived in 1695) might be a preliminary to wider change. But it was not in itself a major landscape change; nor did division, of itself, significantly alter the manner in which townships exploited the land—only restricting the area available for such exploitation. The act recognised that 'discords' might arise from shared use of commonty lands, but did not attach any improving merit to division. A summonds calling for division might be raised by any of the interested parties, and the matter ultimately determined by the Lords of Council and Session.[53] There seems to have been no uptake of this legal possibility in Moray for a century or more. Feuar communities took the lead in pursuing legal division. The commonties of Elgin and Spindle Muir (Spynie) were divided in the initial enthusiasm for improvement before 1800.[54] 'Common heath belonging to Garmouth feuars' was divided under this legislation; while 'Sometime Forres common was divided by arbitration' under the act at the beginning of the nineteenth century.[55] Mundole was not divided until 1822, although shared by three of Moray's leading improvers—the earl of Moray, Sir William Gordon-Cumming and William Leslie of Balnageith. Meanwhile, commonties in Alves and St Andrews-Lhanbryd were not divided until 1837; and Muirton commonty (Kinloss) was divided only in 1846.[56]

Commonty division could prove a protracted process. The busy shieling ground of Faevait (Feith Bhait) at the source of the Don above Inchrory in Strathavon was a commonty enjoyed by Strathavon and Corgarff tenants under an agreement of 1728. After a generation punctuated by disputes among tenants, the duke of Gordon declared, in 1769, a willingness to accept division of Faevait. A plan was drawn by William Anderson; evidence was taken from tenants who had shieled or cultivated improvements on the commonty. In 1776 William Forbes of Skellater urged the duke to settle matters 'before the Grass Season Comes on'. But not until 1786 was decreet arbitral registered and the division of Faevait legally recognised.[57]

The Hardmuir commonty on the western border of Moray was enjoyed by Brodie of Brodie, Sir James Dunbar of Boath, John Gordon of Cluny and The earl of Cawdor. The action for division was raised by Brodie in 1824. As the case progressed, the exasperated clerk to the Court of Session, John Parker, complained that 'proceedings seem to have been lodged ... upon every possible contestible point'. Some 1,500 pages of pleadings were submitted, including the usual evidence taken from elderly peasants who had cut turf, herded cattle, harvested whins or gathered stones on the Hardmuir. The case dragged on for a dozen years before the parties could agree and the muir be divided in proportion to the parties' rentals.[58]

With good will and a shared improving purpose, division of common land was not vexatious. In 1771 Alexander Dunbar of Thunderton and the duke of Gordon affably negotiated the division of a 'Piece of Green Ground (covered by Water from the Loch of Spynie in the Winter Time) which divides your Grace's Lands of Kintrea from the Lands of Crookmuir belonging to me'—without reference to the commonty acts. Thunderton confided, 'My Tennents have dunned me for some Time ... to have this Piece of Ground divided So as that your Grace's Tennents as well as mine may have access to improve it'. Dunbar sidestepped the expense of a legal division, and deferred to the adjudication of the duke's factor on the matter which could be settled 'in a Forenoon'.[59]

The laichland grazings of Alves, Monaughty and Carden remained a commonty into the early nineteenth century—jointly and variously enjoyed by the earls of Moray and Fife, the duke of Gordon and James Campbell Brodie of Kilbuack. The lands were surveyed in 1835 by George McWilliam, Fife's preferred land surveyor. The division was decided by arbitrators consisting of the three noblemen's factors. The commonty was divided by straight lines to make 'regular' boundaries, the proprietors agreeing to 'enclose and appropriate their Lots', under decreet arbitral recorded 29 April 1837.[60] The only hiccup in the process came from Alexander Gentle, minister of Alves, who protested that he '& his predecessors from time immemorial have been in the habit of pasturing their cattle and digging peats on the Common'.[61] Although division of the commonty did not mean an immediate exclusion of the husbandmen who used it, the minister was prescient enough to recognise that enclosure and improvement would follow division, and so he put in an early bid for compensation in anticipation of the erosion of his perquisites—and also obliquely made a plea on behalf of his parishioners, whose rights were also threatened.

The Morinsh commonty remained undivided into the 1840s—shared by Ballindalloch tenants in Glenrinnes and Gordon tenants in Glenlivet under an agreement struck between the two landowners in 1727. When adjacent farms were leased in 1820, Ballindalloch tenants were bound to 'acquiesce' with any changes that a division might introduce. In the event, their enjoyment of the commonty continued without interruption for the duration of their nineteen-year leases. At some point, probably in the early nineteenth century, a Gordon settler broke in an improvement at Badeach on the Glenrinnes side. In 1842 Ballindalloch also complained of overgrazing by the Gordon tenant of Deskie who brought 'upwards of

900' sheep with a shepherd 'from a farm which he rents from Sir Chas. Forbes 17 or 20 miles distant ... in the County of Aberdeen'. Meanwhile, the Gordon tenant of Achoriachan and Tombreachachie, had been 'in the practice of selling sheep off the Commonty and replacing them from ... a hill farm [Glaschoil] 7 or 8 miles from Tombreachachie'. These innovations focused attention on the potential of the commonty for improvement. Its value was further enhanced by the quarries and kilns on Tomlair, which supplied the Ballindalloch estate with lime for agriculture and building works. The commonty was amicably divided. It was not, though, developed for either arable or pastoral farming, except for six rectangular fields at Badeach, and a large enclosure belonging to Craighead—both on lower ground on the Glenrinnes side. The remainder was planted with trees.[62]

In tune with the improving mood of the times, Parliament addressed the hampering effect of entails. An entail secured the descent of an estate to a specified line of heirs; and also restricted a landowner's freedom of action in the development and reorganisation of the property. It has been variously estimated that up to half the land of Scotland was entailed.[63] In Moray, the estates of Brodie and Altyre were among several significant entails. The power of entails was relaxed by the Montgomery Act of 1770.[64] Henceforth it was lawful to grant Tacks or Leases ... not exceeding Fourteen Years ... and for the Life of One Person ... or for the Lives of Two Persons ... or for any Number of Years not exceeding Thirty-One Years. Most significantly, the act specified that such leases 'should contain a Clause obliging the Tenant or Tenants to inclose'. To underline this obligation to create a fully enclosed landscape of discrete fenced fields, it was further specified that no enclosure was to be over forty acres in extent.

The proprietor who laid out money to improve an entailed estate was deemed creditor to the succeeding heir for three-quarters of the cost, provided it did not amount to more than the value of four years' rent. Accounts of monies laid out on improvement were to be lodged with the sheriff.[65] Banffshire records document expenditure on Ballindalloch's mansion places of Kininvie and Kirktown, in Botriphnie, in 1801 and 1808. Improvement under the Act came to Inveravon in 1815, when Ballindalloch expended £209 17s 11^{4}/$_{12}$d on dykes, buildings and drainage at Kilmaichlie, Lagmore and Pitchaish, with dykes for the parks at Ballindalloch.[66]

Charles Grant of Elchies used the procedure in 1815 when renovating his house—'at present in a ruinous and uninhabitable state'—at Carron in Aberlour, and for improving the mains farm. He built a new meal mill on his Knockando estate. He also planted 'the moor called the Drum of Carron' with 300,000 larch trees at a cost of £43 11s 1½d, erecting a house for the 'punlar' (pindler) who protected the plantation from free-grazing livestock. A subsequent revision of the scheme mixed in Scots pine and added 14,000 oaks with 800 ash—at a cost of £52 7s. Elchies also determined 'to erect the present village of Aberlour on that part ... called Allachy ... into a free Burgh of Barony'. Under further schemes during 1813–15, Elchies planted fruit trees around his house; and extended his plantations with larch and Scots pine interspersed with elm, beech and exotic species including spruce and silver fir.[67]

During 1838–39 the duke of Gordon invested in public works with a new road through Glenlivet, and in private pleasures with new houses for his Glenlivet and Strathavon gamekeepers. At Croughly a new threshing mill was built at a cost of £92 13s 1d using timber from the Gordon Castle sawmill. A stone and slate public building was constructed at Tomintoul. In 1840 the farm of Drumin in Glenlivet was improved with '4 barred paling', and with hedges of thorn and whin—shipped to Findhorn by Peter Lawson & Son, seedsmen and nurserymen to the Highland and Agricultural Society of Scotland.[68] Further improvements took place at Nevie in 1840, at a cost of £45 2s 9d.[69]

In the reorganisation of tenure the agricultural revolution in Scotland followed a different path to that taken in England. Scottish estates were seldom encumbered with husbandmen who might claim security of tenure. In England, an Act of Parliament was required (if copyholders and others with secure possession refused to act by consent) to reorganise scattered arable strips into compact blocks and allocate common grazing to create an enclosed and rectilinear fieldscape of discrete holdings. In Moray most tenants enjoyed their possessions under short tacks or at the will of the heritor. A landowner might order a tenant to quit (together with his family, servants, sub-tenants and cottars) with no impediment other than the expiry date on a tack and the need to observe the legal timescale for giving warning. However, even a cursory examination of estate rentals reveals a significant degree of mobility among tenants. It may be that this inclination towards mobility allowed tenants to accept removal when it happened—as just another of the ordinary vicissitudes of the agricultural year. Certainly, there are few records of husbandmen resisting removal during estate improvement.

In general the Scottish landowner could remove tenants, reorganise fieldscapes and reallocate the land by simple diktat, provided he gave the warning specified in an Act of 1555.[70] This ordinary procedure was followed throughout Scotland. For example, in January 1755, George Cumming of Altyre warned eleven possessors of eight townships to 'flitt & remove themselves wives Barnes family Servants Cottars Sub-tenants goods & gear', by 'Whitsunday next to come'. Precepts of warning were delivered in the usual way: placed in the possessor's hand or, if he could not be personally apprehended, planted in a cleft stick before his dwelling or stuck in the lockhole of the door of his house; a further copy was pinned to the door of the parish kirk. Nothing more was required.[71]

The power to remove tenants belonged to a lost world of heritable jurisdictions; and lawmakers (who were also landowners) felt there should be a more modern recognition of landowners' rights, with procedures that specifically addressed the needs of improving proprietors. Thus, in 1756, the Lords of Council and Session passed an 'Act of Sederunt Anent Removeings'.[72] The 1756 act specifically referred to that of 1555, reiterating, amplifying and clarifying procedure for removing tenants. Their lordships—among whom were notable improvers such as the laird of Auchinleck and Lord Kames—noted that 'the Difficulties that have occurred in actions of Removing from Lands have been found to be highly prejudicial to agriculture'. No one seems to have suggested that the promotion of agriculture as a matter of public policy might lie outside their lordships' legal remit. Remedy for the 'great Evill' that the Lords of Council identified, was encompassed in seven paragraphs of procedures for warning and removing tenants in various circumstances: on the expiry of a tack; in the absence of a fixed-term or tack; in case of rent arrears. Clause 3 emphasised the position of sub-tenants, who were clearly obliged to remove along with the principal tenant. Furthermore, the act sought to reduce the law's delay by allowing processes brought before the Court of Session to be dealt with summarily. The Act was not universally welcomed. William Leslie, minister of St Andrews-Lhanbryd, whose improving zeal was tempered with a deep conservatism, lamented the passing of a landlord's unchallengeable power to warn out tenants-at-will. Leslie feared that the new procedure would foment 'a spirit of litigation' and dangerous stirrings of political radicalism:

> for having universally relinquished their legal ancient privilege of warning out tenants by their own authority, great numbers are yearly brought together in the sheriff-court, upon only an act of the Court of Session, to see themselves decerned to remove, where they acquire notions concerning the rights of men, no way favourable to industry, concord or thrift.[73]

In the event, Leslie's fears proved unjustified. Usually petitions for removal went through Moray's courts unopposed. Nor did the new method of clearing tenants result in any perceptible upsurge in revolutionary radicalism

Under the 1756 act, legal removal of tenants fell within the remit of the sheriff courts. In Elginshire, sheriff courts convened separately for the two divisions of the shire of Elgin & Forres; within the royal burghs, magistrates sat with shrieval powers. The provenance of Moray court processes can be traced with some certainty and the series may be complete for the last four decades of the eighteenth century.[74]

Moray removals began with a flurry of legal activity in 1766 as the improvement craze properly kicked in. Eighty-two tenants and possessors were removed in twenty separate processes. These cases included nine petitions presented by tacksmen to remove sub-tenants. The remaining cases were pursued by landowners or their factors: these included the lairds of Muirton (Kinloss), Ballindalloch and Brodie seeking to remove relatively small numbers of named possessors.[75]

All but one of the 1766 cases were undefended, and decreet given in the pursuer's favour. The exception was a case pursued by Robert Grant in Auchterblair, factor to the recently-deceased Alexander Grant of Dalrachnie on Speyside. The forty-five defendants in the case occupied sixteen townships stretching along eight miles of the Spey from Aviemore to Tullochgribban. The case is remarkable for the number of removals sought, and also for the vigorous defence mounted by five tenants of Dalrachneymore. The defendants were unable to write, attesting declarations that were drafted for them, with scratchy initials. The Dalrachneymore five claimed that they had paid grassums for tacks of defined terms. They added that, 'It was Dalrachinie usuall way & practice was to take Grassoms from his Tenents but at the same time gave them no Tacks'. The five urged the sheriff to seek confirmation of this claim, 'by Dalrachinies Lady & Daughters', naively suggesting that proof 'shall be found upon makeing a search through Dalrachinies writes'. The factor countered by declaring that the tenants' petition was 'Contrived to Postpon & Delay the Removing'. In the event, the sheriff declined to interview the Dalrachnie ladies or to order a search of the Dalrachnie muniments. In the absence of documentary evidence, the tenants were decerned to remove in terms of the 1756 act by 'Whitesunday nixt to Come'. The judgement did, though, reserve the tenants' right to sue the Dalrachnie estate for unexpired portions of their 'alleadged Grassoms', amounting to a few shillings each. John Cumming, principal tacksman of Tullochgribanbeg, and his sub-tenant, Janet Cumming, received special notice in the judgement. Cumming, alone among the defenders, was able to produce documentary evidence. Unfortunately, the writings that the illiterate tacksman produced proved, not only that his tack had expired, but also that he was in arrears with his rent.[76]

It is likely that the Dalrachnie case was pursued in order to affirm the legal rights of heirs following the laird's death. Other removal cases too were pursued in circumstances arising from some problem with the estate rather than as necessary for an improvement scheme. For example, the Brodie processes coincide with Brodie's bankruptcy. Twenty-eight Brodie tenants and ten sub-tenants were removed during the period 1768–73: the ten sub-tenants were possessors of Cloves, removed by a major tacksman, Lieutenant John Rose; the twenty-eight tenants belonged to fifteen townships in the laich including Asleesk, Feddan, Coltfield and Kinneddar.[77]

During the period 1766–91, Moray landowners used the 1756 procedure to remove some 324 tenants and possessors.[78] This might represent the legal removal of some 1,500 individuals (including wives and bairns)—equivalent to the whole population of a typical rural laichland parish.[79] This number did not include sub-tenants, cottars and servants, whose presence on most farms might double or triple the total of people dispossessed. John Innes of Blackhills removed fifteen tenants from Blackhills in 1770.[80] The earl of Fife removed 107 tenants including, in 1769: forty-seven from New Spynie; thirty from the Pluscarden valley, Kellas and Mosstowie; and a further thirty from St Andrews-Lhanbryd.[81] There is a mismatch, however, between the earl's court processes and a 'List of Tenents against whom Decreat for Removing is obtained to take place at Whitsunday 1768' among Fife estate muniments.[82] This list was assembled under three headings. Of eleven tenants 'Who have Tacks but in Arrear', only two were named in court processes—in 1769.[83] Of seven named as 'Tenents whose Tacks Expire at Whit 1768' only one appeared (in 1769) in a court process,[84] the remainder presumably accepted their tack conditions. Among forty-one 'Tenents who have no Tacks' just thirteen, mostly in Mosstowie, appeared in a single court processes in 1766.[85] Fife tenants slated for removal who did not appear in court processes, presumably relinquished possession peaceably and without court action. However, as a further complication, the three processes referred to above, named fifty other Fife tenants who were decerned to remove but who were not listed in the 1768 document.[86]

The flurry of legal removals associated with a first enthusiastic eruption of the improvement craze, lasted only until the 1770s. Thereafter, the 1756 procedure was not invoked in rural Moray. From the late 1770s onwards sheriff court processes were concerned rather with removal of tenants from burgh properties. Between 1760 and 1790, in forty-three cases, some 169 individuals were removed: from roods and closes, houses and yards, and from seats in the parish kirks. A handful of cases at the close of the eighteenth century concerned removals from parks, pendicles, crofts, acres and rigs of burgh arable or from peat moss wards—documenting the improvement of burgh land.[87]

Overall, it seems that removal and relocation of tenants was readily achieved without protracted court action. Tenants flitted quietly on receiving a formal warning and on expiry of a tack. Sub-tenants flitted along with principals, unless they could negotiate a new agreement with the incoming farmer. A patient landowner might find that possessions were vacated without trouble to either himself or his tenant by natural wastage, as possessors died or drifted from holding to holding within and out of the estate. The annual Whitsun flittings are not documented. Perhaps the event was too commonplace to notice. Nonetheless the flitting must have represented a considerable spectacle. Husbandmen moved with their wives, bairns, servants, cottars and sub-tenants. They flitted their beasts, in a mixed herd of cows, oxen, sheep, goats, geese and hens on highways and byways between townships. They carried with them their household goods and farming gear; and they might also take the crucks, cabers, doors and door-frames of their houses. They also transported stocks of seedcorn, with the grain, oatmeal and straw that would sustain the family and its beasts until the autumn harvest on their new possession.

Whether they invoked the 1756 procedure or not, landowners derived from the Act of Session a confidence that they did indeed enjoy the right to remove tenants who stood in the way of their plans, and reallocate possessions to farmers who would become active agents of change. This power was fundamental in installing suitable tenants. Landowners might provide vision and encouragement, but it was modernising farmers who would implement the programmes that improving lairds conceived; it was through the daily labour of individual husbandmen that the regular landscapes and agricultural regimes envisaged by the improving tracts would be realised.

5

LANDSCAPE BY THE RULE

Planning for improvement

Experts and commentators such as David Souter recommended 'straighting boundaries' in the interests of agricultural efficiency.[1] Sir John Sinclair concurred, advocating 'fences in straight lines ... fields when large should be square, and when small, of an oblong form', partly to facilitate fencing into strips for feeding turnips off the ground.[2] However the regularisation of farmscapes was also pursued for esoteric aesthetic and philosophical reasons. Rectilinear landscapes of improvement bore the emphatic stamp of Enlightenment rationalism. Landowners' classical tastes preferred straight lines and right angles to the landscapes of curving ridges and straggling head-dykes associated with cooperative agriculture. This rural regularity was triangulated in the field with a surveyor's chain, and drawn to scale with a surveyor's rule. Boundaries were fenced on the ground and indelibly preserved as paper plans lodged in the factor's business room. In this improvers effected 'a face lift which was more thorough-going than in any other country of Europe in the course of the eighteenth century'.[3] Tenants were willing accomplices in landowners' plans, accepting obligations, when farms were divided and tacks granted, to make marches 'more commodious', and to 'straight the marches'.[4] The 1788 tack of the Ballindalloch possession of Blacksboat was typical in obliging the tenant, James Walker, to 'Straighten & Make Marches ... [with] neighbouring tenants'.[5] The tack created, probably for the first time in that district, a discrete farm that did not share grazing or other resources with neighbours.

Thorough rationalisation of the Moray countryside was, however, a protracted business: begun in the later eighteenth century and still continuing in the second half of the nineteenth. Sheriff-substitute Rampini of Elgin dated the 'wonderful advance ... in the way of squaring up farms' as belonging to a generation after 1857,[6] though much had already been done well before that date. Nonetheless, the first Ordnance Survey mapped many landscapes still unenclosed around 1870. For example, the curved common-field strips of Garmouth feuars were a distinctive feature in Speymouth; the new small possessions at Moss of Meft in Urquhart and Crofts of Scalan in Kirkmichael were, for the most part unfenced; and Kellas farms were separated one from another and subdivided internally by the ditches that drained the reclaimed land, with few evident fences.[7]

The regularisation of fieldscapes was not achieved without some conflict. Abrasive relationships between neighbouring farmers and landowners impeded regularisation as each separate project was negotiated to accommodate neighbours' interests. Among the land surveyors who planned the regular landscape, professional rivalries ensured that schemes would be periodically revised as each new generation improved upon the perceived inadequacies of predecessors' work. Meanwhile, the landscape itself passively resisted regularisation: water stubbornly refused to run in regular ditches; topographical irregularities interrupted the geometrical patterns of land surveyors' plans; and local resources often proved inadequate for fencing fields.

Scientific rationalism inspired improvers to map and measure, as a means of asserting mastery of their domains. The cooperative countryside that had evolved organically in harmony with what the land (and jealousies among township neighbours) grudgingly permitted, was over-written with farmscapes redesigned on paper. The passion for estate plans developed in step with the mood of the times. While Scottish explorers such as James Bruce and Mungo Park were mapping Ethiopia and tracing the course of the Niger, Scottish landowners were commissioning plans of their North British domains. Maps conferred dominion. Abroad, James Cook's heroic cartography claimed Australia for the British Crown. At home, estate plans redeemed lowland arable from the grip of a barbarous and ignorant peasantry, and reclaimed the *terra incognita* of waste, muir and bog for rational agriculture.

The surveyor's chain, theodolite and measuring wheel epitomise the age of agricultural improvement just as much as lime, turnips, horse-hoeing husbandry and Bakewell sheep. Always in the vanguard of improvement, Grant of Monymusk bought a surveying chain for estate planning in 1719; and brought in an English surveyor, Thomas Winter, to use it. Winter's *curriculum vitae* included the role of Monymusk baron bailie, and also employment by the duke of Gordon and Grant of Grant.[8] The earl of Fife's men were surveying at Coxtown using the estate's own chain in 1771–72, under the expert supervision of George Taylor, land surveyor: financial accounts for the period included vouchers for 'mending a planning Chain—9*d*', and wages of two men for twenty-six days 'running with the Chain—£1 14*s* 8*d*'.[9] In June 1780, Ballindalloch received an 'improved best 4 inch theodolite' (price fourteen guineas) and 'instrument for drawing in perspective'. The same supplier, Jesse Ramsden, mathematical, optical and philosophical instrument maker, Piccadilly, also provided a portable barometer so that scientific forecasting could replace country weather lore on the rationalised estate.[10]

The publishing industry, ever-sensitive to market opportunities, responded to the craze for land surveying with manuals for amateurs, such as W. Francis *The Gentleman's, Farmers, and Husbandman's Most Useful Assistant in Measuring and Expeditiously Computing of any Quantity of Land* (London, 1818). For do-it-yourself enclosers, Michael Searles published 'useful and correct tables' for calculating land areas.[11] Factors were expected to possess skill in landsurveying, honing their practical abilities with the help of books borrowed from their masters' libraries. Gordon Castle was notably well supplied—with half-a-dozen manuals published between 1673 and 1739.[12] Edward Laurence's manual urged 'a Steward should know the Quality and Quantity of every parcel of Land ... so likewise he should have a *Map* of the whole'. Laurence disparaged 'Surveys done by the *Plain* Table, they ought not to be depended on'. He enabled factors to polish their skills with a lesson in the correct use of the theodolite, recommending 'the best sort of THEODOLITE ever yet invented ... made by MR. JONATHON SISSON, at the corner of *Beauford* Buildings in the *Strand*.[13]

The emergent profession of land surveyor developed rapidly during the middle decades of the eighteenth century as landowners commissioned accurate estate plans as a preliminary to improvement. Previously, surveys had been made by gathering sworn testimony from elderly inhabitants who were supposed to remember details of tenure, landuse and marches. Oral evidence from these 'gray-hair'd herdsmen, skill'd in rural lore'[14] was transcribed as a prose description of the estate. Such rustic imprecisions, jarred with rational inclinations. Underlying this change was the rise of freethinking philosophies that led landowners to wonder whether they could any longer trust evidence under oath in an enlightened age when the kirk was losing its grip, as pagan philosophy and modern science undermined Christian theology.

Modern estate design demanded modern methods. The modern method was the measured plan. In north-east Scotland a notable school of professional land surveyors was associated with the name of Peter May, whose career and connections epitomise the networks that knitted north-east improvers into a coherent movement. Peter, and his brother James, were probably born in Moray. They trained under John Forbes—who had worked as land surveyor for the earl of Findlater. Forbes's apprentices also worked for Findlater. In 1753 Peter May worked for the duke of Gordon surveying at Gordonsburgh (Fort William).[15] He served the Annexed Estates commissioners before moving on to undertake commissions across the north-east, from (among others) the earls of Fife and Findlater,[16] and Dunbar of Grange at Burgie.[17] Lord Deskford recommended Peter May to his cousin Sir James Grant of Grant, as 'the best surveyor in Scotland'; and Peter May subsequently discussed Strathspey improvements over dinner with Lord Kames.[18] May's secondary business as nurseryman reinforced connections with Moray improvers: in November 1763 he supplied the Gordon estate with half a million Scots pines.[19]

Peter May's legacy included at least thirty-four pupils and their descendants spanning three generations, who were convolved in the intimate connections among north-east improvers.[20] May's pupils, Thomas Milne, the brothers George and Alexander Taylor, and George Brown all worked for Gordon. Thomas Milne surveyed Fife's estates. So did George Taylor, during 1771–72, earning six guineas for a plan of Coxtown,[21] which consumed eight yards of green linen at 5*s* 0*d*, and half a quire of lumber paper costing a further 5*s* 0*d*.[22] Alexander Taylor surveyed Badenoch estates for Gordon. The instructions handed to him by the duke's chamberlain, James Ross, indicate the general expectations and principles underlying the measured surveys that were deemed essential concomitants of improvement. Taylor's remit required a plan of each farm with notes on arable, pasture muir and ownership; adding recommendations on any new arrangement or division that might be proper. On moorland he was required to note shieling places and to indicate locations suitable for cultivation that might be annexed to existing farms or settled by small tenants. He was to record all houses, roads, rivers, fords and ferries. Taylor was tasked with making recommendations on drainage; and to note all woodland (with types of trees), and resources such as marl, lime and slate, providing mineral samples as appropriate.[23] Alexander Taylor went on to assist Thomas Milne in surveying Gordon estates in upper Banffshire during 1770–85.

George Brown was a third member of the May school, who assisted Milne and Taylor. Brown was born in 1747, the son of Peter May's sister, Barbara. He was employed in 1770 to survey the west Moray estate of Brodie of Brodie.[24] Brown also worked for Monymusk, and on the north-east estates of the lords Forbes and Saltoun. He succeeded his uncle, Peter May, as the earl of Findlater's factor in Elgin, where he owned the little estate of Linkwood as an exemplary gentleman-farmer, while enjoying extensive influence in local politics and commerce—as a town councillor and (seven times) provost of Elgin, postmaster, Aberdeen Bank agent, and as a capitalist with interests in a linen manufactory, a brewery, and a nursery. He continued working as a land surveyor, and among his trainees was William Marshall the Glenrinnes and Strathavon factor. Brown died in 1816. His son, christened Peter, took over as Findlater's Elgin factor; and was a respected agriculturalist, stock breeder and land valuator. Peter Brown's marriage bound him inextricably into the network of Moray improvers, as son-in-law to William Leslie.[25]

George Brown's land surveying business was taken over by his pupil, George McWilliam, who was Fife's surveyor of choice during the early nineteenth century. McWilliam also resurveyed Strathavon for the duke of Gordon around 1840.[26] He planned improved fieldscapes in Inveravon for Ballindalloch, though in the usual course of professional jealousy, his work was disparaged and revised by a successor Thomas Shier, who complained he could not make his own data 'correspond with Mr M'William's measurement'.[27] Shier was not alone in making such comments, which raise a doubt as to whether early estate plans were any more accurate than the verbal surveys they replaced. Be that as it may, McWilliam trained a further generation of land surveyors including James Falconer and Alexander Murdoch. Another pupil was George Campbell Smith—who used his plan of the estate of Balnageith (belonging to Reverend William Leslie) to illustrate a brochure for distribution among potential clients—which included a scale of charges and a useful table for converting between Scots and Imperial measure.[28]

The initial emphasis of estate plans was to effect a cartographic audit of estate resources. To this end the lands of Lethen were depicted in stylish detail and at generous scale in an opulent atlas during the 1740s. Lethen's plans showed runrig divisions of township lands, with buildings at every social level, from turf township dwellings to the four-storeyed façade of Kilbuiack castle.[29] The plans were, however, disparaged in 1792 by George Brown who, drumming up business for himself, declared Lethen's gorgeous atlas 'far from being distinct, or Compleate, being made at a very Earlie period, in the year 1745'.[30] In 1809 Brown was similarly disparaging of a competitor's survey of East Grange. He declared the work 'quite incorrect, it being measured by a Blundering fello, (Jo Hume) ... I will Cause Jo Sim measure it'.[31]

An atlas similar to Lethen's, though at a smaller scale, was created by William Anderson in 1762, surveying the Gordon lordship of Strathavon—as a sequel to his 1761 survey of Glenlivet.[32] The Strathavon survey was embellished with the Gordon arms and a title page, ponderously lettered in Roman capitals:

A SHORT DESCRIPTION OF STRATH AVIN EXHIBITING ALL THE DIFFERENT
FARMS AND LIKEWISE THEIR EXTENT AND QUALITY WITH MOSSES MOORS
AND PASTURES.

The mapping showed cultivated fields, but not divisions within the arable. Woodland and burns were shown. Township buildings were drawn in elevation, though the schematic depiction bore no relation to arrangements shown on subsequent plans or modern site surveys.[33] Four pages of introductory text perambulated the marches of the lordship. Each of the ten davochs was mapped separately; and each map was prefaced with a prose description of marches, soil types and grazings. Separate tables gave the acreages of corn land, open grass and grass under wood enjoyed by each township. Notes were was included under the heading 'Improveable', for example in Fodderletter:

> There is some small parts would Improve west from the Mains And by the Bridge of Avin where they are Improveing It is confind & Bounded by Avin River on the East And on the west side the Hill is hard Inclineing to Gravel.[34]

The survey of the Fife barony of Coxtown, completed by George Taylor in 1771, was effected in similarly pleasing style, as an impressive single sheet mounted on rollers. It is a map that could be consulted only by ceremonious unfurling: hanging on the wall of a grand house or unrolled on a table such as might be found only in the library of an earl's place—at Innes or Duff House. Taylor's plan mapped the arable and pasture of the barony. Township buildings were shown on plan (Blackhills house in elevation), and probably in their actual dispositions. Runrig divisions were shown. Superimposed rubrics described soils: 'very good fertile soil', 'This Field is of a pretty good Soil with a Clagy bottom', 'Fine Flatt Improveable Moor'. Several vignettes pandered to the earl's classical and improving predilections. A jolly shepherd, a saucy shepherdess and a spotty dog watch over six fat and peaceable ewes and two butting rams. The central vignette shows an ideal tenant farmstead: a neat thatched cottage, a tall barn, and in the distance a windmill and a neat stone bridge. In the foreground a cheerful farmer with a tuft of corn in his hat brandishes a sickle (or hook) while his wife carries home the last sheaf of the harvest. Towering above the cottage roof are the ricks that are the fruits of their improved labours.[35]

Plans of this kind recorded the cooperative countryside on the eve of extinction. Many early plans seem stylish beyond what was necessary, and in formats that were hardly convenient for everyday use by estate managers. Indeed, the physical condition of estate plans suggests that many were not frequently consulted. Arguably, the more extravagant species of plan was commissioned to satisfy the enthusiasm of a heritor in the first flush of improving mania, before he had devised any practical programme for implementation on the ground. A 1789 plan titled on a picturesque vignette 'A DESIGN for the IMPROVEMENT of EASTER ELCHIES the Seat of the Rt. Hon. the EARL of FINDLATER and SEAFIELD', by Thomas White, took the estate plan to the brink of an art-form, with dense colouring and meticulous depiction of coniferous trees in tastefully clumped plantations and natural deciduous woodland. White's design for the estate included winding walks leading from the laird's house down to the banks of the Spey. Stables, farm offices and stackyard were planned at a little distance from the house, surrounded by a screen of trees. An elegantly oval kitchen garden was projected below the house. A picturesquely practical 'nearly natural' serpentine lake fed a mill lade. On the flat terrace above the house arable ground was divided into seven fields by straight hedges planted with standard trees. The scale and references were added on a *trompe-l'oeil* scroll pinned to the foot of the plan.[36]

Within a decade or so of their first mapping, many estates were resurveyed. The new survey of Strathavon in 1773, by Thomas Milne (at a scale of 1 inch : 3 Scots chains, 1:2,880) was a workmanlike exercise, showing the exact arrangement of township buildings (confirmed by modern fieldwork) and the acreage of each division of arable, with further data in a separate book of reference. Milne was meticulous in describing soils: 'a light loam deep in most places, with many loose stones' at Achnahyle; and between Ballintuim and Gaulrig:

> Grass pasture ground with some juniper bushes,—good Clay soil wet in some places, and in other places has a good many Stones.—upon the whole very Improveable Subject.—It is much dug for feal & Divot.

Milne's survey was used for subsequent improvement of Strathavon, which was planned in 1822 by superimposition of emphatically straight boundaries on Milne's base plan.[37] These innovations were developed in a second phase of improvement, documented on a new plan, drawn by George McWilliam (at 1:4,000) in 1840. McWilliam produced two versions of his plan: an immense and unwieldy (7 feet 6 inches by 13 feet) single sheet which the duke might unroll on the ballroom floor at Gordon castle to impress visiting fellow improvers;[38] and a copy in conveniently-sized sections (the largest 50 inches x 30 inches, smallest 30 inches x 26 inches) for reference in the estate office and for use by factors in the field.[39]

Enclosure on the ground

Enclosure on the ground followed site survey. Lines on the map were realised as walls and fences, hedges and ditches: dividing farm from farm, and then separating field from field within each possession. It was generally accepted that 'the first thing necessary in Improvement ... is Inclosing'.[40] James Donaldson urged, that 'farms are enlarged, inclosed and subdivided'[41] as a prerequisite for improved agriculture, which required each tenant farmer to work alone, maximising returns from the land untrammelled by consideration for co-cultivators or neighbours' free-ranging cattle. Internal fencing allowed farmers clearly to identify the divisions within which crop rotation could be practised. The signature division of the improved farm was the *field*—straight-edged, generally rectangular—rather than the rig, strip, butt, shott or acre. Emphatic physical boundaries in the improved landscape drew a symbolic line under the cooperative agriculture of the previous regime.

Enclosure in Moray proceeded haltingly, with practice lagging a good way behind principle. In 1811 William Leslie noted emparkment and walled enclosures in the vicinity of proprietors' houses. He referred also to exemplary enclosures at Kinsteary, on the Nairnshire estate of Gordon of Cluny, by its tenant, a gardener named Skene—as an exception that contrasted with poor progress elsewhere.[42] Leslie did not notice the extensive enclosures on home-farm lands at Moy, Brodie, Innes and Gordonstoun, which were already fifty years old when the *General Views* were composed.[43]

Ten of the first *Statistical Accounts* mention enclosure: negatively in Aberlour, which was 'without any fence'; hampered by 'ancient prejudice' in Rafford; while in Speymouth 'our grounds are almost all unenclosed, and cattle and sheep ... go at large during the winter'. The means by which fields were enclosed was only occasionally recorded, for example by hedgerows on Fife lands in Urquhart.[44]

A generation later a dozen *New Statistical Accounts* noted significant enclosure, though the fencing of fieldscapes was still incomplete: Drainie had 'no complete enclosures'. Inveravon farmers needed 'greater encouragement ... to enclose by means of dykes and ditches'; and Knockando boasted but 'few enclosures'. Oldmills, possessed by the Fife estate factor, John Lawson, was the only farm in Elgin completely enclosed with stone dykes. The Speymouth landscape was 'generally open fields', reflecting the particular circumstances of Garmouth feuars cultivating commonfield strips.[45] Around Forres it was said, as late as 1835, 'square fields are a novelty in this district'.[46] However, a few miles east of Forres, enclosure of the farm of Blervie was certainly complete by 1841: fields of eight to sixteen acres were defined by straight hedges and walls; access roads and tracks had been straightened; burns were canalised and redirected to supplement a rectilinear pattern of drainage ditches.[47] In Spynie, Myreside was 'well enclosed with substantial stone dykes, and formed into neat and convenient lots adapted for modern husbandry' from around 1830; though full enclosure of Spynie farms was not accomplished until the middle of the nineteenth century.[48]

Beyond the margins of cultivation, landowners reserved to themselves the right to enclose muir and rough grazing.[49] Some of this under-exploited land, which included arable improvements on shieling sites, was allocated to settlers who broke in new arable farms. Several settler improvements preserve 'shieling' place-name elements, for example, Bodnastalker and Bodnamoor in Kellas, Oldshields on the Coxtown moor, Rinnamart in Strathavon, and Rynagoup in Dallas. The ongoing labour of the settlers is graphically documented on estate plans as irregularly-shaped improvements—each new ploughed rig probing a separate finger of cultivation into the waste. A settler's labour often involved spade cultivation: trenching (a form of double-digging) that was as toilsome as the work of any pioneer on the American frontier. The actual area of tillage seldom followed the rectilinear boundaries of the holding. Small holdings in Mosstowie were reorganised in the early nineteenth century as regular lots, though the arable ground consisted of oddly-shaped plots that form little islands of cultivation in the unkempt wet pasture. The surveyor's regular grid of crofts and fields was simply inked over a plan of the actual farming landscape. Croft boundaries were presumably marked on the ground with march stones, but possessions were probably not physically enclosed or divided with stockproof fencing.[50] A successful settler improvement of waste land was described in approving terms by the earl of Fife's Elgin factor, John Lawson of Oldmills, in June 1815:

an improvement in the Hill of Quarrywood by Rob. Hardie and his sons ... the old man is dead, but his sons have a Kind of Village upon it, each living in separate houses with Familys Some of them Tradesmen, they entered to the moor about 20 years ago without any arable land ... they have now more than 20 Acres of it under the Plough.[51]

Several generations of nineteen-year leases might be required before the whole of the surveyor's rectilinear farmscape was brought into full cultivation. Indeed, even at the time of the first Ordnance Survey in the late 1860s, many fields were cultivated in patches, rather than ploughed right up to the straight edge of the fenceline. Patches of ploughland within the rectangular fields were still surrounded by tuffocky rough grass—a palimpsest of cooperative arable underlying the regular fieldscape. Some marginal districts were never enclosed. Settlers farming Glack Harness below Ben Rinnes on the Aberlour–Mortlach frontier, used turf and stone to surround their yards, but their fields were irregular unfenced islands of ridged ploughland, fringed with linear dumps of stones, in a tuffocky sea of rough pasture.

The uneven progress of enclosure created conflicts between occupiers of fenced fields and neighbours with unenclosed lands, or who expected unhindered access to common grazings. On Lethen estate an improver's enclosure was demolished because the

poor shabbie Teniment has the whole advantage of the Hill pasture and disturbs the Cattle and Sheep of Clune and Lethenbarr in the Course of their pastureing to and from the Hill.[52]

On the disputed boundary of Kellas, the earl of Fife secured his title by planting an improving settler to enclose ground he claimed at Whitelies, and to guard the march against encroachment by Findlater's tenants and their free-ranging cattle.[53] A couple of years later the positions were reversed. Fife tenants who still enjoyed traditional upland grazings, found access to pasture obstructed by new arable enclosures. They complained of being 'much Crabed' by these improvements, broken in by Findlater's tenants on the Kellas Leys, 'so that they cannot now send their beasts there Safely without Herds, and besides their Passage back and fore would be much Impeded'.[54]

The improving activities of James Skeen, farmer in Auchtertyre, asserted Fife's marches in 1768—on debateable moorland shared with Manbeen, possessed by an Elgin bailie, John Laing. Skeen had been tacksman of Auchtertyre for twenty-four years; his forebears having held the farm 'for upwards of these Sixty years past'. Skene protested his 'Great Expense & Outlay ... in Incloseing Improving & Manufacturing' the possession. He reported on his stout defence of Fife's marches:

I Builded a house on the Eastward estremity ... plewing the Ground & Sowing the Same Bailie Laing Tennants drove their Cattle which I Poinded ... and Cast a Number of Loads of Turff and Peats ... which I Stopt.

Skeen was allowed to engross into his farm the improvements of several 'Transient Tennants' on the moor. But, against his inclination he was obliged to take on one of these settlers,

Joseph Hay, as a sub-tenant. Hay was deemed 'Troublesom & disturbative': clearly he had the grit needed 'to keep the Marches, take in & Improve the Lands' on this difficult frontier.[55]

In 1815 enclosures effected by Colonel Sir George Hay at Westerton Strype vexed Fife tenants at Pluscarden (then not fully enclosed). Factor John Lawson reported on Colonel Hay's 'idle improvements': his planting and palings; and his closing up of loanings that gave Fife's townships access to grazings. Interdicts were sought and Lawson led a gang of Fife's men to make interruption. They 'broke down his palings in 6 or 7 places ... caused horses and Carts to go to the hill and take home fuel along the Roads we had opened'; Hay's men 'gave us no trouble ... we were too powerful'. Lawson's careful account concluded: 'I gave our people 10/- to drink.'[56]

Land taken by the proprietor was often planted with trees. In accepting tacks with a clause that allowed the landlord to enclose and improve, tenants signed away their right to the resources of the hill that had formed an important element in the economy of cooperative agriculture. Early tacks in Strathavon encouraged tenants in the work of enclosing and 'Wining in' new lands: at Dellavorar (1710), Tombea (1719), Dell and Inverchebitt (1735).[57] On Ballindalloch estate too, the proprietor encouraged tenants to improve moorland beyond the old head dyke with leases that allowed farmers to take on sub-tenants to enclose new fields on the 'out skirts' of farms: at Knockan (1785), Glenerder (1787), Stroangalls (1791), and Knockanshalg (1796).[58] The clause became a standard condition in later leases.[59]

Fencing the fieldscape

The first practical stage in estate enclosure was the division of farm from farm, isolating each possession from its neighbours. At Ballindalloch two improving objectives were achieved by separating possessions with ditches that also drained boggy ground on the farms around Tom Farclas. The drains, up to nine feet broad and four feet deep,[60] formed significant linear features in the landscape.

At Brodie a requirement to 'ring fence' each farm was included in tacks from at least 1768, when John Smith received a nineteen-year lease of a 'Tract of Land lying on the North side of the Town of Dyke, Planned off by George Brown Surveyor of Land', under condition that he maintain 'good and sufficient Dykes or Fences around his said Possession'. Subsequent tacks narrate the division and enclosure of the lands of the town of Dyke into discrete parcels according to George Brown's plan. Tack conditions regarding enclosure, were differently worded in each case: 'to inclose the same within one year' (1769); 'sufficiently inclose ... within six years' (1772).[61] A good deal of enclosing had been accomplished at Brodie by the end of the century. Thus in the lease of Wester Claypots (1801), the farm was already bounded by the 'great Ditch' on the south, 'old Dykes of Woodend Farm on the west and north; only on the east was the incoming tenant required to construct, 'a new Dyke to be built at your Expense'.[62] Nonetheless, even in 1832 Brodie was still considering estimates for enclosing each farm with a ring fence, without allowing for subdivision, and noting further: 'Brodie Estates are far behind in general improvements'.[63] Similarly, Lethen's enclosure was far from complete in 1832: farms were not ring-fenced and were still cultivated as detached acres and fields to the dismay of the improving laird and factor.[64]

In 1815 the little estate of Burdsyards, south of Forres, was clearly in transition, exhibiting a telling mix of improved straight-edged fields and irregular unenclosed arable. At the heart of Burdsyards, New Mains farm (formed from the amalgamation of Easter and Wester New Mains) was divided by geometrically straight drains and fences into fields of from thirteen to thirty-five acres. On the eastern margins, Chapelton consisted of irregular fields (from one to ten acres), some with straightened boundaries, around the uncultivable pasture of Wrights Hill. Nonetheless the farmstead of Chapelton was a neatly regular square of building. Sheriffbrae was laid off in four regular three-acre parks. Manachy, though, was almost entirely untouched by enclosure—except for a few straight boundaries within which shapeless islands of arable and pools of water punctuated the rough pasture, occupied by three separate farmsteads.[65]

On many estates, it is likely that the lines that the lines drawn by surveyors and the boundaries that were marked out on the ground with march stones or ploughed furrows—were delineated only gradually with effective fences. There seems to have been some initial uncertainty as to what kind of fencing might be appropriate to enclose the regular farmscape. Of course, there were fences and walls throughout the cooperative countryside: feal dykes on stone founds, stone-faced turf walls, moveable hurdles, and solid rubble walls—surrounding township yards, separating arable from pasture, enclosing tathings, or providing overnight folds. However, walls and fences associated with cooperative agriculture were built to define boundaries; it was the herds' job to prevent beasts straying across the dykes. The enclosures of improved farms were intended to be stockproof, but how this might be achieved was not immediately obvious.

Theoreticians offered a bewildering bazaar of fencing possibilities: turf, stone, hedgerow, palings, single wall, double dyke, ditch, sunk fence, and so forth. William Mackintosh preferred hedges (quickset, whitethorn and crabsets with standard timber and fruit trees) to stone walls.[66] James Anderson urged the use of 'balsam poplar' and 'To add beauty, a few plants of honeysuckle ... and some of the freest shooting roses'.[67] Sir John Sinclair favoured stone walls because 'They are major from their birth'.[68] James Donaldson recommended stone walls, with hedge-and-ditch where stone was unavailable.[69] Donaldson's successor, David Souter, reiterated this advice, while also recommending sunk fences and double drystone dykes.[70] These experts, however, took little account of the difficulty that an ordinary tenant might encounter in nurturing a hedgerow; still less the trouble involved in opening a quarry and carting stone, with the labour only of himself, his sons, a cottar or two, and the small horses and kellochs that were usual on improving farms. Each yard of double drystone dyke would consume up to two tons of stone; and even with stone to hand tenant farmers did not necessarily possess the skill to build it into a stable, stockproof wall. Thus it is likely that even under improving regimes considerable labour was expended in herding cattle, to exclude them from fallow or fields under crop—at least in the short term, while stockproof fences were established.

Farmers may have managed the transition to enclosed fields with temporary hurdling that has left a few documentary records, but no trace in the landscape. The manufacture of hurdles (from the thinnings of Scots pine plantations) was deemed important enough to merit mention in the *Statistical Account* for Urquhart.[71] The routine use of hurdles (flakes) to regulate grazings is documented in the journals of James Badenoch, who farmed near Stonehaven during 1789–97.[72]

Even around 1840 much enclosure involved only semi-permanent fences. Wooden palings were the only fencing mentioned in several *New Statistical Accounts* around 1840.[73] Palings provided the only protection for Gordon's plantations at Drumin in 1824;[74] renewed in 1840 at a cost of £34 3s 1d, with an additional '160 shoot of 4 barred paling', costing £5 6s 8d.[75] Palings were also notable on the Fife estates at Morriston (1801), and around the grass parks of Innes (1802).[76] Grazings at Goosehill, belonging to the burgh of Forres, too were enclosed with palings—combined with sunk fences and feal dykes—in 1814.[77] Palings remained important beyond 1840. Indeed palings may have been usual in districts where stone was wanting. Thus, for example, among the farm stocking of Broomhill, rouped on 23 May 1844, there was 'a large lot of Paling'. Similarly, roups at Gaveney and Cotts of Burgie included 'excellent **PALING**, and **SHEEP HURDLES** of Sawn Larch'.[78]

Improving leases may have unintentionally hampered enclosure. When turf-cutting was forbidden, tenants were denied use of a sustainable building material that was available on the farm, and which husbandmen were skilled in using. Tenants breaking in new arable on moorland and waste might accumulate considerable quantities of field stones. But this came in the shapes and variety that nature provided and might only with difficulty be built into a worthwhile wall. The stupendous effort involved in clearing this stone from the land, and building it into dykes is evident in the famous 'consumption dykes' of Aberdeenshire, or in the boulder walls of the farms below Red Craig in the Cabrach.[79] Field stones were the principal element in the roughly-built walls that enclosed fields and yards on the farms of Strathavon, where few walls were constructed in the stylish double-dyke style, and most also included a large element of feal.[80]

In the search for stockproof fencing several Moray landowners conducted scientific field trials. Experiments in enclosure on the Grange estate around 1780 followed an 'Exact survey ... with lines drawn and measured'. The experiment installed:

> Specimens of each different sort of fence Belnagechs fence for A Anderson & J Duncan Mr Whites Whin hedge for Broomtoun Aberdeenshire Dykes for Laurenceton Blackhills & A whole enclosure of 4 or 6 ackers for a Specimen Garden or Foress bank for W Grange.[81]

Gordon factors too experimented with different combinations of turf and timber fencing. The duke, meanwhile consulted within his network of improving acquaintances. A stone-faced asymmetrical turf wall with ditches in front and behind, suggested by Barclay of Urie, was built to separate township and grazing from arable at Balliecnoic in Strath Avon.[82] Further pen-and-ink drawings among Gordon muniments explored a variety of forms: asymmetric turf-dyke-with-ditch; symmetrical ditch-with-paling-in-the-bottom; asymmetric ditch-with-turf-faced-sunk-wall; and turf-dyke-with-quickset-hedge.[83] Arguably these were intended for the advice of farmers and dykers who had limited experience in the construction of effective enclosures.

Feal dykes were permitted where stone and timber were unavailable. Indeed, feal was recommended for Fife's Pluscarden tenants;[84] and required in leases for new farms carved out of moorland in Aberlour in 1764.[85] This flew in the face of many improving writers' advice: for example Wiliam Mackintosh damned:

> Earthen or Feal Dikes ... [is] the Devil; always a waste, a daily Labour, never can be kept up; yea, can never be made, the very first Day, a Fence against the heayiest (*sic*) or dullest Sort of domestick Fowl or beast.[86]

Turf was the principal material used for enclosing the hard-won arable land of several settler farms: for example, the rectangular fields at Balriannach in Glen Lochy; on farmsteads beside Allt Glander on the border with Kirkmichael: and at the township Innis Bhreac above the Ailnack gorge.[87] Fenced grass fields at Innes (established before 1750) were probably defined by turf walls, which have left no trace on the ground,[88] though the enclosures were significant landscape features remembered in the place-name, 'Parks of Innes'. Fencing here was far from adequate, the factor there lamenting in a letter dated 28 September 1799: 'it is impossible to keep the dykes about Innes in such repair as to keep out Sheep & Geese'.[89]

Turf walls may have been quite widespread under improving regimes, removed when better materials became available. At Lynemore in Knockando, roughly-made walls of turf and field-stones enclosed new fields carved out of the boggy moorland of Glen Gheallaidh. The walls of this outlying Ballindalloch farm were probably never sufficient to exclude the free-grazing beasts of unimproved townships in Glen Tulchan. The poor quality of the Lynemore field dykes make an incongruous contrast with the house and offices, which were regularly built in the most improved style with high-quality quarried granite.[90] Turf field walls are now rare in the laich, though feal dykes survive on roadsides in Urquhart and bounding forestry plantations throughout Moray. William Leslie noted in 1811:

> dykes of sod were pretty generally tried ... but they were found to be wholly insufficient to prevent the inroads ... of black cattle and sheep, and have been for some time generally abandoned.[91]

Hedges were the commonplace of (ancient and modern) English enclosure, but are not now widespread in Moray. In 1791 Isaac Forsyth (founder member and secretary of the Morayshire Farmers' Club) admired English enclosed landscapes, especially in East Anglia where, 'The whole country, in perspective, seems like one vast forest. Every field is enclosed with fine hedges and large trees'.[92] Meanwhile Gordon castle gardeners were investigating the 'common method of planting hawthorn in England'.[93]

Numerous sources suggest widespread planting of hedges in the laich, for example around Forres giving the countryside a 'peculiarly English appearance' in the 1820s.[94] Today notable stretches of hawthorn hedgerow exist on the estate of Westfield in Spynie, planted by Thomas Sellar and his son Patrick. Their comprehensive improvements included:

draining, planting and enclosing ... hedges with belts of wood, were planted, and the fields entirely remodelled, the small holdings done away with, and the estate put into four farms.[95]

Fife estate gardeners planted 'holys and haws', and were employed 'diging the hages' around Innes in 1780. Neglected hawthorn and holly hedges survive in the vicinity today, growing from turf banks along roadsides, though not dividing fields.[96] The pedigree of these hedges may extend back to 1724 when Innes gardener's accounts; included vouchers for 'a cask holding Holy berries mixed with earth' and 'two Casks for holding the seeds mixed with sand'.[97] The Innes hedgerows were nurtured by the Innes gardener who was also paid for 'Prooning' hedges at Darkland, Sheriffston and Torriestown in Urquhart in 1801.[98] A twenty-four year lease on Elgin Town Council lands of Maisondieu obliged the tenant to enclose the property with a thorn hedge.[99] The fields of Blervie, were enclosed with hedges studded with standard trees.[100] Tannachy estate was 'inclosed on all sides by a quick sett hedge'.[101] In highland parishes too enclosures were hedged. Young hedgerows at Nevie in Glenlivet were protected with '500 shoot of Two barred paling' (perhaps 1,000 yards), and at Croughly with '200 shoot' at 4*d* per shoot.[102]

Hedgerows are not now evident in Kirkmichael. Nor are hedgerows widespread, even in the laich. Robert Young declared: 'thorn hedges ... have not succeeded ... as they seldom do in Morayshire'.[103] There is, however, nothing in the Moray soil or climate that is inimical to hawthorn and blackthorn. Nonetheless, even laichland parishes do not offer the extensive prospects of quickset enclosure that characterise other lowland regions. It is possible that hedgerows may have been more widespread, especially in lowland Moray, than is now evident—silently removed when wire fencing became available because: 'much can be said for palings and wire-fencing. They are clean and do not harbour vermin'.[104] Perhaps the availability of palings from estate woodland made hedging unnecessary.

Archibald Grant recommended whin hedging:

> especially on founds of old dykes which don't hurt, and would also save the expence of time. &c. in the yearly building, be fewel, and is the best winter meat for horses and sheep.[105]

Furthermore, whins benefited the soil by fixing nitrogen.[106] Whin seed was sown on Fife lands from the 1720s,[107] This anticipated the advice of an unnamed 'agriculturalist' who recommended the cultivation of whins in 1725, asserting that their use 'takes on mightily ... this improvement comes from Wales, where it has been practised these hundred years.' Whins that now swathe areas of Moray may be the wild survivors of hedgerows or cultivated crops. Whins were planted on earthen banks along roadsides in Urquhart and Speymouth; and to enclose new farmland on the Hardmuir. At Drumin in Strathavon, 1,500 ells of whin hedge were established; with further lengths at Nevie in Glenlivet. The eighty pounds of seed required for this work were purchased on 17 April 1840 from Peter Lawson & Son, seedsmen and nurserymen to the Highland & Agricultural Society of Scotland.[108] Whins trimmed from hedgerows—or specifically cultivated on upland improvements—were valued as cattle feed: for improving milk yields from cows and curing worms in horses. The use of whins as fodder for horses was documented in Rafford around 1790. Stone whin mills, which became widespread in Aberdeenshire from the 1780s onwards,[109] are not evident in Moray, nor are they documented in estate records.[110] However, Moray whins might have been made palatable to cattle by hand-bruising using a mortar or a mallet.[111]

Stone walls became the characteristic fencing of the improved farmscape. 'Dykeing' (or 'dykeing and ditching') was specified for enclosing improvements in highland areas of the Gordon estates from the early decades of the eighteenth century, with the proprietor giving an allowance for the cost.[112] The condition and the allowance became standard in Moray tacks from the 1730s. Dykes constructed under this regime in the highland parishes were usually stone-faced feal, bank-and-ditch, or stone-based turf, with occasional boulder-walls.

It seems that there was no body of professional dykers (practitioners of an ancient mystery) available either to effect enclosure or to advise landowners. It seems that the distinct rural craft of drystane dyking emerged only under the influence of improved agriculture. Monymusk offered a model for enclosers from the mid-eighteenth century onwards, with exemplary fieldscapes defined by walls of drystone construction with a coping of turf.[113] This style of dyke was tried on Fife estates in August 1762 when Alexander Thomson agreed to 5*s* per ell for building 'in a Sufficient & dureable Manner a Drystone Dyke ... to Cope or Cover the said Dyke with three rows of Fail'.[114] Turf copings did not enhance the performance of stone walls; and though these dykes were not generally adopted in Moray, a turf course was added to finish the wall around the Gordon Castle park.

Drystone dykes became an improvement standard after 1760, in all parishes, but especially in the laich. Landowners gave a lead to their tenants, for example at Mains of Burgie where a condition of tack in 1750 obliged tenants to 'lead ... stones for building dykes'.[115] The double drystone dyke is, arguably, the unsung technical innovation of the regular revolution: invented (or perfected) by improvers specifically for fencing regularised fieldscapes. The thirteen-year improving lease of Castletoun of Blairfindy in 1771, obliged the tenant to 'improve into Corn ground out of such pieces of Barron ground ... as will admitt of improvement at lest to the extent of one half Bolls sowing yearly' and to 'inclose, into regular parks or Inclosures of at least four acres ... with a double stone Dyke'.[116] Tenants were encouraged to apply to the duke's 'planner' for help when building their dykes. [117]

The exact structure for a drystane dyke was by no means universally agreed. Factor John Lawson reported on 2 June1802, on dykes built by Thomas Gordon, tenant of Spynie. Gordon's walls were built to a luxurious standard that far exceeded the requirements for stockproofing:

> he is allowed ... £40 for <u>dry stone dykes</u> but the most of the Dykes is built with mud and som of them excellent Mason work ... they will value a great deal of Money & ... of little more value to the Farm than if they had been built of dry stones.[118]

Fife's own enclosures near Elgin were similarly extravagant, using high-grade freestone from the hill of Quarrywood to enclose the earl's woodland, and also for a network of neat double drystane dykes at Quarrywood farm, in December 1762.[119]

Ballindalloch felt obliged to give his dykers several pages of detailed specifications and a sketch plan too, to ensure that walls were built in the proper manner. Specifications for the fence at Delnapot called for:

> pillars of good well beded Materials at ... 8 to 12 feet properly levelled to a hard bottom 3 feet thick at bottom by 4 feet longitudinal & to be 17 inches thick at top and 4½ feet high. The space betwixt the pillars to be filled up with rubble building.

Elsewhere on this fence, the dyke was only 4 feet high, but finished above this with a coping of 'stones set on edge at least 20 inches long'. The coping at Skiradvie was to be one foot high with edges projecting over the wallhead. At Lagmore the walls were only thirty inches thick at base, eighteen inches thick at top and three feet high, not including coping. The double dyke at Delnashach was three feet six inches high, thirty-four inches thick at base, sixteen inches thick at the top, with a coping 'to be Built of good materials laid headerways with a sufficient number of Thorow bands'. At Tomore a further refinement specified a coping of stones:

> 16 inches in height ... to be of such a length as to project over the Dike two inches on each side ... and a course of through bands to be placed at the half height ... one of which in each lineal yard of dyke.

All these walls were supplemented with ditches and variously interspersed with lengths of stone-faced sunk fence in a variety of sizes and profiles.[120]

Tenants throughout Moray and Banffshire were hampered by the expense of enclosing their farms and fields. The cost of dykes and palings was blamed for the bankruptcy of William Mitchell at Drumin—though perhaps more significant in that case was the farmer's incompetence and drunkenness.[121]Some proprietors allowed tenants to reclaim the cost of enclosing. Sometimes this right was written into the tack; if not, canny tenants negotiated future reimbursement before signing a lease. For example, when James Duncan in Kinloss offered in 1771 for the farm of Tambreachs, he demanded, 'I to be paid at the end of my Tack for all fencable Inclosures'.[122] From the 1790s onwards Fife's farmers in the laich were generally reimbursed for the cost of erecting drystane dykes. In 1799 John Forbes in Pluscarden received an allowance for 'what new dykes I have built'; and James Gilzean received an allowance for dykes (over and above meliorations on buildings) when he left his farm of Kintrea in 1805.[123] The cost of enclosing was typically paid at the end of the tenancy—and then it was paid, not by the estate but by the succeeding tenant. If the lease was renewed to the existing tenant the cost of earlier enclosing was not paid at all.

James Donaldson approved the use of ditches and feal dykes in the laich, where stone was not readily available. However, he noted that on the estates of Monauchty, Asleisk and Burgie, there was abundant stone—cleared from arable rigs to '*baulks* or *mearings* ... the stone on which would enclose the whole lands around them, and give a great addition of arable field'. Donaldson noted further that the nineteen years of an ordinary lease gave scarcely sufficient time to raise hedges: 'the only mode by which the country can be enclosed'. He suggested that the proprietor should bear some of the cost of establishing hedgerows.[124]

A survey of Lethen's Kilbuiack estate in March 1793 proposed adding the possession of Moray's Cairn to Gateside because:

> the present tenants ... are Extreemly poor, and not in circumstances to labour it properly It will make ... a convenient addition to Gate side, as it affords plenty of stone for Incloseing— the ground being full of Cairns, and Stones, which an able, and Indousterous tenant, would Remove and turn Into stone Dykes.

The farm was enclosed using rubble won from a Bronze-Age cairnfield—of which a single much-denuded cairn survived, to be noted by the Ordnance Survey and then destroyed by roadworks and forestry.[125]

Today there is little evidence of any kind of physical barrier around many Moray fields—other than post-and-wire. Nor is it possible in most districts to find any vestige of the feal dykes, stone walls, or boundary ditches that might have preceded barbed wire. The neatly lined-out new lands of Mosstowie, and the small farms of Teindland, Cranloch and Coxtown—were probably too poor to repay the cost of paling fences, and are today divided only by post-and-wire, with no indication that they were ever previously enclosed by other means.[126]

There are few if any walls (other than yards beside dwellings) in these districts. In highland and upland parishes too—where the feal dykes of the communal countryside survive—the regular farmscape is now outlined chiefly with barbed wire. It seems that improvers' and land surveyors' vision of fenced fieldscapes remained, in some districts, a paper pipe-dream until the later nineteenth century, when the integration of agricultural and industrial revolutions brought cheap iron wire to farmer, allowing enclosure at last properly to be effected.

Drainage

The extension of enclosed fieldscapes across whole parishes in the laich, broke the contract which cooperative agriculture observed between the husbandman and the land. Improving farmers sought to subject the whole farm to rigorous cultivation and management. However, the surveyor's regular grid of fields and farms within which improving farmers worked overlaid landscapes that were anything but regular. The undulations of arable, the meanderings of burns, the outcroppings of rock, and the hollows of claypots, peatbogs and lochans all defied the regularising impulse. Nonetheless, improving leases obliged the farmer to cultivate his holding within regular manmade boundaries rather than irregular natural features.

Natural drainage might be hampered rather than improved by the superimposition of regular boundaries. The ridging of cooperative arable had been contrived to lead surplus water gently—slowed by the sinuous curve of the furrow—down the natural slope of the

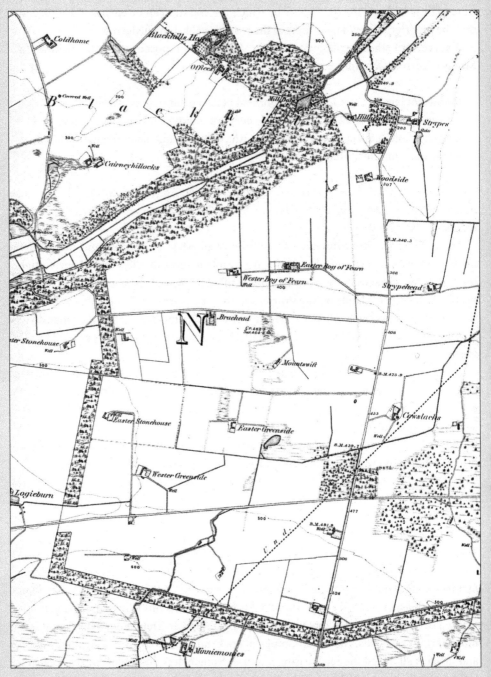

Small farms colonising the muir of Coxtown, sheltered by belts of estate plantation. (*OS, 1:10,560, Elginshire XIII*, 1870)

arable. But expert improvers were in general agreement in disliking curving ridges. Practical farmers were urged to 'Let the Ridges be made as straight as a line ... Water furrs should be all cleared with the Plough and spade';[127] and Lord Kames, while accepting the utility of ridge-and-furrow for drainage, was dismayed by the 'inconvenience of ridges high and crooked'.[128]

Improvers supposed that curving ridges trapped water and chilled or soured the land: William Mackintosh recommended small straight ridges to avoid 'drowning the lower End of our Fields, by reason of the unskilful Plowman's crooked Ridges'.[129] Arguably, though, it was old-fashioned sinuousness that offended improving sensibilities: cleanly classical straight lines appealed to the refined aesthetic sensibilities of modernising landowners as much as any practical benefit of straightened ridges. Where drainage was not a problem agricultural experts recommended levelling ridges. Dr James Anderson at Monkshill, Aberdeenshire, recommended, in 1775, leveling ridges by spade (rather than by cleaving with a plough), reckoning the cost of the work at 18*s* 3*d* per day.[130]

The straight edges of rectangular fields obliged farmers to plough straight furrows and construct straight ridges—or else lose the use of ground at the edges. However, water flowed faster along straight furrows, leaving ridges parched, while perhaps also eroding the furrows. Meanwhile, field dykes created barriers to drainage at the margins of each enclosure. Despite these drawbacks, ridging remained commonplace during the nineteenth century as the ordinary farmer's only feasible method of drainage. While ridging and ditching remained the norm, some experiments with underground drainage were tried. Lord Kames, recommended buried drains consisting of trenches deeply excavated into the subsoil and filled with brushwood.[131] This was a design promoted in print some fifty years earlier.[132] Brushwood drains were tried at Ballindalloch in 1776, together perhaps with underground stone drains: gardener's accounts for work done in the autumn at Craigiecrochan show at least fifty man-days labour 'trenching & Draining', including 'drawing stons broom &c to the drains'.[133] A similar combination of stone and brushwood drains was reported in Alves in 1835.[134] Stone drains were laid in the yards of Brodie's tenants, at the proprietor's expense under an improvement plan proposed in 1832.[135] Beyond the yard-dyke, however, fields were drained by ridging. In 1839 the Gordon factor carefully clipped a column from the *Aberdeen Constitutional*. The article described experimental drains tried in the south of England. These consisted of a trench thirty inches deep, and sixteen inches wide at top. In the base of the trench a slot three inches deep and wide was dug. This was covered with a divot before the whole trench was filled in. The slot was expected to act as an undersoil drain. It is not recorded where (or whether) this system was tried on the Gordon estates—or with what degree of success.[136] All these (and several additional) styles of drain were described in 1801 by John Johnstone, whose *Account of the Mode of Draining Land* was among the handful of improving texts in the Brodie Castle library.[137]

Fired-clay tiles for underground drainage were produced from the late eighteenth century, but were expensive and of inconsistent quality. The duke of Gordon experimented with tile drains in December 1838, when he investigated the use of tiles manufactured using the marquis of Tweedale's 'machinery'.[138] Only after 1840, though, did effective affordable machine-made drainage tiles become available to tenant farmers.[139]

The heroic labour of improving farmers, in managing drainage on their possessions, is writ large in the landscape, in the ditches that skirt the enclosed fields. This anonymous, undocumented, achievement involved detailed planning, survey and levelling, then laborious excavation with pick and shovel, to lead surface water by gentle gradients, through right-angle turns at field edges, until it discharged into a natural burn. Drainage on small farms was undertaken by the farmer, his sons and cottars, and costed only in time and sweat. On larger farms, though, where paid labour was recruited and proper accounts kept, expenditure on drainage was proudly proclaimed as evidence of the farmer's enterprise and expectations of future profit. Thus the minister of Kinloss applauded the vast investment of 'One enterprising tenant ... [who] has expended from L.1500 to L.2000' on 'draining, ditching, and enclosing'.[140]

Ditches and drains constructed by landowners might represent significant features within the improved landscape worthy of mention in legal documents. Thus the lease of Wester Claypots in 1801 defined the holding by its drainage ditches: bounded:

> on the South by the Great Ditch—on the west and North by part of the old Dykes of Woodend Farm, and on the East by a new Dyke to be built at your Expense, in the same direction but about Twenty feet to the westward of the new Dyke running from The Moss to the great Ditch[141]

Ballindalloch expended considerable time and money on drainage works from 1820 until 1840, with major ditches, excavated at the proprietor's expense, serving as marches for improved farms.[142] Morinsh leases in 1820, obliged tenants to keep ditches 'open and clean'.[143] The estate especially favoured sunk fences which served simultaneously as march dykes, enclosure boundaries and drainage ditches. Drains up to nine feet wide were fed with water flowing in the ditches of sunk fences that drained the sloping arable terrace of Marionburgh. The Faebuie, on the foot of Ben Rinnes, however, was not drained, and the possessions at Burn of Whiterashes and Lynriach, both remained as unimproved farmsteads, islanded by bog, until abandoned, probably around 1830.[144]

Drainage schemes carried significant potential for dispute between neighbours. Water drained from one property was discharged onto another, and few farmers would endure inundation by a neighbour's runoff. However, the small negotiations, enduring resentments and oral vituperation that may have accompanied the drainage improvements of tenant farmers were not often recorded. The larger interests and the grandiose schemes of proprietors were amply documented though, chiefly because of the protracted negotiations, and accommodations—copiously minuted by estate factors and lawyers—that were essential to the success of each endeavour.

Drainage that created new arable from waste, moor and bog, also generated minor conflicts between neighbours. When John and Thomas Adam, tenants, respectively of Newmilns and Thistlyflat in Pluscarden fell to be removed from their possessions in April 1768, they sought a nineteen-year lease on 'a New piece of ground ... in the Newlands of Kellas, being a piece of waste uncultivated Ground'. They undertook 'with all the Dilligence and Strength in their power ... to improve & take in the said waste ground'. A report on the property measured the ground at thirty acres:

> of a Watery Strong sward mostly green mixed with heather and interspersed with Moss in several places more than a spit deep ... it would be easily Drained and make a Valuable and Extensive Improvement ... worth double of what is offered.

However, other tenants objected: their cooperative grazings were threatened and constricted by enclosures and improvements:

> as they have no pasturage now left in the Hill Except that Spot nearer than Corrieparnach the whole space being nothing but Rank Heather and Deep Moss much Crabbed by the Improvements begun by Lord Findlater on the Kellas Leys so that they cannot now send their Beasts there safely without Herds, and besides their Passage back and fore would be much Impeded by the proposed Improvements.[145]

This episode stands as an epitome of the landscape revolution. The drainage for cultivation of one small area of moss and moor affected whole communities and provoked conflict between adjacent proprietors, as improvement clashed with cooperative agriculture in an unequal contest which improvement was bound to win.

Large-scale drainage schemes were beyond the capabilities of ordinary farmers, but within the means of improving proprietors, who could afford to pay skilled ditchers from 1½d to 4d per ell.[146] Drainage works in Glenlivet were a significant charge upon the entailed Gordon estate in 1840: £217 18s 2½d was spent at Drumin; £23 9s 7d at Castletown; £43 11s 2d at Blairfindy; £8 11s 11d at Delrachie; £1 19s 8d at Croftness.[147]

Low ground in the laich was reclaimed for arable farming at the proprietors' expense, by rectilinear patterns of ditches, for instance in the low-lying bogs between Buthill and Kirkhill in Roseisle. A couple of miles to the west, the bog between Earnside and Hemprigs was drained for arable cultivation with a broad spinal drain that led water from close-set side ditches and discharged into the canalised Kinloss burn. Drainage at Brodie was improved following a survey of 1824 and a report of 1832 by N. McLean, land surveyor—drawn up over five days at a cost of two guineas per day, plus expenses which included £2 14s 6d for the surveyor's bill at McQueen's hotel, Forres.[148]

In connection with such schemes—and to regularise fieldscapes—natural watercourses were canalised, dredged, embanked and rigorously regulated. Peter May, land surveyor, was employed to supervise drainage for Dunbar of Grange, principally by redirecting and straightening the Soldier's Burn and leading groundwater from reclaimed fields in underground stone drains.[149] Natural streams were straightened and deepened to drain the new farms that colonised the southern slopes of Kellas, improving a landscape of rough pasture into regularity and cultivation. The drainage of land around Sanquhar, south of Forres, was similarly improved by straightening the Marcassie, Manachy and Mosset burns. The Belmack burn was tamed and redirected in a series of straight alignments to allow improvement of the farms of Kincorth and Earnhill in Dyke & Moy. The house of Tannachy and the seven straight-edged fields within which it stood were surrounded by an angular moat of drainage ditches. During January 1811 3,000 ells of drainage ditches were excavated on the Fife possessions of Morristown and Quarrywood.[150]

Drainage of Rosehaugh in the laich was proposed by the earl of Fife's factor on 20 February 1814. The factor urged his master to regard the 'Propriety and Utility' of the scheme:

> to the Proprietors in general & for the good of the Country, as there are a great tract of Moss and Marshy ground which will be laid completely dry with a good leading drain ... [and] there is Marl in the ground which if draind might be wrought to advantage.

The Rosehaugh drainage brought Fife into a partnership with 'Mr Sellar & Mr Young' who urged him to put the work in hand as a matter of urgency, while labour was available: 'there are a good many people looking after the job, which they are afraid may go to the Caledonian Canal if not soon determined'.[151] Improved farming might be more rather than less labour intensive than cooperative agriculture, and periodic local labour shortages were a recurrent unforeseen consequence of improvement. The regularisation of farming that dispossessed the sub-tenants and cottars of communal townships, also freed them to seek work wherever wages were highest.

Money invested in drainage paid a dividend in increased rents as prospective tenants bid against each other for leases. Thus when Fife's trustees cut a drain to improve the farm of Mossside of Meft following expiry of Peter Mitchel's lease in 1837, the improved farm attracted no less than seven offers, for the new nineteen-year lease.[152] A similar rush was recorded for the tenancy of a modest new farm created as a result of the drainage of Bognamoon in January 1838: the land, which had never before returned any income to the estate, was leased for £7 *per annum* under a nineteen-year lease.[153]

In October 1812 Fife's factor, John Lawson, reported to his master on various drainage schemes and suggested further that 'there could be a vary profitable one in Pluscarden'.[154] Here the Black Burn, March Burn and Stripe of Scape were all canalised and straightened at the proprietors' expense during the Autumn of 1814.[155] However, large-scale drainage works required cooperation among neighbouring landowners, and sometimes personal resentments trumped improving predilections, to hamper schemes affecting quarrelling neighbours. Sour relations between Fife and Sir George Hay delayed implementation of a comprehensive scheme in Pluscarden. Fife's factor reported in November 1814 that the Colonel Hay's redirection of the Stripe of Scape was flooding Fife's ground, endangering cattle, and washing silt and stones downstream to clog a ford on the Black Burn.[156] The problem was addressed—and Fife's property improved—by redirection of burns draining his Pluscarden estate, only after lawyers had been involved to devise formal contracts signed during January 1819.[157] The drainage of Pluscarden allowed a replanning of the farming landscape—undertaken by a professional land surveyor. The factor, John Lawson of Oldmills, reported at length on 23 May 1815:

Mr Roy to mark up the different marches, & I suppose you would like much about the same number of Farms Kept up, and the marches made as convenient as possible.

Lawson recommended that the reletting of several Pluscarden farms be delayed while drainage works were underway. He also suggested that when the engineering works were finished an opportunity should be taken to modernise several farms. The cooperative possession of Netherbyre was specifically targeted for improvement: 'Russells farm ... is much scattered amongst some of the other lands part of which he has subset'. Furthermore, Lawson urged that new leases should be devised, with clauses that would allow the proprietor to undertake further drainage works, even where this hampered everyday agricultural operations; and also to oblige tenants to 'pay additional rents according to what opinion of two Honest sensible men think it benefits from drainage'.[158]

Improvement of the bogland and adjacent arable of Mosstowie was probably first mooted around 1760. The district was surveyed by John Home in 1762. His plan shows the lands of Greens and Mosstowie as intensively cultivated runrig with no waste or pasture. Several acres lay under the waters of the Dam Loch and Wester Loch. Hillside was mostly pasture with runrig arable in a narrow strip bordering the moss at the heart of Mosstowie.[159] Drainage of Mosstowie required agreement among landowners including the earls of Fife and Moray. Fife's improving vision, however, extended further than Moray's, and though the matter was discussed between the two earls' factors in February 1798, no action followed.[160] A scheme proposed in January 1811, was hampered by the earl of Moray's reservations. Fife's factor, John Lawson, complained, 'Lord Moray is constantly grumbling'. However, by October 1812 drainage operations were under way.[161] The works continued for several years, the earl of Moray gradually warming to the scheme until, in December 1817, Lawson could report, 'his Lordship has got very keen about the Drainage of Mosstowie'. Difficulties resurfaced, though, over tenants' traditional rights to cut feal and peat in the reclaimed wetland. By January 1819 the major portion of the work was complete.[162] The 'great drain' (Mosstowie Canal) remains a striking landscape feature through Mosstowie carrying water into the Loch of Inverlochtie and thence to the River Lossie. Above the canal, regularly-built farmhouses with steadings bearing new-coined English names (Redhill, Viewhill, Hardhillock, New Alves) perch on hillocks of dry ground beyond the reach of flood waters that periodically refill the Mosstowie basin.[163]

Loch of Cotts attracted notice around 1791, as offering 'encouragement to drain off the water'.[164] This was some twenty years after the earl of Fife had first looked into the possibilities, paying Thomas Milne, land surveyor, £1 16s 0d for 'Taking the Measures and Levells' during the spring of 1774.[165] William Leslie agreed that the loch might be drained, and reckoned the work might be done:

at an expense proportionally inconsiderable; and besides its own extent, which is about 120 acres, a great part of the adjoining swampy plain would be thereby greatly improved.[166]

Late in 1799 a flurry of correspondence in the letter books of the Innes estate factor announced a determined effort to drain the loch.[167] Agreement was reached with neighbouring landowners during November and December 1800.[168] At the same time a report on the farms of Leuchars recommended:

> that the Setting of them be delayed till some proper plan is fixed upon respecting the Loch of Cotts ... and as the Tenants are not improvers they might be allowed to remain from Year to Year untill that was determined.

The report advised the earl of Fife to:

> Advertise for a Man of Skill to inspect the Banks of Lossie and the Propriety of Draining the Loch of Cotts ... there is one Johnston in Aberdeen who understands draining better than any person in the north.[169]

The works were completed over the next two or three years, executed by Moray's exemplary improver, William Young, at a cost of some £1,000.[170] The laborious operation was described by William Leslie:

> The excavation was undertaken at twopence and in the higher grounds threepence the cubic yard ... Pumps of various construction, wrought by the united power of men and by the more persevering labour of horses were found of no avail. The labourers despaired, mutinied and threatened desertion. By fair words and the exhilirating encouragement of the proper quantity of whisky, they were induced to resume their labour ... a dyke of sods was built ... and the rising water was baled over it by manual labour ... with timber scoops. By their united perseverance ... the level [of the excavation] was carried up nearly one foot and a half under the deepest part of the lake ... and in autumn 1804 several hundred quarters of grain were reaped from off ground that had been a lake or unwholesome fen the preceding harvest.[171]

Leslie's account brings into sharp focus the labour-intensive nature of reclamation projects and landscape regularisation, and also the industrial power that labourers might wield. At Loch of Cotts—as on every tenant farm—regularisation was effected by simple muscle-power, without significant mechanical assistance. Loch of Cotts was baled out by hand in a heroic effort of manual labour. In the earlier phase of the project the enterprise seemed hopeless, arguably because the workers were deliberately going slow: either to spin out the job or to provoke their employers into raising their wages. The strategy paid off, though it took the threat of a strike before additional remuneration was won—in the form of a 'proper quantity of whisky'.[172]

The success of the Loch of Cotts project focused attention on Loch Spynie. This represented a more considerable challenge, though reclamation of this landlocked embayment would represent Moray improvers' most significant achievement in landscape remodelling. The drainage of Spynie had been 'long considered as an object of great importance'.[173] The shallowness of the water—reckoned by William Leslie at around five feet—made reclamation seem eminently feasible.[174] In 1750 Loch Spynie covered an area some four miles long by about one mile wide,[175] promising considerable potential addition to the cultivable land of adjacent properties. Leslie noted that the area of the loch in 1798 was probably greater than it had been during the Middle Ages. He noted a drowned crannog near Spynie Palace and the submerged causeway, known as the Bishop's Steps, constructed, he thought, 'to allow the vicar to get from St Andrews ... to officiate at Oguestown'. Leslie also observed ancient roads and cultivation ridges exposed by recent drainage works.[176]

Reclamation and management of Loch Spynie had begun under the medieval bishops of Moray. However, after episcopal land passed to Andrew Lindsay, lord Spynie, in 1590, the works were neglected and the loch refilled. A subsequent attempt to reduce the water level, by diverting the River Lossie, was unsuccessful. During the seventeenth century David Anderson ('Davie-do-a-thing') of Finzeach recommended rerouting the Lossie so that it no longer flowed through the loch.[177] The new channel created under his direction is shown on the map of *Moravia*, by Gordon of Straloch,[178] who sourly noted:

> Lossie is remarkable for nothing except that it does great damage to the fertile fields in its vicinity especially when its waters overflow into the neighbouring Loch of Spynie by reason of which a great deal of fine land is carried away.[179]

Under a contract signed in 1706, interested proprietors agreed to cooperate in maintaining the embankments of the Lossie with 'earth feel stone and creels'.[180] Expenditure appeared in estate accounts, for example £29 6s 0d Scots as Lady Brodie's share of 'Fencing the Water of Losie against its Running into the Loch of Spynie Both for herself and her Tennants in Kinnedar & Oakenhead' in 1757.[181]

Progress in Loch Spynie was hampered by environmental factors. Drifting sand affected laichland drainage, and water that formerly drained into Roseisle loch before entering Burghead Bay now flowed into Loch Spynie. Around 1720 an attempt was made to use wind power to pump water from the lordship of Duffus. The effort was thwarted by litigious neighbours; and when the windmills were wrecked in a storm, they were not replaced.[182] These works were, though, noticed as an enterprise of national significance, by William Mackintosh who applauded:

> *Sir* Robert Gordon of Gordonstoun, *Mr* Dunbar *of* -------- who, I am told *has gain'd many Acres of rich Medow out of a large lake in Murray*.[183]

Determined drainage works, it seems, required the energy (and capital) of a new man. In 1765 a Lisbon merchant, James Brander, acquired the estate of Pitgaveny, while his brother, Alexander, a London merchant, acquired Kinneddar and Aikenhead. The brothers cut a drain on the line of an earlier canal to carry water from the loch into the Lossie half a mile downstream.[184] 'Pitgaveney, by taking off 3 feet 4 inches of the depth of the lake ... recovered 1162 [acres of land]'. Adjoining proprietors also gained new land: Gordonstoun, 104 acres; Duffus, 132; the Crown, 72; Findrassie 51; Westfield, 3. Brander's improvement, sparked a legal dispute with Sir William Gordon of Gordonstoun who secured an interdict to halt the works until Gordonstoun's rights to reclaimed land and compensation for loss of income from the Salterhill ferry could be addressed. Legal disputes continued into the new century. Nonetheless, on 19 January 1801 John Lawson, the earl of Fife's factor at Oldmills reported:

> Mr Brander proposes draining Spynie Loch ... verry practicable ... a great improvement ... of great advantage to your Lo[rdshi]ps lands of Kintrea & Rosehaugh as there is a great deal of low ground at Kintrea often covered with water of the Loch & the whole of Rosehaugh could be made much drier & the moss improved.[185]

In October 1802 Brander's plans were published. The scheme envisaged an exchange of land with Fife and proposals for canals: to Lossiemouth harbour (at a cost of £930); by Oakenhead and Coulartbank (£1,180); or by tunnel under the Lossie 'to Mr Young's canal' (£300).[186] It is unclear how much (if any) of this work was begun. By 1805 yet another new scheme was commissioned from Thomas Telford, with the work contracted to William Hughes, an Inverness engineer, at an estimated cost of £7,000.[187] At the heart of the plan was a canal seven miles long, fed by numerous side drains. Work was completed in 1810. The final cost was swelled by fees to the lawyers who resolved disputes among proprietors—to £12,700.[188] During the summer of 1812 proprietors met to agree finally how the reclaimed land would be shared out.[189] In 1820 a turnpike road through the drained lands joined Elgin to Lossiemouth by a shorter route than the old Kays Brigg road. However, Telford's Loch Spynie improvement proved fragile. The muckle spate of 1829 destroyed sluices and deflected the Lossie into the Spynie canal.[190] Nonetheless, the new lands of the old lake bed were dried out and reported in 1842 to 'consist of rich loam or marly clay and bear heavy crops of every kind of grain'.[191]

As with much of the improvement of Moray, the decisive stages of modernisation in the Spynie basin took place after 1840. In the 1860s techniques employed in draining the Fenlands of East Anglia were employed at Loch Spynie. Self-operating cast-iron sluices were installed and the loch was at last reduced to a bare half mile of open water.[192] This vestigial Loch Spynie lies at the eastern edge of a flat landscape of rectangular arable fields, enclosed with barbed wire, outlined by a regular network of sluggish ditches indicating the former extent of the lakebed. The Spynie drainage was ultimately accomplished by the improvers' descendents, applying industrial muscle to realise their Enlightenment forebears' vision—a vision that sometimes overreached the improver's imperfect scientific knowledge and technical competence.

6

THE REGULATED ESTATE

Farm size

The question of farm size exercised the theoreticians. Indeed, Lord Kames devoted a whole chapter to the subject.[1] Inevitably, local topographical and practical considerations meant that there could never be a national—or even a provincial—standard. Sir John Sinclair admitted 'It is impossible ... to lay down any precise or universal standard.[2] Nonetheless, size mattered, and large farms were felt to be more efficient. In practice, Moray landowners also took some pains to ensure a mix of possessions—large, middling and small—to accommodate different classes of tenant. Nowhere in Moray were farms created in the size ranges most admired by Sir John Sinclair: 1,000—2,000 acres for 'commercial farms'; 600—1,000 acres for 'turnip arable' farms.[3] In 1794 James Donaldson reported that the most extensive of Elginshire farms covered 100–150 acres, though the 'general run ... contain only thirty to fifty acres'. He noted too the pioneering improvements of settlers, breaking in new land: the farms of these 'poorer people, particularly in the hilly and more remote parts of the country, extend only from five to about fifteen or twenty acres'.[4] Farms in Banffshire were of similar extent: 'many ... contain from 100–200 acres of arable land ... the general extent ... 40 to 60 arable acres'. The remainder comprised small tenants 'who possess from five to fifteen acres'.[5]

First *Statistical Accounts* recorded no precise acreages. In Bellie, Duffus and Speymouth 'small farms' were said to predominate.[6] William Leslie amplified the *Statistical Accounts*, describing progress in establishing appropriately large farms in both laichland and upland areas. In Edinkillie, Speymouth and Rafford, Leslie noted 'several farms in the low grounds pretty extensive; but ... of small extent in the hilly parts'—perhaps not taking into account upland grazing allocated to each farm or shared with neighbouring townships. In Duffus Leslie identified only two farms exceeded 100 acres; and in Forres farms were 'not of very great extent, few or none exceeding 60 or 80 acres'. In Rothes there were 'several farms of very commodious extent'; and in Inveravon the improvement of Ballindalloch created 'many farms of very respectable extent'.[7] In Alves, Elgin and St Andrews–Lhanbryde farms of 100 acres or larger, were reported—cultivated by farmers on a scale that allowed them to claim the status of gentlemen.

Under improving regimes, the conversion of a holding from scattered strips into compact possessions created farms in which economies of scale and the possibility of innovation, unhampered by consideration for neighbours, promised handsome incomes for both tenants and landowners. The character of the farmer mattered at least as much as the size of his possession. Abraham Gordon, minister of Spynie, observed, 'The industry of the farmer will often increase the value of a farm, where the sluggard will starve'. To prove his point the minister cited the 'remarkable' example of this in the improvement of Murraystown (Morriston) by a Mr Donaldson, who took on the farm with a nineteen-year lease following the bankruptcy in 1764 of its four joint tenants. Modern agricultural practice and the energy of the tenant brought the farm into enviable profitability. In the 1792 Donaldson's successor, James Duncan, was earning, 'besides the profit of his crop ... for milk and butter 150 l. yearly'—a handsome income by any standard.[8] However, Dr Richard Rose, minister of Drainie, painted a dismal picture in 1842 of the ill-effects of amalgamating farms:

> About the year 1800, the mania for augmenting farms spread from south to north, and in 1809 the farms in this parish were reduced from the number of 68 to 38. Only three or four tenants in the whole parish of Drainie now remain on farms occupied by their fathers at the date of the old Statistical Account. Little discernment was manifested in the choice of their successors. The highest bidders, men without capital, were preferred. They were perfectly satisfied with the terms and duration of the lease, and well they might, for before the expiration of it, four-fifths of them were bankrupts and rouped out.[9]

Even the most draconian improvement regime was unlikely to convert a whole estate into farms of ideal size—even if the experts could have agreed on what that size should be for every permutation of soil type, aspect and elevation. Thus the division (and redivision) of lands continued throughout the improvement period. The viability of farms was reassessed when leases expired. Size was generally less important than 'convenience'—a word much favoured when farms were assessed or advertised for let. And convenience was what landowners and surveyors sought in defining the bounds of a possession to encompass a proper mix of arable, pasture and improvable ground, with access to water, links to the road network—all in a compact unit within undisputable boundaries.

Convenience was not always achieved at the first attempt. A number of single-tenant holdings were established on Fife's Elgin estates as improvement took hold during the first decade of the nineteenth century. However, a plan drawn in 1815 showed many inconveniences requiring remedy. George McWilliam was employed to rectify matters. At Quarrywood, McWilliam noted two crofts: one occupied by William Thompson, 'an old man', the other by John Gillan's widow. He recommended that these small parcels be added to the flourishing Quarrywood farm, while allowing the sitting tenants to remain in their houses.

At Pluscarden, two discrete farms had been created by drawing a straight line through the lands of Auchtertyre. This facile line had also simply sliced through the township. The two new (single-tenant) farms were now inconveniently possessed: 'the tenant residing in

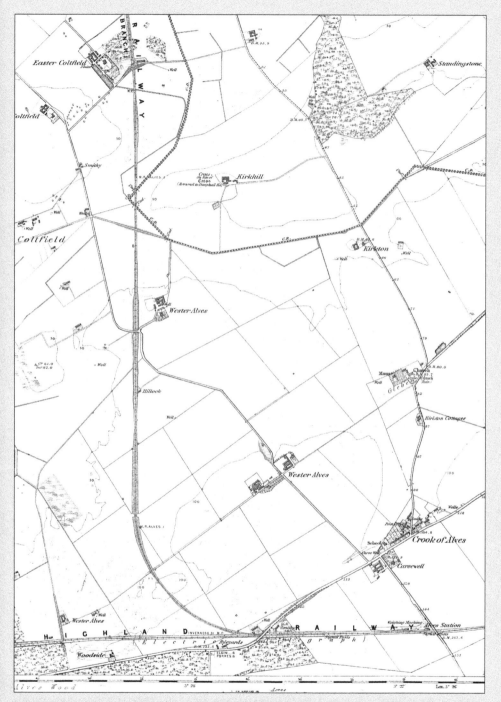

Farms with regular steadings and fenced rectangular fields in Alves. Improvement has left the parish church isolated. A new linear settlement has been planted on the Great Road. The curve of a road between Kirkton and Crook, however, preserves a boundary belonging to the vanished cooperative countryside. Railways spread through Moray from the 1850s onwards. (*OS, 1:10,560, Elginshire VI, 1870*)

the East Houses, having the greatest part of his land on the West side; and *vice versa*'. A new line of march was proposed, though still the dwellings and farm offices of the two farmers remained as a clustered township. As an additional convenience a fourteen-acre lot of the neighbouring farm of Stonewalls, possessed by an Auchtertyre tenant, was earmarked for inclusion as part of his Auchtertyre farm at some time in the near future. A further detached lot of Stonewalls was also noted for future division into two portions, destined to be added to Crossley and Auchtertyre. However, to avoid 'the disagreeable business of puting out the present Tenant, who appears to be a sober industrious man', this improvement was deferred for the time being. Crossley had been divided into two discrete farms in the same manner as Auchtertyre—with a straight line drawn by an armchair surveyor. The Fife estates land surveyor, George McWilliam, declared that these two farms were divided in a 'very irregular and inconvenient manner each having lots in different parts' (presumably a relic of former runrig possessions). The township of Crossly remained in its established situation at the focus of the cooperative farm. McWilliam recommended division of the Crossley land into two 'regular' lots; and 'Russels houses, being old and ruinous, should be rebuilt near the west end of the young plantation'—to create discrete farms each with a farmer's house and new steading at its heart.

Meanwhile, Factor Lawson had declared, Incharnoch 'is by no means convenient'. Incharnoch comprised two farms, created by simple division of the former township and its lands. Lawson reported, 'The houses are not very good. The other possession of Incharnoch comes too close ... a different arrangement is absolutely necessary'. Lawson also noted:

> The houses of Incharnoch are Situated close ... to those of Croy, with the march of the possessions running through them which makes them very inconvenient ... a different arrangement would be very desireable.[10]

Similar redrawing of the landscape was effected at Barnhill where marches were straightened and adjusted to create five small holdings. A sixth lot was reserved for a new church; and a patch of 'bare moor ground' was identified as 'a pleasant and convenient scite for dwelling house and steading, which, if tastefully executed, would have a nice effect from the Abbey'. The fifty-five acres of Whitree, however, remained largely unregularised, cultivated as several irregularly-shaped patches of ridged arable, variously subset among a number of possessors.[11]

A rare episode, in which division was resisted by sitting tenants was documented in Mosstowie where Fife's joint tenants disputed the actions of Lawson and the local ground officer who 'divided the farm ... giving each of them that part most convenient for their Houses in place of run rig'. The women of the two households gave Lawson such 'a great deal of Abusive language' that the matter was at last was referred to the courts. The women 'continued to object ... & ... had the Indiscreation to abuse the Shirriff & the whole Court'. In the event the division was enforced and the tenants ordered to keep the peace on pain of eviction. The Mosstowie wifies were probably not exceptional in their quarrelsomeness, though it was not usual for such neighbourly squabbles to reach the courts. It was even more unusual for the abolition of runrig and the creation of single-tenant possessions to be so vigorously resisted. The Mosstowie squabble was, though, a serious matter because it threatened to hamper regularisation; perhaps the matter was brought to court as a warning to others.[12]

The protracted process of creating convenient single-tenant farms is particularly well documented on Fife lands in the laich.Landscapes were redrawn (and redrawn again) in the pursuit of convenience into the 1830s. This trial and error revision of fieldscapes was possible because early enclosure in many districts—using palings and flakes—was relatively insubstantial. When surveyed by William Urquhart in 1785, the farms of Aldroughty, Morriston, Oldmills and Sheriffmill were already regularised into single-tenants farms with rectilinear fieldscapes, the different divisions named with the telling suffixes 'Park' or 'Inclosure'. Kintrea, Leggat and Ardgay, by contrast, were farmed in runrig by multiple possessors. Kintrea was owned partly by the duke of Gordon (with five tenants) and partly by Fife (with six tenants). Under Urquhart's plan Fife's part of Kintrae, with Leggat and Ardgay were each cut up to form single-tenant holdings: Ardgay and Leggat into four lots each; Kintrea into fourteen lots. The sizes of the new farms ranged from around twenty to around forty acres; their boundaries followed the curving edges of the fields and furlongs of the cooperative farmscape.[13] However, it took more than fifty years before the redrawing of this part of the laichland landscape was completed: the principal Kintrae farm was regularised with a new layout of rectangular fields before 1834; then redivided into yet another new arrangement of fields, and access roads in 1843.[14] Inchbroom, covered over 500 arable acres with pasture besides, and comprised the townships of Backley, Carse, Folds, Room, Claypots and Milltown. George McWilliam, land surveyor, recommended a comprehensive reorganisation, for 'more convenient & advantageous cultivation'. His plan created a suite of single-tenant farms in a range of sizes. McWilliam carved out a large farm embracing the lands of Inchbroom, Milltown and Carse (265 acres arable, 107 acres pasture and water). Smaller farms were created from the remainder: Folds of Innes (124 acres); Room, with part of Folds in two farms (104 acres and fifty-five acres); Backleys (sixty acres); Milltown (sixty-two acres); and a small croft (five acres arable, eighteen acres pasture) at Carsehill for a subtenant.[15]

Sometimes, however, the continuing regularisation of boundaries was undertaken as much for aesthetic delight as for agricultural convenience. For example, at Viewfield and Kempston where 'The Marches ... is Very crooked ... which looks bad from the public Road ... the southmost hedge now forms the Natural boundary ... and ... should be continued'.[16]

Tacks and rents

Written tacks became widespread, particularly in southern Scotland, from the 1630s onwards. This trend was only tenuously ancestral to improvement, though some early tacks urged tenants to maintain soil fertility by means of lime and basic crop rotations.[17] As elsewhere, tackholding in Moray was not a revolutionary change that suddenly surfed in on the improvement surge of the 1760s. Tacks were not unusual in the cooperative countryside, though they were far from universal. However, only rarely did Moray tacks before 1760 impose improving obligations. One of these rarities concerned Newton of Struthers in Kinloss, acquired by Ballindalloch in 1732. Newton was possessed by five tenants holding equal portions, allocated as runrig, under separate nine-year tacks. These leases, granted by the previous owner, Ludovick Colquhoun of Luss, forbade absenteeism and subsetting—and thus might be regarded as taking a tentative first step on the path to improvement.[18]

Written tenancy agreements became commonplace in Moray only during the later eighteenth century, when their spread was both a symptom of and a spur to improvement. Secure tenure under a tack was a positive factor in encouraging (and enabling) tenants to adopt new practices that demanded heavy short-term investment (of both labour and capital), but promised handsome profits in the future. William Leslie opined:

> security of possession is the indispensible pre-requisite for the improvement of a farm ... Without this pre-requisite neither fallow, nor turnip, nor cultivated grass, can be admitted into the rotation.

Leslie was, however, doubting the value of prescriptive leases continued:

> any degree of controul in the management by the proprietor must repress [the tenant's] ingenuity, must encumber his operations.[19]

Written tacks regulated and regularised relationships that had previously been flexible. The tenant was no longer at the mercy of a heritor, who might be capricious or carefully patriarchal; but he was contractually bound by conditions in his tack. The landlord too was legally bound into a relationship that could not readily be broken within the term of the agreement. Only occasionally, though, was legal action threatened to enforce conditions of lease: for example by Brodie of Lethen who was exasperated by tenants who continued customary practices into the 1830s: 'exhausting the soil ... by casting and carting away Peats and Turfs', and also burning the muir. He threatened offenders with prosecution 'not only for breach of their Tacks, but also at Common Law.[20] In general, law cases were raised only when rents fell into arrears.

The question of what constituted the proper period for a tack, exercised minds as the improvement craze took hold. Francis Grant, minister of Knockando recommended in 1790, 'the condition of the people might be much meliorated by granting them leases for 38 years, and a lifetime'. The minister thought, landlords should support long leases by giving tenants 'good examples of husbandry'.[21] Lord Kames articulated an argument in favour of long leases:

> because a man never loses hope of living longer ... By this means, the tenant is deluded into a course of management, equally profitable to himself and to his landlord.[22]

Leases of thirty-eight years duration had been granted by Lord Findlater in the 1750s to 'intelligent, active and substantial tenants' in lower Banffshire, who 'became bound under penalty' to adopt improved methods.[23] The policy crossed into Moray, though thirty-eight year improving leases were not adopted conspicuously beyond Findlater's estates at Myreside ('the first nineteen years at a nominal rent') and Newfield in Spynie.[24] Moray landlords, however, recognised the need for tenants to enjoy some security within which they could improve their holdings and also reap a reward from their investment; few, though, were willing to bind themselves into contracts that might encumber their estates for a generation into the future.

In the Ballindalloch heartland of Inveravon, written tacks were commonplace from the 1730s: granted variously for three, seven, nine, eleven, fifteen and seventeen years, but with a trend towards a nineteen-year term—which became general at Ballindalloch (as throughout Moray)—in the closing decades of the century.[25] A significant minority of the duke of Gordon's early tacks were for nineteen years, for example Dell (1713). Gordon's nineteen-year tacks, moreover, included clauses encouraging modest improvement of the possession. A signal change achieved in the nineteen-year tacks for Tombae and Blairfindy (1719), was the payment of rents entirely in money. By the 1730s a more or less standard form of tack had emerged for Gordon's Kirkmichael possessions, where tack conditions included: money rents (with converted values for custom wedders and hens); requirements to plant trees, extend arable ground; fence and ditch new improvements; all with a promise of meliorations on buildings.[26] These conditions were additions to, rather than reforms of, cooperative regimes, and in most respects township life was undisturbed by improvement on the margins. Robert Willox, the Strathavon forester and tenant of the Gaulrigs, meanwhile, took an old-fashioned view of tack-holding. He recommended, in 1773, giving 'no tacks but During the Good payment of there Rents it Will always keep them in fear and make them pay the Rent'.[27]

Nineteen-year tacks were agreed on Fife estates east of the Spey during the 1740s, and also in Fife's Moray estates of Dipple (where twenty of the sixty-seven tenants held tacks for from twelve to nineteen years); Teindland (ten out of thirty-two tenants); and Coxtown & Barmuckity (eighteen out of seventy).[28] A judicial rental of George Duff's lands of Milton, Bilbohall, Waukmill, Barmuckity and Scotstonhill, compiled in September 1764, listed forty-five tenants of whom ten held under tacks for eighteen or nineteen years, agreed from 1750 onwards.[29] In the western laich, a handful of possessions on the Brodie estate were enjoyed under nineteen-year tacks from the early eighteenth century.[30] Nineteen-year tacks became usual in mid-century, though most holdings, remained runrig possessions in cooperative townships.[31]

The popularity of nineteen-year tacks spread rapidly through Moray from the 1760s. All of the thirty-one possessions of Strathavon were leased under nineteen-year tacks in 1765–67.[32] The earl of Fife's Brodie lands of Leuchars, Dunkinty, St Andrews, Calcots and Harvieshaugh were possessed by some fifty individuals all of whom enjoyed long leases granted from 1770 onwards. However, written tacks spread patchily through Fife's other estates, with tenural improvement on some lagging a decade—or even a generation—behind the leaders. In Kellas only a handful of tacks were agreed before 1798, when every tenant received a nineteen-year lease. In 1800, six Pluscarden tenants enjoyed seven- or eleven-year tacks, but a further seventeen tenants held no tack at all. Only in 1802 did all Pluscarden tenants receive tacks for eleven, fifteen or nineteen years. Mosstowie was covered by nineteen-year tacks from 1788; but possessors of the adjacent lands of Hillside enjoyed no tacks until 1810. Quarrywood's thirteen tenants held nineteen-year tacks from 1786. On the barony of Coxtown, nineteen tenants held nineteen-year tacks from the 1780s; but a further twenty-two remained tenants at will. All held tacks in 1800. The twenty tenants of Lochs, Finfan and Pittensier received their first leases (for sixteen or nineteen years) in the 1790s. The four Leggat tenants enjoyed nineteen-year tacks from 1786; as did the eight tenants of Kintrea. The principal tenant of Morriston was granted a nineteen-year tack in 1788; but five Morriston crofters had none, and continued without security until the mid 1790s when they were dispossessed and the estate reorganised into two large farms (under leases for twenty-five and nineteen years) and one croft (with no tack). Innes estate in 1790 was occupied by eight tenants with tacks and twenty with none. The estate was reorganised during the decade with major tenants receiving tacks in 1797; though twenty-nine crofters and small possessors on the Moss of Meft held no tacks into the early nineteenth century. Monaughty (including Cloves) was possessed by thirty-two tenants in 1800: one tenant held a nineteen year tack (granted in 1788); a further six held ten-year leases (granted 1794–97); and Asleesk was held precariously under an eleven-, fifteen- or nineteen-year tack (granted 1796). The farm of Spynie was a single tenancy under a nineteen-year tack (granted 1783). Throughout the Fife estates, special conditions and short leases applied to marginal districts and land undergoing reclamation and improvement.[33]

Written tacks issued under improving regimes, were agreed between the landowner and a single tenant. Only rarely was a joint tenancy contemplated, and then, typically, the joint possessors had the same name and were presumably near relatives, occasionally identified as father and son. For example, On the Fife estate of Hillside of Mosstowie, where written leases were not general until 1816, three of the seven possessions were leased to joint tenants: James & Douglas Robertson; James & William Douglas; and William Clark & James Simpson, who in 1824 shared the holding with a third joint tenant, Alexander Stewart. This density of joint tenants was exceptional under improving regimes in Moray.[34]

By the 1830s, *New Statistical Accounts* could report nineteen-year leases as the norm in eight parishes. Probably, nineteen-year leases were usual elsewhere, but too commonplace to merit notice.[35]

The nineteen-year tack was the improving landowner's chosen instrument for imposing regular regimes upon his tenants. The tack might itemise the agricultural practices to be implemented, or refer to general regulations. These regulations, enshrined in a separate document, were favoured as a means by which written leases might be shortened and the parties saved the expense of many pages of stamped paper. 'Articles and Regulations'[36] for Gordon tenants were devised by the duke's Edinburgh law agent during 1783, adopting a suggestion by the Gordon Castle cashier:

> I beg leave to submitt to you whether it would not be proper to make General Conditions etc in a paper apart ... as might be referred to in a lease, and which would shorten it considerably.[37]

Estate regulations published for Fife tenants in 1772 observed:

> it would be of general use, benefit, and advantage to all industrious tenants, and promote
> the general improvement of the country, to have laws for the preservation of sown grass,
> turnep, hedges, planting and inclosures, put strictly into execution. [38]

The 1772 rules were amplified in 1776 in four pages of 'Articles and conditions' for Fife
estates in Aberdeenshire and Banffshire.[39] The new regulations were printed in quantity for
distribution along with leases. Among the eighteen conditions, tenants were obliged to: erect
stone buildings; plant trees; grow turnips; rotate crops, sow grass; straighten boundaries
and enclose fields. Under these regulations the tenant was recruited as an apostle of
improvement: by fulfilling his obligations he would 'distinguish himself visibly, as a faithful
and industrious improver in the country, exemplary in so doing to the neighbourhood, and
others of the country'. The regulations forbade killing game, cutting turf, and selling dung or
lime, and keeping sheep or sub-tenants without permission. A postscript sugared the pill:

> Particular encouragement is always given to the tenant who has a good field of turnip
> fallow, and a fine laid down field of grass, inclosed with stone, or properly with hedges.

The 'encouragement' was not financial. It perhaps materialised in the form of a favourable
consideration when leases fell to be renewed or in more nebulous expressions of patriarchal
approval from the earl.

Regulations published in 1776 for Fife's Elginshire estates contained similar regulations
and prohibitions but couched in language—and with frequent references to Acts of
Parliament—that harked back to an earlier age of imperious lords with rights of pit and
gallows. Indeed, the regulations were uttered with all the ponderous authority of the baron
court. The conditions included moral injunctions, for example against harbouring sturdy
beggars (contrary to a statute of 1424[40]); and set scales of fines for 'using unlawful oaths, and
pronouncing of God's name in vain', and 'drinking or tippling in any inn, victualling house,
or ale house, or haunting any tavern'. The rules applied to 'tenants, sub-tenants, cottars
and others living in the said lands', with a suggestion that Fife's Moray properties generally
lagged behind those east of the Spey—at least in respect of the prevalence of sub-tenants,
and perhaps also in the progress of improvement. The baron court ordered 500 copies to
be printed, distributed throughout the estate and published at kirk doors four times a year.
Even the mode of publication suggests a somewhat old-fashioned approach. This may relate
to the conservatism of the earl of Fife, or the factor, or the tenantry—or any combination of
the three.[41]

By the first decade of the nineteenth century most tacks on Moray estates contained
clauses which specified, in more or less detail, agricultural practices that the incoming tenant
was obliged to implement. For example, Brodie of Lethen specified a six-course rotation
around 1810,[42] revised to a five-course rotation in 1848.[43]

Rents

Written tacks, shifted the emphasis of a landowner's relationship with the tenant—and with the land—into a money transaction. Money rents were fixed, typically, by a calculation based upon the market value of the grain and small customs paid previously. This conversion was under way in the laich by 1766, when Blervie's bear rents were converted at £10 per boll. Thus Hieron McGillivray in Sourbank paid £112 10s as the converted value of 11 bolls 1 firlot; and John Petrie paid £100 as the value of 10 bolls. The tenants paid in addition £4 11s and £3 6s 8d respectively for the converted value of labour service and other customs.[44]

Highland estates did not necessarily lag behind the laich. Gordon rentals in Strathavon were assessed in money from the late seventeenth century, perhaps as a result of a cash nexus established by the widespread use of wadsets in the district.[45] The rental of 1752–54 shows that the sub-tenants too, for the most part, paid a money rent for their holdings, supplemented with labour services and various small payments in kind—of hens, sheep, eggs, butter, &c.[46] The rental of Glenlivet and Strathavon in 1772, was simply a list of money payments. Rents ranged from £3 6s 8d (presumably an original 5 merks) for Eskiemore in Glenlivet, to £106 2s 3d for Camdale and Fodderletter in Strathavon.[47]

The conversion of rents into cash took time to effect. The 1773 rental for Cloves (part of Fife's Brodie lands) itemised payments from twenty-two tenants: a complex confection of money (from 4s 9d to 5½ merks), victual (from 2 firlots to 21 bolls 2 firlots), lint work, hooks at harvest, hens and poultry. However, looking forward to a change to money rents, a table of conversions (men in summer and at lint work at 6d each, hens at 2d, poultry at 6d) suggests that tenants might opt to pay cash in lieu of services.[48]

Lethen's lands at Burgie and Asleesk were occupied as late as 1829 by tenants paying rents calculated in money, hens, oats, barley, chickens, wedders and cuts of yarn, though a half-hearted attempt had been made to modernise estate income: 'Victual Rents in Morayshire are payable at the Fiars of that county. The Meal of Nairnshire is deliverable in Kind'.[49] On the estate of Burgie, the new laird, Lewis Dunbar Brodie, granted nineteen-year leases to all his tenants in 1796. However, he did not fully modernise the rent structure. The 1802 rental shows fourteen farms paying from six to twenty-eight bolls of victual and also from £8 4s 6d to £38 19s 2d in money. Tenants also paid from a dozen to twenty hens and chickens. The total Burgie rental was 194 bolls of victual and £238 9s 2d. Twenty years later rents had risen, indicating both an increase in productivity and tenant prosperity, and a rise in prices largely as an economic consequence of war with France. However, though the 1796 leases had expired and the farms had been relet (the majority to new tenants) still the estate income came in the form of both money and victual. Notably though, new holdings on Hill of Burgie paid only money (£5 or £7 10s) but with six chickens and one hen for the single reeking lum on the croft. Total rental in 1822 was 154 bolls of grain and £499 18s 3d.[50]

This pattern was repeated at Altyre. Tenancy agreements before the 1790s were by simple letters of acceptance. A tack on Begstoun taken by Alexander Smith (an outsider from Granary in Rafford) repeated the kinds of conditions specified in agreements a generation earlier, with no significant addition of improving clauses. The tack on Miln of Altyre, dated

1. Bailechnoic, Strathavon: stone foundations preserve the ground plan of a cooperative township of turf-walled houses, byres, yards and kilns; several buildings remained roofed and in use in the 1860s. (*J. Barrett*)

2. The Strathvon Survey team ('the Other SAS') at the deserted township of Milton in Glen Lochy. (*J. Barrett*)

3. The kirkton and cooperative countryside of Longbride (Lhanbryd) on the earl of Fife's Coxtown estate, showing the division of arable fields into strips possessed by township husbandmen; drawn by George Taylor, 1771. (*J. Barrett, Fife, MS3175/RHP31002, reproduced by permission of Aberdeen University Library*)

4. Tomnacroik of Belon, Strathavon: Turf-covered founds of township houses in the foreground; beyond are rectangular yards surrounded by walls of turf-and-stone, planted with yard-dyke trees. (*J. Barrett*)

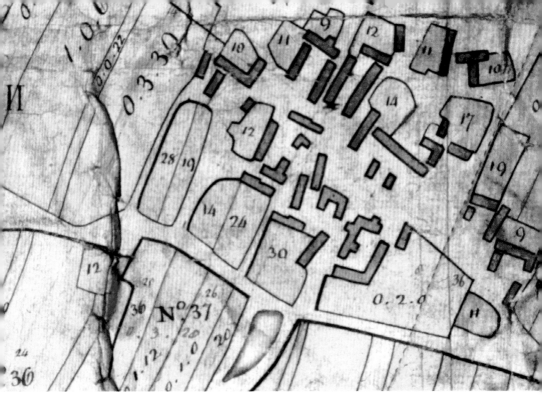

5. Oldtown of Roseisle: a large laichland township. (*D. Iredale, reproduced by permission of MDRO, Forres*)

6. Baile Gean: an experimental reconstruction of turf-and cruck buildings forming a cooperative township—at Highland Folk Museum, Newtonmore, Inverness-shire. (*J. Barrett*)

7. The stone foundation for a turf-walled shieling hut occupied seasonally by the men and boys who tended township cattle—and laichland herds sent for summer grassing – on the flanks of Ben Avon. (*J. Barrett*)

8. Roseisle estate: colours indicate runrig lands owned by the laird of Gordonstoun, the duke of Gordon, and others; surveyed by Alexander Taylor, 1773-5, to facilitate redivision prior to improvement. (*D. Iredale, reproduced by permission of MDRO, Forres*)

9. Roseisle estate: stone walls and wire fences define and enclose the regular fields of improved laichland farms. (*J. Barrett*)

10. An ideal improved farm: vignette illustrating a plan of Coxtown estate, surveyed by George Taylor in 1771 for the earl of Fife. (*J. Barrett, Fife, MS3175/RHP31002, reproduced by permission of Aberdeen University Library*)

11. The double drystane dyke was the expensive new development that defined and divided the regular landscapes of the regular replanned countryside—here erected around 1820 to enclose plantations at Delnapot on Ballindalloch's Knockando estate. (*J. Barrett*)

12. Hedgerows with hardwood trees flourished on the field margins and roadsides of Innes estate, despite a popular belief that hawthorn would not grow in Moray. (*J. Barrett*)

13. Blairfindy, Glenlivet: a regular farmhouse and steading with a ragged row of yard-dyke trees in front. (*J. Barrett*)

14. Oldshields, St Andrews-Lhanbryd: the farm began as a shieling improvement on Coxtown muir before 1760; the house and steading—built of clay-and-boule around 1800 (originally thatched)—are arranged in a regular square. (*J. Barrett*)

15. Stocktown, Glenlochy: the granite farmhouse is in regular improved style; traditional turf-and-stone yard walls support several yard-dyke trees; the old-fashioned cruck-framed barn and steading are arranged in a modern rectangle. (*J. Barrett*)

16. Ladderfoot, Glenlivet: the modest regular dwellinghouse and yard-dyke trees of a settler farm colonising a rectangular croft improved from moorland at the limit of cultivation. (*J. Barrett*)

17. Ballindalloch's kiln at Morinsh provided lime to sweeten the acid soils of improved farms in Inveravon and Knockando. (*J. Barrett*)

18. Lynemore, Knockando: a milldam provided water power for a threshing machine in the barn of a farm established on a shieling site around 1750, and fully modernised after 1800. (*J. Barrett*)

19. Water wheel at Knock farm in Strathavon to power a fanner and threshing machine in the barn. (*J. Barrett*)

20. The improved plough was the essential implement of regularised farming—manufactured by local smiths who freely copied, adapted and improved the design originated by James Small in the 1780s (*J. Barrett*)

21. Dykeside, Birnie (*c.*1750): regular rural housing for a progressive tenant. (*J. Barrett*)

22. Whitefield croft, Elgin (*c.*1800): a regular stone house in the new vernacular style for the tenant of a small possession on the fringes of the reclaimed land of Mosstowie. (*J. Barrett*)

23. Innes house (*c*.1646): a combination of traditional and modern elements—defensible and convenient—the Moray seat of the earls of Fife. (*J. Barrett*)

24. Tannachy/Invererne (1818): a model of neoclassical convenience for an enlightened gentleman. (*J. Barrett*)

25. Pitgaveney (1776): a towering classical statement for James Brander, a Lisbon merchant and improving laichland landowner. (*J. Barrett*)

26. Elgin High Street (1684): regular facades and classical details were embraced by burgh merchants during the seventeenth century. From 1703-22 this house was the place of business of William Duff of Dipple and Braco, banker, landowner, and ancestor of the earls of Fife. (*J. Barrett*)

27. Braeriach, Forres (1821): regular and mildly classical convenience for a burgh merchant. (*J. Barrett*)

28. Inveravon manse (1775 & 1834): the minister's house, rebuilt in the style of an improved farmhouse, seemed old-fashioned to a later generation, and was extended and reoriented with a smart new wing in the style of a scaled-down laird's house. (*J. Barrett*)

29. Dyke parish kirk (1781): 'a handsome commanding structure', typical of the plainly regular Georgian buildings that replaced medieval churches throughout Moray. (*J. Barrett*)

30. St Giles parish kirk, Elgin (1825-8): a polite classical temple reflected the enlightened taste of the burgh community. (*J. Barrett*)

31. Urquhart parish kirk (1843): regular gothic style was chosen to dignify the improved landscape of the earl of Fife's Innes estate. (*J. Barrett*)

32. Forres tolbooth (1838): Scottish traditional style, reinvented by William Robertson for a modern prison and courthouse—overshadowing regular dwellings in the closes of the royal burgh. (*J. Barrett*)

33. Dr Gray's hospital, Elgin (1815-19): classical style was favoured for public institutions—here closing the vista along the burgh high street. (*J. Barrett*)

34. Craigellachie bridge (1814): improved communications supported the regular revolution; Thomas Telford combined modern cast iron and fashionable gothic style to span the River Spey. (*J. Barrett*)

35. Lossiemouth seatown (1784): regular terraced dwellings for fishermen in a new town replanned in 1784 as an outport for the burgh of Elgin. (*J. Barrett*)

36. Charlestown of Aberlour (1812): the central square of Charles Grant's new village was dignified by William Robertson's regularly Romanesque church—replacing the medieval parish kirk of Skirdustan/St Drostan. (*J. Barrett*)

1786, gingerly required some reorganisation of rigs and, significantly, reference to a lime kiln; it also converted rents into cash. Perhaps these modern elements reflected progressive inclinations appropriate to a millowner, who, as a businessman connected to wider commercial networks than the ordinary husbandman, was open to the improving spirit of the age. It took a new factor, Donald Smith, in 1796 to introduce, as part of a modernising regime, formal leases (a tack for Blairs and Kirktoun) on stamped paper.[51]

Ballindalloch tenants paid the main part of their rents in money from the 1730s, though labour services and carriages were exacted into the closing decades of the eighteenth century; and carriages were still required under tacks signed in 1801 when most of the possessions on the estate were set under improving leases. Payments of peats, reek hens, chickens, hoggs and wedders, and various services, persisted, in leases signed during the first decades of the nineteenth century.[52]

On Fife's Moray estates the shift to money rents was accomplished piecemeal as improvement progressed. The change from grain and services to money was not, though, necessarily accompanied by other changes either to the cultivation of the soil or the appearance of the landscape. On the Kellas estate, by 1790, almost all farms were held under tacks, possessed by single tenants paying money rents. Mosstowie was frequently reorganised as land was reclaimed from moss and allocated, chiefly in small crofts. From 1792 onwards Mosstowie rents were paid solely in money. A similar pattern obtained at Hillside of Mosstowie. At Pluscarden, money and grain were evenly balanced in 1790 (£246 and some 260 bolls of bear, oats and meal). Thereafter the balance shifted sharply towards money rents: in 1795 to £376 and 116 bolls; 1813 to £800 and 93 bolls; 1824 to £1,020 and no grain. During the period 1790–1802 money rents for the barony of Coxtown rose sharply (from £496 to £712), while the total for bear, oats and meal rose only modestly (379 bolls in 1790, 487 in 1802) as new holdings were created under leases requiring only a money rent. At Monaughty, money rents rose between 1790 and 1802 (from £266 to £438) while victual rents fell (255 bolls to 120 bolls). Eight tenants with nineteen-year leases in Kintrea paid £118 and 87 bolls in 1786. Some rents in kind were converted to money in 1795; and when the leases expired, the property was reorganised into one large farm with four small crofts paying, in total, £101 and 12 bolls. Most tenants were granted new nineteen-year leases in 1827, when grain rents were finally ended and the total money rent was £128. The changing balance between grain and money on the Fife estates in Moray is shown below. Rents, in general, rose during the period; though the picture is complicated by the acquisition, amalgamation and reorganisation of properties.

1792 £3,474 + 2,488 bolls
1795 £4,066 + 1,740 bolls
1800 £4,391 + 1,712 bolls
1802 £5,727 + 1,769 bolls

Totals for the estates of Kellas, Pluscarden, Mosstowie, Hillside of Mosstowie, Kintrea and Quarrywood:

1811   £2,047 + 125 bolls
1815   £2,261 + 117 bolls
1817   £2,864 + 80 bolls
1819   £2,861 + 34 bolls
1825   £2,860 + 34 bolls

The residual payments in grain by Quarrywood and Kintrea ended in 1826, leaving only one small payment in kind due from Pluscarden:

1827   £2,976 + 10 bolls[53]

The change to cash from kind left estate girnels empty and new uses were found for the redundant buildings. In 1842 Fife estate trustees agreed that the Morristown granary should be fitted with seats and with glass instead of timber windows, prior to being leased for nineteen years as a meetinghouse.[54]

Money rents relieved the landowner of the need to find markets for the tenants' grain: he was saved the cost of shipping grain to merchants, at the mercy of changes in price between dispatch and receipt. Money rents transferred this obligation onto the tenant who, to meet his rent, was required to find a buyer for the output of his farm. Of course, husbandmen had always been involved in buying and selling (of cattle, surplus grain, whisky, etc.) to generate the cash they needed to buy the things they could not make or grow for themselves. But, arguably, the tenant of an improved farm—paying a money rent and employing regularly waged labour rather than dependant cottars—was engaged in a qualitatively different relationship with the land. The improved farmer perforce became a businessman as well as a primary producer. Cooperation with the land gave way to exploitation of the land. The improved farm became a capitalistic business, securely tied into the cash economy of the nation.

The clamour for tenancy

The turnover of tenants continued under the cash economy of improved agriculture: subtenants rose to tenancies; and tenants declined into subtenancy, or, as subtenancy vanished from the scene, into obscurity among the agricultural workforce. The established culture of tenant turnover enabled landowners to select the most apt candidates from among prospective tenants. John Dunbar, minister of Dyke & Moy, recommended:

> proprietors to make farmers of the most judicious and thorough bred of their farm-servants. When these could be observed to profit by the new methods ... hundreds would copy from a thriving farmer.[55]

Thus social mobility might be written into agricultural improvement.

Altyre rentals document and almost complete turnover of tenants every couple of decades as improvement proceeded—continuing a trend that seems to have been general in the cooperative countryside. Of the estate's 1775 tenants, only nine survived among the thirty-one listed in 1796. Nineteen of the 1796 tenants were listed among twenty-four in the rental for 1808–09: the greater number of survivals between these two latter rentals reflects the introduction of nineteen-year leases in the final decade of the eighteenth century.[56] Among the fourteen possessions in the Burgie rental for 1802, only four were held by the same tenants in 1822.[57] Similar turnover occurred throughout Moray, including the Fife estates, though the phenomenon was less pronounced as improvement and long leases reached upper Strathavon.[58] Ballindalloch tenancies followed the general pattern, with vigorous bidding for farms and significant turnover of tenants at each renewal of tacks. For example, thirty farms of Morinsh in Glenrinnes were allocated under tacks commencing 1820: thirteen possessions went to the existing tenants; twelve to new tenants—all of whom came from another part of the Ballindalloch estate; five farms went to tenants whose location at the time of bidding was not specified. Similarly, of the four possessions of Kilmaichlie in Strathavon leased in 1820, only one was allotted to the sitting tenant.[59]

Land-hunger allowed landowners to retain people on their estates despite the creation of single-tenant enclosed farms from cooperative townships. Settlers could always be found to break in new land, creating new farms in the waste, at minimal cost to the proprietor. For example on the skirts of Ben Rinnes a wilderness of 'heather, rushes and bent' was 'studded over with substantial dwelling houses and small steadings without costing the proprietor a penny'.[60] These new possessions are clearly identified by their new-coined English names: Greenmoss, Parkhead Crofts, Shoulder, &c., which contrast with the Gaelic names of older farms and settlements. In the long run, though, many of the new farms proved unviable: 'hunger for the soil drove the people there and the insatiable hunger of the soil drove them away again'.[61]

Significant pressure for extending cultivation onto the moorland fringes of each estate came from ambitious cottars and sub-tenants who seized opportunities to become farmers of new improvements. William King requested 'a piece of moorish ground' in the hill of Pluscarden, 'alongside of the muirs being taken in by the Tennants of Different Towns'. He undertook to improve the ground and bring it into cultivation, rent free for five years and thereafter at a valuation set by birleymen. William Grigor in Newton of Kellas offered £20 a year as rent for a nineteen year tack of an 'Improvement in the Hills of Kellas called Whiterashes ... upon getting the first five years Rent Free'.[62] Arrangements of this kind became usual on the Fife estates from the 1760s, and continued into the 1830s. Low rents encouraged the settlement and improvement of marginal lands. This extension of arable increased the number of farms. Even when the improvement was enjoyed rent free for several years, the new farmer paid a heavy price for his status—earned at the cost carving a farm out of stone-strewn moorland and undrained bog.

The Muir of Essil was transformed into arable under tacks that recognised the time it might take to earn a return from the land. Alexander Gowans's tack in August 1769 gave the possession rent free for five years, then at 20*s* yearly for seven years, and at £2 for a final seven years.[63] A similar encouragement attracted settlers to improve the Muir of Kellas, where, in 1763, Robert James paid nothing for seven years, then 20 merks (Scots) for six years, and £20 (Scots) for a final six years.[64] Reclamation of moorland at Cranloch was effected under rents with a sliding scale. The lots, of different sizes, were rented at 1s per acre for the first five years; 2s for the second five years; and 5s for the final nine years.[65] Similar sliding-scale rents were reported in the Gordonstoun barony of Dallas (under Alexander Penrose Cuming Gordon of Altyre) during the 1790s: tenants of new improvements received timber for their buildings from the landlord and paid for their first rent one hen in token of their single firehouse, increasing by one shilling for every crop thereafter until the nineteenth year, 'when the land was let of new, at the value to which it had then been brought'.[66] Land hunger among husbandmen meant that prospective tenants might accept onerous conditions, committing themselves to astonishing toil in improving unpromising land into arable. William Burgess, tenant of Little Coxtoun, signed a tack in September 1799 which obliged him each year to cover two acres of his possession with mud carried from Hill of Cotts at the rate of 800 loads per acre.[67] This condition was exceptional. Nonetheless, it underlines the fact that, after all the theorists had put away their pens, and after all the improving landowners had completed their plans, it was the heroic hard labour of landhungry tenants—toiling with basic handtools and muscle power—that subdued an intractable land to effect the regular revolution in the Moray countryside.

As nineteen-year leases became available, tenants, sub-tenants and strangers scrambled to take advantage of the new security. From the late 1760s Fife's tenants began bidding for tenancies as they became available, offering grassums and additional rents. Many offers did not come from the existing tenants. In accepting offers, the earl seized opportunities to create more convenient farms, end joint tenancies, or convert rents into cash. Especially the earl grasped the increased rents that prospective tenants offered. In 1768 Robert Gordon in Pluscarden offered £15 of 'Complement' and £1 additional rent for a nineteen year tack of Thistlyflat, possessed by Adam and Alexander Pettrie at a rent of 16 bolls. Gordon's offer included a request (apparently granted) for: 'Liberty to Improve a bols sowing of the comon hill on the west side to keep me Skeath of some other Improvements there'. James Meller in Mosstowie offered a guinea of grassum and £4 Scots additional rent for a tack on his holding (held jointly with George Cook). Cook 'who is an old Man' was provided for in the agreement, with a house for life. Alexander Taylor offered £10 grassum and £1 additional rent for a nineteen-year tack of the town and lands of Westhill of Pluscarden; failing which he requested to be continued as tenant of 'eastend of Barnhill' in Pluscarden, with the addition of a tack of Hill of Whiterashes and a part of Overtown. James Wright, weaver in Westhill of Pluscarden, offered the same £10 grassum, plus £1 additional rent, for a tack of the cooperative town and lands of Westhill, possessed by John Taylor, James Hardie and their sub-tenants—at a present rent of 16 bolls, 11s 2d and two wedders. John Irvine offered £24 Scots additional rent 'either in money or laid out upon any improvement in Incloseing &c.' for Auchtertyre; failing which he lodged an interest in Whiterea where, he believed, the tenant was in arrears. Peter Milne in Wester Bracton offered 'either Yearly Additional Rent or Grassom and that as much as any other man will give In Reson' for a 'Six Boll Tack ... which is intermixed and run Ridge ... on Acc[oun]t that it lies so mixed with my own'. His offer provided an opportunity to rationalise a piece of cooperative countryside and to profit the estate. A footnote to Milne's petition noted that a subtenant, James Craig, William Scot's 'mellener' [mailander/cottar], had also offered for the holding, hoping to rise in the social scale to tenant farmer.[68]

Would-be tenants felt entitled to negotiate terms. Thus James Christie began a correspondence with the Lethen factor, Duncan Campbell, over the farm of Kilbuiack (present rent 16 bolls and £11 6s 11d). On 24 March 1794 Christie wrote:

> if the man that was before ws did not agree to your terms; my sone would get the farm at Georg Mors Rint which I would have liked better then Killnbuiack at 20 pound per annum ... likeways if you and my Son make a bargain for the farm of KillnBuiack I wnderstand Miss Brodie was to allow a years rint for building A duelling hous and the Offices to her Standirt[69]

Offers and vigorous bidding for tenancies became an established feature of tenure on the Fife estates. As leases expired, factors considered streams of offers from hopeful applicants. Few of the offers received (and accepted) in a round of bidding during 1815 came from the existing tenants. The relentless rise in rents during the improvement period was driven, in great measure, by a hunger for tenancies—and the estate did little to discourage tenants from bidding up the price of farms. In a flurry of offers for some fifty farms falling vacant in 1815, offers from prospective tenants pushed up rents. The smallest increases were at Torehead (existing rent £28 15s) where a bid of £33 16s was accepted; and Bogbuie (increased from £20 to £24). Most rents were at least doubled; some tripled. For example, a ten year tack on Reddarie (existing rent £10) was granted at £30. Crofts at Bodnamuir (Kellas) proved especially popular: lot 22 jumped from £6 13s 4d to £22; lot 20 leaped from £2 to £8.[70] Factor John Lawson was contemptuous of tenants who bid more than they could afford or the farms return: if tenants' rents were too high—as in Kellas—and if tenants failed as a result, it was 'from their own folly'.[71] Perhaps Lawson's opinion was justified. Nonetheless, into the 1830s, offers were consistently above the valuations fixed by the Fife land surveyor, George McWilliam;[72] and the estate generally accepted the highest offer, however extravagant.

Tenants seem to have adopted a relaxed attitude to the possibility of being unable to pay the rents they had offered. Indeed, most rentals seem to have carried a burden of arrears. Some arrears were recovered by compounding with the tenant; many more were written off as irrecoverable. Litigious landowners might seek to recover unpaid rents through the courts. An example from 1769 shows Brodie of Brodie—his estate drowning in debt—suing twenty-eight former tenants for arrears. The sums involved (for example £11 15s 8d sterling owed by Janet Brown in Asleesk, £151 0s 10d Scots by Alexander Cook in Coathill) were, however, unlikely to save the estate from sequestration. Eleven defendants had already left their possessions: most had moved to other Brodie lands; several had left the estate altogether. A handful of the tenants vigorously defended themselves—or at least tried to delay judgement by clouding the issue with references to payments by sub-tenants. It is not recorded whether any of the defendants ever paid their arrears. Perhaps none did.[73]

In general, a tenant who could not pay his rent or make a living from his possession, felt entitled simply to resign his lease. William Leslie recognised this conceit, persisting as an unwritten caveat in every lease even in the early nineteenth century:

> the poor tenant considers himself at liberty to throw up the lease, and speaks of his privilege to give in a renunciation, as a most important advantage.[74]

Brodie's Asleesk factor, Robert Anderson of Linkwood, reported on deficient bolls in 1767. The tenants sought to renegotiate the terms of their tenancy, asserting, 'they Cannot live and pay the rent in victuall but at the former Conversion of Five pounds Scots p. boll'. Meanwhile, 'The two greatest tennants', Thomas Johnson in Asleesk and Michael Fimister there, simply abandoned their possessions. Among the many unpaid rents that vexed Anderson in 1770, were the arrears of twenty-two tenants whose debts dated back to 1756. Half of these remained in their possessions with an insouciant unconcern for their arrears. The remainder had moved away, several leaving the estate altogether.[75] James George, factor at Innes House, vented his exasperation with tenants' fecklessness in a letter to the earl of Fife, dated 24 June 1791: frustrated by problems in filling vacant farms at Kempston, the factor complained 'the Tenents are always turning out Bankrupt'.[76] A tenant who abandoned his holdings might slip into subtenancy; or he might move away with his seed corn, cattle, household furniture and farm gear and take up a possession elsewhere. Mobility among tenants was a usual part of rural life.

The sale of a bankrupt tenant's goods, gear and cattle might recover some of the rent arrears, but at the risk of pauperising a family, who then became a burden on the poor's fund, which might need support from the landowner. Roups to recover arrears are unusual in estate papers, perhaps because landowners maintained patriarchal concern for failing tenants—or because the value of a failed tenant's possessions was not worth realising. Alexander Brodie of Brodie (perhaps because he was himself in financial difficulties) squeezed tenants hard, especially when the debtor owned goods and chattels of some value. James Sinclair, dyster at Brodie, owed £19 10s for unpaid rent due in 1757. In 1759 he was obliged to dispone to Brodie all his:

> goods Insicht Plenishing, Goods and Gear ... one Horse one Mare one Cow, with my Corn and Straw presently Stack'd ... Drying Loomes and Utinsells vi[delicet] one Big Fatt, one Coper, Two Skezers, one Press and a Big Table with all my Houshold Furniture.

Sinclair's gear was rouped in 1762.[77]

During difficult years tenants' hands were strengthened in negotiating (and renegotiating) rents. The Fife factor, Francis Stewart, complained to his master in a tone of some dismay in 1763. He was clearly vexed by the tenants' casual attitude to rent arrears—and frustrated in his attempts to collect them following a poor harvest in 1762. He submitted to the earl 'a list of those to be warned ag[ains]t next Term. I would have insert a good many more ... on Acc[oun]t of bad payments but cannot find Tenents to take their possessions'. Two

Morriston tenants petitioned for rent reductions 'offering a Renounciation'. The Morriston tenants' brinkmanship paid off. Stewart caved in, accepting:

> its better to give them some Deduction as I cannot find Tenents for the possessions tho' I have been offering them to Severalls—Robert Anderson Writter in Elgin has likewise thrown up the Possession of Knockmarioch & others are threatning to throw up their Possessions as last Cropt has reduced many to low Circumstances.[78]

In the end, though, the two Moristown tenants declared they 'Could not make bread upon their Possession at the Present Rent'. They renounced their tenancies and walked away.[79]

Sub-tenants continued to aspire to the status of farmer during the early decades of the nineteenth century. Thus, in 1815, William Hardy, subtenant of the Easter half of Newton (present rent £8, present tenant John Nairn) offered £13 for a lease. His offer was accepted with the provision that Nairn was accommodated as subtenant (probably employed as a labourer) with a house, yard and two acres.[80] For the farm of Gladhill, tenanted by the widow of Thomas Grant in 1839, a subtenant of Grant's named Cosmo Reid, offered to take on a new lease, which he secured at the existing rent of £45.[81]

Amid the flux of tenancies, the earl of Fife seems to have taken some patriarchal care of several casualties, though doubtless reaping a dividend of good will and self-satisfaction from his investment in charity. In 1768 James McIntosh offered 'Double rent and perhaps something more' for two crofts. The factor noted:

> Tho[ma]s Russell and George Cook whose crofts he wants were the Improvers of these Crofts. They are now very Old very Poor and very Helpless and if Turned out must go abegging—So that for ane Incouragement to others as well as an Act of Charity ... My Lord should allow them to Die out. This need not hinder his Lordship Granting McIntosh a Tack if he Pleases Burdened with their Lifetime I mean his Entry to Commence at their Deaths which in the Course of Nature must be soon.

Similarly, two aged tenants in Mosstowie were rewarded for their exemplary record with a ten-year renewal of their tacks (at double the rent) in response to their semiliterate petition:

> we have lived upon our possessions wich was taken in By ourselves & has paid rent for it ever since except the first year which we had free And as we are now turned very old and unfit to improve neu Ground and rather than flite we humbly make offer of Double rent for our present possessions.[82]

Thomas Laing was allowed to continue in his tenancy at Asleesk 'owing to the long period he has been upon the Estate, & his now advanced age'—despite being deeply in arrears.[83]

Typically, Fife ensured that the deserving poor among his tenantry were not sent abegging as tenancies changed. Thus at Hillside in 1815, when James Douglas successfully offered £20 for the holding he had shared with John Grant, Katherine Thain and Widow Dow (at

£15), his lease obliged him to allow his previous joint tenants to stay on in their own houses. Seven offers were made for Mosside of Meft in the 1837 round of bidding. A nineteen-year lease was awarded to the highest bidder, James Miln from Bishopmill—who was obliged to allow 'two poor infirm women', Magdalen and Margaret Simpson, to remain in their houses. Similarly, a house and yard was reserved at Wester Brochlach of Blervie for two sisters of a previous tenant.[84]

Offers for tenancies were reinforced by character references, and by the improving credentials of potential tenants. When William Hardie in Blervie offered £20 in grassum and £20 rent for a tack for Whittree, he justified his generous offer, by emulating the earl of Fife's improving enthusiasm, declaring 'Some men will tell your Lordship the possession is not worth what I have now offered but believe them not for I see now how to make it worth it by improving and Inclosing'.[85] On 19 June 1816, when the prospective tenant of Whiterashes in Kellas, decided to take up another vacancy in Altyre, he suggested an alternative candidate, 'a young lad well recommended' whose father gave security.[86]

A prospective tenant might be excluded by bad references. When John Adams and James Grigor, joint tenants at Mains of Kellas, fell to be removed in 1768, they complained of the 'Badness of the place', but claimed too that they had made improvements. They pleaded against removal on account of their 'numerous young Families'. But especially they denigrated the prospective new tenant, William Wink, a stranger from Birnie, as 'a very Indifferent Character'. The opinion was reinforced by a letter from Wink's previous landlord, James Hay, to Fife's factor. The letter contained a catalogue of 'Fraud and Villainy' and impugned 'likewise the honesty of the woman he is married to'.[87] Prejudice against foreigners from other parishes was a strong factor when considering competing offers. Local men, already resident on the estate, or known to the factor, were generally preferred. Thus William Gillan's offer in 1837 of £30 for a lot of Incharnoch was accepted with a note also that Gillan was a 'very industrious good tenant'; a rival offer (of £41) from William Duncan in Birnie was dismissed, because Duncan was 'an entire stranger and reported fickle'.[88]

In the 1837 round of Fife estate renewals, existing tenants were given the opportunity of matching the highest bid received. It seems likely that some would-be tenants received a hint of the rent expected so that he might lodge a successful offer—typically a few pounds above valuation. Thus canny factors conspired to push up their master's rental income, while retaining on the estate good tenants who had proved their improving mettle.[89]

The lease on the marginal Coxtown farm of Sauchen Burn expired in 1836, and the sitting tenant offered first £12 (the present rent) then £15 and finally £20. But his bid was unsuccessful as he had 'difficulty in paying the present rent' on the farm, which lay at the very farthest limit of cultivation on Brown Muir of Tiendland. A lease was eventually given to William Hay who offered £25 10s; the factor presumed that Hay could improve the farm and increase its value—and also make a profit himself—'having several active young sons to assist him'.[90]

Bidding on other estates followed the same aggressive trend. Several offers for leases of Lethen farms seem to suggest that competition for leases pushed rents higher.[91] Competitive bidding also pushed up rents in Strathavon. For example, Alexander Innes offered, on 31

July 1802, £17 10*s* and half a wedder for half of Achlichny (present rent £8). He supported his application with a declaration that targeted the duke of Gordon's military enthusiasm: 'I am Brother of Serjeant James Innes in your own Regiment And had it not been owing to Coinachy that prevented me I made Offer to your Grace to go Also'.[92] John Duncan offered £3 for a croft in Camdelmore which he 'brook in out of heather', supporting the application with an appeal to the duke's compassion for his 'small numurs family'.[93] The recommendation of the forester, Robert Willox, was the key to success in securing a Strathavon tenancy. When Alexander Stewart, tacksman of Upper Cults, offered £5 10*s* for Lower Cults, seeking to amalgamate the possessions, he was supported by Willox who declared him 'Substanchall and under a Good Character'. This testimonial satisfied criteria laid down by Sir John Sinclair who advised landowners to have regard to both the character and capital of potential tenants.[94] A man of substance was generally preferred under improving regimes. Sinclair thought that a reliable tenant should possess capital of £10 for each acre of his farm and could 'hardly be safe unless he has a sum equal to one year's rent, over and above all his outgoings'.[95] The initial costs of improved agriculture were high, but the money invested could be expected to yield a return within the period of a nineteen-year lease.[96]

Cottars and labourers

Under improving leases the various classes of subtenant vanished. Only occasionally, and during the early stages of improvement, were sub-tenants were continued. For example, in 1768, James Skene, holder of a nineteen-year tack of Achtertyre, was obliged to keep on two sub-tenants. However, Skene protested the condition, claiming that his cautioners (who were clearly men of progressive views) insisted he 'have the whole Management of my own possession'.[97]

In general, those who did not rise to tenancy, declined to become agricultural labourers—living on the margins of the farm or in new villages. Improved agricultural regimes might be significantly more labour intensive than communal husbandry: fences and ditches had to be built and maintained, and cattle herded until fences were established; arable crops required relentless ploughing, liming, dunging, harrowing, hoeing and weeding. Some township cottars retained their turf-and-cruck houses and kaleyards—with perhaps the right to graze a cow with the tenant's cattle—on the margins of the farms. Many might, perhaps, feel that little was changed by their conversion to agricultural labourers.[98] Possibly their employment was more secure, during a six-month term, with an assured money wage that bound them into the cash economy. Rising wages during the period seem to show that dispossessed small sub-tenants might prosper as agricultural labourers. William Leslie thought the price of labour 'exorbitant', noting:

> About 40 years ago, the average price of a boll of grain was 12s. and the yearly wages of a ploughman about L.2: at present, though less industrious and more expensively maintained, his wages have risen about 300 per cent. and the value of grain not quite 30.[99]

Many mailanders and cottars flitted, along with township craftsmen, to new houses (with lotted land attached) in new villages built to soak up surplus population. Here, arguably, they were better housed with greater security of tenure. Meanwhile, agricultural reform expanded employment opportunities, for example, ditching, dyking, and planting the proprietor's new woodland.

Township craftsmen too enjoyed enhanced opportunities arising from the new agriculture. The great rebuilding that replaced turf-and-cruck with masonry in rural buildings, provided work for quarriers, sawyers, masons, joiners, plasterers, thatchers and slaters. The manufacture and repair of iron implements—and of iron fittings for the new architecture—required blacksmiths. New ploughing regimes required farriers and saddlers to maintain draught animals and their increasingly sophisticated tack.

Clearance, population and emigration

Robert Hay's exemplary study of township reorganisation on the Altyre estate in Rafford concluded: 'There is no evidence that the final removals were anything other than peaceful'. Several displaced husbandmen were relocated to settler farms; others were accommodated in 'a new community of semi-skilled workers in tied cottages'. A few moved away; but many did not move far from Altyre, and reappeared periodically on the estate, for example 'for paid forestry work'.[100] Even though the Rafford population declined by 8 per cent (from 1,072 in 1790 to 987 in 1841), Hay concluded, 'the Altyre removals cannot be classed as "lowland clearances"'. Hay's investigation highlights a need for family reconstruction for other estate populations.

In general, the Altyre model seems to have obtained throughout Moray. Parochial populations declined in Urquhart, Alves and Dyke & Moy (by from 3 per cent to 10 per cent), perhaps as a result of very determined improvement at Brodie, Moy and Innes, and the extinction of large townships such as Easter Alves and Oldtown of Roseisle. Everywhere else population increased (by from 20 per cent to 40 per cent.) between 1790 and 1841.[101] Spynie rocketed by 86 per cent, boosted by 621 souls in the new village of Bishopmill.[102] Rothes population was also increased by the erection of a new village.[103]

Birnie's population was thought to have declined—from 460 in 1781 to 402 in 1791. The minister noted:

> besides 24 persons who have emigrated to America, two farms ... possessed by tenants who do not reside in the parish, for the purpose of pasture, where 4 tenants formerly lived. Besides there are 4 tenants who possess as much land as 8 did before.[104]

Emigrations continued and the population remained stable with 408 souls in 1831.[105]

Rural folk were, it seems, shallowly-rooted in the soil of Moray. Even without estate reorganisation flittings were frequent and commonplace—within the parish or estate, within Scotland and to overseas destinations. Kinloss people were notably infected with 'the spirit of travelling' in 1790.[106] From Dallas some twenty young men emigrated to America between 1778 and 1790.[107] In Aberlour it only was 'aspiring young men, who have had a more liberal education' who emigrated to seek fortunes in London and the West Indies.[108] From Duffus, it was said in 1792, 'there is, and always has been a constant succession of adventurers issuing forth to the British Capital, the East and West Indies, and other parts of the empire'; though 'some individuals [who] went to North America ... returned and settled at home, bringing bad tidings of the country, which their imaginations had figured to be the *fairy*-land'.[109] Among the various *Statistical Account* responses to questions on emigration, none identified a major problem. There was no enforced emigration from Moray. Indeed landowners seem to have been careful to retain population on their estates. The individuals who did leave Moray (and the north-east lowlands generally) emigrated to 'push their fortune'—drawn by opportunities, rather than driven by despair.[110]

There was no significant resistance to regularisation, beyond a few niggling difficulties caused by quarrelsome individuals. As estates were reorganised, opportunities and rural prosperity increased. More farms were available—and more chances for social advancement into the farmer class. Expanding demand for labour and rising wages ensured there was neither distress nor unemployment as cottars were transformed into agricultural labourers. Township husbandmen who were mobile and accustomed to periodic changes in status had no reason to oppose regularisation. Most embraced change.

7

REGULAR REFORESTATION

Destitute of forest

Samuel Johnson was famously curmudgeonly on the subject of Scotland and the Scots. In this persona he was notably disparaging regarding the shortage of trees in North Britain. Travelling through the eastern lowlands in 1773 he noted small plantations around gentlemen's places, 'but these are few, and those few all very young'; and later he declared, A tree might be a show in Scotland as a horse in Venice.'[1] By the time Johnson reached his ultimate destination in the treeless Hebrides he facetiously insisted that his missing walking stick must have been stolen: 'Consider, sir, the value of such a *piece of timber* here!'[2] Johnson saw, but did not much admire, 'Lord Findlater's wood' at Cullen;[3] and he found little between the Spey and the Ness to change his opinion regarding Scotland's lack of trees—though his account of the journey from Cullen to Fort George is muddled and misremembered, so somewhat suspect. The orchard and a plantation of oaks at Gordon castle were worthy of remark, but the earl of Moray's Darnaway forest was not noticed. Extensive plantations at Brodie were, it seems, passed while Johnson's attention was distracted by the forthcoming prospect of Shakespeare's blasted heath—which tourists were shown on the Hardmuir commonty.[4] Nonetheless, the extent of Darnaway forest at the time of Johnson's tour is amply documented,[5] as were mature pine plantations around Brodie castle and within sight of 'Mack Beaths hill'.[6]

Johnson's day-trip through Moray was notably punctuated by a disgusting breakfast (dried haddocks broiled) in Cullen and an inedible dinner in Elgin;[7] and arguably the irascible lexicographer's observations were coloured by indigestion. Johnson's analytical powers were certainly blunted; he seems to have accepted uncritically a general prejudice regarding Scotland's lack of trees, his preconception growing from earlier travellers' accounts. Edward Burt's *Letters* (a generation before Johnson's tour) noted that even in the south of Scotland were 'but few Birds except such as build their Nests upon the Ground, so scarce are Hedges and Trees'.[8] Similarly, William Mackintosh (a generation before Burt) declared Scotland 'intirely destitute of Forest'— even though at the time of writing industrial forestry was under way in upper Spey.[9]

Early travellers, in search of anthropological oddity and highland scenery, found Moray uninterestingly cultivated, and so they passed rapidly through the laich missing the woodland that grew in places off the main routes. Lowland Moray was, indeed, relatively poorly forested. Its climate and soil were so suited to arable husbandry, that it would have been a waste of resources to plant trees except on heathland waste; but this land was valuable for grazing, feal and fuel. The main tourist routes led to Fort George and thence to Inverness and Loch Ness. Few travellers took the roads south along the Spey, Avon and Findhorn, and so they never saw upland woodland that supplied the laich. English tourists also failed to appreciate the value of the woodland that they did see in Elginshire and Banffshire.

Managed semi-natural woodland in the cooperative countryside—growing along burnsides and in odd corners of the laichland fieldscape—had an unfashionably disorderly appearance that jarred with rational tastes in landscape. Furthermore, regular architecture, improved designs of agricultural implement, and enclosure with palings, all required timber in sizes, qualities and quantities that traditional woodland could not supply. Meanwhile, refined sensitivities were offended by naked landscapes that might benefit from the shelter trees provided, or which seemed underexploited when used only for cooperative grazing. For some commentators the potential value of timber was less important than aesthetic and secondary agricultural considerations. Thus, for example, the minister of Kinloss expressed a general view when recommending 'a belt of planting ... where there is nothing at present but a coarse kind of bent, it would add greatly to the beauty of the landscape and the mildness of the climate'.[10]

Highland pinewood

Before the improvers' planting craze developed, laichland demand for timber might be supplied from natural pinewoods on the fringes of Moray. These resources were possessed by a handful of major landowners: Gordon owned Glenmore; Ballindalloch owned Glen Feshie; Fife owned Mar. Industrial-scale exploitation of highland timber probably began during the seventeenth century. Around 1630 John Grant of Freuchie sold timber cutting rights in Abernethy forests to Captain John Mason. In 1658 a lease for timber exploitation in Rothiemurchus forests was given to the English entrepreneur Benjamin Parsons—who subsequently also took a lease on Abernethy. Parsons, in partnership with Samuel Collins of London began building ships at Garmouth but the enterprise was abandoned—leaving an unfinished ship on the stocks—in 1672.[11] Around 1680 Sir Robert Sibbald operated a sawmill within the 'great Firrwood' of Duthil, where, it was said, local husbandmen neglected agriculture in favour of wage labour in the forest. Presumably the wages offered by forestry contractors were better than those paid by tenants for the day-labour of their cottars. The willingness of rural folk to work in the forest rather than on township lands suggests that some were only loosely connected to the soil—and flexibly willing to abandon agricultural for industrial employment. Timber was floated from Duthil, down the Spey to Garmouth, and used to build at least one ship before the enterprise collapsed.[12] Meanwhile, timber belonging to the Grants of Tulchan in Inverallan was also being cut and rafted down the Spey to the laich, guided by a floater in a *curach*. The rafting technique is said to have been devised by the poet and traveller Aaron Hill (1685-1750). Be that at it may, Hill was certainly involved with the York Buildings Company, and was energetic in realising a vision of commercial exploitation of highland forests:

> High up upon the mountain of her native shore,
> The gummy pine shall shed her pitchy store,
> Tall firs, which useless have long ages grown,
> Shall fight the seas and visit lands unknown.

Following the 1715 rising, English energy and capital industrialised Scottish forestry. The York Buildings Company secured title to the forfeited Mar estates, with a view to exploiting the Deeside pinewoods. From 1726 York Buildings entrepreneurs secured the right to cut 60,000 Scots pine trees in the woods of Rothiemurchus. The company erected sawmills, built roads, constructed sluices, canalised watercourses and floated timber down the Spey to the laich.[13] In a similar speculation, John Gage, a Banff merchant, and Donald Tayliour, a London entrepreneur, contracted with the duke of Gordon to cut timber in Glenmore for floating down the Spey to Garmouth.[14] The success of Gordon's first float was celebrated in June 1710 with a feast for all concerned in the operation.[15] Payments to floaters continuing through the eighteenth century, indicate significant volumes of timber extracted from Glenmore. In 1733 James Grant, alias Miller, in Gortans at Boat of Pitchaish was paid for floating timber to Fochabers. In the same year Robert Grant in Tulchan was paid for a float of 118 deals, four 'Gists' and ten nineteen-foot spars. Peter Miller in Knockanbuie of Tulchan was paid for floating 134 deals, 202 flake bars and fourteen spars (up to twenty-two feet long); and for a second float of sixty-eight deals and forty-two spars.[16] In 1737 the Strathavon chamberlain's further payments to floaters, including a chopin of 'aquavitae' as a bonus.[17]

Timber floated from the upper Spey was used in 1718 for building the neoclassical mansion of Balvenie: Donald Grant at Boat of Elchies on the Spey received £32 Scots on 13 May 1718 'for bringing down six flots of timber for roofing the house of balveny'. The timber was presumably carried by packhorse for the final three or four miles of its journey. In the same year John Moir and Donald Our were paid thirty-four merks (Scots) 'for bringing down four floots of timber bought from Grants Chamberlain ... brought byus & John & Dannell Mores Currockers also to the boat of Skirdustan'. Elchies and Skirdustan (kirkton of Aberlour) seem to have been usual trans-shipment places where highland timber was landed.[18] The floating trade continued for over a century, providing significant, if seasonal, employment especially for men on the Ballindalloch estate in Inveravon.[19]

Though Speyside pine was acceptable for a second home such as Balvenie, discerning aristocrats felt that this local timber fell below the standard required for prestige buildings. The earl of Aberdeen declared Abernethy pine 'too knotty' for use in Haddo House.[20] Similarly, William Baxter rejected Speyside timber as being 'of the roughest coarsest kind' and unsuitable for the new Gordon Castle, which instead was built with Norwegian, Swedish, Russian and Prussian timber shipped from Leith to Garmouth.[21]

Rothiemurchus timber extraction continued after the end of the York Buildings Company contract in 1732. Subsequent contracts were worth some £370 yearly in the 1770s—doubling the rental of the estate. Between 1769 and 1771, 13,823 lengths of spar wood were floated to Garmouth, together with a proportionate number of sawn deals and planks, and 4,000 wooden pipes for London water works. Further timber was carted by road through Dava to Forres and the western laich.[22]

In 1784 the duke of Gordon signed a twenty-six-year contract with Ralph Dodsworth, a York merchant, for timber extraction in Glenmore. Dodsworth, in partnership with William Osbourne and Thomas Hustwick, both from Hull, developed the industry, founded the town of Kingston at the mouth of the Spey, and established (in 1786) a shipbuilding industry that flourished until the 1850s. Twenty-five vessels were built in the first decade of operation. 190,000 tons of shipping was built by 1806. When the English company ended operations at Speymouth in 1815, several redundant shipwrights emigrated to Miramichi in New Brunswick to work in the shipyard of William Davidson of Inverness.[23]

During the mid-eighteenth century Mackintosh of Mackintosh negotiated a contract to exploit timber in Glenfeshie.[24] The operation resulted in periodic disputes (and agreeement in February 1807) between Aeneas Mackintosh and George Macpherson Grant of Ballindalloch over floating rights affecting Ballindalloch's Invereshie estate.[25] Extraction lasted for nearly a century under successive contracts, earning significant income for the estate. For example, Sir Aeneas Mackintosh made a new agreement in 1819 with Alexander Duncan, woodmerchant in Garmouth, who paid £2,350 for 10,000 trees in Inshriach and Glenfeshie.[26]

Highland pinewoods might have been endlessly renewable, and might have satisfied the whole demand for timber in the laich.[27] However, the Rothiemurchus woods at least were not sustainably exploited, and in the latter decades of the eighteenth century were significantly depleted and in need of respite to regenerate. Furthermore, Rothiemurchus timber operations were hampered by disputes with Gordon over damage caused by floating to the duke's salmon cruives; and also by impediments arising from an entail drawn up in 1787.[28]

The planting craze

The supply of highland timber was controlled by a handful of great magnates. Laichland landowners and small proprietors owned no extensive pinewoods. There was, meanwhile, no incentive for tenants to plant trees, either for their own use or as a cash crop, because the landowner could claim all the timber on his estate under legislation amplified progressively from the fifteenth century onwards.[29] Progressive commentators regarded this legislation as an anachronism and a clog on improvement. William Leslie reported that the laichland was 'naked, and the fields unsheltered', because 'impolitic and oppressive' laws prevented tenants from planting the:

> irregular patches of uncultivated ground, either skirting or interspersed among the fields of each farm, of no value to the proprietor, and of very little to the tenant ... by the effect of these laws the tenant is prohibited from planting such unproductive ground, and which must be therefore transmitted from generation to generation with increasing sterility.[30]

A decade later, Leslie again argued the advantages of allowing tenants to plant 'the sides of their fields, or uncultivated corners of their farms' and to enjoy woodland as 'their own property', with the proprietor obliged 'at the termination of the lease, either to purchase the trees ... or that the tenant shall have the privilege of felling and disposing of them to the best account for himself'.[31] Leslie overestimated landowners' self-interestedness: few were inclined to relinquish a profitable monopoly on estate timber.

Early in the eighteenth century, while any change in the law lay far in the future, Moray landowners used the tacks that were being agreed in increasing numbers to enhance timber resources on their estate. While yard-dyke planting continued, clauses inserted into tacks obliged tenants to plant copses on their farms. The trees that tenants nurtured belonged, of course, to the laird. For proprietors this was planting without responsibility, and at very small cost. Strathavon tacks may have pioneered the practice in 1710, when the Dellvorar tenant was obliged to plant twenty trees yearly, with an obligation 'to nurse and Conserve the Same'. This became a standard clause during the 1730s: forty trees a year at Dell (1735); sixteen a year at Glen (1734).[32] The large tack of Cleeves, in the Brodie barony of Monaughty, was granted for twenty-seven years, from 1740, to Robert Dunbar of Bethnal Green, under condition that he 'drain ditch and inclose the meadows ... and plant them with Hedges & a Row of barren Timber ... to be furnished Him by ... Alexander Brodie'.[33] Lord Kames might not have approved, believing that standard trees deprived the hedgerow of water;[34] but perhaps Brodie was guided by William Mackintosh who was firmly convinced of the merit of planting timber along hedgerows.[35] Hardwood trees, planted along roadsides and field margins became a feature of the landscapes created by several laichland improvers: for example on Fife's estates in Urquhart and St Andrews-Lhanbryd; on the Sellar estate of Westfield; the Duff property of Orton; at Moy and Brodie; and the earl of Moray's property on the Findhorn. Elsewhere field-edge standards were not usual.

By the second half of the eighteenth century, landowners in southern counties of Scotland had long since taken to heart the advice of a Scotch laird to his son: 'Be aye sticking in a tree, Jock; it will be growing whilst you are sleeping'—and begun to create significant plantations on underutilised land.[36] Monymusk began planting in 1716;[37] and Daniel Defoe commented upon the 'new and laudable method of all Scots gentlemen' in planting 'firr-trees' in Fife around 1720.[38] The disparity between Defoe's observations and Dr Johnson's, probably arises from the different emphases and predilections of the two travellers: Defoe was engaged upon a survey of economic resources; Johnson's interests were literary and anthropological. Defoe saw the value and significance of these innovatory softwood plantations; Johnson, perhaps, dismissed pine plantations as unworthy of notice in comparison with proper ancient English oak forests. When invited to explore plantations on Findlater's domain, which was:

> indeed admirably laid out ... Johnson did not choose to walk through it. He always said that he was not come to Scotland to see fine places, of which there were enough in England; but wild objects,—mountains,—waterfalls,—peculiar manners.[39]

Be that as it may, significant commercial plantations had been established in Scotland by the middle decades of the eighteenth century. The Blair Adam estates in Fife and

Kinross are often cited as a pioneering model. In 1733, it was said, there was just one tree on the estate; by 1792 1,144 acres was covered with plantations—though Defoe's observation suggests that Blair Adam did not lead the planting craze in Fife. Meanwhile, rivalry between the improving dukes of Atholl and Argyll accelerated the creation of plantations on their estates, with a particular preference for larch in Atholl. A planting frenzy swept through Perthshire from the early decades of the eighteenth century. The estates of Breadalbane and Scone were reforested, notably with exotic larch; and at Blair Drummond Lord Kames completely redesigned his own local landscapes by planting the reclaimed mosses of the Carse of Forth. The laird of Invercauld was said, in 1800, to have planted 'vast ... woods and firs ... in incredible numbers ... Few proprietors have done more towards the improvement of their estates than Mr Farquharson [who has] planted 16 million firs and two million of larch'.[40] Moray landowners were not behind the fashion; and some were ahead of the trend. In part the planting craze was a response to the rising cost of buying in Highland timber,[41] which was increasingly in demand for improvement purposes—both for building work and for fencing. The earl of Findlater took a leading role in the plantation craze, perhaps because he did not own enormous highland pinewoods.

Highland forests, provided seed for planting in the laich. In August 1715 Scots pine seedlings from Strathspey were planted in a 'parkque' at Gordon castle;[42] in 1730, a dozen men worked for three weeks, planting Scots pines in a rectangular enclosure on Stynie muir.[43] Conifer plantations established at Brodie by Mary Sleigh in the mid-eighteenth century were shown as mature woodland in 1770: sectioned by a tasteful radial pattern of rides focused upon the castle. 104 acres of mature pinewood and twenty-five more of 'young firs' grew on Hardmuir; two plantations, totalling 113 acres, fringed Brodie's northern marches; at Feddan there was a wood of 'Allars'.[44] By 1764, 205 'backgoeing' trees in Fife's fir plantations near Cowfords (planted perhaps in the 1740s) were ready for cutting, the thinnings going to nearby improvers for houses and fences.[45] William Leslie also noted the early forestry plantations of Sir Robert Gordon at Rininver in Dallas. However, he thought that it was not until around 1770 that 'proprietors ... began generally to form plantations'.[46]

As the general improvement craze took hold during the 1760s a mania for tree planting gripped the Moray gentry. Trees were planted for both economic and aesthetic reasons as landowners embraced the principle that an unplanted landscape was a waste of land and an affront to rational sensibilities. Trees were deemed 'both profitable and pleasant'; and trees were a crop that could be persuaded to grow on the soils of hills, moors, bogs and commonties—and at elevations—that resisted improvement into arable.[47] The fourth duke of Atholl (1755–1830) whose tree-planting enthusiasm earned him the nickname 'Planter John', declared 'Planting ought to be carried on for Beauty Effect and Profit'.[48] Similarly, William Adam of Blair Adam gave equal emphasis to the economic and aesthetic or recreational value of planted woodland.[49] Plantations changed landscapes more than any other innovation of the regular revolution. The irregularities of rocks, hillocks and gullies were softened by tree cover. Open moorland vanished beneath ranks of trees. Local drainage patterns were affected as tree cover interfered with run-off after heavy rain. Clumps of trees in the laich exaggerated the prominence of the hillocks on which they grew. Everywhere, the hard-edged boundaries of rectilinear blocks of planting—extravagantly defended by stone walls, more usually bounded by paling fences and turf dykes—regularised and reclothed the Moray countryside.

The *Statistical Accounts* suggest that by the 1790s considerable plantations had been established in Moray, supplementing managed semi-natural woodland. Some plantations were already reaching maturity. The minister of Aberlour noted 'some firs lately planted'.[50] In Inveravon there were thriving fir plantations.[51] In Kirkmichael, however, natural alder and birch were not supplemented with pine plantations.[52] Ten parochial reporters noted plantations of larch (a key marker of an improving heritor) and/or Scots pine. These were supplemented with belts of beech trees at Burgie.[53] In Dallas there was oak woodland (managed by coppicing), as well as the 'inclosures of planted firs, of pretty old standing'. There were further managed oak woods, in addition to softwood plantations, at Quarrywood in Spynie.[55] Few coastal parishes were so well provided with planted and natural trees as Dyke & Moy, where alder was harvested for ship-building; birch for agricultural equipment; ash, elm, beech and 'plain' for export; 'firs' for local house-carpenters and English buyers.[56] However, neither plantations nor natural timber were mentioned in Alves, Birnie, Drainie, Kinloss and Rothes, though both Kinloss and Rothes had possessed significant deciduous woodland when surveyed in the 1740s. William Leslie, writing in 1798, confirmed these surveys, and added several details including the availability of oak, birch, hazel and 'plane' in Birnie, 'but not in sufficient quantity for the implements of husbandry'.[57]

New Statistical Accounts reported thriving plantations in almost every parish (with the exceptions of St Andrews-Lhanbryd (a short and sketchy report);[58] and Speymouth (where timber was consumed rather than produced, especially in the Garmouth shipyards).[59] In Elgin, an additional comment declared that 'seventy years ago, the lowland district of Moray was one of the barest in Scotland. Scarce a tree was to be seen, except a few ashes in the avenue leading to the mansion of some old family'.[60] Most of the wood in Forres was less than forty years old in 1842.[61] In Kirkmichael in 1842 there were still no plantations; and the 'natural growing birch and alder, which adds so much to the beauty of the scenery'—and which had been a major resource in the cooperative countryside—was deemed 'of little value'.[62]

Tree-planting mania developed as a numbers game in which commentators itemised with relish the achievements of their favourite improvers. The ninth earl of Moray was admired as 'a great arborealist'. Within two years of succeeding to the title in 1767 he had planted thirteen million trees including 1,500,000 oaks at Doune, Darnaway and Donnibristle. In planting parks at Drumincruch, Tornagrain, Mid Coul and Fisherton on his Nairnshire properties in Petty, the earl planted 1,400,000 Scots pine and 103,000 beech, oak, ash, elm and plane. His gardener, William Lindsay, boasted on 26 May 1780 of the 7,646,000 trees planted 'at his sight and direction at Darnaway and Petty'.[63] William Leslie reckoned that 2,500 acres of deciduous trees alone had been planted by the earl to restore the ancient forests of Darnaway and Drumine; though Leslie downgraded the total to 10,591,000 trees. Even at this rate the Darnaway forestry operation earned £400 per annum. Elsewhere, Leslie reckoned the original extent of the Darnaway forest at 1,000 acres 'to which the earl has added an extent of plantation ... of nearly 3000 acres'.[64] The earl of Moray's example inspired his neighbour at Altyre. Before 1770 plantations were established at Mains, Newtyle and Ramflat. From 1776, the new laird, Alexander Penrose Cumming, ordered a programme of enclosure and planting that continued to the end of the century, when his Altyre estate contained some thousand acres of timber, with further plantations at Relugas.[65]

Notwithstanding early efforts by Brodie and Moray, James Donaldson described the 'low part of the district ... [as] naked and exposed' in the 1790s. He applauded Fife's efforts at 'ornamenting the country' with belts and stripes of native trees; and he noted Findlater's plantation at Birkenhill, near Elgin—where the sale of thinnings was earning the earl a steady £40 per annum.[66] Rather than waste good rentable arable land, proprietors sensibly established their plantations in areas which were not suited to grain production. To do this they invoked a clause which had become commonplace in tacks, which reserved to 'The Proprietor ... full liberty to inclose plant or improve ... heath or barren ground on the possession ... or on the adjoining Muirs'.[67]

Commonties were prime candidates for planting. Thus trees spread across the grazings of Hardmuir, Alves, and the Gordon portion of Morinsh. Elsewhere, high moorland was planted. Teindland became one unbroken forest, spreading to Findlay's seat above the limit of cultivation on the Coxtown estate, southward into the Glen of Rothes, and east towards the Spey at Orton. The lower moorland of Coxtown (below 200 metres) meanwhile was comprehensively reorganised: with a broad belt of forestry plantation sheltering a regular landscape of discrete small farms that were intended to be self-supporting without the benefit of communal resources formerly enjoyed beyond the head-dyke. Notably, there was almost no tree planting on the shingle banks between Lossiemouth and the Spey;[68] and there was only small-scale planting, late in the improvement era, on the Culbin sands in Dyke & Moy, comprising belts of trees established by Grant of Kincorth in 1837, and some 200 acres of pine and larch planted by John Grigor, nurseryman in Forres, around 1840.[69] However, successful experimentation had long since proved that trees might be persuaded to grow on unpromising sands. At Myreside in Spynie, Findlater made 'a very considerable improvement' in 1772:

> by planting about 15 acres with Scotch fir. It was moorland, and very bleak producing no pasture ... and did not bring in a farthing of rent. The droppings of needles ... enriched the soil, and, after the lapse of thirty years an experiment was made in attempting the improvement of a few acres. It was found that the ground made tolerably arable land ... The farm of Newfield has been made out of the ground covered with wood ... yeilding good crops of corn, turnips, and grass.[70]

Estate records suggest a competitive spirit among improvers as they vied to plant the most extravagant acreages. Sir Archibald Grant, who was seldom falsely modest about his own achievements, boasted his arboreal prowess in a letter to Grant of Ballindalloch in February 1769:

> To satisfye you, I am no contemptible planter in some sense, I have actually planted on my small Esteats above 35 million of Trees—this is more than any two in Britain and Ireland have done.[71]

This figure probably owes more to bombast than accurate measurement. At a typical density of 2,500 trees to the acre this would mean that Monymusk claimed to have planted some twenty-two square miles with new woodland.[72]

Fife tacks reserved to the proprietor the right to 'make drains and plant the hills'.[73] This right was realised around Innes in 1771–72 when the earl planted firs, alder, beech and birch in stone-walled and feal-dyked enclosures: at Kempston, Shearerston, Lochhill, Whinhill, Elginshill and Rutherhill. Timber sales from planting in 'clumps' at Meft and elsewhere, in 1780, won a small cash income from glacial hillocks of sand and gravel in the eastern laich that otherwise yielded only scanty pasture and divot for building. The care of the clumps fell to the Innes house gardener.[74] In an enclosed park at Lochnabo, Fife planted 1,010,000 firs, with 3,500 oak and beech.[75] As the woodland matured, Lochnabo was frequented by picnic parties from Elgin. The 'fairy abode' of the lochside was admired as were the many 'clumps of wood' that improved prospects in Urquhart—contrasting with 'the barren hills and dark gloomy woods of Scotch firs'.[76] Fife's woodland at Stynie was already well established at this date; and trees and sneddings were sold from the wood in September 1772.[77] A considerable extent of unenclosed grazing, however, remained at Stynie even in 1810, when the bleakness of the place was invoked to give additional thrill to accounts of the murder of Elspet Lamb—ravished and bludgeoned to death as she herded her father's cattle on the moor. The murderer, Alexander Gillan, was hanged and gibbeted on the spot, and subsequently buried in a wood established on the common grazing by the earl of Fife.[78]

Forres Town Council was an enthusiastic early planter. On 6 March 1766 the council ordered the planting of the moor between Muiryshade and New Forres. In November 1792 the council agreed to planting the Cloven Hills on the eastern margin of the town. New Forres moorland remained available for grazing and communal use until 21 October 1816, when the town council and Sir William Gordon Cumming of Altyre agreed that 'the moor of the Drum ... is quite useless', and should be planted with trees.[79]

Planting at Ballindalloch seems to have begun with a modest plantation of 19,800 trees established during April 1770.[80] In April 1775 estate labourers worked for 155 days 'planting Firs in [th]e Hill of Over Arn'. In 1779 a dozen men worked for a fortnight sowing acorns on the north side of the Spey. Some of these oaks flourish as stands of mature trees in rectangular stone-walled parks on the slopes below arable terraces.[81] Otherwise the estate and its tenants seem to have managed well enough on local resources of managed natural woodland, supplemented with timber floated from the Ballindalloch pinewoods of Invereshie.

Large-scale planting at Ballindalloch was initiated around 1815 as the proprietor exercised his right to:

> enclose, plant, or improve such pieces of heath or barren ground on the possession, or on the adjoining muirs ... reserving to the Tenants a loaning to give them access to the unimproved or unplanted muirs, excepting ... where the plantations already lined off exclude such access.[82]

In spring 1815 300,000 larch and Scots pine were planted for Ballindalloch on the north side of the Spey. A further 289,000 pine and larch were planted at Elchies, together with 14,800 oak and ash. 140,000 conifers were planted on the Drum of Carron.[83] Ballindalloch's hardwood sales (both plantation and semi-natural timber) yielded a modest income, while also supplying local farmers and craftsmen: in May 1813 fifty-seven lots of oak were rouped, raising £26 19s 0d. Separate sales of ash raised £11 0s 6d; and a further twelve lots of oak from Ballieheiglash and Bragach were knocked down to John Laing, cartwright in Fochabers, for £14 4s 6d.[84]

A wide range of native and alien species was planted under estate schemes. Usually, conifers were planted along with deciduous species, the quicker-growing softwood providing shelter for the hardwood. In 1780 Fife planted saugh, beech, elm and ash—sheltered by 217,000 larch at Crooked Wood in Urquhart.[85] Initially, Fife's pine trees were regarded as of little value, 'except as nurses to ... other trees'.[86] However, plantation softwood soon proved its utility and value. One of the largest vessels constructed at Speymouth, the *Lord Macduff*, was built with larch from the laichland plantation of Bin Hill—its launch applauded by a party of ladies and gentlemen from Innes house. Laichland larch framed with plantation oak became (briefly) usual in Speymouth shipbuilding during the 1850s. This locally-sourced timber combination might have superseded highland pine—but it was itself superseded by cheaper imported timber from North America. Moreover, the design specification of 1834, for the first steamship to ply the Moray Firth, called for English and African oak, mahogany and pitch pine; and the ship was built in Glasgow. The vessel, named *The Duchess of Sutherland*, ushered in the new fashions and technologies that would eventually kill off the Speymouth shipyards.[87] Laichland softwood was used in shipbuilding meantime; but increasingly it was harvested for parochial palings and house-carpentry.[88]

Native deciduous planting included oak, ash and elm. Lime was not a usual plantation tree, though specimens were grown in the gardens and policies of proprietors' houses. A rare reference shows lime trees sold—with ash, plane and fir—in a roup of Gordon timber at Stynie in 1783.[89] Smaller native deciduous species, deliberately planted, included birch, with alder and willow for wet ground. Aspen (formerly used for furniture, barrel staves and turned ware) was not, it seems, planted or encouraged under improvement regimes. Hazel, which coppices readily, had been valued for wattle, hurdles, basketry, hoops, stakes and charcoal); but the tree was not planted in improved forests, its utility having declined as changing fashions reduced demand for creelwork.[90]

Beech is native to England but not to Scotland; 'plane' (sycamore) is a central European tree, introduced from England in the sixteenth century. Beech does not readily seed; sycamore seeds readily. The sycamores that now grow as prolific weeds on Scottish roadsides are the feral descendants of trees deliberately planting during the late eighteenth century. Their troublesome ubiquity proves the wisdom of Oliver Rackham's cautionary comment: 'it is a tree which no responsible person should plant without carefully considering the consequences'.[91] The unrestrained spread of sycamore was already causing difficulty in 1775 when Alexander Christie, gardener at Ballindalloch, recorded many days' work, 'rooting out' self-seeded ash and plane in the castle policies.[92] William Leslie was aware of the invasive nature of sycamore. He introduced a caveat in his advice to landowners, urging them to allow tenants to plant 'the ordinary kinds of deciduous trees, plane-trees only excepted'.[93]

Native 'fir' (Scots pine) was planted in roughly equal numbers with alien larch. The European larch (*Larix decidua*) had been introduced into England in the late sixteenth century, grown as a specimen tree. Larch seed was listed in London nurserymen's stock by 1700. The tree was probably planted in southern Scotland before 1700, and may have reached Moray around 1710. Larch was formerly supposed to have been first planted in Scotland by the duke of Atholl during the 1720s. Although this is incorrect, Atholl's enthusiastic larch planting was probably instrumental in popularising larch as a plantation tree among Scotland's improvers.[94] William Leslie thought larch superior to Scots pine and 'better fitted for every purpose in building than the best timber from the Baltic'.[95]

Estate records indicate the introduction of other exotics into planting schemes. The alien species represent a fundamental change to the Moray landscape. There are sweet chestnut growing alongside native trees in woodland at Orton, some isolated specimens among old beeches near Urquhart, and further specimens at Darnaway. Sweet chestnut was included among 16,000 trees planted at Pluscarden in 1819—together with Turkey oak, scarlet oak and beech. However, most of the exotic deciduous species (apart from beech and sycamore) did not become common in the north-east. After felling they were replaced with conifers; and there are now no forests of sweet chestnut or scarlet oak. Laburnum was recommended to practical farmers in 1766: 'It carries a beautiful yellow flower and Cods. The timber very hard and valuable in house hold furniture'.[96] 200 ells of roadside planting on Fife lands near Elgin during 1819 included laburnum, grey poplar, Darlington willows, and silver fir, mixed with native alder. However, the exotic species did not thrive or survive, and there are, today, no roadside laburnums at Pluscarden, Kellas and Innes.[97] Ballindalloch too experimented with exotic trees, planting 300 acres around 1806, mixing spruce with larch, oak, ash, elm and beech. The planting of Elchies in 1813-15 also experimented with spruce, varying the planting of 3,600 seedlings with 100 silver fir.

Seedsmen and nurseries

Seeds and saplings for planting were sourced from commercial seedsmen, from neighbours, and from dedicated nurseries on the estate—usually under the care of the proprietor's gardener. Fife's men were gathering tree seeds, presumably for planting in estate nurseries, in 1724— ordering 'a cask for holding Holy berries mixed w[i]t[h] earth two Casks for holding the seeds mixed with sand'.[98] Otherwise, however, records of nursery work before the planting craze of the 1760s are scarce. The networks that knitted together the interests of north-east improvers were useful in supplying tree-planting schemes. For example, in January 1763 the duke of Gordon purchased 500,000 Scots pine plants from Peter May, 'Planer in Aberdeen'; and in October and November 1763 the duke purchased a further 527,000 two-year-old Scots pine plants, with twenty-five pecks of birch seed, from Monymusk.[99] Within Moray, provost George Brown of Linkwood, included a commercial nursery in his portfolio of business concerns.[100]

The earl of Findlater's nursery at Colleonard, managed by William Reid, covered up to twenty acres in 1762, and established a pattern for neighbours to follow.[101] By 1780 the earl of Fife's nursery operation was well developed, raising a range of species including oak beech, birch, holly and hawthorn.[102] In 1787 Fife raised Scots pine seedlings in 'flying nurseries' and heathland seedbeds.

I order different pieces of moor to be trenched where the soil is best, and most sheltered, and lay on a little lime and dung on it, and in those places I sow seeds as a nursery. I also plant in beds, year old trees of different kinds, taken from my other nurseries; I nurse them for three years, and plant them all over my plantations.[103]

Gordon castle gardeners operated similar nurseries, though details of their early operation are not recorded. However, nurseries of tree seedlings were well-established by around 1780 when they were the subject of a detailed report.[104]

Estate gardeners and foresters returned an income and cemented relationships among improvers by supplying neighbours with seed and nursery-grown plants. This trade may be traced back to the beginnings of estate forestry operations in the early decades of the eighteenth century—albeit for planting at Banff. On 3 April 1722 Lord Braco wrote:

I heave gott the seeds from My Lord Forglen with ass Mainie Broom seeds as will serve six or seven bolls souing of oats, also ten unce of fresh funn seed, five unce of firr seed and three unce and an half of arn seeds, the firr and arn seed ar to be sown in the Gairden, and the broom and fun seeds on the faice of the hill of Down betuixt the funs that is planted. [105]

When the planting craze took hold in earnest, Fife's own nurseries produced most of what was needed. However, the estate purchased a small supplement of 100,000 seedlings from William Lindsay, gardener at Darnaway, in 1787.[106] Altyre too was planted with Scots pine bought from Darnaway: thirty-three pounds of seed were supplied between 1776 and 1784; and 22,000 pine seedlings in 1788. Further supplies were purchased from the gardener at Kinsteary in Auldearn.[107] Scots pine and larch seed from Findlater's Colleonard nursery was brought to Ballindalloch in April 1809, though Mr Reid was unable to supply, on that occasion, either beech mast or acorns.[108]

The trade in seed probably helped to vary gene pools and strengthen plantations. The Moss of Urquhart was planted in 1780 with Scots pine from Kininvie.[109] Acorns from Oakwood in Spynie were demanded for Fife's estates in Braemar, though the factor, John Lawson, noted on 10 November 1818 a shortage of seed in that year. He added that there was 'difficulty in getting a kiln to dry them', though, as a miller he certainly operated a kiln. Perhaps he was just being obstructive to prevent a loss of seed that he required for local planting.[110] Seed and seedlings sourced from further afield—and especially from outside the closed circle of improving Moray landowners—further varied genetic variety. The Ballindalloch gardener received a cargo of seedling trees imported through Findhorn in 1774.[111] On 9 April 1816 Ballindalloch's gardener asked his master to send acorns from London, urging the laird to 'endeavour to get them of the best quality—fresh & genuine as they are very deceiving'.[112] Dickson & Brown, seedsmen in Perth, supplied the Fife estates with larch and ornamental trees in 1776.[113] Dickson's firm may have been a regular supplier: Dickson & Turnbull supplied Fife with further ornamental trees from Perth in 1819. In the same year Dickson & Gibbs in Inverness supplied Fife with 16,000 hardwood trees to be planted on ground cleared during the thinning of firs at Pluscarden.[114]

Timber sales

Plantations yielded steady income for estates throughout Moray. Local sales provided palings for newly enclosed farmscapes. The sudden availability of straight, plantation-grown softwood facilitated a great rebuilding and an architectural revolution of rafter-and-sarking roofs that could support coverings of slates. Estate sawmills supplied timber for farm houses offices and estate buildings. Records of plantation timber sold out of Moray and Banffshire are not very evident, though Thomas Newte noticed in 1791 that the earl of Moray had planted 12,000,000 trees, with Scots pine sheltering young oaks. The pines were felled when twenty years old: 'These he exports to good advantage, from the port of Findhorn to Newcastle and Sunderland, where, it seems, they are of use in the coal-mines'.[115] Scots pine from Dyke & Moy too was destined for export as pit props to Newcastle and Sunderland.[116] Exports of timber had begun quite recently when William Leslie surveyed the province of Moray. The timber laded at Findhorn represented, presumably, a first harvest of plantations established in the initial flurry of aboreal enthusiasm. Leslie was confident that 'as the plantations in the country advance, this branch of traffick will probably be enlarged'.[117] The earl of Fife's Quarrywood and Pluscarden timber—both hardwood and Scots pine—was sold to local people in 1838–39; while a further 3,994 trees 'blown down in gales' were bought, presumably for use as pit props, by a 'Mr Dow Newcastle', for £199 14s 0d.[118] As Darnaway timber reached maturity it was sold by roup, for example the lots exposed at the castle on 28 November 1843 included:

OAK WOOD ...About **5000** feet, from 8 to 14 inches on the side of the square, fit for Ship-building; also, about **3000** feet of very superior **CROOKS** for Boat-building, and about **2000** feet well adapted for Cartwrights.[119]

The Fife woodland at Quarrywood (known as Oakwood) supplied bark to tanneries in Elgin—where leather-working is well documented as a major industry from the seventeenth century onwards. Oakwood bark was also supplied to fishermen—including the earl of Fife's fishers at Garmouth in 1764—for steeping nets to stop them rotting.[120] The high value of the bark is perhaps indicated by the seriousness with which thefts were viewed: a five guinea reward was offered—posted on the door of the kirk in August 1799—for information leading to conviction of men who had cut three oak trees and barked several others at Pluscarden; and a reward of two guineas was offered in May 1800 for information leading to the arrest of those who had stolen bark from the wood of Scroggiemill.[121] Nineteenth-century records suggest that oak woods were managed to yield an annual harvest. Wood and bark sold from Quarrywood in 1799 was worth £323 18s 3d; in 1800, £206 11s 0d; in 1801 £204 8s 7d.[122] Ten tons of bark were sold in July 1814. Three thousand stones of bark were sold by roup at Aldroughty in August 1815. However, bark sales raised only £33 15s 5d in 1821.[123] Sales continued into the 1830s—earning £30 7s 6d from Pluscarden in 1839.[124] These sales seem to follow the national trend, which saw native tan bark priced out of the market by cheaper imports after 1815.[125] Home-grown bark declined as imports increased: 140 tons of foreign bark entered through the port of Lossiemouth in 1838.[126]

Orchards

In noticing the orchards at Fochabers, Boswell and Johnson drew attention to a characteristic aspect of Moray agriculture.[127] Fruitful laichland orchards were noticed in the writings of George Buchanan (1506–82), quoted in the first *Statistical Account* for Duffus: 'Moray, for pleasantness, and for the profit arising from fruit trees, surpasses all the other counties of Scotland'. The *Account* went on to lament: 'In modern times, we have much neglected this culture; and our orchards are at present often found about deserted castles and religious houses, nearly as much in decay as the buildings they surround'.[128] Moray's orchards were admired in Arthur Johnstoun's '*Elginum*':

> CORCYRA, *Aples* unto *Thee* hath sent,
> DAMASCUS, *Pruns*, CERASUS, *Cherries* lent.[129]

Later references among landowners' records, suggest orchards in flourishing (and profitable) condition, supplying proprietors' households and producing a surplus for sale. Books on fruit trees formed a significant element among agricultural texts in the Gordon Castle library.[130] The Fife estate purchased three bundles of fruit trees—together with 6,000 'aller trees' and 'hoop saughs' from Alexander Catanach, merchant in Rotterdam in November 1724. The following year 1,000 red and white 'hoop saughs' were shipped, together with a dozen each 'half stand apple', cherry and 'plumb' trees.[131] Further evidence of laichland fruit-growing is suggested by the petty customs levied in the Elgin market, published on 24 August 1752: 6*d* on each firkin of apples or pears; 4*d* on cherries, geans or plums; gooseberries, red or white currants and blackberries; 2*s* per boll on juniper berries; with further duties collected on cyder perry.[132]

William Leslie admired the orchard and fruit wall and greenhouse at Orton in 1811.[133] There was also a famous orchard on Fife's estate at Pluscarden, sheltered by the medieval walls of the monastic precinct, where William Leslie observed an ancient fig tree, which 'continued to blossom in it within these few years'.[134] In February 1810 the tenant was supplied with fruit trees from Duff house, to replace old and unproductive trees.[135] Fife's own fruit orchards were replenished in 1812 with trees supplied by Dicksons & Gibbs, from their nursery at Millburn, Inverness. Dickson's stock included 102 varieties of apple, 104 pears, eighty-one gooseberries, thirty-five peaches, thirty-four plums, with currants, strawberries, nectarines and a range of forest trees, grass seed and garden flowers.[136]

A similar range of fruit was grown even in highland Inveravon, where, in 1768, the Ballindalloch castle gardener planted apples, pears, cherries, apricots and gooseberries, supplied from the commercial nursery of Alexander Christie, Elgin.[137] Further fruit trees and bushes came from the nurseries of Alexander Grigor in Elgin, and Dickson & Gibbs at Inverness. Orchard trees supplied to Ballindalloch in 1813 comprised fifty apples, twenty six pears and pearmains and various cherries; more apples and pears were ordered in 1814.[138] Meanwhile, the Logie orchard, planted by Robert Cuming around 1780 covered:

> 4 acres, sheltered by groves of forest trees ... A number of ash trees have shot up to ... almost
> 100 feet: but the fruit trees stand open to the reverberated power of the southern sun, and in
> general the crop is plentiful.[139]

Job creation

A key economic benefit from the forestry boom was in job creation. The earl of Fife was adamant that 'the most regular attention must be to the weeding ... the value and property of the wood depends upon the unremitted attention to weeding'.[140] Thus, labour-intensive forestry provided paid employment that might soften distress arising from agricultural and tenural change. Husbandmen displaced from cooperative farms at Altyre are particularly documented as daylabourers, employed to plant trees and fence plantations on the estate after they left their township possessions.[141]

Plantations were supervised by paid keepers. These foresters kept up the fences and prevented encroachment by the cattle that strayed across imperfectly enclosed farmland, as well as reporting thefts of wood and bark by local tenants. In the spring of 1815 Ballindalloch appointed a 'punlar' (pindler) to protect a new plantation: the pindler's remuneration comprised a house in the plantation and an annual salary of £24 (Scots).[142] Plantation guardians may have been recruited from the labour pool of displaced cottars, who, failing to appreciate the rigour of modern forestry regimes, demanded the usual cottar perquisites. In 1817, the prospective candidate for the post of caring for Pluscarden plantations demanded firing, ale money and a cow, in addition to his house and salary.[143] John Lawson, factor at Oldmills encountered similar demands; and he reported, in May 1813, 'I have not yet fallen in with a man suited for a Forrester & ground officer, they think the wadges too little unless they had liberty of keeping a Cow in the woods'.[144]

Plantation labourers seem to have exercised significant industrial muscle. They recognised that there was some urgency involved in getting the bare-rooted seedlings planted before they wilted and while weather permitted. At Ballindalloch in 1816 it proved impossible to get male labourers, and the women who came forward demanded the men's rate. It is not clear whether this was because of a general shortage of labour, or perhaps because the men hung back, thus strengthening their wives' bargaining position. The forester reported:

> I dismissed the weakest of my squad and picked 15 or 16 of the Stoutest women (to make the pitts) but they would not hire with me under /8 per day—Now because I could get no men ... I agreed with 8 or 9 of the best hands at /8 per day.[145]

Forestry workers might come from some distance away, demonstrating the same easy mobility that also allowed harvest gangs to travel the country, following the work. Tree-planting gangs typically were organized in pairs: a male worker opened pits, women putting in the seedlings. These working methods provided ample opportunities for flirtation and ribaldry. Planting on the Dallas estate around 1840 was joyfully celebrated in verse by one of the labourers, the local poet, Danie Ross.

> The Planting it is now begun,
> A wite we got some little fun,
> For many a ane to it did run,
> They thocht no travel weary ...

Its Betty Stuart and the Finn,
To him the plants she did put in,
She will do richt if she get him
When she was at the Plantin ...

Its Douglas frae the Lenoch cam,
He thocht it was the wisest plan
To work for money frae han to han,
When he was at the Plantin.

Its 'Inna the plants to him put in,
An tho she was a tract most grim,
I never believe that she'll get him
Tho she was at the Plantin ...

A problem arose in respect of the planters' wages, which was resolved, it seems, when the workers, flexed their industrial muscles, backing their demands with a threat of violence:

We gotna our wages for a week,
Because the same we didna seek,
But got it all withoot a cleek,
For fear we wid grow crazy.[146]

The planting craze transformed Moray landscapes, clothing muirs and heathland with a profitable cash crop. The planting of Moray also lay at the heart of the regular revolution. Plentiful supplies of straight sawn softwood timber facilitated an architectural revolution: rafters and sarking replaced the turf-and-cruck supplied from yard-dyke plantings and seminatural woodland. Pine panelling or lath-and-plaster replaced interior creelwork won as wattle from coppiced willow and hazel. Moorland landscapes that were a fundamental element in the economy of cooperative townships were clothed with timber. As moorland resources became unavailable, township husbandmen were, perforce, obliged to adopt alternative agricultural regimes. Meanwhile, woodland provided the palings that defined their improved fieldscapes. Plantation timber, furthermore, was a privatised resource: woodland was no longer a communal amenity enjoyed by adjacent townships, but the exclusive, industrialised economic resource of the proprietor supplying demands that were both local and national. Ancient laws devised to conserve a communal resource, were applied in defence of this valuable private property. Paid keepers and stone dykes denied access to woodland grazing; and exemplary prosecutions extinguished the cooperative concept of woodland 'fit for common use'.

8

FARMING BY NEW RULES

Science in agriculture

Improved agriculture was based upon regimes that were supposed scientific; though
Enlightenment natural philosophy provided only the shallowest understanding of soil
chemistry and plant biology.[1] The discovery that 'fixed air' (carbon dioxide) contributed
the major constituent of a plant's substance was tentatively suggested only in 1804.
Photosynthesis did not begin to be understood until the mid-nineteenth century. Scientific
description of carbon and nitrogen cycles belongs to the late nineteenth century. The role
of trace elements in plant biology was unknown (as were some of the elements themselves)
to the experts who devised the cropping regimes that underpinned improved agriculture.
The low level of scientific knowledge is illustrated by the minister of Dyke's opinion that
the virtue of lime lay in its 'attracting the dews, [to] bring a more copious supply of nightly
moisture'.[2] William Leslie believed in the virtues of simple water as a manure. He urged:

> proprietors to retain one or more labourers merely for the purpose of spreading rills
> of water ... over the sides of heathy mountains. By this simple means, a vast extent of
> unproductive territory would in the course of a few years be converted into a verdant and
> valuable pasturage.[3]

Leslie rode his hobby-horse further in 1811, declaring that 'the whole fertilising quality of the
water .... itself is a kind of vegetable nutrition, which the plants draw out and assimilate to
their own substance'.[4]

Science in agriculture consisted, for the most part, of numberless trials (and errors) by
individual improvers. Around 1780 Dunbar of Grange investigated experimentally several
different fencing types and crop rotations.[5] John Lawson at Oldmills undertook 'Comparative
experiments in the sowing of wheat'.[6] On 17 November 1818 the Ballindalloch gardener
recorded observations of experimental sowings of timothy grass with red and white clover.[7]
Energetic managers at Gordon Castle conducted field trials of oats on home farm fields
during 1836–39. A crop reaped from eighteen acres of land 'formerly a Lake' was analysed

and growing conditions minutely noted: 'soil is poor mostly sand drained with peats in the shape of a drain'. A strain of oat 'first discovered in ... Rhynie' was found 'from their Earliness & great quantity of straw ... to be Superior to any other oat for the North of Scotland'. Twenty seven acres of 'Potatoe Oats' yielded 72 quarters 6 bushels while twenty-nine acres of 'Common Oats' yielded only 59 bushels. Further experiments compared yields of 'Chevalier barley' with 'Dovetailed barley'; and round white American potatoes' with 'black kidneys'.[8] These efforts favourably impressed tourists with an impression of agriculture: 'studied as a science; and every possible method tried to render the earth productive'.[9]

Scientific theory seldom troubled the ordinary husbandmen, who rarely possessed the literacy, leisure or inclination to access technical publications. He acquiesced in newfangled methods to please his laird, and because they were specified in his lease—though it might take a full nineteen-year term before he began to reap the benefits of a reformed regime.

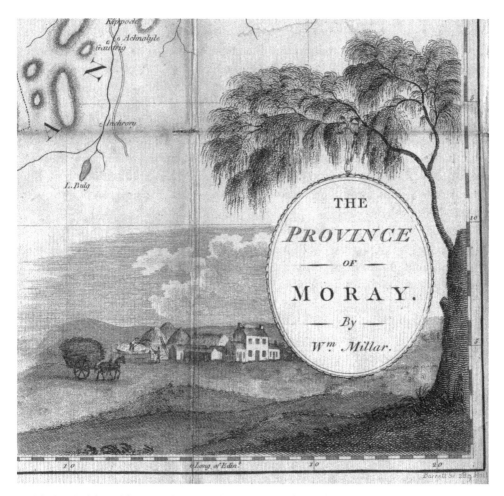

An idealised laichland farmstead, depicted by W. Millar. (*Survey of Moray, 1798*)

Crop rotation

Reason suggested that rest might refresh the soil. How this happened was unclear; and mysterious indeed was the magical manner in which some crops might actually enhance soil fertility. This marvel of nature had long been recognised. The nitrogen-fixing properties of legumes were unknown; but the beneficial effect of a season of peas was an ordinary part of agricultural lore. The use of clover as a 'Meliorating Cropt' was, though, an innovation. Sir Archibald Grant recommended that seasons of peas, beans, vetches or clover—should intervene between sowings of 'scourging' grain crops: offering practical farmers four- five- or six-shift rotations, which alternated grain with fallow and vetches.[10] A decade later, Lord Kames devoted a whole chapter of his grand thesis to crop rotation and clover.[11]

Moray's improvers, however, anticipated the theoreticians. This proves that practical landowners were the drivers of improvement, building new systems through experiment within the supportive network of fellow enthusiasts—while the swarm of published treatises followed in support or simply cashed-in on the mood of the times. From the 1750s Fife estate tacks, imposed crop rotation under a general condition of not allowing successive 'scourging' crops in five-shift regimes.[12] Regulations published in 1776–79, remedied 'very irregular' practices, specifically protecting the 'turnep, kaal and … the fallowed and turnep fields in winter' of those who had embraced modern cropping from free-ranging cattle belonging to neighbours who had not.[13] A pioneering lease of 1775 for the Brodie farm of Darklass obliged the tenant, Alexander Alves, 'to leave at outgoing one third in Grass & one third in Barley or any fallow Crop'.[14] Brodie regimes became more rigorous as improvement progressed: in 1812 a nine-year lease on the farm of Flockleys, obliged the tenant to sow one-third of his possession with grass, turnips and potatoes; and not sow more than six firlots of wheat—and that laid down with clover.[15]

The adoption of regular rotations was patchy, with larger laichland farms scarcely ahead of upland and smaller farms. The *Statistical Accounts* merely hint at crop rotation in the 1790s, and James Donaldson reported 'there is no fixed or steady rotation on any farm in the country' [of Elginshire]; but he added:

> in all large farms, some proportion is annually fallowed, some laid down with turnips, and other green crops, and the whole grass amounting to a third or fourth part, consists of sown clovers, rye-grass, and rib-grass.

Smaller farms too seem to have sowed sequences of grain, grass and green crops that conformed in general terms to the improvers' model.[16] To encourage those who had not yet taken to crop rotation, James Donaldson quantified the benefits of improved regimes: Banffshire barley yields in 1794 were said to have become 'much more abundant';[17] while Moray barley yielded six bolls per acre, representing an eightfold return on seed sown.[18]

The patchy spread of rotation is illustrated by data from different estates. Ballindalloch lagged somewhat behind laichland landowners. Ballindalloch leases around 1800 forbade tenants taking 'more than two white or corn crops in succession'. A hefty fine of £2 was levied 'for each acre so mislaboured'—though no regular rotation was specified.[19] Rotation was not, it seems, imposed on Lethen's Moray estate until around 1826, when a lease on Gateside in Alves bound the tenant, James Stuart, 'to ... manage and labour the lands in a proper manner and agreeable to the most approved system of husbandry adopted in the County of Elgin and Forres'. The lease, recognising that some time was needed to establish a proper regime, allowed Stuart until the 'last five years of the lease' before he was expected fully to 'manage the land according to the five-shift course'.[20]

By around 1840, laichland leases generally required five- or six-course rotations; though four-shift rotations obtained in Duffus.[21] In Kirkmichael the minister reported, 'The Duke of Richmond now restricts his principal tenants to a five shift rotation'—replacing six-shift cropping.[22] Even at this late stage in the regular revolution, the landscape of regular rotation, in upland and laichland parishes, was notably patchy: Knockando's agriculture was 'still ... in its infancy' in 1835; Inveravon had 'Of late ... made rapid progress'; Drainie too lagged behind, and in 1842, 'Only one farmer, Mr John Stephen of Coulard Bank, adopts the rule of never growing two white corn crops in succession'.[23] This fundamental rule was routinely broken also in Forres, where the 'common rotation' was '1st, fallow or green crop; 2d, corn; 3d and 4th, grass; 5th and 6th, corn'.[24] William Leslie sensibly observed the need to frame rotation regimes to local climate and soil;[25] and landowners' trial-and-error experimentation with four-, five-, six-, and even occasionally seven-course rotations continued into the nineteenth century—experience slowly teaching what worked best in particular districts.[26]

White crops

Rotation was practised using the usual grain crops. A typical balance is represented by the contents of the stackyard at Blackhill of Altyre, which went under the hammer on 7 February 1839, comprising: seven stacks of early Angus oats; ten of Hopeton oats, three of barley and two of peas. Growing crops at Muiryshade, near Forres, rouped on 28 February 1843, comprised: common oats, sandy oats, wheat and barley.[27]

Oats and barley remained the principal grains on Moray farms, with oats the staple in popular diet; barley supplying bannocks, ale and whisky. Oatmeal and barley continued to be exported through the Moray ports. Innovation came in the adoption of particular strains and species of seed, which scientific trial had proved to be hardier or more productive than traditional varieties. Hardiness was probably more important than enhanced yield during the later eighteenth century; improving weather during the nineteenth century reduced risks from early frost and excessive rain and allowed farmers to pursue the goal of increased yield. Donaldson noted the introduction of new strains of early oat into Banffshire, by the earl of Fife in 1783—which ripened a fortnight earlier than the strain used west of the Spey.[28] In Elginshire, traditional 'common white, and the black-bearded oat; or, more properly, the grey oat' persisted.[29] Two principal varieties of barley were grown in Moray in 1811: four-row Scotch bear and two-row barley; though some distillers preferred English barley—especially in the Forres area where, presumably, imported grain entered through the port of Findhorn.[30]

Wheat was cultivated generally in the laich around 1790: yielding 'superior crops' in Duffus.[31] William Leslie suggested an extraordinary yield: 'a little more than 3 bushels is the quantity of seed allowed to the acre; the return about 5 or 6 quarters'.[32] Donaldson agreed, estimating a bountiful (thirteen-fold) return on seed, but nonetheless noting a 'recent' decline in production in favour of barley.[33] Wheat was mentioned in *New Statistical Accounts* for most lowland parishes. It was 'generally cultivated' in Bellie (where barley had declined as a result of changes in demand from the distillers) yielding a nine-fold return on seed. In Urquhart farmers raised 'as much wheat as possible ... wheat is the grain most easily ... converted into money to meet the rent'.[34] Wheat was third in order of importance (after oats and barley) in upland Edinkillie; a 'very little' was harvested in Inveravon, though it was 'of excellent quality in favourable seasons'.[35] Farmers' reluctance to concentrate upon wheat stemmed in part from a cultural prejudice in favour of a popular diet based upon barley, oatmeal and pulses. Furthermore, barley and oat straw was valued for feeding cattle, while wheat straw contained little nutritional value.[36] Fluctuating demand for barley from distillers (under changing excise laws) also affected wheat cultivation.

Rye declined under improvement regimes and was, by the 1790s, grown only in small quantities, in the laich,[37] though more widely on acidic highland soils.[38] Rye featured in an experimental rotation for light soils tried at Grange around 1780; though apparently without success as it was not noticed in the *Statistical Account* in 1794-5.[39] Rye survived on smaller farms (sown with oats in Speymouth)[40] but declining in 1811, and insignificant in *New Statistical Accounts*.[41]

In general, it seems that even at an early stage of agricultural improvement, grain yields had increased. Under improved regimes, famine would become a thing of the past and starvation no longer the inevitable consequence of crop failure. However, more important, in explaining the end of periodic dearth and distress were, arguably, changed attitudes to poor relief and also improved communications. Starvation was averted in 1782–83 because grain and meal were imported to areas affected by shortages, and distributed timeously.

Pulses provided a staple in husbandmen's diet during the early decades of improvement. Following harvest failure in 1782, pease meal was distributed (with oatmeal) as an appropriate form of food relief. Gordon castle archives record the arrival of five cargoes (495 bolls—perhaps 31 tons) of pease meal at Speymouth. The meal was sold on credit, or for ready money, and distributed gratis to Gordon tenants.[42] Pease were sown in small quantities, fairly generally in Banffshire in the 1790s.[43] In Elginshire, meanwhile, pease and (horse) beans were both grown, with a recently-introduced species of 'early pease'. Yields might be generous (up to nine-fold), though sensitive to weather.[44] Pease and beans continued to feature in the cropping of improved farms, though in declining quantities. *New Statistical Accounts*, noticed pulses as grown only on fifty acres in Kinloss; and thirty-five in Edinkillie; and 'from necessity' in Drainie—and probably also in other parishes—where 'the poor farmer has not capital to wait a distant though more ample return'.[45]

Exotic roots

Exotic new crops took root as pease and rye declined. Turnips head the list. Introduced into England during the sixteenth century, turnips were grown, initially, as a garden crop and served as a delicacy on polite tables. As a field crop, turnips were fed off the ground to sheep from the mid seventeenth century onwards, the animals manuring the soil as they ate.[46] Henry Home (1696–1782) was credited as the first landowner to grow turnips to feed cattle in Berwickshire.[47] Already, though, turnip cultivation had leapfrogged to tenants in north-east Scotland: paid in rents to feed cattle at Craigievar during the mid-seventeenth century;[48] and on sale in Elgin by 1709, where petty customs were levied at 4*d* per peck or 1*s* on each 'load of … carrots, turneips and parshneips'.[49] Lord Kames was fulsome in praise of turnips and all who cultivated them:

> It animates me to have opportunity for giving directions about a crop, that the best farmers have now taken into their plan of husbandry; and that does not altogether escape even small farmers … no person ever deserved better of a country than he who first cultivated turnip in the field.[50]

In Banffshire that credit was deferentially granted to the earl of Findlater, for promoting turnip husbandry from around 1748.[51]

> The gentlemen of the neighbourhood who visited his lordship, and several of the farmers, were, of course, led to see and consider the example thus set before them: and they were soon convinced of the advantages.[52]

Turnip seed was sold from Cullen home farm from (at least) the 1760s.[53] Turnips were presumed to be general under Fife estate regulations and tacks in the 1770s.[54] Dunbar of Grange planted turnips in experimental rotations around 1780.[55] In upland Ballindalloch, the gardener, Alexander Christie, raised turnips in the castle nursery during 1778–79.[56] The first *Statistical Accounts* recorded turnips in fourteen parishes: 'on every farm' in Aberlour and Bellie; 'a few for family use' in Dallas; 'by gentleman farmers' in Dyke & Moy; and by 'the best sort of farmer' in Speymouth where they were said to grow well, though cultivation was hampered by sheep grazing commonfields and unenclosed pasture.[57] *New Statistical Accounts* suggest that turnips were routinely included in cropping regimes by around 1840. At this date turnip cultivation was a usual condition of lease, for example in 1842 under five, six, or seven-shift rotations on Ballindalloch farms throughout Inveravon and Knockando.[58]

　　Records are unclear regarding the species of turnip cultivated under early rotations. Scottish farmers eventually preferred the hardy Swedish ruta baga, encouraged among British farmers from around 1760 by the Royal Society of Arts.[59] A roup at Burgie Mains in 1829 included 159 drills of 'Yellow turnips'—together with lots of implements including a turnip harrow.[60] Laichland farms might grow both white and yellow turnips and ruta baga too.[61] Mangel wurzels, introduced on English farms during the mid nineteenth century, were perhaps tried by the earl of Fife in 1792;[62] but they did not enter the repertoire of Moray farmers.

Potatoes may have been introduced into Scotland during the 1740s: enjoyed as a luxury by the quality, while servants were treated to the skins.[63] By the end of the century the potato had effected a dietary revolution with wide social consequences. James Donaldson thought potatoes were introduced in Moray 'soon after the famine in 1740', adding that potatoes broke from the kitchen garden into the fields only 'a few years' after their first appearance. Potatoes were traded in the Elgin market by 1752.[64] A red-skinned variety was the strain first planted, though this was abandoned after a couple of decades in favour of 'the white kidney kind'.[65] The Ballindalloch gardener cultivated potatoes routinely from at least the 1760s.[66] The health of his crop was maintained by periodic introduction of seed from distant sources, including, in April 1809, Findlater's model farm at Colleonard.[67] The Gordon estate exploited a wider supply network, for example importing 'Early Bradford' potatoes from Goodwood in 1837.[68]

Lord Kames approved of potatoes as 'good and wholesome food for horned cattle, hogs and poultry, adding 'of late years [potatoes] have been ... a great support to many poor families, as they are easily cooked, and require neither skill nor mill'.[69] However, William Leslie noted that potatoes were eaten by the poor 'only through necessity, not through choice ... and in many families the servants do not eat them at all'.[70] Famine helped to dispel the popular aversion to potatoes, which were distributed as food relief from Gordon Castle in 1783.[71] By the 1790s potatoes had descended from high status as a 'vegetable of the greatest delicacy ... served up on the tables of the opulent' to become a popular staple.[72] William Leslie noted that potatoes supplied:

> a large proportion of the food of the labouring class. They form for 8 or 10 months of the year one dish at dinner, and frequently also at supper, on the tables of those who in this quarter are accounted wealthy.

And he helpfully added several serving suggestions: steamed; boiled in water; boiled in milk; fried in butter; mashed with butter, cream and 'spiceries'; baked with oatmeal or flour into thin cakes.[73]

In Drainie, potatoes throve 'admirably well ... and serve for the subsistence of the poor, at least a third part of the year'.[74] In Rafford they were chiefly fed to horses and poultry; and the lower classes of the human population.[75] However, Leslie added the alarming caveat that cattle sometimes choked on potatoes, which could also burst their stomachs.[76] In Dyke & Moy potatoes were 'little known before the year 1745', thriving only in lazy beds. However, by 1793 the minister could report 'Now, nobody misses plentiful crops': 228 bolls planted in that year, yielding an eight-fold return on seed. Potatoes were grown by as a commercial field crop, and also on plots allocated by farmers to their cottagers. With potatoes as a dietary staple, the subsistence of a labourer on an improved farm required less land than his cottar predecessor. Labourers' potato plots yielded more calorific value per acre than rigs of oats. This 'greatly lessened the consumption of grain', increasing surplus corn for the farmer to sell.[77]

Grass

William Mackintosh declared in 1729 that fallow was the essential partner of enclosure in improvement regimes.[78] Fallowing and haymaking were both already practised under cooperative regimes in some districts of Moray. However, when landowners planted moorland pasture with settler farms or forestry, the grazing available to farmers was reduced. The loss was supplied by improving the quality of pasture through regular sowing of selected grasses within the enclosed fieldscape—refining practices already established within cooperative regimes.[79] Improved rotations called for grass and clover seed to be sown along with the grain crop, to be grazed as pasture or cut as hay in the following year. Practical farmers were recommended: 'To a Scots Acre sow—16 lb. of red Clover, four of white and two bushels of Rye grass'; and for sheep pasture 'add a few pounds of narrow-leafed Planten'.[80]

On the Grange estate, regular fallow breaks were introduced in regulations imposed soon after 1760:

> as the resting of ground keeping their Cattle at home and making clean Dung is the only way to insure clean Crops of Grain if the Tenant neglects such management the Proprietor reserves power to himself to rest or lay down to grass a proportion of the arable field ... the whole produce not only of the Grass but the Crops of Corn after breaking up shall belong to him[81]

Sown grass was specified by Brodie leases from 1785, when a letter of lease granted a nineteen-year tack on part of Drumduan with the requirement: 'Five acres of the last Crop ... to be laid down with Grass seeds at the rate of One Boll Rye Grass & Eighteen pounds Dutch weight of red Clover each acre'.[82] By the turn of the century Brodie farms routinely incorporated sown grasses into their rotations.[83] Grass and clover seed was sold to Gordon tenants, at favourable rates, by the castle gardener from 1783.[84] Fife's tenants were encouraged with free seed in 1765: a few pounds each to small tenants in Mosstowie and Pluscarden; 24 lb for Alexander Thomson at Hatton of Longbride, 40 lb for Alexander Young in Mains of Coxtown, and 85 lb for Thomas Craig in Longbride.[85] Progressive landowners provided examples for tenants to follow. The Ballindalloch Grants were enthusiastic haymakers from the 1770s onwards, with some eighty man-days spent cutting home farm meadows in 1774.[86] Ballindalloch's seed, consisting of rye grass with red and white clover, was purchased from the firm of Mason, Teesdale & Minier, seedsmen, in The Strand, London.[87] Gordon castle home farm accounts record hay harvests from 1782, when two mowers earned £8 2s 8d for cutting sixty-nine acres; nineteen women and one man who assisted the haymaking earned 5d per day for several days. The home farm meadows were then reseeded with 360 lb of red clover, 218 lb of white clover and 120 bushels of rye grass.[88]

The revolutionary greening of the landscape with sown grass was enthusiastically documented in *Statistical Accounts*: 'on a large scale' in Alves; on 'every farm' in Bellie; 'daily gaining ground' in Elgin.[89] Not all farmers, however, readily adopted hay as winter feed.

There was straw aplenty from grain crops and many, it seems, continued to winter beasts on this customary fodder. Sown grasses were embraced only 'by the best sort of farmer' in Speymouth; only on large farms in Inveravon; and by gentlemen farmers only in St Andrews-Lhanbryd, Edinkillie and Spynie.[90] In Birnie there was 'very little' sown grass; and poor tenants in St Andrews-Lhanbryd continued to rely upon 'natural ley grass'.[91] William Leslie asserted, 'Among many of the poorer tenants ... it is not cultivated at all; though ... its cultivation is spreading farther every year.'[92] A decade later smaller tenants continued grazing their beasts upon 'such natural herbage as the soil itself may spontaneously produce'.[93]

Sown grass was cultivated primarily to feed the farmer's own cattle, and the subletting of grazing was discouraged. Surplus grass was, however, harvested for sale—even in upper Strathavon, where the forester, John Stuart, possessor of Torbain, sold 132 stones of hay 'to Glenfiddich' for £4 8s 0d on 16 December 1794, with a further shipment worth £4 11s 0d shortly after.[94] The extent of the hay trade is somewhat unclear. Sanguine reports in 1794 observed 'more hay stacked for the market, than perhaps in any other district of the kingdom'.[95] Four years later, however, it was said—perhaps following a poor season—'There is not a great quantity of hay stacked, either for the market or private consumpt'.[96] Hay sales and grazing rents earned significant income to landowners. Grass parks at Innes returned a rent of £51 14s 6d in 1778. These parks were periodically ploughed and reseeded. For example, in January 1796 the factor ordered a six-acre park to be sown with '12 Bushels of Rye grass seed ... sown with Lib 10 of Red & Lib 6 of White Clover.[98]

Soil improvement

Even the most rational farmers relied upon the most fundamental of materials to fertilise their fields. Lord Kames declared, 'dung is of great importance in husbandry, a farmer cannot be too assiduous in collecting animal and vegetable substances that will rot'.[99] Dung for the fields was produced by the farmer's own beasts, seasoned with whatever the family could contribute, and compostable material from the kitchen. The admirable Mr Jamieson acknowledged 'without cattle, he could not convert his straw into dung',[100] though there was nothing new in this:

> when Grounds are all inclosed, and the laid down Fields well stock'd with Cattle, to return, by their frequent pissing and dunging on it ... 'tis quickly ... inriched.[101]

Archibald Grant offered a list of materials that might be added to the dungheap, including: malt dust; refuse of tanners' pits and slaughterhouses; hoofs, horns and hair; raggs, 'those best which are improper for paper milns'; sawdust; and 'sudd from wash houses'.[102] Grant also declared 'Sea weed amongst the best Manures we have';[103] and kelp harvesting continued into the 1840s.[104]

Edward Laurence urged, in 1763: 'Manure bred on every Farm should (by the watchful Eye of the Steward) all be laid on the Lord's Lands', and not wasted.[105] Dung conservation was written into improving regulations, for example at Lethen where, in 1811, a prohibition was imposed on selling or otherwise removing dung from the farm.[106] Clarification of the regulation was required in 1831 when James Stuart, tenant of Gateside, sought to set aside the condition that forbade the sale of turnips. The turnips the tenant wished to harvest would normally have been eaten where they grew by cattle that dunged the field while feeding. The matter was discussed in a letter from the factor to the laird, then in Edinburgh:

> I think your proposal of adding an obligation to bring back as much Dung as the Turnip crop would have produced may be a sufficient antidote for the evil, should the Turnip be carried away ... I may almost venture to say the Tenant of Gateside has not sold a single acre of Turnip ... Gateside or any other of the Lethen Farms have not like those in the vicinity of Towns the command of a market for Turnips and a supply of extraneous manure in their stead. I can easily conceive ... your views on this point residing as you do in Edinburgh where Turnips command a ready market and high prices and where an abundant supply of manure can be had in their stead.[107]

Laichland farmers bought in muck from nearby towns. In 1772, Grange estate regulations recognised the particular quality of burgh manure, by providing that 'all who lay on ordinary straw muck to pay the rent as usuall. All who Dung with Ashes ... or what ordinarily goes under the name of Forress muck to have the cropt rent Free'.[108]

Estate improvement disrupted traditional nutrient transfer. Under improved regimes cattle were kept at home, on the farm, all year round. No longer were lowland cattle sent to highland pastures for the summer. A consequence of this (apart from a loss of income for highland tenants) was a reduction in the amount of dung added to their shieling improvements—which were gradually lost as supplementary arable. Nor were cattle driven daily out of lowland farms for promiscuous grazing on common pasture to return at night with bellies full of moorland or outfield grass which fell as dung in the byre, yard or field; thus local nutrient transfer was diminished.

Improving regulations furthermore ended the importation of moorland turf for mixing with dung. Turf-cutting was restricted on Brodie farms from around 1785.[109] The earl of Fife pursued an exemplary process in the sheriff court during the spring of 1798 against a tenant, George Smith, who was engaged in 'practices detrimental to the farm'. These included: not leaving land fallow; exhausting the farm; and mixing only very little dung with 'fail' spread as manure— with a 'determined resolution to scourge and reduce the said farm previous to his quitting the same.'[110] Lethen regulations of 1811 stated: '[tenants] shall not cast up any green ground ... for Turfs for fire or flags for middens'.[111] The end of turf-cutting accelerated an architectural revolution: turf walling was abandoned in favour of stone; divot-and-heather roofing was superseded by straw-thatch or slate. As an unintended consequence of architectural change, the farm lost the nutrient benefit of organic building materials periodically recycled through the dungheap. Rigorous fallowing was required to make up the nutrient deficit.

Acid soils might be improved with lime: replacing the calcium that leeched from the soil over time, leaving it hostile to 'meliorating' crops, including the clover that was crucial in fallowing. The chemistry of liming was not understood, though its practical value had been appreciated since the Middle Ages;[112] and limestone was burned for agricultural use in Strathisla kilns during the early seventeenth century.[113] At Brodie a wood-fired kiln burned lime (for fertiliser or mortar) in 1739: George Grant in Findhorn supplying 'three Pound of [gun] Pouder for blowing up ... old roots to burn the Lime'.[114] Lime was used agriculturally by Fife tenants at Slap of Fintry, where nineteen-year leases on the cooperative township in 1740 and 1752 itemised, intown, outfield, rich meadow, shieling, 'Triangle Park lately improved', and 'limed ground'.[115]

In the 1790s lime had 'by no means come into general use as a manure' in Banffshire— notwithstanding an abundance of limestone and the determined enterprise of Strathisla folk, who produced 50,000 bolls a year at the 'low price of 6*d*. or 8*d*. the boll'. James Donaldson disparaged this industry as inefficiently small-scale and wasteful of fuel.[116] These concerns were also the subject of an anonymous letter to the earl of Fife in 1774:

> [to] Let you know of A wonderfull Loss that ye are att. Lime Especially the peple in the paroche of Keith to Make and Burn ... the Imployment all Rownd from hill to water this has been all the Imployment of peple ... this three years past in Making and Burning Lime to the Duke of Gordons Building and his New Lands ... they have Distroyed More of your Lordships Moss then all your tennants ... would have don this thirty years to Come ... They Neglect All there owne Labour att home ... Call in All and Every Man before A Smeart and Sharp Judge ... and Seuerly fine and punish the Limemakers and peat sellers ... Lous not on days time[117]

No action was taken. Indeed, the earl was himself a customer, purchasing Keith lime for building work at Oldmills and for his granary at Corriewood (Quarrywood) in March 1771.[118] The Fife estate operated its own kiln at Banff, burning imported limestone in at least twenty-seven firings during 1767–69.[119] Vouchers for agricultural expenses at Innes during the summer of 1771 included payments of wages for 130 man days spent 'at the lime work' or 'Bracking Lime Stone and Burning the Kiln', and for 1,050 stones of Scots coal supplied by Alexander Young at Oldmills to fire the kiln.[120] Meanwhile, the cost of liming was allowed as a rent rebate for small tenants and settlers on Fife lands.[121]

In the 1790s, farmers in the laich were importing lime, overland from Banffshire or by sea from Sutherland, though William Leslie thought this latter trade of little significance.[122] The cost of carting (from Boharm or Keith) was reported as a factor limiting the use of lime in Speymouth. In Dyke & Moy lime was used by 'Gentleman farmers'; and though limestone was available in the parish, at 'the Boat-pool' on the Findhorn, 'for want of fuel, it is more eligible to purchase lime than burn it'—because lime 'could be had from Sutherland at 4*d*. per meal firlot'. In Kirkmichael, where limestone and peat were both abundant, lime was applied by most farmers.[123] In Strathspey, up to 3,000 bolls of lime were being manufactured annually for local consumption 'which, when applied as manure, has in every instance answered expectation'.[124] Lime kilns became a feature of the improved farmscape, notably surviving in the Kirkmichael, strategically sited to serve several adjacent farms. Most are simple peat-fuelled, flare kilns, typically built into a natural slope of the ground to facilitate loading at the top of the kiln-bowl, and unloading through the drawhole at the base. At Torbain and at Bailecnoic typical small kilns, constructed of quarried granite blocks, each served one side of upper Strathavon. A similar kiln, of local quartzite masonry stands below the track connecting the farms of Lyne and Altnaha with Belon and Knock.[125]

Large-scale limestone quarries were established in Glenrinnes. On 6 September 1773, Robert Gordon wrote to the duke of Gordon's factor declaring that he had 'for some time past Quarried Limestone on Lord Fife's interest in Glenrinnes'. Now he requested permission to work on the duke's property, where 'there are inexhaustable Quarries ... more than would supply all Scotland ... the Stones ... are above Ground almost everywhere & upon uncultivated places'.[126]

William Young of Inverugie developed a commercial lime manufacture supplying laichland farmers, and also producing a surplus for export: multiple coal-fired kilns allowed continuous production, while a railway connected the operation with Hopeman harbour.[127] Ballindalloch established industrial-scale lime burning on the Morinsh commonty, probably before 1800.[128] The moorland is pocked with quarry pits where limestone was won. A substantial kiln was constructed with local stone that was unsuitable for burning, including a sugary white quarzite built into a soaring buttressed façade with a generous arched drawhole. Ancestors of this enterprise are documented in vouchers for September and October 1774 when John Nicolson was paid 6*s* for six days work 'Building the Lime Kiln' and James Wright received the same payment for 'Twelve days work at Braking a Kilne of Limestone'.[129] Separate kiln accounts were being kept by 1788.[130] From about this time Ballindalloch's Knockando tenants were obliged by their tacks to spread specified quantities of lime on their fields.[131] New nineteen-year tacks of Morinsh farms, signed in 1820, revived customary carriages—to serve the lime kiln. Tenants of twenty-five farms were obliged to send their own carts and horses to carry from ten to ninety-six loads of limestone to the kiln—a total of 615 loads annually.[132]

By the time of the *New Statistical Accounts* lime was in more or less general use even where this meant carting it some distance. Improvement of Knockando farms was 'much aided ... by the facility with which lime is procured from Mortlach, in consequence of the building of Craig Elachie bridge, and the improved state of the roads.' Aberlour farmers imported lime from Glenrinnes, Glenlivet and Mortlach. In Edinkillie farmers bought in lime burned at Cothall near Forres or imported by sea through Findhorn. In Glenlivet, peat-cutting and quarrying to supply the small kilns on 'almost every farm', diverted farmers' energy from 'cultivation of his farm and the care of his stock'.[133]

An alternative to lime was available to estates near the coast. Rents paid by Brodie's Maviston fishermen were rendered partly as sacks of shells from around 1730 until the 1760s. The shells were either crushed and applied directly to the fields, or burned in kilns and applied as slaked lime. Shells were also purchased in 1766 to make lime mortar for repairing Brodie's Monaughty granary.[134]

Marl was used, where available, as a substitute for lime. It was not carried great distances; rather it was used where it was found. A marl pit at Tomalinan in Glenlivet was particularly mentioned in both *Statistical Accounts*.[135] Marl was also noticed on Findlater land near Elgin and on Gordon property near Bridge of Spey.[136] Some little excitement was generated by the discovery on 20 February 1814 of a lode of marl on Fife's Rosehaugh property in the laich, 'which ... might be wrought to advantage'.[137]

Trial and error—rather than awareness of plants' need for phosphorous and calcium— proved the value of bonemeal. The earliest records of this fertiliser in Moray are in Birnie and Speymouth in 1835.[138] On 10 June 1837 the ship *Anne* of Crail unloaded 'bone dust' worth £376 6s 6d at the mouth of the Spey. This shipment, by the Edinburgh Bone Mill Company, had been ordered for Gordon Castle, though there had been difficulties in obtaining the supply, as bonemeal became the soil-improver of choice among progressive farmers. Alexander Balfour in Kirkcaldy explained to William Walter, the duke's land steward, on 24 February 1837, that there was a shortage of bones: 'we are paying about 50 p[er] c[en]t more for Bones than ordinary, from encreased demand & diminished Supply'.[139] To meet Moray demand, the entrepreneural Fife factor at Oldmills began producing 'Bone manure', selling 'Drill & Dust mixed' at between 2s 6d and 3s 6d per bushel. Most was purchased by farmers in the laich, notably on Fife lands at Pluscarden, Cloves, Kellas, Urquhart and Blackhills. Bonemeal also went to Roseisle and Findrassie, and was sold into Dallas. Small quantities were carried to Rothes, Dundurcas and Knockando, with more notable supplies to the improving lairds of Ballindalloch and Wester Elchies.[140] Bonemeal had spread generally through Dyke & Moy by 1842; it was too expensive, though, for smaller farmers in Urquhart.[141]

Farmers were adventurous in their use of fertiliser. In 1842 Bellie farmers' repertoire included herring soil—a waste product from the duke of Gordon's fishery at Portgordon.[142] Meanwhile, Mr A. M'Donald, corn merchant at Moy, was agent for 'Clarke's dessicated compost', advertised as a 'superior turnip manure'. This 'preparation of Night Soil with Animal Matter' was said to give 'most luxurient returns of Barley and Clover Grass ... and the results will be found to be far superior to what is produced either by farm-yard, or bone manure'.[143] The Gordon castle home farm experimented with 'Animalised Carbon' imported probably from the south of Scotland: the first cargo weighing 14 tons 5 cwt was unloaded at Kingston on 7 June 1839.[144] However, Gordon's imports were exceptional: for most purposes, Moray was self-sufficient in manure down to 1840.

Animal husbandry

Improvements in animal husbandry marched ahead of arable innovations. Traditional goat-keeping had declined to insignificance by the time of the *First Statistical Accounts,* when just 310 goats were counted—all in Kirkmichael. However, enterprising Dallas farmers capitalised upon the health fads that accompanied increasing prosperity, by keeping milking-goats 'for the accommodation of tender people'.[145]

The improving impulse, and the promise of profit, trumped ancient prejudice against pigs.[146] Berkshire pigs were introduced from Aberdeenshire, probably before 1800, though most cottagers were said still to 'prefer a dog which is of no kind of use'.[147] A new generation proved more practical. By 1809 Patrick Sellar was planning industrial-scale pork curing at Burghead.[148] Fifty pigs were counted at Wester Elchies and Ballintomb in Knockando in 1835, while in Elgin pigs 'of every variety' were 'very abundant in every farm-yard, and there are very few of the poorest cottagers without one'.[149]

Poultry continued as commonplace farmyard inhabitants even after customary hens were converted into money payments. Though 'spirited farmers' regarded poultry-raising a 'mark of inferiority',[150] fowls were reared for sale in the 'families of the smaller tenants, cottagers, and rural artisans';[151] and eggs were shipped in quantity from Burghead and Findhorn to London—at 3s 6d per chest.[152] Improvers were willing, though, to raise species which possessed an aura of modernity. Thus turkeys supplanted geese in the stock of gentlemen and progressive farmers.[153] Ballindalloch turkeys were shipped (like coals to Newcastle) to General Grant's Florida plantations in 1775, along with clothing for his negro slaves.[154] Turkeys were raised elsewhere on Ballindalloch land, the tenant at Kilmaichlie reporting some dozens killed in a storm on 22 May 1802.[155] And turkeys ousted hens from Brodie rentals: tacks signed in 1811 required 'a fat young turkey at Christmas', or 'against New years day'.[156]

Alien sheep entered Moray somewhat ahead of other improvements: on 4 August 1755 Brodie of Lethen wrote to his man of business in Edinburgh:

> I am very deserous to get Some Sheep this Season from Selkirk to mend the breed of our own ... If they can get me but thirty or forty lambs, and ten or a dozen of yearold Rams ... I would Gladly send for them.[157]

By the 1790s, several commentators nostalgically lamented the supplanting of the native whiteface.[158] The immigrant 'large bodied, black faced sheep, whose fleeces are of a very rough and inferior nature'—did, however grow more mutton for the butcher and a wool that suited machine spinners.[159]

Some four thousand whiteface still grazed in Duffus and Alves around 1790[160]—though under threat from alien invaders that had thoroughly penetrated Moray: Bakewells in Alves and St Andrews-Lhanbryd; cross-bred Lintons in Bellie; 'a very hardy kind ... called Badenoch' in Dallas; 'Black faced Tweedale' in Edinkillie'. Lintons 'with black faces and feet' mixed with the natives in Inveravon; and with whiteface and Bakewells in St Andrews-Lhanbryd. Lintons had been tried in Speymouth, but found 'not to thrive'.[161] Ballindalloch improved his flocks in 1806 with five English ewes at two guineas each and one ewe hog at 25s—purchased from Arndilly.[162] The earl of Fife asked his factor to write to Patrick Sellar on 16 April 1819 'to get a ram of the meirn breed and of a dark colour to make my black sheep a little more fine—any young one of the brownish kind would do'. The factor felt that 'a south down ram would be better—cross with the black faced sheep and improve the wool'; but he deferred to the judgment of Sellar whom he supposed was more expert in sheep.[163]

Sheep were generally regarded as incompatible with improved arable farming: they cropped the pasture, damaged trees and invaded growing crops in imperfectly enclosed fields.[164] The Elgin minister noted: 'plantations of wood, and sown grasses, have thrown sheep so much out of the low country, that thirty years ago, more hundreds were sold out of it than there are now scores in it'. Sheep were forbidden on Fife's Banffshire farms under regulations of 1777-9;[165] and severely restricted under Lethen regulations of 1848.[166]

Hardy new breeds of sheep that required no housing, however, could earn an income from high grazings. Sheep husbandry increased in upland parishes: in the 1790s Inveravon grazed 2,500 head, Knockando 5,000, and Kirkmichael 7,050.[167] By the 1830s the native breed was all but extinct: Cheviots predominated in Rafford; brown-face/Cheviot crosses in Speymouth; blackface grazed Edinkillie and Aberlour. Birnie Cheviots were managed by 'shepherds brought from the border counties'. Kirkmichael hill pasture supported 6,536 head of unspecified breed.[168]

Improvement continued as breeds were crossed and selected. In September 1836 the duke of Gordon introduced Southdown and halfbred Leicester tups—supplied by a Mr Elman in Lewes, Sussex:

> to give persons in your country the opportunity of seeing the description of stock which we breed upon the Southdown Hills ... Cheviot wool is too coarse ... the Leicester and the highland sheep is also objectionable ... altho' the mutton is good ... I am sure that the South down ... will answer as they can withstand the inclemancy of an American climate.

This enhancement to the Moray bloodline was facilitated by developments in the wider economy, the rams travelling north and returning home in comfort and style—by steam packet via London.[169]

Moray's landowners did not adopt the policies that made Patrick Sellar notorious in Sutherland. Alien breeds might replace native whiteface. And, to a degree, sheep replaced cattle in Kirkmichael. But nowhere did sheep drive out people. Landowners sought to retain people on the estate and to promote commercial mixed agriculture rather than sheep farming. Ballindalloch hesitated to expand sheep farming in Glenfeshie after the minister advised 'if it is laid waste for deer or put under sheep ... it will prove a thorn in the side of the tennants and gall them exceedingly'.[170] The duke of Gordon too rejected large-scale sheep farming, declining in December 1776 an offer from James Bryden at Kailzie near Peebles: of £100 sterling *per annum* for a nineteen-year lease on the forest of Glen Avon (for sheep-farming)—bidding also for Robert Willox's farm at Gaulrig 'In order to have a stock of Hay for the support of his Sheep in severe weather'.[171]

Cattle were crucial in improved agriculture. They provided dung. The importance of this was such that, in 1833, Lethen leases contained a clause that obliged the tenant to 'keep a sufficient number of Cattle ... upon the farm'.[172] Cattle sales brought in ready money both to farmers and estates: factor John Lawson sold some 200 Fife cattle every spring during the early decades of the nineteenth century.[173] Cattle trading also connected ordinary farmers with the wider economy: cattle sold to drovers fed urban populations in the south—and during war years also supported armies and navies fighting Napoleon. Money earned from cattle sales was paid in rent and expended on imported manufactures such as salt, coal and ironmongery, and luxuries such as broadcloth, crockery, cotton goods, sugar and tea. Cattle also provided the chief motive power on the farm until the 1790s, though the rising fashion was for horse-power. Lord Kames appreciated the value of the ox, which was 'as tractable as a horse ... going as sweetly without a driver as a couple of horses; directed by voice alone'. He also appreciated that oxen produced dung, were cheaper than horses, needed no shoeing; and furthermore, 'they can be sold to the butcher when past the vigour of work, and their price will be more than sufficient to put young oxen in their stead'.[174] The sentiment was shared by Sir John Sinclair[175] and articulated locally by John Dunbar, minister of Dyke:

> It would be more profitable to carry on the farm-work altogether with oxen, which are fit for every work ... are much more easily maintained, are less liable to sudden diseases, and, in the end, fetch a good price for beef: when old horses must be given to the dogs.[176]

The first *Statistical Accounts* counted up to 1,000 cattle in each laichland parish. In Knockando there were 3,000 head; in Kirkmichael 1,400.[177] Income from cattle sales made up for deficiencies in grain production in upland parishes such as Dallas.[178] Upland parishes continued to earn an income from summer grassing. Though declining, this traffic continued into the 1790s, when around 1,000 head were pastured in the forest of Strathavon.[179]

The breed kept under improving regimes was 'black cattle'. William Leslie explained:

> When the breed of black cattle began to be attended to in this country, a coarse Dutch breed was first introduced: they were more weighty than the native breed, but less handsome, and more difficult to maintain and feed. They gradually disappeared; and the Lancashire breed became for some time a great favourite. They also have been for some time given up, being accounted less handsome and more delicate than the true Scots breed, which is now only raised. Very handsome bulls of this kind have been introduced from the isle of Sky and the Western Highlands.[180]

Black cattle continued predominant in the *New Statistical Accounts*. This was the breed demanded by English graziers.[181] Moray breeders concentrated upon perfecting this native strain, which contained considerable genetic variation, and thus also potential for improvement. An inventory of forty-five beasts owned by the earl of Fife in 1771 included: a black rigged steer; a brander rigged steer; a brown-backed bull; a black white-faced quoy; a white humble quoy, a white scarred steer, and a brown white-faced quoy—though all were of the basic black breed.[182] Similarly, John Anderson's black cattle rouped at Darklass (Dyke & Moy) in 1817 included red, white, brown and dun beasts.[183] Ballindalloch expended particular care upon the home farm herd from around 1800 onwards; and lending out a 'handsome' two-year-old black bull to a fellow enthusiast.[184] During December 1823 the laird of Ballindalloch was in correspondence with Sir John Sinclair on fatstock matters,[185] laying foundations for the estate's famous herd of polled cattle managed by James Mackay from 1835 onwards.[186] Ballindalloch blood eventually flowed in herds worldwide, beginning in 1842 when two of Mackay's 'Durham bulls' began a journey to Australia, on the Moray Firth steamer *Duke of Richmond*.[187] In Speymouth, meanwhile, farmers experimented with cross breeding 'the Highland and Aberdeenshire ... sold when two or three years old to the graziers in Aberdeenshire, and other counties to the south'.[188] Rafford farmers raised 'Highland, polled Aberdeenshire, and short-horned' cattle: 'Much attention' was paid to their improvement, rewarded by 'many of the prizes from agricultural societies'.[189] Alien genes also improved the Gordon castle herd, following the purchase, in 1838, of a 'short horned' bull whose pedigree could be traced back five generations.[190]

A couple of hundred horses were counted in each parish around 1790: 'of the common sort reaching 13 hands' in Dyke & Moy; 'small and of a very indifferent quality' in Edinkillie. The Duffus minister amplified: 'We plough all with horses, and these are of an indifferent breed'.[191] The spread of iron ploughs after 1800 required an improved breed of horses to draw them; and with the modern implements, the new mystery of the horseman emerged. In Birnie the native breed of horse persisted, admired as: 'small, but very active, and admirably adapted for ploughing the light land of which this parish is chiefly composed'.[192] Horses also replaced oxen for drawing carts, though William Leslie thought the change was not for any practical reason but because:

> servants, who in any journey beyond the farm, prefer driving carts, as their superiors do the barouche or curricle, much beyond the speed of the ox ... An ordinary tenant could not hire servants at all, were oxen only to compose the teams.[193]

The duke of Gordon engaged in a profitable breeding business, advertising in the public prints: for example on 28 April 1783—'To cover at Gordon Castle ... YOUNG SOUTH & an Arabian' for half a guinea plus half-a-crown to the keeper;[194] and in November 1837—a pair of carriage horses, several mares and a colt sired by Tam o' Shanter.[195] Commercial breeders travelled Moray with their stallions. John Boswell in Aberdeen offered a remarkable Clydesdale, named 'Flare-up', to improve the 'poor breed of farm horses' in Moray, in 1837.[196] Forres farmers were spoiled for choice around 1840. Nigel, 'a strong black horse of beautiful symmetry ... sixteen hands high', was advertised by the farmer of Gervallie at Relugas. The 'young horse Noble' was recommended for his pedigree: 'got by that far-famed Horse, LEIVLY, who gained two successive premiums in the Carse of Gowrie and was sold in England for a ransom ... his Dame ... from the purest Clydesdale Breed'. Young Lively (no relation) 'was got by that celebrated Horse Chance ... his Dam was an excellent Clydesdale Mare'. 'That celebrated horse, Highland Laddie, was bred ... near Coldstream ... got by Mr Frame's celebrated Clydesdale Horse Glance, out of an English Mare'—and available in Moray for 'One Pound each Mare, and One Shilling to the Groom'.[197] Heavy horses were, though, already at work on laichland farms. For example, farm stocking rouped at Wester Alves, advertised on 10 April 1838, included '4 Pair of powerful Work Horses, being a cross breed betwixt the Clydesdale and Perthshire'.[198] And in Elgin, 'inferior' horses had been replaced before 1835 by 'The best breeds of horses from the southern counties ... more compact, active, strong horses are seldom to be met with than those in the possession of the Morayshire farmers'.[199] Many of these traced their ancestry to a stallion named Montalto, who was made available to farmers, during the first decade of the new century, by the Morayshire Farmer Club.[200]

Tools and power

New tools and equipment were required to conduct the new farming regime and to cultivate the new crops. The headline innovation was horse-hoeing—introduced in the tract *Horse-Hoeing Husbandry* (published, 1731).[201] Its author, Jethro Tull, was apotheosed in his own lifetime into the firmament of improvement, and embraced into the Scottish pantheon of improvers when 'A treatise on horse-hoeing husbandry' in the *Scots Magazine* during 1748,[202] urged the method as the 'best manner of preparing and dressing of land'. The technique, introduced an ethos of intensive cultivation, with relentless ploughing and harrowing, reducing soils to the finest tilth and eradicating weeds. Horse-hoeing and the sowing of crops in straight-line drills inscribed the arable fieldscape with a new straight grain. Horse-hoeing was notably practised for the cultivation of turnips—the headline crop of improved agriculture, though, in the transition from old methods to new, some adopted the 'barbarous practice' of sowing broadcast.[203] However, once sown—and even with a horse-hoe—turnips required laborious thinning, normally with a hand hoe, ensuring work in spring for agricultural day-labourers.[204] Nor did the eighteenth-century farmer understand why intensive cultivation gave increased yields. Indeed, it was commonly believed that hoeing pulversied the soil into particles of a small enough size to be absorbed directly by the plant; 'also that the continual stirring with the hoe facilitated the passage of dew to the roots—the reverse of what we now know about capilliary action'.[205]

'But it was the ploughs that they talked about most ... in the early days of the new farmtouns'.[206] The improved iron-mouldboard (or all-iron) plough designed by James Small was 'boldly' recommended by Lord Kames;[207] while Sir John Sinclair declared 'James Small is the artist to whom hitherto Scotland has been most indebted'.[208] Kames encouraged Small to publish *A Treatise on Ploughs and Wheeled Carriages* (Edinburgh, 1784). Detailed plans in the book ensured that Small's implements could be copied by any provincial blacksmith who chose to ignore the author's patents.[209] Thus Small's design was refined by the Grants of Craigellachie into the 'Standfast' ploughs, which became standard equipment throughout the north-east.[210] By the time Small's plough was approved by the king, 'farmer George' in 1791, it had been known to Moray improvers for two decades. In 1771, a plough of this improved kind illustrated a plan of Coxtoun estate—though perhaps the depiction represented aspiration rather than observation as the surveyor George Taylor, pandered to the improving predilections of his noble client.[211] Improved ploughs were certainly used on laichland farms by the 1790s: 'generally used' in Speymouth, though drawn in the old manner by '2 horses ... with 4 oxen, or a mixture of oxen and cows'. Improved and Scotch ploughs were both used in Urquhart, while 'Those whose farms are in good order' in Rafford were said to plough with two horses—perhaps implying a Small plough. In Knockando, however—just a ferry ride across the Spey from the Standfast works—there was only one modern plough among 'about 150 ploughs, all of the Scotch kind'.[212]

Improved equipment cemented the mutual relationship between agricultural and industrial revolutions. While improved agriculture supplied industrial populations with food, expanding industry supplied the iron that was increasingly important in agricultural machinery. The new equipment required skills beyond the handicraft of a tenant farmer, who turned therefore to specialist manufacturers. Iron tools were expensive. James Donaldson reckoned that an improved plough cost 30s to 50s (compared with less than 10s for a Scotch plough). An iron-toothed harrow cost 8s or 10s (compared with half a merk Scots for a wooden-toothed implement). A dung cart with an iron axle cost from £6 to £7 (compared with 4s 6d for a kelloch—which the farmer might construct for himself).[213] Costs rose even higher during the next generation. In 1835 the prices quoted (in Knockando) were, £3 6s for an iron plough; and £6 10s for a full mounted cart. Unsurprisingly, it was reported here at least that improvement was held back by 'want of capital'.[214] Faced with such costs tenants were naturally cautious regarding the benefits of a new agriculture, whose implementation seemed ruinously expensive. The minister of Dyke & Moy noted:

> proprietors ... are too apt to complain of the slow progress of new methods among their farmers, which they erroneously impute to stupidity or obstinacy; but, considering how many richer people have suffered deeply, by new experiments and speculations in husbandry, it is a lucky circumstance for landlords that tenants are not so venterous.

Nonetheless, even here it was reported: 'Box-carts are coming in use for kellochs'.[215] The earl of Fife incentivised tenants to invest in improved equipment, urging his factor:

> I think the Experiment might be tryed upon my giving [the tenants] 10 or 12 good Murray Carts [costing about £4 Scots each] ... And that every Tenant that gets a Cart from me should be obliged to buy another for himself.

Moray carts represented only a slight improvement on the kelloch, and a subsequent note recommended more substantial vehicles mounted with iron.[216] An inclination to 'industry and frugality' among Dallas craftsmen exploited the demand for sturdier carpenter-made equipment. However, the output of Dallas 'cart and cart-wheel wrights', noticed in 1790–91, did not develop into a lasting industry.[217]

Mechanical fanners for winnowing grain were developed from the early eighteenth century, notably in developments of James Meikle's design, which sold in southern Scotland from 1737. The fanner indirectly influenced farm architecture. With a machine to generate an artificial wind, the farmer was no longer obliged to site his barn so that opposed doorways could catch a through-draught for winnowing.[218]

Andrew Meikle (son of James), an East Lothian millwright, took the mechanisation of the barn a stage further with his threshing machine—invented around 1743—with an improved and water-powered version patented in 1788.[219] By the 1790s threshing machines were commonplace in Moray, especially in eastern parishes where 'almost all the extensive corn-farms ... are provided with these machines: they are turned by 2 or by 4 horses, or by the power of water; and they cost from L.40 to about L.60'.[220] At this price a threshing machine represented a considerable capital investment. It says much for the profitability of agriculture (albeit unsustainably enhanced by high wartime prices)—and the sanguine expectations of some farmers—that, even before the turn of the century, so many embraced expensive mechanisation. By 1842, most Forres farms used horse-powered threshing mills, and in Rafford the minister declared: 'Thrashing mills are now almost universal'.[221]

Threshing machines were mainly made of wood, and might be fabricated by parochial wrights, with ironwork supplied by local smiths.[222] However, the iron capstans and driveshafts, with gearing, and bronze bearings required installation by professional millwrights.[223] The horse-gang that powered the threshing machine is the ubiquitous feature of early improved farmsteads: typically surviving as circular raised platform behind the barn, with a culvert to contain the driveshaft.[224] At Altnaha in Inveravon a horse-powered threshing mill in a turf-walled barn remained in use within living memory.[225] Prosperous farmers provided a roofed building, blistering obtrusively from the barn wall, to protect the gin horses from the elements—and to advertise their own modernity. The Ballindalloch specification of 17 July 1808 is typical:

> Horse Shade ... Built in the form of an Octagon with the Pillars 8 feet each, 2 feet thick and 8 feet 3 inches high the deamiter to be 29 feet 6 inches within walls.

The works cost more than £100, which included £55 0s 7½d to Alexander Naughty, miln wright, from Whitefield by Elgin, for installing the machinery, with a further £7 10s 1$^{6}/_{12}$d for additional smithwork, cast iron brought from Aberdeen, Swedish bar iron, and 8 lb. of brass for bushes.[226]

From the 1830s water power was increasingly applied to threshing, especially in upland parishes; even on settler farms such as Quirn below Carn Daimph in Glenlivet, or the marginal improvement at Lynemore in Knockando.[227] The weirs, dams and lades of these works are significant landscape features, the result of detailed surveying, considerable excavation and subtle calculations. Skilled masonwork was required for the substantial buildings to support the iron mill wheels that epitomise the industrialisation of agriculture. These works, beyond the means of ordinary tenants, received financial support from the landowner. Thus, in autumn 1837 Fife's trustees considered allowing £50 towards the cost of a new threshing mill at Marcassie, Rafford; and £24 for erecting a dam and making 'a cut bringing water' to Alexander Lumsden's 'thrashing mill' at Blervie Mains.[228] The entailed Gordon estates paid for: 'mason for excavation of lead' and 'covering wase lead [and] water wheel' to finish a threshing mill at Drumin in 1840; also £92 13s 1d for a mill building at Croughly, Kirkmichael in 1839; and a 'Threshing Mill House' costing over £150 at Minmore in Glenlivet.[229]

Sir John Sinclair noticed in 1814 a new phase in the mechanisation of farm work. He observed, 'where coal can be had at a moderate expence, some would reckon steam power superior even to water'. A handful of engines already provided power to the barns of the 'most improved' farms in southern Scotland. However, Sir John was lukewarm in his recommendation of the new technology; and his estimate of the costs involved (£300 for an engine plus £100 for a threshing machine, with the cost of coal on top) placed such mechanical marvels beyond the reach of most Moray farmers during the 1820s and 1830s.[230]

By about 1840 new crops, new beasts and new regimes were firmly established in the Moray farmscape. Innovation was encouraged by the zeal and practical support of improving proprietors; but effected by the toil and enterprise of the tenant farmer. The new agriculture required a radical change of mind among husbandmen, who became capitalistic producers, investing time, money and energy in the short-term, in the expectation of future profit. Tentative mechanisation laid foundations for industrialised agriculture, though the superstructure of thoroughly mechanised farming would be constructed by subsequent generations. Meantime, the new agriculture involved relentless physical labour; and the vigorous activity of the improving farmer struck a contrast that might make the routines of the cooperative countryside seem like licensed indolence. This regime of continual busyness was well established in the laich by around 1800.[231]

The improvers established a technological paradigm for agricultural operations. Iron ploughs sliced deep, surgically-precise, straight furrows. Iron harrows scarified the ploughsoil to a tilth, raking in a measure of caustic lime. Relentless ploughing, hoeing and harrowing eliminated wildflowers—redefined as weeds in the improvers' agricultural lexicon. High-stepping Clydesdales made an energetic contrast with the humble garrons and plodding oxen that powered the cooperative countryside. Horsedrawn carts with iron axles and spoked wheels brought a briskness—even a sense of dash and style—to humdrum activities such as spreading dung or lifting turnips. The clatter of mechanical threshing replaced the dreary tyranny of the hand-flail; while fanners in the barn made a breeze at the farmer's convenience, without waiting upon the caprice of providence. In Moray—as in Scotland generally—no one broke the machines or opposed their introduction. Indeed, modern equipment and highly-bred ploughteams were a lure to attract the best farm workers; thus capital investment yielded an instant dividend.[232] Even modest technological change might have significant consequences. Smooth-bladed sickles replaced serrated hooks, significantly speeding the harvest; then, from around 1805, English scythes accelerated the pace again and the female shearers were replaced by male scythemen.[233] But no one rioted to suppress the innovation.

Mechanisation and retooling on the farm created employment opportunities, and new hierarchies and skills within the rural workforce. The ploughman was 'the craftsman of the old farmtouns';[234] and he was supported by associated artisans, including farriers who serviced the horses; saddlers who supplied the tack. Rural craftsmen—smiths, millwrights, cartwrights, wheelwrights—manufactured and maintained the farmers' increasingly complex gear. Agriculture, however, remained dependent upon hand labour. The endless toil of field work under improved regimes, ensured employment for Moray's displaced sub-tenants and cottars, as well as drawing in harvest gangs that included highlanders and locals—all in search of the rising money wages that were generated by Moray's agricultural revolution.[235]

9

BUILDING REGULATION

Classicising the laird's house

The domestic ideal for a rational gentleman was epitomised poetically by John Pomfret (1667–1702):

Near some fair Town, I'd have a private Seat,
Built Uniform, not Little, nor too Great:
Better, if on a Rising Ground it stood;
Fields on this side, on that a Neighbouring Wood.
It shou'd within no other Things contain,
But what were Useful, Necessary, Plain.[1]

Archibald Grant of Monymusk picked up the theme in 1719 when he recorded his dismay at the irregularity of his own seat. Expressing himself in the persona of an exasperated gentle-everyman, Monymusk's catalogue of inconvenience spoke for the whole towerhouse-owning class of north-east Scotland.

The house was an old castle with battlements and six different roofs of various heights and directions, confusedly and inconveniently combined, and all rotten, with two wings more modern, of two stories only, the half of the windowes of the higher riseing above the roofs, with granaries, stables and houses for all cattle, and of the vermine attending to them, close adjoining.[2]

In fact many laird's houses (including most of Monymusk) were, in the first half of the eighteenth century, scarcely 150 years old, the product a great rebuilding during two or three generations following the Reformation. Few towerhouses, probably, were structurally unsound; and many successfully combined defensibility with comfort. Indeed, Innes house (built around 1645) accommodated, behind a defensible façade, interiors that were suitable without fundamental alteration (as a second home at least) for the earl of Fife in the late eighteenth century—when the house was admired as a happy conjunction of 'the magnificence of the Gothic castle to the elegance of the modern seat',[3] 'ranked among the most elegant mansions of the county'.[4]

Defensible mansion places, such as Burgie, Blervie and Kilbuiack, were far from comfortless or incapable of being upgraded at least to the Innes standard. Indeed, fortalices at Brodie and Ballindalloch were both successfully enlarged and modernised. Bawm walls were removed and courtyard offices relocated.[5] This left towerhouses impressively and picturesquely isolated in the landscape: making space for the addition of new wings with politely symmetrical façades; and opening vistas onto landscaped policies, civilised with careful planting and artificial lakes. The small laird's houses of Kilmaichlie and Easter Elchies were readily modernised by removal of bawms and insertion of symmetrical fenestration with regular twelve-pane sash windows.[6]

In general, though, as landowners' military role evaporated following the union of 1707, their cultural horizons expanded, and genteel tastes increasingly regarded ancestral fortalices as barbaric anachronisms. Reasonable gentlemen in a peaceful and rational age, preferring to live their enlightened lives in domestic comfort behind an orderly façade, initiated a new spasm of rebuilding. Moray landowners shared sentiments articulated in 1734 by John Drummond of Quarrel in Stirlingshire: 'I desire no more vaults nor any grates to the windows'. Rather than 'echoes of ruins' Moray lairds yearned with Drummond for 'a convenient little habitation ... done frugally and effectively'.[7] 'Convenience' became a defining concept for internal arrangements: indeed, 'convenience' remains a key term in the estate agents' lexicon. Convenience implied, of course, an absence of physical discomforts in the form of smoke, draughts, smells, damp, dark rooms, and space shared with domestic staff; but convenience also encompassed the moral and psychological comfort of a dwelling that was not just a shelter—far less a military stronghold—but a suitable setting for a gentleman of wealth and taste, and also a home.[8] The rational design of William Young's exemplary house at Inverugie, especially attracted William Leslie's approval as: 'a neat, clean and commodious dwelling in which convenience more than show has been studied'.[9]

Convenience was delivered by the emerging architectural profession. The new mystery was dominated by men educated in the neoclassical style that was the Enlightenment design standard. A national architectural template was founded in the regular mansions of Hopetoun House and Kinross House, designed by William Bruce during the 1690s.[10] The new house of Balvenie, in Mortlach, designed by James Gibbs in 1722 for William Duff, Lord Braco (later earl of Fife),[11] epitomised regular style and rational convenience—and was applauded even half a century later as 'a handsome regular modern seat'.[12] Its symmetrical pedimented front was echoed in the houses provided for the senior officers at Fort George, designed in 1747 by William Skinner, built by William Adam.[13] Thus Moray improvers might look south, east or west for models which country masons might follow.

New builds in Moray were scarcely behind national trends. In Elgin's high street, houses turned through ninety degrees to present symmetrical façades to the high street; regular fenestration, pedimented dormers, and street-front 'piazzas' supported by couthy Ionic capitals, all appeared before 1700.[14] Stair turrets were relegated to the rear; or staircases were absorbed into the heart of the house. Meanwhile, the plain, harled, three-storeyed block of Duffus House, commissioned by Archibald Dunbar of Thunderton in the early eighteenth century, earned an improver's approval nearly a century later when described as 'a handsome modern seat'.[15] Extravagant round squares of service buildings, erected for the polymath Sir Robert Gordon at Gordonstoun and Dallas, introduced radical (and rational) architectural style simultaneously into laichland and upland Moray. Gordonstoun house also experienced early classicisation with a makeover that smoothed irregularities of the fortalice façade and added matching two-storeyed wings around 1730.[16] William Bruce's pupil, William Adam, brought cosmopolitan classicism north with a flamboyant palace near Banff, designed in 1735 for Lord Braco. In the event Duff House proved a white elephant, subject to legal dispute, during its first owner's lifetime. Though never completed, Duff's house demonstrated what might be done by the determined application of money and modern taste.[17]

Moray's landowners absorbed modern architectural concepts during their normal peregrinations within Scotland, into England and through Europe on the grand tour. Stay-at-home proprietors discovered modern design in architectural publications, which formed a significant genre within the Enlightenment information boom.[18] Architectural pattern-books were marketed on the basis that their exemplary designs were sufficient for landowners and provincial craftsmen to follow and adapt. James Gibbs' *Book of Architecture* (London, 1728) was specifically advertised to be 'of use to such gentlemen, especially in the remoter areas of the Country, where little or no assistance for Designs can be procured'. Gentlemen were encouraged to mix and match architectural styles, using designs generously shared by E. Hoppus in *The Gentleman's and Builder's Repository* (1737); by William James in *The Gentlemen's or Builders' Companion: Containing ... Useful Designs for Doors, Gateways, Peers, Pavilions, Temples, Chimney-Pieces* (1739); and in several William Halfpenny publications, with plans and details ranging from farmhouses to modish chinoiserie. Robert Morris and T. Lightoler offered in *The Modern Builder's Assistant ... Regular Plans ... for Noblemen, Gentlemen or Tradesmen with Large or Small Families* (London, 1757). George Jameson published *Thirty-three designs with the orders of architecture according to Palladio* (Edinburgh, 1765) with plans of double-pile houses with symmetrical façades, which he intended should be 'in the hands of every mechanick concerned in a building' thus ending the 'prevailing abuses' and 'monstrous enormities' of inept architects.[19] John Cruden compiled a guide to *Convenient and Ornamental Architecture ... beginning with the farm house, and regularly ascending to the most grand and magnificent villas* (London, 1770). *The Rudiments of Architecture* (Edinburgh, 1778), enjoyed seventy years in print. *The Rudiments* included 'Twenty-three Elegant Designs of Buildings', and pedantic instructions on correct proportions, for example: 'stairs should be large and spacious ... the number of steps at every landing be odd ... the bigness and number of windows be proportional to the rooms they enlighten, and their height double their breadth ... all principal chambers of delight be placed towards the best prospects of the country, and, if possible to the east'.[20]

Moray's nurturing of architects did not match its prolific spawning of land surveyors, though three were recognised in Elgin in 1825.[21] The work of only one is clearly identifiable. William Robertson, 'Architect in Elgin' (1786–1841), was a native of Aberdeenshire. He may have trained under John Paterson in Edinburgh, or perhaps with William Playfair—connections that joined him to the mainstream of polite architecture. Robertson's work spanned a large range of domestic and public buildings, in a variety of neoclassical and native styles throughout north-east Scotland. His client list included leading improvers. His public buildings dignified both Elgin and Forres. He designed an Italianate school building at Auldearn, under Brodie patronage. He designed Hopeman Lodge, around 1840, for William Young of Inverugie; and added airy drawing rooms for the Duffs at Orton. In 1828 he was commissioned by Charles Grant (who made his pile in Canada as a supplier to the Navy) to add a convenient new wing to his castle at Wester Elchies;[22] and, in 1830 Roberton designed a suburban townhouse for the family in Elgin, with conveniences including 'Hot Shower baths and two Water closets'. Robertson designed manses at Grange (1814) and Rothes (1838). He also designed a new house in laichland sandstone for Alexander Grant at Aberlour: 'a mansion of architectural merit that holds its own by British as well as by Scottish standards'. In the grounds, Robertson erected a Doric gate lodge, sister building to his pontage house at Boat o' Brig—and a sixty foot high 'Tuscan column'.[23]

In the main, Moray's great rebuilding was effected by ordinary masons, who never adopted the title architect and who often rémain anonymous—but who competently plundered pattern-book designs to satisfy clients' specifications. Only rarely was the architect role of a mason or wright acknowledged in records. Usually these men appear only as craftsman-contractors: unusually, James Ogilvie, master mason, is recognised as the designer of Pittensier in 1735; and James Robertson, carpenter in Fochabers, was credited as a designer—'Laying down a plan and Specification' for Gordon tenants' houses and farm buildings at Tomballie, Auchenhalrig, Oxhill, Byres and Tulloch.[24]

The craze for classical modernity among landowners was expressed in regular, double-pile houses with symmetrical aspects, ashlar façades, and assemblages of pediments, columns and pilasters. Low-pitched pavilion roofs (or gabled roofs with plain stone skews) were preferred in a reaction to the steep pitches, turrets and crow-steps of towerhouse architecture.

Grant Lodge, the Elgin townhouse of the lairds of Grant, offered a model of neoclassical convenience for the laich in the 1750s. At Moy, in 1762, Sir Ludovick Grant firmly planted the new classicism in the countryside: replacing an inconvenient two-storey laird's house with a 'handsome manor'—a neoclassical mansion of three storeys, designed by John Adam and built by Colen Williamson (subsequently architect of the White House in Washington).[25] Forres House, in similar style, was a 'magnificent modern structure', occupied as a townhouse by the Cummings of Altyre, who purchased the place from Lady Tannachy in 1789.[26]

Comfortable classicism was embraced by smaller landowners in the laich from the 1770s onwards, using a template that was becoming common throughout Scotland. The symmetrical, double-pile, stone-and-slate box of the laichland mansion, typically comprised two principal floors—with attics above hidden by pediment, parapet or balustrade, and a semi-basement below containing kitchens and service rooms. The front door stood at the head of a sweep of stone steps; and some architectural trouble was taken to dignify the doorcase. A fireplace was provided for each principal room: this convenience was advertised externally in matching slabs of chimney stack, usually rising from the end walls. A double-pile design with central circulation made a feature of the entrance hall and principal staircase, located at the heart of the house, in a specific reaction to the inconvenience of the towerhouse turnpike. This, with separate circulation for servants (who were segregated to constricted stairs at the rear) underlined social differences within the household and emphasised a new fashion for privacy. Cosmetic variations personalised the design with a pick-and-mix of neoclassical features: pilasters, balusters and urns for Sir Archibald Grant at Dalvey (*c.* 1770); giant pilasters and rusticated basement masonry at Grange Hall (1805); Venetian windows for General James Grant of Tannachy (1818).[27] A spartan lack of ornament and austere ashlar dignified Highfield, the suburban Elgin townhouse of Sir Archibald Dunbar (*c.* 1820), which provided a model for subsequent suburban villa developments.[28] William Leslie admired the house of Grange as representing a pinnacle of convenience and taste:

> a new fabric, a quadrangle of 60 by 40 feet. The walls are of freestone, smoothly cut, and jointed accurately by the chisel ... The two great rooms are on the principal floor ... they are large well-proportioned apartments, elegantly finished ... The square form of the building admits of having all the rooms more commodiously disposed to one another, than houses with more extended and more varied fronts.[29]

Pitgavney (1776) and Orton (1786) stood taller than their neighbours, with three full storeys, in a 'high classical cube' above basement service rooms—a style that suggested Moray builders had learned a lesson taught by Robert Adam (1773) at Letterfourie in Rathven.[30] On a smaller, three-bay, frontage, the style was adapted for the master of Lochinver, who could afford only one-storey living, though with basement below and lofts above. Social aspiration was expressed in architecture as prosperous tenant farmers and professional men adopted the lairdly template (usually single-pile), with pedimented façades and classicised porches on the outskirts of Forres. Stynie farmhouse also has a pedimented central bay, and is built double-pile with a fireplace in every room. 'The Cottage' in Archiestown was constructed in 1790 of squared Ben Rinnes granite with projecting pavilion wings, in the manner of a regular gentleman's place, but single-storeyed.[31]

It is tempting suppose that new lairds' houses were built on foundations of agricultural improvement: 'as agriculture became more profitable, generating more capital that could be directed to house building'.[32] However, Moray's building boom was driven by fashion, not by increased income. A regular house proclaimed the proprietor's enlightenment, and his integration in the British cultural mainstream. A new house, anticipating the profits of improvement, advertised a heritor's confidence in the ultimate benefits of agricultural reform. The new house of Lethen was finished in 1788—at which date written leases had scarcely begun the regularisation of Lethen's Moray estate.[33] Gordonstoun House was comprehensively classicised in 1775 with a Corinthian doorcase, an ashlar façade and regular fenestration offering views to enclosed parks and a linear water-feature (established a generation earlier)—even though agricultural improvement had scarcely begun among tenants.[34] The expense of rebuilding the laird's place could be met, it seems, from surplus rents accruing even from an estate largely under cooperative agricultural regimes; or rebuilding might be founded upon external sources of income including business ventures and public office. Nor was a new house oppressively costly. A small laird's house might cost no more than £300; and this price might be covered by the ordinary landowners' usual budget for luxuries.[35] However, fixtures, fittings and furniture might cost as much as the house: significantly, the Gordonstoun interior was not completed.

Nostalgic romanticism was an inevitable reaction to regular classicism. Elizabeth Grant of Rothiemurchus was charmed in 1809 by the 'romantick' ruin of the old Burgie tower, but disappointed by the convenient 'tea cannister' (1802) house that replaced it:[36] the same house was admired by William Leslie as possessing 'all the splendid elegance of modern architecture ... much symmetry ... and a strikingly just proportion'.[37] A taste for the picturesque and for medieval style, at least in a gentrified regular form, took hold even as towerhouses were being abandoned. The fashion was reinforced by gothic novels and romantic poetry, as an inevitable reaction to regular neoclassicism. Early architectural exemplars included Inveraray (1745) and Douglas Castle (1757), which gave aristocratic legitimacy to faux medieval style;[38] and in Moray it was the great magnates who most conspicuously embraced gothic architecture. Alexander, fourth duke of Gordon, insisted that the six-storeyed tower of his house at Bog of Gight be retained as a focal feature of his new palace, designed by John Baxter in 1769.[39] In this Gordon shared an inclination with the earl of Mar who preserved his own ancestral tower when renovating Alloa House, because 'There is something in the old Tower ... which is venerable for its antiquity and makes not a bad appearance, and would make one regrait being oblig'd to pull it down'.[40] The new Gordon castle was built of laichland freestone, extending symmetrically outwards from its irregular centrepiece. William Leslie declared the castle an exemplar of 'superb and elegant ... modern architecture', surpassing 'the most splendid English palace'; admiring its fashionable gothic details and handsome battlements. Charles Cordiner approved of the design, which, 'though still in character of a castle, it is at once an elegant and majestic edifice'. Lord Cockburn, however, 'despised' the building, and felt that an hour spent visiting the 'contemptible' castle in 1839 was an hour wasted. The magnificence of the interiors impressed Leslie and also the authors of early guidebooks, though none applauded the house for its convenience.[41] Darnaway castle, seat of the earls of Moray, was rebuilt 1802–12, preserving the medieval hall and adding convenient Georgian apartments in 'a huge pile of building' combining 'a Grecian front, and window ornaments of a Gothic character', trimmed with crenellations and 'dinky turrets'.[42] To some observers, however, aristocratic gothic seemed like architectural excess, though cautious critics were careful not to identify offending lords by name.

> ... see where yon modern Gothic pile,
> But lately rear'd—its huge fantastic stile
> Bespeaks the owner's poor perverted taste;
> The passing stranger smiles to see such waste
> Of stone and mortar.[43]

Colonel Hay of Westerton built in gothic style: a style above his station, which irritated other landowners, and exacerbated poor relations with neighbours. Westerton's provocative place—encrusted with towers, turrets, hood-moulds, crenellations and a vast perpendicular window—was built of granite, carted from Speyside at extravagant expense.[44] Despite classicists' disapproval, regular gothic style became established in the fashionable repertoire and appropriate for the most modern erections. Thus castellated piers decorated Telford's iron bridge across the Spey at Craigellachie, completed in 1815, and admired for its 'utility of lightness' by the romantic poet Robert Southey.[45]

A new vernacular

Stone walls, slate roofs, double fronts, symmetrical façades, gable-end chimney stacks, square quoins, and occasional classical details to dignify a doorcase, descended the social scale in both town and country. The renewal of ordinary rural tenants' houses (and subsequently the homes of labourers) from around 1760 fully conforms to the defining criterion for a 'Great Rebuilding' as: 'The changeover from building for a limited life to building for an indefinite life'.[46]

Several prosperous tenant farmers adopted regular architectural style ahead of their betters. The tall farmhouse of Dykeside in Birnie, was probably built around 1750, with gable-end chimney stacks and copings typical of the early eighteenth century, serving fireplaces on both the lower and upper floors. It stands two full storeys high, with central doorway and symmetrically arranged windows with distinctive moulded margins beneath a roof of schistose stone slates. The dwelling shares features with a 1696 house in Elgin; also with Pittensier in St Andrews-Lhanbryd, built in 1735.[47] This small-house template is seen outwith Moray at Old Auchentroig, Stirlingshire (1702) and Udrigle, Ross-shire (1745).[48] James Gordon (1726–1812), the aspirational tenant of Croughly in highland Kirkmichael, built his regular stone farmhouse with flanking wings (and tasteful Georgian panelling on box beds in the principal room) around 1760.[49] Other early regular buildings may remain to be recognised, perhaps to push back the starting-date for the regular revolution in Moray building.

Older estate customs hampered improvement of housing insofar as they allowed tenants to claim, at the end of a tenancy, only the value of woodwork in buildings. Furthermore, the uncertainties of a tenancy at will and short tacks—and the relative mobility of township folk—meant there was little incentive to invest in long-lasting stone-walled buildings. Nonetheless, some Ballindalloch tenants occupied stone-walled buildings by 1742, when the baron court noted a nineteen-year tack granted for the possession of Francis Grant in Kirktown of Inveravon. Under this, the laird reimbursed the cost of masons' work on Grant's house, but not the value of stones and lime; the heritor also repaid the cost of masonwork in Grant's barn, stable, kiln and byre at 5s Scots per ell. The court further noted, in 1749, 'the old Stone Chamber' at Wester Bellilleglash, where the tenant was due the value of:

> any stone walls of the houses to be built by him ... at the rate of five shillings Scots for Each Eln thereof in length that Shall be one Eln and one half Eln in height Sufficiently built with dry Stone or Stones with Clay or lime.[50]

In general, allowances for the cost of stone walls and masons' work (in addition to structural timber) came only slowly into Moray leases as improvement took hold. Strathavon tacks of

1765 occasionally encouraged improvement of dwellings from turf-and-cruck to stone-and-rafter. Donald Martin accepted Mid Tomachlagan with the proviso:

> if the houses be meliorate by Timber he is to be paid therefore ... or have Liberty to carry away the same, And if they be Meliorate by Mason work, he is to be paid for Lime & Workmanship.[51]

The condition was, at first, conferred only grudgingly, and insofar as it served the estate's immediate interests. Thus on 17 December 1772 the duke wrote:

> to encourage John Steward in Torbain, my Forrester in Strathaven & Glenlivat, to keep good houses upon that possession, I shall allow him meliorations at his removal to the Extent of One years rent—in which nothing is to be considered for walls but such as are built sufficiently of Stone & Lime.[52]

The Urquhart schoolmaster, George Morrison, probably spoke for the whole community when he wrote to the duke of Gordon's cashier on 6 July 1776. Morrison advised that he intended rebuilding his turf house with 'good stone and mud walls', provided he received the value of the new walls at the end of his tack. He pointed out further that 'there has been no allowance hitherto in this place for walls, which makes us live in hutts rather than honest houses'.[53]

Improvement of housing stock was achieved by improving leases on other estates, marching more or less in step with Gordon from the 1770s onwards. Allowances for the value of masons' work, stone, wood, glass and iron in tenants' houses were inserted into Brodie leases from at least 1791, when William Smith was promised up to £60 in respect of a possession rented at £55 per annum.[54] Ballindalloch conditions of lease, published around 1800, allowed all tenants to receive the value of house walls, 'provided that such houses are ... built of stone and lime or stone and clay pinned with lime'.[55] Typically an allowance for meliorations, which included dwellings, farm buildings and sometimes also stone enclosure dykes, was limited to one year's rent. The cost of rebuilding tenants' houses in stone did not necessarily fall upon the estate. Usually, leases specified that the value of a farmer's meliorations were charged, when the improver's lease expired, to his successor. Of course, if the tenancy was renewed, the farmer got nothing. This condition appeared in Fife tacks for laichland farms agreed in 1798, under which outgoing tenants were guaranteed a sum equivalent to one year's rent for:

> lime and workmanship of Sufficient Mason work, built with Stone and Mud with or without Straw and harled with lime and for sufficient timber and Straw thatch Covering the same.[56]

The condition was standard in Fife tacks granted 1798–1823, as the estate followed a general trend.[57] Lethen estate allowed 'Meliorations for Buildings .... to the amount of a years rent'; and as estate regulations, around 1800, forbade the cutting of 'feals or divots for biggings', tenants had little choice but to build with 'stone and lime, or stone and mortar sneck-pinned with lime, and covered with slate or bent thatch, and not divot'.[58] In practise, though, divot continued to be cut, to provide an underlayer for thatch, long into the nineteenth century. Thus on 4 July 1837 a Forres craftsman, Alexander Smith, was employed by Lethen 'to finish … the Carpenter Work Divots and Bent of Angus Finlays House at Wester Cottertown'.[59] Elsewhere, for example among the small farms of Coxtown, divot insulated corrugated iron roofs even in the twentieth century.

The accelerating pace of rebuilding was not widely recognised in the first *Statistical Accounts*. Indeed it was the 'meanness' of houses that attracted notice in Duffus. Several Rafford farmers had built 'decent' houses, though the dwellings of Grange tenants were 'mean'. In Spynie, though, Mr Russel of Westfield had 'built houses for the inhabitants', presumably in regular modern style.[60] By contrast, William Leslie reported in 1798:

> on every farm of considerable extent, the buildings are sufficiently commodious and neat, of substantial masonry, stone and lime, and for the most part slate, two stories in height … …The dwellings of the mechanics and labourers begin to assume the same neat and substantial form.[61]

A decade later laichland houses were:

> in general of two stories, though in some the upper part is but an attic story. The windows are handsome casements, the roof in general slated … doors, chimneys, windows, and timber ornaments are always painted … they consist of a parlour and drawing room, and 2 or 3 bedchambers. The kitchen is in general a thatched building of one story, adjoined as a wing, with a similar building as a store room, or cellar, on the opposite side.[62]

It had taken a generation to reach this happy situation, which Leslie certainly overstated: turf-and-cruck survived into the nineteenth century in many districts. Be that as it may, an exemplary two-storey regular farmhouse, with matching service-room wings, was the focal feature of a vignette on W. Millar's map of Moray, tipped in to Leslie's *Survey*. In general the one-storey-with-lofts was the standard for Moray farmhouses. A truly prosperous farmer might declare his status with two full storeys; two storeys with lofts was rare in Moray farmhouses, though not unusual for professional men, ministers and burgh merchants. Few if any tenant farmers in Moray achieved the standards of accommodation that gave most satisfaction to possessors of the large farms of Lothian: 'of three stories, the kitchen-story half sunk'—like a Moray manse or small gentleman's place.[63]

New housing was an ornament and an asset for an improved estate. Brodie invested in building works 'to induce persons of sufficient means and respectability to settle as tenants': spending £80 on new houses at Maviston and Penreance; £150 at Moss-side, Easterton and Claypots; £90 at Blinkbonny and Muiryhall.[64] Lethen advanced money for building works to tenants, but at a swingeing 7 per cent interest rate.[65] Lethen also exercised strict control over building standards. Thus in 1834 the settler who tenanted a croft colonising Lethen's waste under a sliding-scale rent, agreed to build:

a good dwelling House framed with wood and built with stone and harled with lime—The side walls not being less than seven feet high ... Wood ... to be provided by the proprietor's forester and five percent to be paid on that value.[66]

New Statistical Accounts reported regular stone houses as commonplace, but nonetheless worth remark. In Alves tenants of large farms possessed 'substantial dwelling houses, of two storeys'. In Drainie tenants' 'old butts and bens, with kitchen and spens, were abolished' during wartime boom years, replaced by 'mansions with dining-rooms, drawing-rooms, and parlours, which they could not afford furnish': though in reality these palatial dwellings were modest two storeyed, single-pile stone-and-thatch (more rarely slate), cottages. In rural Duffus both 'ordinary' and gentleman farmers were 'comfortable in their ... dwellings', and their houses 'cleanly'. Upland rebuilding lagged behind the laich: 'improved of late years' in Knockando; while the Inveravon minister proudly reported:

> Many excellent slated dwelling-houses two storeys high, are to be seen ... Those at Wester Deskie ... are the admiration of strangers ... and would attract attention in any part of the country.[67]

Between turf-and-cruck and stone-and-slate there was a transitional architecture, chiefly evident among settler dwellings, but perhaps once more widespread. The house on the new improvement of Tom Cruim (Bogg More), and its near neighbour above Allt Glander in Strath Avon, constructed around 1770,[68] combined old and new features. Surviving walls were of roughly-coursed, quarried quartzite blocks, with corners regularly square inside and out. Doorways were centrally placed with (probably) a window symmetrically placed on either side. However, the clay-bonded stone walls stood only to sill height, with gable walls rising barely shoulder high. Upper courses of the walls were of turf; the roof was supported on crucks. The fire burned in a hearth on the floor at one end, the gable wall protected with a hearthback slab, and smoke carried away by a hanging lum. The house was probably divided internally by insubstantial partitions, or perhaps by furniture such as box beds. The remains of houses in similar transitional style, some with turf still capping the wallhead, survive elsewhere in Strathavon, for example at Dalbeithachan and Balrianach. None of these transitional houses is now inhabited or entire.[69] Dwellings of this kind have not previously been noticed in Moray, though a somewhat similar style was described in Buchan:

> side-walls are scarcely five feet in height. The door ... is so low that an ordinary-sized person ... requires to bend ... the gables ... are built of turfs ... the roof ... is covered with turfs, which are overlaid with straw ... There are two small windows in front, each containing four panes of glass. There is no ceiling ... Nor is any attempt made at separate apartments by regular partitions. One or two bedsteads, placed in the middle, divide the building into two portions, familiarly denominated a *but* and a *ben*.[70]

In Moray these transitional-style dwellings were occupied by settlers and smallholders: sub-tenants and cottars who, 'deprived of their possessions, were forced to betake themselves to the improvement and cultivation of a piece of waste land ... at a nominal rent for a stipulated number of years'.[71]

A more substantial style of settler house survives at Oldshields on the moor of Coxtown. The house was built of lime-harled or pointed clay-and-bool, the wallheads capped with a deep course of turf. The original dwelling comprised a single room with a door and window in the front wall. The house was dignified with a gable-end fireplace served by a flue in the thickness of the wall and a chimney stack in stumpy early eighteenth-century style. The roof was of unsquared timber and thatched. A house in this style is depicted in a vignette on the Coxtown estate plan of 1771, which celebrates the regularity and prosperity of the improved farmscape.[72] Subsequent extension at Oldshields added a further room, perhaps occupied as a separate dwelling, heated by a clay-and-bool fireplace, freestanding against the gable wall with a timber lum above.

From these early (and arguably experimental) transitional styles, a formal standard developed—and rapidly became the dominant vernacular style in Moray and throughout the north-east. Walls were of stone, usually built as random or roughly-coursed rubble. Dressed stones formed quoins, skews, window dressings, doorways and chimney stacks. Corners were sharply square inside and out. Poorer houses were clay-bonded with lime pointing; larger farmers could afford lime mortar. More pretentious dwellings might boast a front of ashlar or coursed squared stone, perhaps laid in fancy Aberdeenshire bond (of pink granite blocks with grey schist snecks). The new houses were gabled, emphatically rejecting the old-fashioned hips of turf-and-cruck architecture.[73] Stone skews might finish with a fancy skewput: sometimes incised with a date; embellished with scrolls in towns and paper-sailors near the sea; though most were plain. The façade comprised a door with a window on either side, symmetrically arranged, fitted with twelve-pane sashes. Doorcases might be dignified with carved mouldings. The classical symmetry of rural houses, however, was disrupted by addition of a lean-to room attached to the gable, which served as a dairy or toolshed.[74]

The interior of the improved house was divided by timber, lath-and-plaster or plastered wattle-and-daub partitions into two main rooms with a lobby between. The central cell might serve as a bed closet or scullery; it also contained ladder or staircase leading to loft rooms under the thatch or sarking. A fireplace in each gable wall heated the two downstairs rooms. Fireplaces were usually served by flues in the gable and a stumpy chimney stack; though hanging lums may have survived long into the nineteenth century, their former existence masked by subsequent improvements. Labourers' dwellings built at Peterfair above Ballindalloch, around 1820, had low clay-bonded stone walls, and gabled ends with a hearth beneath a hanging lum—a design that was subsequently improved upon when the dwellings were heightened and re-roofed (perhaps replacing crucks with rafter roofs); and hooded masonry fireplaces were inserted with flues contrived within reconstructed gables. Built-in box beds were typically located against the partition wall in downstairs rooms: surviving *in situ* in Kirkmichael: in the high-status farmhouses of Croughly and Ballantruan; in the small farmhouse of Tomlay; and in dwellings among the Crofts of Scalan.

Classically-proportioned houses were embraced by tenants and promoted by landlords as demonstrations of an aspiration to Britishness and conformity with the improving ethos.[75] Regular houses represented a new vernacular, embraced so comprehensively that (apart from castles) no popular memory now survives of any other rural architecture. Houses in the regular style were specified by Elgin town council in 1784 for its fishermen in the Seatown of the replanned town of Lossiemouth:

> Eight of them 30 feet Long within walls 13 feet wide within walls seven feet high from the soul of the Door to the Upper bed of the wall tabling ... all one streight Line each house to be Divided with Stone Gables the Gables at the Extreamity, of each end ... to be Finished with sque Tabling the rest of the gables to be Thatched over ... the whole of the Buildings to be built with Clay ... Thatched with Divots and Clay & Straw ... Each house to have sixteen coples sawen out of 24 feet spars of Abernethy wood And Cabered or Lathed with Backs or Lath sawen from spars ... each house to have Partition of lath Clay and Straw and outer door of Inch Deals with aLock & Key ane Inner Door in the partition with a sneck Crook & bands for each Door ... each house a Timber Lumb.[76]

The joining of houses end-to-end in a terrace, with common gables, (a characteristic of new-town classicism) was an innovation. Otherwise, though, the fisher house specification might describe any small farmhouse in Moray. Houses built to this pattern remain—largely unaltered except for reroofing with corrugated iron or slate—throughout rural Moray; and also generally in new villages, coastal and inland, in the laich and the upland. Houses in this style—with regular façades, stone-and-mud walls and divot-and-thatch roofs—were the basis of the rebuilding in the village of Dyke and the hamlet of Bankhead in 1759, paid for by the laird of Brodie.[77]

Larger farmhouses might boast two full storeys with fireplaces in upstairs rooms, and even a small grate with separate chimney to heat the bed closet behind the stairs. However, even these seldom included a back door, though there might be a rear window to light the bedcloset. Small gable-end windows might light the loft rooms. Slated roofs, nailed to sarking of sawn softwood planks, allowed the insertion of iron-framed skylights. (known as 'Carron lights', because the design was first produced at the Carron ironworks, near Falkirk).[78]

The new vernacular was adopted in town as in the country. Stone houses with gable-end chimneys and regular façades, one or two storeys high, with roofs slated or thatched according to the wealth of the occupant, became the urban norm. High Street properties in Forres were largely rebuilt, two- or three-storeyed in regular style from the 1770s onwards. A few single-storeyed seventeenth-century buildings survived, end-on to the street in the medieval manner; but increasingly street-front properties were rebuilt (some built double-pile) and reoriented to present their regular faces to the highway. Façades were linked, though nine-inch customary gaps were preserved behind. Regular style was further asserted in terraced rows of cottaging—with regular façades, and with the further revolutionary innovation of common gables—curving along the roods behind high street frontages. Occasionally domestic convenience clashed with traditional urban values—breaching medieval building regulations. For example, in 1777 John Young's regular new house irritated neighbours by opening a rear window 'for afternoon sunshine', overlooking the close behind. Young offered to 'Iron stanchion' the offensive light; and he undertook never 'to ... throw anything from that Window'. But Forres was not yet ready for such dramatic innovations.

The 'immemorial Statutes ... of the Burgh' prevailed and the window was blocked up.[79] These considerations did not apply when modern regular dwellings were constructed in new suburban developments, as burghs cautiously broke from their medieval bounds. Houses built in the new vernacular around 1820 rose to two full storeys with drawing room on the first floor and attics above, on the outskirts of both Forres and Elgin.[80]

The town of Findhorn, rebuilt after translation from its older site in 1701, enjoyed a regular rebuilding from around 1770 as dwellings were replaced or renovated in the new vernacular. Regular style was adopted in Garmouth before 1770, perhaps reflecting the relative sophistication of its mercantile community, and the security of feu tenure.[81] Prosperous residents embraced the improved model with regular façades and neoclassical doorcases. However, stone quoins, skews, chimneys and dressings, and slated roofs often dignified dwellings built in vernacular cob or clay-and-bool.

> The houses, many of them three storeys high, are built of clay, kneeded up with straw, in a frame ... they are plastered, or roughcast, with lime, so as to present an extremely good exterior.[82]

Manses

Established-church manses were rebuilt in polite style, from the 1760s onwards, in step with the pace of parochial improvement. The new manses were two storeyed, usually larger than a prosperous tenant's house—their size emphasising the minister's social status. The size of the buidings and the style and opulence of their fittings varied according to the means, taste and generosity of the heritors who funded redevelopment.

The 1775 specification for Inveravon manse required a symmetrical two-storeyed dwelling with a 'tympany Gavel' (a nepus or wallhead gable). The contract, signed by James Anderson, mason in Keith, and Alexander Duffes, wright in Cullen, on 22 and 26 June, called for gable-end chimneys with 'Six Vents for fire Rooms', including a gable-end fireplace for servants in the attic. Stairs were accommodated in a rear 'projection'. The kitchen was a separate detached building.[83] The manse of St Andrews-Lhanbryd was built in similar style, with wallhead gable and gable-end chimneys, but with a larger five-bay frontage.[84]

By about 1840 all the manses of Moray had been rebuilt, the ministers using their *Statistical Account* reports to declare themselves satisfied with the accommodation: 'neat and handsome-looking ... in the cottage style'; 'very handsome and comfortable'; 'excellent'; and 'elegant and commodious'.[85] Urquhart boasted a neoclassical doorcase, fanlight and cornice. Rafford and Aberlour, like little lairds' houses, were entered by a sweep of stairs and a neoclassical doorcase. Forres manse was a tall regular townhouse with a neoclassical doorcase, though, standing end-on to the high street, facing the blank back wall of its neighbour across the close.

Once implemented, improvement engendered its own momentum of ever-rising expectations. This is particularly documented among ministers Thus the Dallas incumbent, jealous, perhaps, of the more modern conveniences enjoyed by brother ministers, complained in 1842 that his house, built in 1783, was 'in very bad repair, and, owing to the miserable state of the interior, a new one is required immediately'.[86] Similarly, though Kinloss manse was rebuilt in 1820 and renovated in 1839, to a 'very neat' design by 'Mr. Gillespie [Graham] of Edinburgh', the minister carped that his accommodation was 'not extensive'.[87] In 1834 William Robertson added a new front to re-orient Inveravon manse, dignifying it with a neoclassical aspect that would have suited a minor laird. Robertson removed the detached kitchen and created a new one in a basement below the new front. He demolished the tympanum that had seemed so gracefully modern to the preceding generation. The projecting stair at the rear of the 1775 house became a servants' stair, establishing separate circulations. Attic accommodation for servants remained as originally built: accessed by a ladder; with only the sarking for a ceiling and internal division by timber backs (with bark still attached) saved from the rough squaring of principal rafters.[88]

Materials and workmanship

The rebuilding of Moray was facilitated by technological, economic and agricultural developments associated with improvement. The builders of Balvenie had lacked suitable local timber in the 1720s; but pinewood for the new house was readily imported as floats from Rothiemurchus, the spars and deals transported from the Spey at no cost by invoking tenants' obligation to undertake carriages.[89] As agricultural improvement progressed, the unsophisticated rafter roofs of ordinary houses were readily framed with the small softwood timber that became available from estate plantations from the 1780s onwards. The same timber was particularly suitable for sawing into joists, panelling, floorboards, washboards and sarking.

Stone has double the density of turf: however, the carriage of building stone was facilitated by the introduction of iron-mounted carts, and also by improvement of road surfaces to meet the needs of the new vehicles. Quarry pits are commonplace in Moray landscapes, indicating where building stone and mud for mortar were won, often within sight of the building site. Fieldstones accumulated on the baulks of runrig land were gathered for rubble work. Freestone for window dressings, doorcases and fashionably square quoins came chiefly from the laich—the building boom supporting significant employment for quarriers working coastal sandstones.[90]　Laichland sandstone was preferred wherever it could be afforded: laid as polished ashlar on the front; but perhaps built as random rubble at the rear, covered with harl for a more genteel finish. Brick was rare, though there is a reference to the burning of 'a first kiln' of 10,000 bricks for the duke of Gordon in 1710;[91] and also to 40,000 bricks made by John Turner, bricklayer, for Brodie of Brodie on 13 October 1749.[92] Brick was used sparingly in Moray, chiefly in internal walls or as fireproofing for chimneys.[93]

Frugal landowners recycled stone from their ancestral castles, cleansing the landscape of uncomfortable reminders of a barbarous past. Blervie Mains (1776), and Burgie House (1802) were built with stone from predecessor castles whose towers were, however, spared as picturesque conversation-pieces.[94] Quarrywood castle was quarried away to build new farmhouses.[95] Stone from Aslesk castle is identifiable in nearby farm buildings; and other castle masonry was used to build an estate granary at Bishopmill.[96] Stones in steadings at Hemprigs are probably recycled from the old castle. The tower of Drumin was partly dismantled, to provide material for the Gordon factor's farmhouse and steading in its shadow. Kilbuiack castle was removed because it was surplus to the requirements of its Brodie mistress, and its stones were reused in local farm steadings.[97] Castle stones are also evident in farm buildings at Hemprigs. Agricultural lime kilns supplied lime mortar, plaster and whitewash—the improvement of houses and land advancing together in step. Transport of materials for the lairds' works was provided by tenants: for example a usual condition of Ballindalloch tacks from the 1740s onwards obliged tenants to transport slate for the heritor's building works.[98] Within the emergent cash economy meanwhile, money became available to the improving tenant, to pay for materials, transport and craftsmen on his own house and steading. Though the cost of rebuilding might fall heavily upon the tenant, he might look forward to some reimbursement at the end of the lease—after having enjoyed up to nineteen years of modern home comforts.

Reroofing Moray presented some challenges. Slate was unavailable in many districts: 'Sandstone slates' from Slatehaugh in Rafford, and schistose stone 'slate' from Dallas, which covered burgh roofs, and lairdly towers from before 1700, were a shabby alternative.[99] And a stone-slate quarry at Clunie in Rafford was worked for a generation from 1798, supplying Moray's main phase of rebuilding, supplemented with mica-schist quarried at Kellas. True slates from Enzie in Banffshire entered eastern laich in quantity after bridging of the Spey in 1801 reduced carriage costs.[100] Gordon estates regularised slate working on the estate in response to growing demand. On 8 February 1782 a quarry at Minmore in Glenlivet was formally leased to Alexander Laurence, slater in Keith.[101] On 7 February 1802, the Gordon factor noted the irregular manner in which the schistose stone of Cnoc Fergan was being exploited: 'people ... has been Quarrying Slate for several years past and there wase never apenny sterling of rent payed'.[102] Extraction was regularised with a nineteen-year tack under which William and Joseph Leslie, slaters in Rothes, paid two shillings per thousand for slates produced at the quarry. The slaters insisted on a monopoly with 'power to keep other people from Quarrying Slate'; and they paid compensation to local husbandmen 'as the Quarrys is on the out pasture ground of two Small Crofts'.[103] Cnoc Fergan stone was the usual roofing for the improved dwellings of upper Banffshire, and the quarry operated until the 1930s.[104]

Wherever the cost of transport could be afforded, builders specified grey slate. This true slate split thinner for a lighter roof; and lighter roofs consumed less timber. Neatly-trimmed grey slates were also preferred as a fashion statement, in genteel contrast with stone tiles. Initially, grey slate was laid with several courses of small second-grade slates at the ridge. This penny-pinching expedient evolved into a general fashion for roofs of slate graded in size from ridge to eaves. Grey slate from The Scalp above Glenfiddich covered roofs in the earl of Fife's new town of Dufftown in Mortlach (founded 1817). Grey slate from Aberdeenshire entered Moray during the early decades of the nineteenth century, but west-coast slate was preferred, after it became more cheaply available, shipped through the Caledonian canal that shortened the route from Argyll to Moray.[105] By 1842, the minister of Rafford was able to report that in his parish at least, local slate was entirely superseded by 'Easdale or Ballachulish blue slate'.[106] The import was a significant element in the trade of Findhorn, selling at from £2 10s to £3 per thousand in the generation 1810–42.[107]

The rebuilding of Moray resulted in an employment boom for building workers. Masonwork was beyond the capability of an ordinary tenant: a master craftsman was required to erect clay- or lime-bonded walls, and to dress stones for gables, skews, skewputs, sills, lintels, quoins, ridges and chimney stacks. Skilled wrights were required to build roofs and staircases suitable to regular architecture, using machine-sawn softwood and iron fixings. Unskilled building workers were readily recruited from among township cottars, easing their conversion into wage-labourers. As tenants' expectations rose, professional joiners were required to fit out the house with comforts and conveniences including sash windows; and with skirtings, soffits, doors and box beds, all panelled in the modern style and finished with tasteful mouldings. Plasterers were required to finish interiors, though often their work ended at the head of the stairs with attic apartments unceiled beneath the thatch or sarking. Slaters were required to cover new roofs. Even thatch underwent improvement, and it is likely that improved thatching with clay stob, which superseded divot and heather, required expert installation.[108]

Regular farmsteads

Farm buildings were regularised to complement improved farmhouses. The earl of Findlater was applauded for encouraging improvement of farm steadings in Banffshire during the 1750s, following precepts and plans advanced by Lord Belhaven around 1699:[109] 'The offices, which generally form three sides of a square, are also built of stone and lime, and either covered with slate, tyle, or a substantial thatch of straw'.[110] This became a model for improved farmsteads: barn (housing threshing machine and fanner), granary, root store, byre and stable were arranged as a rectangle of building, with the farmhouse, perhaps forming one side, and a dungpit in the centre. This characteristic farmstead provided secure storage (for grain and implements) and dry accommodation for cattle. The high value of heavy horses meant that comfortable stabling with well-drained flagged or cobbled floors made commercial sense. Architecturally, the steading matched its farmhouse: built of clay- or lime-mortared stone, with rafter roofs, thatched or slated according to the farmer's taste and resources. Quoins were sharply square; end walls gabled with plain stone skews.

'Mr. Donaldson, a tenant of Lord Fife's, at Moneton near Elgin' was applauded as 'the first who built a regular set of farm offices' in Moray'—some time before 1794.[111] Neatly-square steadings were certainly built by tenant farmers in the laich before 1790, for example at Barmuckity and Sheriffston in St Andrews-Lhanbryd.[112] Masonry steadings were usual in the laich by around 1800:

> The farm-offices are built in ... [a] substantial manner ... in some cases they are slated, but more generally thatched with a thick, neat cover of straw, put on in the manner of slate, the upper half of each course securely embedded in clay: they are disposed in the form of a square court, nearly connected with the mansion house.[113]

Progressive landowners set the standard. William Leslie noted an 'excellent suit of offices ... announce that Moy is a dwelling of taste and opulence'. The steadings at Grange formed 'a handsome square court'. At Logie the home farm steading was 'a showy building of three stories ... containing a thrashing mill, a meal mill, a kiln, and a large granary ... procured at a cost of nearly £600'. Numerous 'neat commodious offices, impressing the idea of thrift and of rural plenty' evidenced the earl of Moray's influence upon his tenants. William Young built an exemplary suite of offices at Inverugie: 'conveniently disposed, and the barns, stables, and cattle feeding-stalls, are arranged with much taste and judgment'.[114] However, improvement of home farm buildings at Gordon Castle, though projected from the 1760s, was not realised until the 1830s when offices as extravagant as the Gordon brand demanded were erected to a design by Archibald Simpson and sycophantically applauded as 'buildings which for amplitude, utility and elegance are certainly unrivalled by any in the north'.[115]

Tenants were encouraged to improve farm offices with the promise of reimbursement of the cost at removal.[116] The valuation in 1811 of Darklass in Dyke & Moy, appreciated a typical steading, probably erected after 1792, at the beginning of a nineteen-year lease. The masonry buildings included a dwellinghouse, barns, stables, winnowing barn, grass barn and kiln. All were built of stone with roofs of bent thatch, worth in total £85 3s 3d. A solitary Darklass millander (cottar), however, still occupied a turf house containing timber worth just £1.[117] Cottertown farm, similarly improved during a nineteen-year lease, was comprised in 1814. The valuation described a lime-harled stone 'New Dwellin house', with 'vents' (masonry chimney-flues) and 'Hew stones' (dressed stonework); a lime-harled masonry kiln with stone stairs; a barn, stable, henhouse and a 'cotter house' also of stone.[118] Ballindalloch paid for a fully slated steading for Newton of Struthers around 1830. Byres, stables and threshing barn were arranged around three sides of a square to a design by George Brown, under a specification requiring masonry of Covesea freestone.[119]

Though there was no practical imperative that demanded a regular plan, the fashion for farm squares pervaded even upland and settler farms, far removed from the gentleman-farming of the laich. The steading of Lynemore, Knockando, on the marginal new land of Ballindalloch, enclosed three sides of a rectangle, with the two-storeyed farmhouse outside the square of offices—all built of quarried granite, roofed with Cnoc Fergan slate. At Stocktown in Glen Lochy the improved farmhouse formed one side of a rectangle. Behind the house stood an open-fronted cartshed with stables and byres; a detached barn at right angles completed the regular farm, with a dungpit occupying the central area. The house was built in regular style, but the offices were of drystone rubble with cruck-framed roofs. At a respectful distance a turf-and-cruck cottar's house stood on undrained moor beyond the old head-dyke.[120] At Oldshields of Coxtown, an improver's steading was built of clay-and-bool, the barn and henhouse, stable and byre arranged in parallel ranges at right-angles to the house, to form a regular rectangle, open at one end.

Small tenants occupying suites of building too small to make a square, continued to occupy house and barn/byre in longhouse style. Accommodation for small farmers at Scalan was constructed in regular gabled stone-and-rafter style, thatched or slated, with house and barn/byre joined longitudinally, though with separate roofs and no access from house to offices. Upland farms on new lands in Kellas too were regularly arranged: at Badiemichael with house and stabling in longhouse style, without internal connection; and with byre and barn forming a parallel range behind.

Regular settlements

Professor Tom Devine declared: 'Edinburgh new town is a metaphor in stone for the Scottish Enlightenment'.[121] This metaphor—of terraced houses and regular unified façades dignifying grids of streets and squares—became a cliche during a craze for village foundation that established nearly 500 new settlements throughout Scotland during the century1750–1850.[122] Urbane landowners sought (literally and metaphorically) to civilise their people. A lead came from the government which urged Annexed Estates Commissioners to pay 'particular attention ... to the Enlargement, or new erection of Towns and Villages ... [to] Reclaim the Inhabitants from their long habits of Sloth'.[123] Banffshire and Aberdeenshire especially required villages to wean the inhabitants 'from their idle and wicked practices to commerce and trade';[124] and in 1767 the commissioners applauded:

> My Lord Findlater [who] has ... carried the plan of erecting villages into execution upon his estate. The surprising effect that it has had in his lordship's village of New Keith has induced many others to follow this example.[125]

On the eve of improvement, Moray already possessed several significant towns, notably the royal burghs of Elgin and Forres, and their outports at Garmouth and Findhorn. Elgin's new outport at Lossiemouth, founded in 1698 on a barren corner of the Brodie estate, though not a populous place, was commercially important, with wharfage, warehouses and a number of fisher families working the town's large and small boats.[126] Westwards along the coast, Burghead contained some 400 souls around 1800, 'most of whom follow a seafaring life'.[127] Old Fochabers contained some 150 households in 1764, though it was judged a 'wretched town' when visited, on the eve of improvement in 1771, by Thomas Pennant.[128] Several laichland townships, with their mixed communities of husbandmen, cottars and craftsmen, were large enough to bear description as villages: for example, Easter Alves, Oldtown of Roseisle, Kirkton of Dyke and Urquhart.[128]

A new village was a fashionable—and rational—accessory for an improved estate, contributing to the regularisation of rural life and landscape.[130] A new village accommodated displaced cottars and sub-tenants, retaining families on the estate to work at established crafts and new industries, and especially on the improved farms. Sir John Sinclair declared:

> proprietors who erect villages on a *proper plan* in order to keep their countrymen in the Kingdom deserve better of the public than those who set them adrift without the least recourse.[131]

Sinclair also expected that new villages would enhance rentals and create wealth through commerce and industry.[132] Optimistic proprietors hoped that the village environment would elevate the inhabitants' morals.[133]

Modern historians usually describe improvers' new settlements as 'planned villages'. Improvers' new towns were, indeed, rigorously planned; but not more so than cooperative townships—arranged to accommodate diverse agricultural and industrial activities; or royal burghs—whose inch-perfect Anglo-Norman plans survived through half a millennium of development. Villages founded by Enlightenment landowners are distinguished by rigidly rectilinear plans expressing the taste of their rational and classically-minded promoters. Indeed, village foundation was driven, in large measure, by aesthetic considerations as an element in the replanning of rural landscapes. Neat new villages formed a pleasing prospect—and a marked contrast with the disorderly appearance of cooperative townships, which seemed (to an improver's eye) to have:

> originated in accident, been put down at random, and for the most part extremely irregular. Dwelling-houses, barns, byres, meeting-houses, cart-sheds, dung-steads, pig-sties and privies, are huddled up alternately on the street, in such confused groups, as to appear ridiculous, and shew a total want of taste.[134]

Moray's thirteen regular villages were established by the region's improving luminaries:

1760	–	Archiestown—Grant of Monymusk
1766	–	Rothes—earl of Findlater, extended by Grant of Grant (1790)
1775	–	Tomintoul—duke of Gordon
c. 1775	–	Fochabers—duke of Gordon
1784	–	Kingston—Osbourne and Dodsworth
1784	–	Lossiemouth—Elgin Town Council
1795	–	Bishopmill—earl of Findlater
1805	–	Hopeman—William Young
1808	–	Burghead William Young, Thomas Sellar, duke of Gordon, & others
1808	–	Cummingstown—Sir William Cumming Gordon
1811	–	Dallas—Alexander Penrose Cumming
1811	–	Duffus—Sir Archibald Dunbar
c. 1811	–	Covesea—Sir William Cumming Gordon
1812	–	Aberlour—Charles Grant of Wester Elchies
1830	–	Branderburgh—James Brander of Pitgaveney
c.1830	–	New Elgin—Elgin Guildry Society[135]

Among these, many were created through the regularisation, transplantation and extension of existing communities. Several, though, were entirely new, including Hopeman (a name not known before 1805); Kingston (founded by entrepreneurs from Kingston-upon-Hull); and Archiestown, Cummingstown and Branderburgh (named for their founders).[136]

Leasehold tenure was usually preferred, sparing villagers the legal cost of transferring feus on inheritance. This was a clear break with ancient previous urban landholding practice, indicating that landowners expected that their villagers would be poor labouring folk rather than merchants and wealthy capitalists. Alexander Boswell, lord Auchinleck, advised the duke of Gordon on 16 December 1763, recommending 999-year leases 'The Rent being but a Trifle in order to enforce a regular payment'.[137] In the event there were no 999-year leases

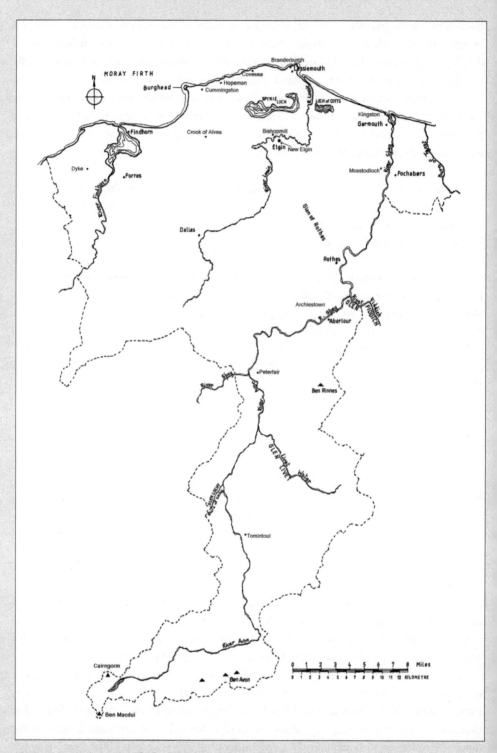

Moray: new settlements. (*C. Clerk*)

in Moray: though long tenure (thirty-one years in Aberlour, ninety-nine years in Hopeman) gave some security. Lossiemouth tenements (each one rood in area) were, however, feued, reflecting the burghal connections of the development.[138]

The regular rectilinear ground plan of a 'planned village' makes a striking feature, which seemed extraordinary when the settlement was brand new. Regular settlements complemented a rectilinear landscape, in which newness and straight lines were admired: the two-street village of New Duffus—three rows of single-storeyed houses in parallel lines stepping up a steep slope—was said to be 'neat, regular, and cleanly ... the prettiest, probably in the county, except the beautiful and picturesque little town of Rothes'.[139]

Most new villages were planned along a single straight street, perhaps dignified with a focal square—intended to accommodate fairs and market activities. Grids of streets crossed by side lanes gave a determinedly urban regularity to larger settlements such as Hopeman and Burghead. Lossiemouth too was a grid, but, distorted in the Seatown quarter where rows of fisher houses, placed end-on to the estuary, in a traditional manner, ran across the grain of the plan. Regularity of aspect was enhanced by obligations imposed upon the inhabitants to build their houses in modern style, fronting the street, and with doors opening directly onto the thoroughfare rather than onto a foreland where dungheaps might accumulate. Tomintoul's regulations specified houses 'in a regular manner, all fronting the street of equal height and as uniform as possible'.[140] At Cummingstown, Lossiemouth Seatown, Duffus, Kingston, and in the quarrelsome community of Urquhart, houses faced the street on one side, and backed onto the street on the other, in the medieval manner, as a sensible precaution against neighbourly nosiness.

Township cottars were relocated into colonies of labourers and craftsmen, rehoused in regular houses lining the straight roads of the regular countryside. Ballindalloch labourers occupied dwellings built gable-on to the straight road at Peterfair, each within a two-acre plot. Smaller plots were provided at Crook of Alves, a linear hamlet on the new Great Road: accommodating six agricultural labourers, four shoemakers, and other characteristic township trades including blacksmith, house-carpenter, cartwright and tailor. Another linear Great-Road hamlet at Mosstodloch accommodated a similar mix of township callings, including three shoemakers, a tailor, a weaver, a salmon-fisher, nineteen agricultural labourers, and six men who claimed the title of farmer.[141]

A new village of Urquhart was created in 1800 as a transplantation and regular rebuilding of a cooperative township. The happily-named land surveyor, William Urquhart, measured and mapped the old town and land in 1793, before marking out new regular stances each containing thirty-two falls on a 'conspicuous level situation'. Stones from township dwellings were recycled to build regular houses on the new site. Tenants' runrig possessions were reallocated as fifty-nine rectangular, two-acre, enclosed lots, 'divided in as commodious and regular manner as the ground would admit of'; and in 'small farms so as to accommodate six tenants'.[142]

New Fochabers, like Urquhart, was transplantation, but on a larger scale and for specifically aesthetic reasons: relocating Bog of Gight castletown (comprising over 150 dwellings) 'on account of its inconvenient nearness' to Gordon Castle.[143] The town was shifted to straddle the Great Road close to where it crossed the Spey. Tenementers were bought out in individual negotiations, which lasted until 1802, the feuars receiving from £5 to £52 each, and 'Materials of ... present houses and dykes'.[144] The neoclassical mercat cross (with jougs) of Old Fochabers survived as a garden feature in the enlarged ducal park. New Fochabers was planned by John Baxter as a grid of three parallel streets with a square and cross-lanes, and boasting 'several good inns'. It was, however, despised by Lord Cockburn who visited in 1842, disliked its regularity, and deplored its use as 'a kennel for the retired lacqueys and ladies-maids of the castle, and for the natural children and pensioned mistresses of the noble family'.[145] These drones were presumably among seventy-two inhabitants enjoying 'independent' means in 1841. The remainder of Fochabers folk followed a usual range of occupations: tailors, blacksmiths, cartwrights, innkeepers, merchants, masons, plasterers and house carpenters; with 172 farm servants, two butchers, two bakers, a cabinet maker, a surgeon, a brewer, an artist and two musicians.[146]

The transplanting of Fochabers underlines the contrast between Moray's consensual clearances and vexatious evictions elsewhere—including the distressful enclosure movement in England. Fochabers was removed, not by force, or even by law, but through robust negotiation. The removal left in its wake none of the bitterness that spices folk-memory of the Strathnaver removals. Nor do Fochaberians today feel any mawkish nostalgia of the kind voiced by Oliver Goldsmith—though Lord Harcourt's clearance of Newnham in Oxfordshire was identical with the duke of Gordon's park extension scheme.[147]

> ... The man of wealth and pride
> Takes up a space that many poor supply'd:
> Space for his lake, his park's extended bounds,
> Space for his horses, equipage and hounds:
> The robe that wraps his limbs in silken sloth,
> Has robb'd the neighbouring fields of half their growth;
> His seat where solitary sports are seen,
> Indignant spurns the cottage from the green.[148]

Village foundation was usually driven by visions of commercial activity and industrial development. Most villages failed to fulfill their founders' hopes. None flowered as a Moray rival to New Lanark. Tomintoul was typical. Planned as a street-and-square-with-back-lanes in the late 1770s to civilise upper Strathavon,[149] and lining the military road linking Strathspey with Strathdon, the duke of Gordon envisaged a prospering linen manufactory. Spinning wheels and lintseed were distributed. A spinning mistress was employed to instruct the villagers. A lintmill was built on the Conglass. However, despite subsidies from the Board of Trustees for Manufactures continuing into the 1790s, the town, in its first generation at least, was a social and industrial failure.[150] A local farmer, Thomas Stuart, 'meditating on what might encourage the proposed village', identified 'an excellent mineral well ... better than that at Paninich on Deeside'.[151] A new inn was built by John Mackenzie in 1777, comprising 'a house of seven feet high in the walls with two rooms to accommodate passengers'—improving upon the old Camdelmore establishment which made such a 'poor appearance' that passengers were 'unwilling to enter in ... until they are prevail'd with'.[152] But Tomintoul

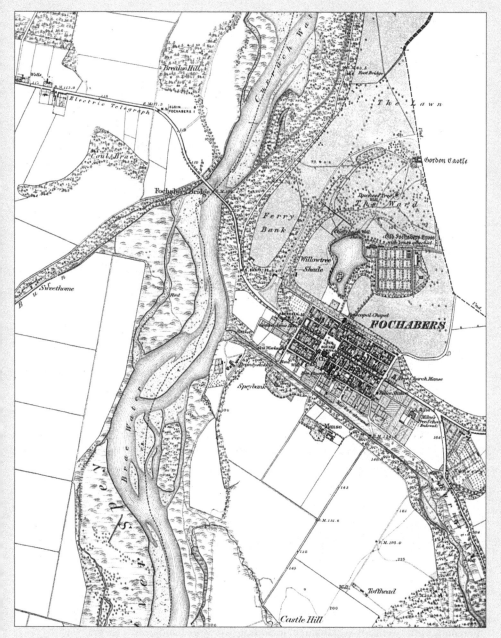

Gordon castle park: the mercat cross marks the centre of Old Fochabers; the neat grid-plan town of New Fochabers stands beyond the new park wall. (*OS, 1:10,560, Elginshire XIV, 1870*)

did not develop as a tourist spa either. Kirkmichael's minister, meanwhile, despaired of the idleness and lax morals of Tomintoul folk in 1791:

> All of them sell whisky, and all of them drink it. When disengaged from this business the women spin yarn, kiss their inamoratos, or dance to the discordant sounds of an old fiddle.[153]

As with many other new towns, Tomintoul found a role chiefly as a dormitory for agricultural labourers who commuted to work on local farms, and craftsmen serving local markets. Some Tomintoul folk supplemented their income with the produce of lotted land. However, the 120 two-acre plots were possessed by just fifty-six of the 143 families in 1841; and Tomintoul housed a sizeable landless and workless underclass including forty-one widows, and nineteen paupers.[154] Queen Victoria commented that the village was a 'tumbledown, poor looking place ... dirty looking houses and people with a sad look of wretchedness' when she passed through it in 1853.[155] The hilarity of the 1790s had perhaps evaporated along with any modest prosperity when local (illicit) whisky production collapsed following excise reform in the 1820s.

Archiestown, founded in 1760, was similarly disappointing. The village comprised a single street with back lanes and a square, sited upon an uncultivable boss of granite that bulged through the schist beneath the moor of Ballintomb in Knockando. Sir Archibald Grant advertised for settlers to his new town in the public prints, emphasising the 'inexhaustible Moss and good Water and Stone for Building, and very convenient and healthy pleasant Situation'. Land for houses and yards, with lotted lands for agriculture were available as feus or—recognising that the legal costs involved in feuholding could be beyond the means of labouring men—under leases. As a further inducement, Grant offered interest-free loans of up to £1,000 to assist manufacturers in establishing their businesses. High moral standards were a basic qualification required from those who wanted to participate in this progressive development: newspaper advertisements for settlers were particularly directed to 'honest and sober tradesmen and virtuous, industrious labourers'.[156] Grant's vision for Archiestown was industrial linen manufacture. He attracted weavers from as far away as Huntly, Cullen and Portsoy, with settlers coming from a mean distance of thirteen miles.[157] Archiestown, however, suffered from the collapse of the linen industry and a disastrous fire in 1783. The village had not recovered by 1798, when many houses were still roofless and 'instead of continuing progressive, it has for several years been rather retrograde'.[158] By 1841 industry had departed. Archiestown now contained nineteen agricultural labourers, one crofter, one farmer and one merchant, with twenty-two craftsmen, including just three handloom weavers.[159]

This pattern of population was reproduced elsewhere, as industry and commerce failed to thrive. The Covesea hamlet of fisher families on Gordonstoun land around 1811 was replanned as a regular, single-street village. However, lacking a harbour, the place failed as a fishing station. By 1841 Covesea's fourteen households comprised sixteen agricultural labourers, a blacksmith and a mason; a further four inhabitants had engrossed a sufficient acreage of lotted land to claim the status of farmer.[160] Similarly at Cummingston, Sir William Cumming Gordon's new creation, advertised in 1808 as a fisher town, also lacked a harbour—or even a beach: its fishermen were expected to commute to Burghead.[161] By 1841 the community comprised just six fishermen and four coopers. Otherwise the village was a dormitory for fifteen agricultural labourers, with a further dozen who, having engrossed most of the lotted lands, claimed to be farmers. Coastal quarries supplying stone for the Moray building boom employed a further fourteen Cummingstown men.[162]

Most of Moray's inland new towns—including Dallas, Duffus, Rothes, Charlestown (Aberlour) and Tomintoul—absorbed adjacent kirktons and castletons, as well as families displaced by improvement and township extinction in the wider parish. Unsurprisingly the range of callings followed by the inhabitants reflected the usual mix of township trades: smiths, tailors, weavers, shoemakers, dressmakers, wrights, and building workers such as masons and thatchers, with a leaven of merchants and professionals, including midwives and schoolmasters. Around one-third of the working villagers in 1841 were agricultural labourers, who commuted to work for wages on improved farms, and who cultivated lotted lands attached to their villages—enjoying a lifestyle scarcely different from that of a township cottar or subtenant.

Coastal new towns proved more successful where harbours and sandy beaches allowed trade and fishing to develop. Kingston alone possessed a specifically industrial identity. The village grew from a scatter of dwellings, planted on the beach in 1810 into three rows of cottaging for workers, who worked for wages in the Speybay shipyards, without the benefit of lotted lands.[163] Sixty fishermen gave Lossiemouth a basis for prosperity, which supplemented a commercial harbour as the town became Moray's principal port. However, Lossiemouth was also a dormitory for some sixty agricultural labourers who commuted to work on local farms.[164] Hopeman and Burghead were both devised as business ventures by landowners in the laich. Hopeman was the exclusive project of William Young of Inverugie. He advertised the development in 1808, offering stone, lime, clay and slates 'on the premises'; excellent soil; and an 'excellent Fishing Ground' with Burghead Harbour nearby from which cod and other fish were shipped to London.[165] Fishermen were recruited from Campbeltown (Ardersier) and Avoch to kickstart the Hopeman industry.[166] Young sold the town in 1817. When Hopeman was purchased by Admiral Duff of Drummuir in 1837, 'there was only one slated house ... and the harbour was little better than a natural creek'.[167] Nonetheless, there were forty-eight fishermen in 1841, in a community supported by the usual craftsmen; also including eighty-three labourers (half of them agricultural), and fifteen masons, employed in coastal quarries.[168] William Young was also involved in redeveloping Burghead, in partnership with the duke of Gordon and a cadre of laichland improvers including Thomas Sellar and Brander of Pitgaveney. Burghead absorbed an existing maritime community which provided a secure foundation for the development of a significant trading port under the sole ownership of William Young from 1819 onwards, while thirty-nine fishermen worked from the northern-beachfront.[169] In general, though, prosperity for coastal new towns would come—despite the decline of coastal shipping following the coming of railways—with the fishing boom of the later nineteenth century.

Regularisation in Moray's burghs was hampered by feuholding in medieval townscapes governed by conservative planning and building regulations. Nonetheless, high-street

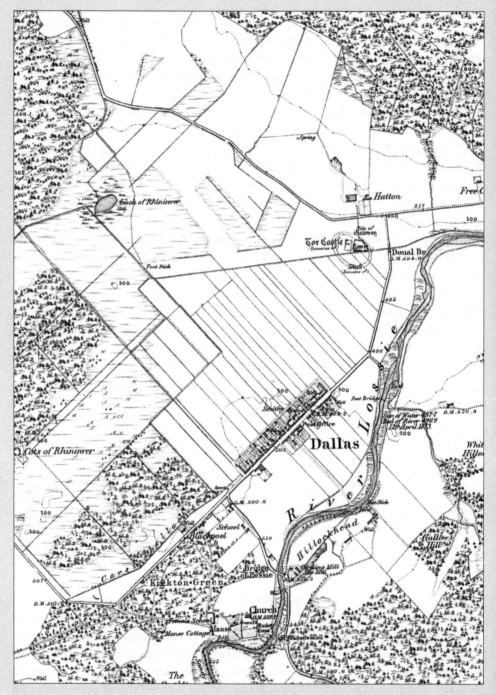

Resettlement of Dallas folk left the parish church isolated. The new village was planned as a linear settlement with generous house plots, and straight strips of lotted land nearby. (*OS, 1:10,560, Elginshire XVI, 1871*)

building lines were allowed to move forward by up to ten feet; and, from around 1720, houses were routinely built to face (and open front doors onto) the highway. Elgin's arcades were engrossed as shop windows to the properties they fronted.

In Forres, private agreements between adjacent feuars allowed the creation of double-width vennels (half a rod wide. Houses in the closes were rebuilt in regular style, linked in terraces, facing each other across the close in a revolutionary departure from medieval habit. An amalgamation of two feus behind the Tolbooth (and a further two on the north side of town) allowed revolutionary cross-street developments: L-shaped regular dwellings in Caroline Street (from around 1768); regular dwellings, end-on to Tolbooth Street (from around 1780). Duncan Urquhart of Burdsyards developed five adjacent feus around 1770 as a new street on the south side. Urquhart's wynd curved along the line of its central rood, with regular houses on either side—built end-on to the street in the burghal manner and thus against the grain of the medieval plan.[170]

In Elgin, the demolition of Calder's townhouse, which extended across three roods on the north side, allowed a cross-street (North Street) to be driven through.[171] Partial demolition of the royal lodging of Thunderton allowed another cross street opposite. This attempt to superimpose a grid plan, however, progressed no further; and North Street was not a classically straight thoroughfare, but a lane curved along a medieval rood. Around 1825, contemplating the replacement of St Giles, burgh officials proposed radical redevelopment, emulating Edinburgh's new town. The scheme proposed a straight street, piercing the heart of the burgh from north to south, to enter vast square, where the new parish kirk would stand. A broad east-west thoroughfare through the square would form a new straight high street beyond the southern back passage.[172] This radical vision was doomed to remain a planner's pipedream as feuars' interests trumped classicising inclinations. It would be another generation before Elgin decisively broke its medieval bounds; and when this did happen, new streets lined with detached villas traced the curve of burgh arable rather than spreading as a rational suburb of neoclassical circuses, grids and squares.[173]

Public building

Regularisation of the built environment was completed by replacing and classicising public buildings, thus applying a stamp of official and ecclesiastical approval to the regular revolution. Architects of national standing were employed to enhance Moray's urban and rural prospects and ensure that this corner of the kingdom conformed to the national template. Laichland sandstones were exploited to present a public face of unblemished ashlar.

Urbane urban public buildings established classical foci that emulated the architectural vistas of Edinburgh's New Town. Funding for these redevelopments came from the community's wider network of commerce and enterprise. Dr Gray's Hospital (1815–19, by Gillespie Graham) triumphantly terminated the west end of the High Street with a Doric portico and a dome, financed with £20,000 earned in India.[174] The fortune of a rags-to-riches Elgin loon, General Andrew Anderson, dignified the burgh's eastern boundary with a domed, neoclassical, Doric and Ionic 'Institution for the support of Old Age and Education of Youth' (1830–33, by Archibald Simpson).[175] William Robertson added a courthouse and council chamber behind a portico of Corinthian columns in 1841,[176] as a 'rational' replacement for the towered and turreted town-centre tolbooth.[177] On the royal-castle motte an 80 foot Tuscan column, erected by public subscription in 1839, honoured the last duke of Gordon: 'Patron and generous promoter of agriculture ... a Nobleman deservedly popular with all ranks of society'.[178]

The poor-sister burgh of Forres was redignified with more restrained public architecture. In 1823 William Robertson designed Jonathan Anderson's Institution, at the east end: a school for 'children of Forres, Rafford and Kinloss', with pediment and spire, funded by income from landed estates near Glasgow.[179] The freemasons' hall was classicised as a town hall by Archibald Simpson in 1829, with an elegantly pilastered double-cube principal chamber.[180] Forres demonstrated its wider vision with the castellated Trafalgar Tower, built in 1806 as one of the first public monuments in Britain to honour Lord Nelson. When Forres tolbooth was condemned as dilapidated beyond repair,[181] William Robertson designed a replacement with a neoclassical courtroom, a modern prison, and accommodation for the reformed police—housed in a baronial structure, embellished with a graceful spire. However, 'many gentlemen of undoubted taste' insisted on a '*fac-simile* of the OLD DOME', which Robertson duly provided. The cost was met through a handsome donation from Thomas Davidson of the British Linen Bank—whose reward was official permission to rebuild his own premises several feet forward of the old building line on the public street.[182] As the tolbooth was completed, public opinion decided something more dignified was required in place of the stone stump of the mercat cross. The new cross, selected from competing plain and fancy designs, was a gothic confection of crocketted finials, by Thomas Mackenzie, as a diminutive version of Edinburgh's Scott monument.[183]

In a century of rebuilding, almost all of Moray's churches were replaced. Only Birnie escaped demolition, perhaps because its Norman chancel arch and Pictish and episcopal associations imparted a sanctity with which even rational Presbyterians venerated.[184] Other medieval kirks, which had survived the Reformation with little more than cosmetic change and reorganisation of furnishings to accommodate presbyterian worship, could not resist the enlightened zeal of improvers in the pursuit of convenience. The irregularity of medieval buildings, their interiors dimly lighted only by splayed lancets, conflicted with rational predilections. Prevailing attitudes were epitomised by William Leslie's disparagement of the thirteenth-century Dallas kirk: 'a very ancient fabric, thatched with heath, and without windows, save 2 or 3 narrow slits which yawned to a very disproportioned wideness within'.[185]

Church rebuilding began with the red kirk of Speymouth, erected in 1731 in a central location to serve the combined congregations of Essil and Dipple.[186] During the same decade the medieval parish church of Spynie was demolished and its stones reused for a plainly regular new kirk on a more convenient, 'centrical, but bleak', site at Quarrywood.[187] Most parish churches were renewed during the general spasm of improvement, 1760–1830. Typically, replacement kirks were airy Georgian boxes with large, regular, round-headed windows (occasionally with tentative gothic tracery) and perhaps some classical detail around the door. Roofs were gabled, covered with grey slate, and topped off with a stone bellcote. Duffus, exceptionally, retained a sixteenth-century porch and the lower storey of a medieval tower within a structure largely rebuilt in the eighteenth century.[188] The 'commodious' kirk of Dallas (rebuilt 1793) preserved a floreated medieval cross in its kirkyard.[189] The kirks of Dallas and Duffus both survived removal of their kirktons to new settlements nearby: because both churches had been regularly rebuilt before the new villages were established; and the new villages were designed with neither polite squares nor urban pretensions.

Elsewhere, parish churches were relocated to provide an architectural focus for the square of a new town that absorbed the kirkton population: plainly Georgian in Rothes (1781), recycling stones from its predecessor;[190] replacing 'mean ancient' St Drostan's kirk of Aberlour, (1812)—with a 'Saxon' (Romanesque) tower, added by William Robertson;[191] with columned porch, pediment, spire and 'European sophistication' in Drainie freestone, by William Baxter (1798) in Fochabers, for Bellie parish.[192] Elgin's new church imposed exemplary classicism in the heart of the royal burgh. A Grecian temple replaced medieval St Giles in 1828, as an architectural statement of the burgh's progressive credentials.[193] Archibald Simpson's design—subsequently judged 'the equal of any Greek Revival church in the country'—was finished with a tower which the burgh's cogniscienti appreciated as a homage to the monument of Lysicrates in Athens.[194]

After a generation of improvement, polite taste was suffering from classical overload. The demolition of old St Giles—damned by classicists as 'a low mis-shapen fabric, at once deforming and encumbering the street'[195]—sparked protests from modern romantics. Already William Robertson had provided, in 1825, a gothic church for Elgin's Episcopal congregation—the design inspired by his measured survey of Elgin's Holy Trinity cathedral (published 1826). The crocketted south gable of Robertson's Holy Trinity church formed a visual termination for the burgh's new North Street.[196] A similar vista was contrived by Archibald Simpson with a gothic chapel for Fochabers Episcopalians.[197] Meanwhile, gothic style made an architectural statement in rural areas: for example the Roman Catholic Church of the Incarnation at Tombae (1829);[198] and James Gillespie Graham's 'handsome and commodious' (1826) regularly gothic confection for the established kirk in Rafford, which deserted the ancient kirkyard for a more picturesque site, in 1826.[199] The earl of Fife, a beacon of improving taste and style, translated Urquhart parish church in 1843. The new kirk, designed by Alexander Reid (William Robertson's nephew) in Gillespie Graham gothic style, was sited for maximum picturesque effect: oriented north-south as a focal feature in the hedged and tree-studded enclosed landscape that formed the setting for the earl's second home at Innes.[200] The regular perpendicular church on Gas Hill, nicely balanced a Bronze Age stone circle that was permitted to survive as an antiquarian curiosity, where straight new roads converged on the hilltop above Innes Mill. Thus Fife added a finishing flourish to the first, and revolutionary, phase of improvement in this corner of the laich. The Innes landscape epitomises Moray's regular revolution: reorganised into retilinear regularity for agricultural efficiency; but replanned also to satisfy the improvers' enlightened ethic, which was equally economic, moral, social, cultural and aesthetic.

10

CONCLUSIONS

In 1771 George Taylor finished his opulent plan of the barony of Coxtown with a vignette depicting a classically-draped figure—a goddess or muse—who trumpets a clarion call for change.[1] The genius of improvement sounds a last trump across a landscape of runrig arable and common muir, announcing the extinction of the cooperative countryside. Taylor contrived his allegorical conceit as a compliment to his employer, the classically-minded, improving earl of Fife.

Nearly 250 years later, this image gives a sharp focus to two headline conclusions. The first concerns the cooperative countryside—depicted in Taylor's plan and discussed in Chapter 2. This landscape was the product of an effective, organic, self-sufficient agricultural system, operating at a level well above mere subsistence. Cooperative husbandry had endured for generations—even centuries; and it might have persisted for further decades or generations, drawing upon inbuilt flexibilities and commercial dynamism to meet new challenges and changing circumstances. Adaptability, though, is not incipient revolution. There was no tendency towards radical reinvention within the cooperative countryside. Thus the impulse for fundamental change had to come from outside.

The second conclusion follows from the first. The regular revolution was introduced from outwith the townships of the cooperative regime; and this is allegorically affirmed in Taylor's vignette. The regular revolution was imposed from above: not through a supernatural *deus ex machina* intervention—but by the unconstrained determination of visionary lords and lairds. Coxtown was improved by the earls of Fife. The improvers' inspiration was Enlightenment rationalism—an ethic developed within the landowning elite. Regulation (in every sense) was embraced by enlightened landowners as a new cultural paradigm. The ethos was realised in a regular revolution that transformed agriculture, architecture and landscape—satisfying imperatives that were both cultural and commercial.

The regular revolution was implemented in Moray, as elsewhere, through the unconstrained exercise of proprietorial power: by 'landowners [who] were probably the most powerful in the whole of Europe'.[2] The cadre of wealthy individuals who imposed Moray's regular revolution comprised some thirty or forty major heritors. These landowners were connected by a shared passion for improvement; closer knit by family relationships;

linked too in wider networks, with the intellectual and social centres of Edinburgh and London, and with the European polite culture. Moray's landowners swam in the cultural mainstream, and their regular revolution was shaped by templates adopted throughout the Scottish lowland counties. Models for Moray's regular landscapes, regulated agriculture and comfortably classicised buildings came from the same patternbooks—and the same cultural predilections—that informed landowners in Lothian and Angus. Moray's landowners did not actively seek guidance from the flood of published tracts and agricultural handbooks that capitalised upon the improvement craze. Rather, it was networking among practical improvers—including gentleman-farmers and their wives, factors, land surveyors, grieves, builders and ploughmen—that drove the regular revolution forward and disseminated new practices within Moray, and thence into other regions. The regularisation of Moray was accomplished in step with the other lowland regions: beginning with eccentrically progressive improvements before 1740, for example at Brodie and Gordonstoun; burgeoning into a general craze during the following generation—with 1766 perhaps as the turning point.

Legal sanction was not required (or sought) for most aspects of estate improvement. However, landowners did find that legislation designed to ensure sustainable management of woodland in the cooperative countryside, could be invoked to protect plantations and effectively to privatise woodland previously enjoyed as a communal resource. With this legal protection, the planting craze—pursued for both commercial and aesthetic ends—effected one of the most dramatic transformations in the Moray landscape.

Where several proprietors' interests were co-mingled or blurred, heritors, of course, used the courts to establish property titles. Thus law business was unavoidable in disentangling proprietorial runrig; reorganising dispersed acres of burgh arable into discrete holdings; dividing commonties; and distributing new land created through drainage. The 1756 Act of Session,[3] which defined procedures for removal of tenants, was invoked in a flurry of litigation in 1766, marking the beginning of determined regularisation in Moray. These processes, though, chiefly affirmed legal possession on estates experiencing particular difficulties. Litigation soon ceased. From the 1770s onwards, estate reorganisation did not depend upon decreets from the sheriff courts of Elgin & Forres. Estates were regularised and people transplanted through the simple exercise of landlord power. Meanwhile, the legislative substructure that had evolved to support the complexities of the cooperative countryside fell quietly into dissuetude.

The cooperation of tenants was a key element in landowners' schemes. Ordinary husbandmen in Moray proved eager recruits to the regular revolution. They readily accepted written leases, single tenancy and money rents; and the same husbandmen who had sturdily cultivated the cooperative countryside, just as sturdily reshaped their farmscapes to accommodate the improvers' regimes. Tenants' compliance was a consequence of landhunger among husbandmen. Prospective tenants for discrete farms on regularised estates willingly accepted tack conditions that imposed reformed agricultural regimes as the price that had to be paid for the security of a nineteen-year tenancy. There was also a financial price to be paid. Rents were driven sharply upwards by the tenants themselves, who engaged in vigorous competitive bidding for leases, and for the social cachet of being called a 'farmer'—even if that meant breaking in a settler farm on uncultivated moorland. For some farmers (though by no means all) the prices paid proved a sound investment that yielded a handsome dividend.

The cottar class too accepted change without apparent disquiet or distress. The establishment of crofting communities (for example at Scalan in Kirkmichael) and small farms on the margins of improved farmscapes (for example in Urquhart) allowed a significant number of cottars to enter the tenant class. Otherwise, redefined as agricultural labourers, cottars flitted to new towns or inhabited their existing houses on the margins of the new farms. C. Smout's general observation holds true in Moray:

> those who remained on the land, or who were evicted from the land and had to depend on waged labour, living maybe in some little cottage with a plot of ground to grow potatoes and a few hens ... were no worse off than they had been before.[4]

Labouring families in Moray—rehoused with secure tenancies in regular dwellings in new villages, with access to lotted land—were, arguably, better off than they had been before.

Throughout the period 1760–1840 resistance to change was extremely rare, though several petty squabbles were documented. Some conflicts were clearly rooted in personal resentments and professional jealousies. Others arose in situations where the patchy progress of regularisation meant that one man's local improvement hampered a neighbour's cooperative husbandry. Certainly, in Moray as elsewhere in the arable lowlands of Scotland:

> There was neither rick-burning nor riotous assembly ... an indication perhaps that the Scottish farm worker, ill-paid and ill-fed though he was, may have been more at one with the farming revolution.[5]

A tenural revolution dismantled the social hierarchy of the cooperative countryside: subtle gradations of tacksmen, tenants, sub-tenants, mailanders, grassmen, cottars and servants were rationalised into two distinct classes—those who had a farm and those who did not. T. Devine noted this social change, observing that 'social dislocation in the rural lowlands ... has virtually been overlooked ... the Lowland Clearances still await their historian.'[6] A foundation for a historiography of lowland clearances was laid by C. Smout's provocative assertion that 'There was tremendous suffering and problems and resentments as well as tremendous amounts of money to be made.'[7] However, in Moray, social change did not lead to social unrest, perhaps because problems and resentments were defused by rising living standards. Meanwhile, the abandonment of cooperative husbandry and the establishment of single-tenant farms was effected in a manner and at a pace that ensured township folk were neither violently evicted nor forced to go abegging.

The term 'Lowland Clearances' has an attractive timbre, which, however, jars with the low-key and dourly practical tone of Moray's regular revolution. In contrast with the drama and pathos of some island and highland clearances, profound change was accomplished in Moray without causing popular dismay at the time or disapproval since—and without mass emigration. Established habits of social and geographical mobility eased transitions when estates and farms were reorganised, while also, perhaps, masking from the individuals involved the extent of the changes that were under way. Increasing population during the period 1760–1840, considered with the absence of animus at the time—and the absence today of any folk memory of clearance—suggest that, although Moray's cooperative countryside was comprehensively obliterated and every cooperative township razed, the dispersal and redistribution of township folk still does not merit the 'clearance' label. 'Lowland Clearances' is a value-heavy description that does not sit comfortably upon the consensual regular revolution in Moray.

By around 1840 Moray's regular revolution was deeply entrenched. The most intense phase of eradicating the old and inaugurating the new had occupied two or three generations. The *New Statistical Accounts* suggest that regularised agricultural practices were everywhere established in the radically reshaped landscapes of Moray. The regular paradigm was firmly inculcated upon the consciousness of Moray's farmers and set in stone within the built environment. However, the revolution was by no means complete in 1840. The great rebuilding was unfinished: turf-and-cruck houses and farm buildings were still occupied in the laich until 1830;[8] and into the 1860s in Kirkmichael.[9] Patterns of enclosure for fields and farms—the *sine qua non* of improved agriculture—were marked out on the ground in accordance with the land surveyors' plans, but imperfectly effected in most parishes. Although hedgerows had become established in a few districts, and stone walls had been built by those who could afford them, paling fences and feal dykes remained commonplace. In poorly-fenced fields, herding remained an essential feature of agricultural practice. Stockproof enclosure became possible only after iron wire became affordable. Iron post-and-wire fencing was tried as a luxurious innovation at Ballindalloch in 1843;[10] and on 18 October 1850 tenants agreed to pay interest on the cost of wire fences separating Fife's farms from Pitgaveney's in Spynie.[11] In general, though, the land surveyors' fenced fieldscapes were fully realised with posts and wire only from around 1860—with barbed wire added to the encloser's toolkit a decade later.[12]

Improved breeds of sheep and horses were comfortably accommodated on Moray farms by 1840. However, thorough improvement of cattle—crossed with or selected from the black-cattle gene pool—belongs, in Moray, to the decades after 1850. The 'Ballindalloch era' for Aberdeen-Angus cattle, though founded upon the work of James Mackay in the 1830s, began properly with a cow named Erica, purchased in 1861—whose calves established the premier family of the breed.[13]

In 1840 farmers generally looked no further than their own cattle and limekilns for soil enrichment. After 1840 Moray farmers were able to supplement farm dung with exotic products transported unimaginable distances or manufactured by astonishing chemical processes. Guano arrived in Scotland from darkest Peru and Chile in 1842.[14] It was documented at Mary Park in Inveravon where Ballindalloch reported, on 12 January 1844, 'my first field has now assumed a workmanlike appearance with the aid of <u>Guano</u>';[15] and an early shipment imported at Findhorn was rouped at Fraser's Hotel, Forres 'immediately after the CATTLE SHOW' on 28 October 1845.[16] Within a decade or so Moray fields could receive their first dressing of superphosphate, produced by the reaction of bone ash or mineral phosphate with sulphuric acid, and manufactured by John Bennet Lawes from 1843.[17] Industrial origins gave added glamour to this most modern fertiliser, underlining how far farming had come from the sustainability and localism of cooperative regimes, at last to enter the realm of science.

Improved agriculture was labour intensive. Rational regimes relied upon horsepower and relentless hand labour. Dunging, dyking, ditching, moorland improvement, trenching sand-blown soils, haymaking, turnip-hoeing and harvest were all done with basic handtools. Iron ploughs and harrows and new designs of cart—with the heavy horses that drew them— imparted a gloss of modernity; but the basic operations of tilling the soil on the ridges of an enclosed farm field were little different from those on cooperative arable. While labour remained relatively cheap, labour-saving innovation was not the improvers' prime concern.

Ridging remained usual for field drainage, and a notable landscape feature down to the 1840s. Effective and affordable ceramic tile drains became available from 1843 onwards, manufactured using the technical developments pioneered by Josiah Parks in Warwickshire.[18] This innovation reached Moray during the mid nineteenth century, allowing farmers at last to level their ridges and mechanise fieldwork in a second surge of agricultural advance that embraced farmers more fully into wider industrial revolution.

Once the ridges were levelled, it was practicable to deploy reaping machines.[19] The machine of choice would be American—albeit descended from a Scottish ancestor— designed by Cyrus McCormick and exhibited at the Great Exhibition of 1851.[20] Steam power, which had arrived on the Moray Firth, driving the steamships *Duke of Richmond* and *Duchess of Sutherland* during the 1830s, appeared on Moray's agricultural horizon in 1842. The Forres minister blandly reported 'on one farm there is a threshing machine ... worked by a steam engine', perhaps failing to recognise the step-change promised by this innovation.[21]

Eighty years of determined regularisation effected sweeping landscape redesign, tenural reform, an agricultural revolution, and a great rebuilding. Yet, around 1840, as the *New Statistical Accounts* took stock of progress, the work remained unfinished. The uneven pace of change among the numerous and disjointed estates of Moray left gaps in the fabric of improvement. Meanwhile, as industrial and technological advances offered a tantalising promise of endless further progress, improvement became a continual process, extending far beyond anything that might have occurred to Lord Kames's rational foresight or Monymusk's rashest imaginings. Our recognition that the great work of the Moray improvers was still incomplete in 1840, sounds again the keynote struck by Sheriff Clerk Rampini in 1898,[22] and invites a final conclusion—that improvement in Moray, between 1760 and 1840 was 'almost a [regular] revolution'.

GLOSSARY

acre	land measure, in Scotland comprising 6,150.40 square yards imperial measure, later superseded by imperial acre of 1,760 square yards; also a term for a parcel or strip of land in a common field.
allar	alder tree.
aqua vitae	'water of life'—whisky.
American fir	coniferous tree of the species *abies alba* or *abies nigra*.
anker	measure of capacity containing ten gallons.
annual rent	interest paid on money lent.
ashlar	smooth-faced, square-hewn masonry, sometimes cladding rougher work.
banner/benner	inner or best room of a house.
barn	building where grain is stored and threshed.
barren	native (tree species).
baulk	untilled ground between commonfield strips or other parcels of land.
bear/bere	hardy six- or four-row barley.
ben	inner room of a house (*be-innan*).
birk	birch (tree).
birleyman	reliable tenant operating under the jurisdiction of the baron court to decide minor disputes and value property.
boll	a unit of capacity for grain containing 18 pecks or 4 firlots or 6 imperial bushels; the boll of flour weighs 140 pounds, and of wheat 14 stones 3 pounds; 2 bolls equal one English quarter.
bruntland	land cultivated after paring and burning the surface peat or turf.
burgh biggid land	land available for building within a burgh; land within burgh boundaries, as distinguished from extra-mural burgh arable.
but	outer room of a house (*be-utan*).
but	corner of ploughland.
but-and-ben	a two-roomed house.

byre	building or part of a building where cattle are housed.
caber	small roof timber extending from ridge to eaves.
carucate	*see* **plough**.
chalder	measure of capacity containing 16 bolls.
chamber	inner room in a house, perhaps unheated, used as a sleeping apartment.
commonty	land possessed in common by two or more proprietors, typically moorland used for grazing.
caoraich mora	'great sheep'—Cheviot, Bakewell and other large breeds of sheep that displaced native whiteface.
cot	building in which sheep are housed.
cottar	subtenant possessing very little land, perhaps only a house and yard with grazing for a cow, and depending upon income from craftwork or wages earned by working for other tenants or sub-tenants.
couples	curved pairs of timbers, joined at the apex, to support a roof and form the structural fame of a house.
crucks	couples.
curach	light boat, framed with wood and covered with hide—a coracle.
cut	a certain quantity of (linen) yarn—properly containing 120 rounds of a legal reel extending 91 inches in length.
dabhach	land measure, notionally containing 416 acres, but in practice varying in size according to the quality of the soil—containing 4 ploughs or 32 oxgangs; Anglicised as **daugh** or **davoch**.
deal	sawn softwood planking.
decreet	judgement (of a court of law).
decreet arbitral	judgement consequent upon an arbitration.
divot	thin turf, typically cut for roofing.
doocot	building to accommodate nesting pigeons harvested for their meat—a dovecote.
dyke	wall.
easter	downstream (in place-names).
ell/eln	unit of length extending 37 inches.
entail	legal settlement limiting the descent of an estate.
excambion	contract whereby one piece of land is exchanged for another.
fall	unit of area covering 1/240th of a rood and containing 6 square ells; also a unit of length equal to 1/40th of a furlong or 1 rod, pole or perch.
fanner	machine generating an artificial draught for winnowing grain.
feal	turf.
feu	heritable real estate held under feudal tenure from a superior on payment of an annual feu duty.
feuar	person possessing a feu.

fir	Scots pine tree.
firehouse	a room in a house with a hearth.
firlot	unit of capacity containing one quarter of a boll.
flag	thin turf.
flake	hurdle.
flitting	removing.
found	foundation of a building.
fun	whin or gorse.
gean	wild cherry tree, *prunus avium*.
girnel	place where grain or meal is stored: a granary building or a domestic chest/kist.
glen	valley; also a shieling place.
grassing	practice of sending cattle away from lowland farms in summer to be grazed on highland pasture; usually involving a money payment
grassum	payment made by a tenant at the commencement of a tack.
grip	small structure attached to a township firehouse, stable or byre (exact meaning not known).
guano	bird dung imported from South America for use as a fertiliser.
hanging lum	smokehood, made of timber, located over an open hearth and venting through the ridge of a roof.
harling	external wall coating of lime, perhaps mixed with gravel.
harping	sieving or sifting grain.
head dyke	wall dividing infield land from outfield grazing and waste.
herd	person—often a boy or girl—responsible for watching cattle to prevent straying.
heritor	proprietor of a heritable subject; a landowner.
hog	young sheep not yet shorn.
hook	short sickle with serrated edge; also the man or woman who wields it.
horse gin	horse-powered engine, specifically to turn a threshing machine and/or fanner.
horse gang	circular track of a horse gin.
improvement	a piece of waste land broken in for arable.
infield	the arable land of a township.
interdict	court order preventing any action complained of as illegal.
kilnbarn	building incorporating grain storage and processing areas, with a kiln for drying and malting grain, all under one roof .
Lammas	Christian festival and legal term falling on 1 August.
lease	mutual contract between a proprietor and a tenant in respect of lands, mills, fishings, etc.
lint	linen.
little house	privy or latrine
lower	downstream (in place-names).

lum	chimney.
mail	rent.
mailander	low status inhabitant of a cooperative township, perhaps occupying land subset by a subtenant.
malt	grain that has been steeped in water, allowed to sprout, then dried in a kiln as raw material for ale and whisky.
march	boundary.
marl	lime-rich clay used as fertiliser on acid soils.
Martinmas	Christian feast of St Martin and a legal term day falling on 11 November.
meliorations	improvements to buildings; payment made to reimburse the cost of improvements.
merk	monetary unit (and occasionally a coin), worth two-thirds of one pound, 13s 4d.
miduell	timber element, probably forming part of the roof, in a turf-and-cruck dwelling (exact meaning not known).
muirburn	burning of vegetation on grazing land to improve the quality of the grass or as a preliminary to ploughing.
multure	a payment, usually in kind, to a miller for grinding grain.
nether	downstream (in place-names); equivalent to **easter**.
outfield	township land beyond the permanent arable, used mainly for grazing, but periodically ploughed.
oxgang/oxgate	land measure, notionally containing 13 acres, but varying in practice according to the quality of the soil—containing one-eighth part of a plough.
peck	measure of capacity containing seven and three quarter pints in Scotland and two gallons in England.
pindler	official who protected woodland, specifically by poinding straying cattle.
plain/plane	sycamore tree.
plough/ploughgate/ ploughland	land measure, extending to one quarter of a *dabhach*.
poinding	impounding.
pole	land measure containing 30.25 square yards (imperial measure); also a unit of length extending 16 feet 6 inches.
pound Scots (£ Scots)	unit of monetary value, worth one-twelfth of one pound sterling during the early eighteenth century. The pound sterling was generally used for accounting purposes from the 1760s onwards, though evidence of recent conversion from Scots pounds is preserved in values including twelfths of a penny.
process	collection of writs, forms and pleadings comprising a court case.
quey	young cow up to three years old, which has not calved.

quern	hand-turned millstones for grinding grain into flour.
quoin	external corner of a building; a dressed stone making the cornerr.
reek hen	poultry hen paid in rent; typically one hen for each reeking (smoking) chimney belonging to a possession; thus notionally (or originally) equivalent to the number of dwellings on the holding.
rod	unit of length extending 16 feet 6 inches; the basis for burgh planning, in which feus were one-and-a-half rods wide.
rood	land measure containing 240 falls, extending to one quarter of an acre; the size of a royal burgh feu.
roup	auction.
rig	ridge in ploughland; also a strip in a common field; occasionally a land measure containing one quarter of a Scots acre.
runrig	the division of arable land into strips allocated among several cultivators or possessors.
sarking	boards covering the rafters of a roof, to which slates are nailed.
Saugh	tree of *salix* species; willow.
shieling	grazing site at a distance from a township, to which cattle are taken in summer.
shot	division of infield, equivalent (though not in area) to a furlong.
side	timber in a turf-and-cruck house, probably in the roof, perhaps equivalent to a purlin (exact meaning not known).
silver fir	*picea pectinata* or *pinus picea* native trees of central Europe and northern Asia.
skew	slope of a gable wall from ridge to eaves—finished with a **skewput** at the wallhead.
skirret	water parsnip, cultivated as a garden root vegetable.
smearing	treating the fleeces of sheep with tar to prevent maggots and other parasites.
sned/sneddings	lopped off branches.
souming	limit set on the number of beasts allowed to graze a pasture.
spar	length of timber, typically the trunk of a pine tree of a length and quality suitable for carrying a sail on a square-rigged sailing ship.
spence	inner or best room of a house; a parlour; also a room in which victuals are kept, equivalent to a buttery.
stilt	handle of a plough.
stirk	young bullock or heifer between one and two years of age.
stot	young castrated ox; also sometimes a heifer.
subset	subtenant; **subsetting**—subletting.
summer town	dwellings on a shieling site.
superior	feudal overlord.
superphosphate	soil improver manufactured by treating bones or mineral phosphate with sulphuric acid.

tack	lease.
tathing	area of waste upon which cattle had been folded to manure the ground prior to ploughing.
thirlage	obligation to have grain ground at a specified mill—to which tenants were **thirled**.
thrammel	chain for tethering an ox in its stall.
upper	upstream (place-name), equivalent to **wester**.
usquebaugh	'water of life'—whisky.
wadset	pledge of land in security for a debt, the debitor having the right to recover the lands on repayment; a form of mortgage.
washboard	skirting board.
wedder	castrated ram.
wester	upstream (place-name).
whin	gorse or furze.
Whitsunday	Christian festival of Pentecost, a moveable feast celebrated on the fiftieth day after Easter; also a legal term falling on 15 May.
winnowing	separating grain from chaff using a natural or mechanically-generated draught.

NOTES

Abbreviations

APS—T. Thomson and C. Innes (eds), *The Acts of the Parliaments of Scotland* (Edinburgh, 1814–75). Acts of Scottish Parliaments are also online at https://www.rps.ac.uk, though *APS* is preferred in *A Regular Revolution* as being less infected by silent editorial alteration.

AUL—Aberdeen University Library.

Ballindalloch—Grant and Macpherson-Grant of Ballindalloch muniments, at Ballindalloch Castle, Banffshire (NRAS771).

Brodie—Brodie of Brodie muniments, at Brodie Castle, Moray (NRAS770).

District of Moray (1987)—C. McKean, *The District of Moray: an illustrated architectural guide* (Edinburgh, 1987).

Fife—Duff house/Montcoffer muniments (Earl of Fife's estates), at AUL (MS3175).

Gentleman Farmer (1776)—H. Home (Lord Kames), *The Gentleman Farmer* (Edinburgh, 1776).

Gordon—Gordon castle muniments, at NAS (GD44).

Grange—Grange estate muniments, at NAS (GD298).

Lethen—Lethen estate muniments, at NAS (GD247); also at Lethen house, Nairnshire.

MA—Moray Archives: including Moray District Record Office; Moray District Council Department of Libraries, Local Studies Section; The Moray Council Archives; and The Moray Council Heritage Centre.

NRAS—National Register of Archives (Scotland)

NRS—National Records of Scotland (formerly National Archives of Scotland and Scottish Record Office).

NSA—*New Statistical Account of Scotland*, vol. XIII, Banff—Elgin—Nairn (Edinburgh, 1845).

OS—Ordnance Survey.

OSA—*The Statistical Account of Scotland, 1791-1799*, edited by Sir John Sinclair, (the 'old statistical account'), reprinted edition: D. J. Withrington and I. R. Grant (eds) *Banffshire, Moray & Nairnshire*, vol. XVI (Wakefield, 1982).

Practical Farmer (1766)—A. Grant, *The Practical Farmer's Pocket-Companion* (Aberdeen, 1766).

RCAHMS—Royal Commission on the Ancient and Historical Monuments of Scotland.

RHP—Register House Plans (at NRS).

Roy's map (1747–55)—William Roy and David Watson, military survey, 1:36,000 (1747-55)—online edition http://www.scran.ac.uk.

SAS—Strathavon Survey, conducted as part of the Scotland's Rural Past project, supervised by RCAHMS: finished plans and site descriptions lodged in the National Monuments Register; field notebooks and further information retained by SAS members.

Scottish Farming (1953)—J. E. Handley, *Scottish Farming in the Eighteenth Century* (London, 1953).

Strathavon (1960)—V. Gaffney, *The Lordship of Strathavon* (Aberdeen, 1960).

Survey of Moray (1798)—W. Leslie, *A Survey of the Province of Moray; historical, geographical, and political* (Aberdeen, 1798).

View of Banff (1794)—J. Donaldson, *General View of the Agriculture of the County of Banff* (Edinburgh, 1794).

View of Banff (1812)—D. Souter, *General View of the Agriculture of Banff* (Edinburgh, 1812).

View of Elgin (1794)—J. Donaldson, *General View of the Agriculture in the Counties of Elgin or Moray, lying between the Spey and the Findhorn; including part of Strathspey, in the County of Inverness* (London, 1794).

View of Moray (1811)—W. Leslie, *General View of the Agriculture in the Counties of Nairn and Moray* (London, 1811).

1 An Introduction

1. Groome, *Ordnance Gazetteer of Scotland* (1882), vol. 1, p. 27; vol. 2, pp. 338, 454, 552; vol. 3, p. 46; vol. 4, pp. 295, 433, 445; vol. 6, p. 470. These measures are imperial acres, standardised in 1824 at 4,840 square yards; Scots acres, in common usage during the eighteenth century, contained 6,150.40 square yards, or 4 rods/poles/perches.
2. *View of Moray* (1811), p. 16.
3. Macaulay Institute for Soil Research, *Soil Survey of Scotland, Sheet 5, Eastern Scotland: land capability for agriculture* (1981). The map is amplified by Walker (and others) *Soil and Land Capability for Agriculture: Eastern Scotland* (1982).
4. Defoe, *A Tour through the Whole Island of Great Britain* (1962—first published, 1724–26), pp. 404-5.
5. Gordon, *Moravia*, in Blaeu, *Atlas Novus* (1654); also <https://maps.nls.uk/atlas/blaeu>.
6. Kirk, *The Books of Assumption of the Thirds of Benefices* (1995), p. 467.
7. Macgregor, *The Buried Barony* (1944), pp. 2-3; Ross, *The Culbin Sands* (1992), pp. 64, 70-2, 159; *APS*, vol. IX, pp. 452-3.
8. *Survey of Moray* (1798), p. 124; *OSA*, vol. XVI, Duffus, p. 504; NRS, RHP2004. This sandblow forms a distinct layer—exposed and documented in archaeological excavations at Clarkly Hill on the margins of the former Loch of Roseisle in F. Hunter *Excavations at Clarkly Hill, Roseisle, Moray, 2011, 2012* (2012, 2013).
9. *NSA*, Duffus, p. 39.
10. *Survey of Moray* (1798), p. 124.
11. OS, Elginshire, second edition (1905).
12. Institute of Geological Sciences, *Elgin*, sheet 95 (1969).
13. Gordon, *Moravia* (1654).
14. The Meteorological Office, *The Climate of Scotland* (1989), pp. 6, 12-14, 16-18.
15. Smout, Macdonald and Watson, *A History of the Native Woodlands of Scotland, 1500–1920* (2005), p. 389: Simmons, *An Environmental History of Great Britain from 10,000 years ago to the present* (2001), p. 121.
16. Johnstoun, '*Elginum*', in *Poemata Omnia* (1642), translated by John Barclay in Alexander Skene, *Memorials for the government of royall-burghs in Scotland* (1685).
17. Gordon, *Moravia* (1654); text translation by National Library of Scotland, <http://www.nls.uk/maps/atlas/blaeu>. The 'open threshing areas' seem unlikely: threshing barns with opposed doorways to create a through-draft for winnowing are usual in Moray townships.
18. Defoe, *Tour through ... Great Britain* (1962—first published 1724–26), p. 405.
19. Sunspots and solar flares may have influenced weather in 1829: exceptional aurora borealis in July was followed by torrential rain on 3 and 4 August causing the 'muckle spate' and widespread flooding in Moray. Lauder, *The Great Floods of August 1829*, third edition (1873), p. 1.
20. Volcanic effects are discussed in Dodgshon (and others), 'Endemic stress, farming communities and the influence of Icelandic volcanic eruptions in the Scottish highlands', in Geological Society, *Special Publications*, vol. 171, pp. 267-80; also in Ross, 'Improvement on the Grant estates in Strathspey in the later eighteenth century: theory, practice and failure?', in Hoyle (ed.), *Custom, Improvement and the Landscape in Early-Modern Britain* (2011), pp. 289-311.
21. *Survey of Moray* (1798), pp. 102-3. Leslie recycled this statement in his *View of Moray* (1811) changing the place of origin of the people buying Moray grain from Aberdeen to Angus (p. 14).
22. *View of Elgin* (1794), pp. 10-1.
23. 'Letters from a young farmer to his father', in *The Farmer's Magazine* (1807), p. 369.
24. Watson, *Morayshire Described* (1868), p. 4; also in Gordon, *Moravia*<http://www.nls.uk/maps/atlas/blaeu>.
25. MA, ZBFo A97/930/1, Forres burgh guidebook (*c.* 1930).
26. Hamilton, *An Economic History of Scotland in the Eighteenth Century* (1963), p. 76.
27. The Meteorological Office, *The Climate of Scotland* (1989), pp. 6, 12-14, 16-18.
28. *View of Moray* (1811), p. 14.
29. Macaulay Institute for Soil Research, *Soil Survey, Sheet 5* (1981).
30. *View of Moray* (1811), p. 17.

31. Data from 1:10,560 OS maps.
32. British Geological Survey: *Glenlivet*, sheet 75W and *Glenfiddich*, sheet 85E (Nottingham, 1996); *Knockando*, sheet 85W (Nottingham, 1997).
33. Beaton, 'The pattern of Moray building', in Sellar (ed.), *Moray: Province and People* (1993), pp. 225-52.
34. Macaulay Institute for Soil Research, *Soil Survey, sheet 5* (1981).
35. British Geological Survey: *Knockando* (Nottingham, 1997); *Glenfiddich* and *Glenlivet* (Nottingham, 1996).
36. *View of Moray* (1811), pp. 18, 21.
37. *Strathavon* (1960), pp. 282-9.
38. *OSA*, Aberlour, p. 4.
39. Barrett, *Mr James Allan* (2004), pp. 108, 116.
40. Johnson, *A Journey to the Western Islands of Scotland* (1924—first published 1775), p. 35.
41. *OSA*, Inveravon, p. 624; Edinkillie, p. 587; Kirkmichael, p. 293.
42. The relentless all-year-round travels of a peripatetic minister during 1688–90, documented in Barrett, *Mr James Allan* (2004), include journeys: Elgin—Aberdeen from 15–18 January 1690, pp. 148-9; Aberdeen—Edinburgh from 27–31 January 1690, pp. 153-4.
43. Barrett, *Mr James Allan* (2004), pp. 39-40, 211, 218.
44. MA, ZVSt 633/722/2, Stoneyforenoon estate, transport of a coach by sea from Leith to Findhorn (1722); ZVSt 60/725, repairs to coach (1725).
45. Boswell, *The Journal of a Tour to the Hebrides with Samuel Johnson* (1955—first published 1785), pp. 80-3.
46. Ballindalloch, bundles 47, 358, 360, 481, 507, 555, 717, 720, 729, 747, 761, 1093, 1116, 1169, 1195, correspondence with Stafford and Sellar (1808-18).
47. Richards, *Patrick Sellar and the Highland Clearances* (1999), pp. 17-18.
48. Hall, *Travels in Scotland* (1807), p. 453.
49. Census 1841.
50. Warde, discusses the linguistic implication—largely from an English perspective—in 'The idea of improvement, *c.* 1520–1700', in Hoyle, *Custom, Improvement and the Landscape in Early Modern Britain* (2011), pp. 127-48.
51. *Oxford English Dictionary* (1933). The word 'improvement' is notably used in this sense in the sixteenth century in 'An Act concerning the Improvement of Commons and Waste Grounds', 3 & 4 Edward VI, chapter 3.
52. Quoted in Warde, 'The idea of improvement' (2011), pp. 139-40.
53. This terminology is borrowed from *OSA*, Dyke & Moy, p. 540, in which the reporter refers to a 'mode of cultivation ... reduced to established rules, or a regular succession of crops'.
54. Mitchell, *Historical Geography* (1954), p. 4.
55. Adams, 'The agents of agricultural change', in Parry and Slater (eds) *The Making of the Scottish Countryside* (1980) pp. 155-75; *Scottish Farming* (1953).
56. *OSA*, Dyke & Moy, p. 537.
57. *Scottish Farming* (1953) p. 145; Macmillan, *Letters of of Patrick Grant, Lord Elchies* (1927), p. 61.
58. 'Letters from a young farmer to his father', in *Farmer's Magazine* vol. viii (1807), pp. 369-75; Ballindalloch, bundle 1234 (1816).
59. *District of Moray* (1987), p. 166.
60. Gordon, GD44/24/33/3/6 (6 July 1776).
61. *View of Banff* (1812), p. 101.
62. *General View of the Agriculture of ... Aberdeen* (1794), quoted in Campbell, 'The Scottish Improvers and the course of agrarian change in the eighteenth century', in Cullen and Smout, *Comparative Aspects of Scottish and Irish Economic and Social History, 1600–1900* (1977), p. 209.
63. *OSA*, Birnie, p. 467; Aberlour, p. 6; Drainie, p. 484; Duffus, pp. 500-1, 510.
64. A single exception to this is documented among the independent-minded feuholders of Fochabers, who planted a fashionably revolutionary tree of liberty in their village at the Gates of Gordon castle in 1792: Logue, *Popular Disturbances in Scotland, 1780–1815* (1979), p. 149.
65. Whatley, 'How tame were the Scottish lowlanders during the eighteenth century?', in Devine (ed.), *Conflict and Stability in Scottish Society, 1700–1850* (1990), pp. 1-30; Whatley, *Scottish Society, 1707–1830* (2000), pp. 142-83; K. J. Logue, *Popular Disturbances in Scotland, 1780–1815* (1979).
66. Ferguson, *Scotland 1689 to the Present* (1978), p. 166-72.
67. Whyte, *The Changing Scottish Landscape, 1500–1800* (1991), p. 130.
68. Devine 'Social Stability in the eastern lowlands during the Agricultural Revolution, 1780–1840', in Devine (ed.) *Lairds and Improvement in the Scotland of the Enlightenment* (1978), p. 59.

69. A similar process, characterised as a 'land-rush', occurred on Grant estates in Strathspey during the 1760s—described in A. Ross, 'Improvement on the Grant estates' (2011).

70. This is the tone was set by early commentators such as Hugh Miller in *Sutherland as It Was and Is, or how a country may be ruined* (1843), quoted in Fry, *Wild Scots, four hundred years of highland history* (2005), pp. 170-1. It is continued in more modern histories such as Prebble, *The Highland Clearances* (1969) and Mackie, *A History of Scotland* (1978), but moderated in Richards, *The Highland Clearances* (2008). 'Clearances created a permanent sense of injustice against the Highland landlords and their managers ... which has hardly yet recovered ... much of the historical literature is filled with indignation and rhetoric'— Richards, *Debating the Highland Clearances* (2007), p. 3.

71. *Survey of Moray* (1798) pp. 341-2; Devine, *The Transformation of Rural Scotland: social change and the agrarian economy, 1660–1815* (1994), p. 144; Devine, *Clearance and Improvement: land, power and people in Scotland, 1700–1900* (2006), p. 106.

72. Fife, MS3175, vol. 9 (20 Feb 1814)—see chapter 5.

73. Brereton, *Gordonstoun: ancient estate and modern school* (1968), p. 112; Ballindalloch, bundle 1234 (1816); MA, DBA A97/2, 'The Planting' (*c.* 1840).

74. *OSA*, p. 565.

75. *Ibid.*, p. 677.

76. *Survey of Moray* (1798), pp. 341-2.

77. *OSA*, p. 277.

78. For example many improvement schemes initiated by the fifth duke of Argyll were more or less abandoned in the duke's own lifetime: Fry, *Wild Scots* (2005), pp. 162-4.

79. Richards, *The Highland Clearances* (2008), p. 286; the Barra story is distilled from pp. 265-88.

80. Crofts were created only on a limited scale in Moray, though some small settler farms were scarcely larger than Hebridean crofts. Most Moray crofts are in Kirkmichael including: a dozen or so dwellings forming a roadside crofting settlement at Auchnarrow; a further scatter at Scalan; and some small settler farms at the head of Glenlivet.

81. Branigan, *The Last of the Clan: Gereral Roderick Macneill of Barra, 41st chief of Clan Macneil* (2010), pp. 80-3; Richards, *The Highland Clearances* (2008), p. 268.

82. Richards, *The Highland Clearances* (2008), pp. 274-84.

83. This account is distilled from Prebble, *The Highland Clearances* (1969), Richards, *The Highland Clearances* (2008), and Richardson, *The Curse on Patrick Sellar* (1999).

84. Mackenzie, *The History of the Highland Clearances: containing a reprint of Donald Macleod's 'Gloomy Memories'* (1986—first published 1883) p. 119; Macleod quotes from Beecher Stowe's *Sunny Memories of Foreign Lands* (London, 1854).

85. Fry, *Wild Scots* (2008), p. 161.

86. Quoted in Lockhart (ed.) *Scottish Planned Villages* (2012), p. 27.

87. *Ibid.*, p. 167.

88. Prebble, *The Highland Clearances* (1969), p. 56.

89. Richards, *The Highland Clearances* (2008), p. 177.

90. Sellar wrote in 1820: 'Morayshire is by no means a well improved country. I think it is now, generally speaking, far behind Sutherland as now peopled, but at that time Sutherland seemed a century behind it'—quoted in Richardson, *The Curse on Patrick Sellar* (1999), p. 110.

91. David Stewart of Garth, *Sketches of the Character, Manners, and Present State of the Highlanders of Scotland* (London, 1822), quoted in Richards, *Debating the Highland Clearances* (2007), pp. 27, 160.

92. Richards, *The Highland Clearances* (2008), p. 181.

93. *Ibid.*, p. 194.

94. Quoted in Fry, *Wild Scots* (2005), p. 169.

95. Richards, *The Highland Clearances* (2008), pp. 186-99. This episode is emotively described in Prebble, *The Highland Clearances* (1969), pp. 58-94.

96. Tindley, *The Sutherland Estate, 1850–1920* (2010), p. 13.

97. Richards, *The Highland Clearances* (2008), p. 78.

98. Devine, *The Transformation of Rural Scotland* (1994); Devine, *Clearance and Improvement* (2006).

99. Devine, *The Scottish Nation, 1700–2000* (1999), p. 147.

100. Aitchison and Cassell, *The Lowland Clearances* (2003).

101. Iredale and Barrett, 'The lowland clearances', in *The Scots Magazine* (September, 1992), pp. 633-40.

102. Aitchison and Cassell, *The Lowland Clearances* (2003), p. 70-1.
103. *Ibid.*, p. 27.
104. Devine, *The Transformation of Rural Scotland* (1994), p. 47.
105. Devine, *Clearance and Improvement* (2006), pp. 49-50.
106. *Ibid.*, p. 94.
107. *Ibid.*, p. 97.
108. *Ibid.*, p. 99; Devine, *The Transformation of Rural Scotland* (1994), pp. 130-2.
109. Aitchison and Cassell, *The Lowland Clearances* (2003), p. 60; Devine, *The Transformation of Rural Scotland* (1994), p. 151.
110. Devine, *The Transformation of Rural Scotland* (1994), p. 141.
111. Devine, 'Social stability' (1978), p. 66; Devine, *The Transformation of Rural Scotland* (1994), p. 105.
112. Quoted in Aitchison and Cassell, *The Lowland Clearances* (2003), p. 150.
113. Quoted in Devine, *The Transformation of Rural Scotland* (1994), p. 140, and also in Devine, *The Scottish Nation* (1999), p. 147.
114. Devine, *The Scottish Nation* (1999), pp. 99-100.
115. Aitchison and Cassell, *The Lowland Clearances* (2003), p. 99.
116. Devine, 'Social stability in the eastern lowlands of Scotland during the agricultural revolution, 1780-1840', in Devine, *Lairds and Improvement in the Scotland of the Enlightenment* (1978), p. 59.
117. Devine, *The Transformation of Rural Scotland* (1994), p. 36.
118. Devine, 'Social stability in the eastern lowlands' (1978), p. 66; Devine, *The Transformation of Rural Scotland* (1994), pp. 128-32.
119. Aitchison and Cassell, *The Lowland Clearances* (2003), p. 99.
120. Watley, 'How tame were the Scottish lowlanders during the eighteenth century?', in Devine (ed.) *Conflict and Stability in Scottish Society, 1700–1850* (1990), p. 23.
121. Aitchison and Cassell, *The Lowland Clearances* (2003), p. 107.

2 A Cooperative Countryside

1. Population estimates from *OSA*, which includes Webster's census of 1755.
2. *OSA*, Elgin, pp. 588-9, Forres, pp. 617-8.
3. RHP2004, Roseisle map (1773); *Survey of Moray* (1798), pp. 126, 149-51.
4. Graham, *The Social Life of Scotland in the Eighteenth Century* (1950—first published, 1899), pp. 166-7.
5. Devine, *The Transformation of Rural Scotland* (Edinburgh, 1994), pp. 1-2.
6. Quoted in Cameron, *The Ballad and the Plough* (1987), p. 19.
7. The cooperative nature of the early-modern township is highlighted in Smout, *A History of the Scottish People, 1560–1830* (1969), pp. 114-16.
8. This legislative underpinning is discussed in Whyte, *Agriculture and Society in Seventeenth-Century Scotland* (1979), pp. 94-112, though, arguably it does not support the conclusion that seventeenth-century legislation provided a basis for improvement.
9. Graham, *Social Life of Scotland* (1950—first published 1899), p. 157.
10. Grant, *Essays on the Superstitions of the Highlanders in Scotland* (1811), p. 27.
11. Quoted in Dodgshon, *The Origins of British Field Systems* (1980), p. 3.
12. The general picture is drawn from Smout, *History of the Scottish People* (1969), pp. 111-45; *Scottish Farming* (1953), pp. 33-73; Graham, *Social Life of Scotland* (1950—first published 1899), pp. 146-227; Whyte, *Agriculture and Society in Seventeenth-Century Scotland* (1979).
13. Whyte, *Agriculture and Society in Seventeenth Century Scotland* (1979), p. 63.
14. *Ibid.*, p. 65.
15. *APS*, vol. VIII, pp. 494-5 (1685).
16. *Ibid.*, vol. II, p. 134 (1426), vol. VIII, p. 494 (1625).
17. Brereton, *Gordonstoun* (1968), pp. 101-2.
18. Whyte, *Agriculture and Society in Seventeenth-Century Scotland* (1979), p. 215.
19. The system is discussed in detail in Dodgshon, 'The nature and development of infield-outfield in Scotland', in *Transactions of the Institute of British Geographers*, number 59 (1973), pp. 1-23.
20. MA, ZBEl B2/1, Elgin burgh court book; the regulations were reiterated into the eighteenth century.
21. Allardyce, *Scotland and Scotsmen in the Eighteenth Century*, vol. II (1888), p. 193.

22. J. Anderson, *General View ... of Aberdeen* (1794), quoted in *Scottish Farming* (1953), p. 40.

23. Fife, MS3175/939, tacks (1735); NRS, Gordon, GD44/43/101: 'flaughtering ... is frequently done with a flaughter spade & the turff so cast is dry'd & burnt on the ground before plowing' (1773).

24. *APS*, vol. II, p. 242 (1503); III, p. 35 (1567).

25. The word 'tathing' is used to describe a piece of outfield or muir that has been enclosed and dunged for cultivation.

26. Roy's map (1747-55); also see, for instance, Hoskins, *The Midland Peasant* (2008—first published 1957).

27. RHP2004, Roseisle map (1773).

28. Fife, MS3175 RHP31002.

29. OSA, p.541.

30. Fife, MS3175/F30/3/1.

31. Grange, GD298/406.

32. Grange, GD298/412.

33. Roy's map (1747–55).

34. RHP2488, 'A Short Description of Strath Avin' (1762).

35. Smout, Macdonald and Watson, A History of the Native Woodlands of Scotland (2007) p. 392.

36. RHP2488, 'Description of Strath Avin' (1762), 'daugh of Inverourie'.

37. Aitchison and Cassell, The Lowland Clearances (2003) p. 100.

38. Laichland strips seem to have been significantly larger than those of classic English commonfield arable—which measured from half a rood to half an acre and were typically around one rood in area: Hoskins, The Midland Peasant (2008—first published 1957), pp. 65-6.

39. View of Elgin (1794), p. 16.

40. Dixon, Puir Labourers and Busy Husbandmen (2002), pp. 32-6; estate plans naming possessors of individual strips include: MA, Lethen atlas (1746) and RHP1423, Garmouth lands (1772-73).

41. Dodgshon, 'Scandianavian 'Solskifte' and the sunwise division of land in eastern Scotland', in Scottish Studies, vol. 19 (1975), pp. 1-13.

42. Dodgshon, The origins of British field systems (1980), pp. 3, 40; Grant, Highland Folk Ways (1995—first published 1961), pp. 89-90; Whittington, 'The problem of runrig', in Scottish Geographical Magazine no. 86 (1970), p. 70, doubted that strips were distributed so as to ensure equal possessions.

43. Scottish Farming (1953), p. 48; Hodd, 'Runrig on the eve of the agricultural revolution', in Scottish Geographical Magazine, vol. 90:2 (1974), p. 130.

44. Grange, GD298/412.

45. OSA, vol. XVI, Elgin, p. 597.

46. MA, ZBE1 A2/16/2-5, feu charter, (1794).

47. Grant, 'Description of ... Monymusk', in Miscellany of the Spalding Club, vol. 2 (1842), p. 96; Birnie, 'Ridge cultivation in Scotland', in The Scottish Historical Review, vol. 24 (1927), pp. 95-8; ridge-formation is discussed at length in Taylor, Fields in the English Landscape (1975), pp. 75-88, and illustrated throughout Slezer, Theatrum Scotiae (1693).

48. J. Robertson, View of ... Southern Perthshire,p. 64, quoted in Grant, Highland Folk Ways (1995—first published 1961), p. 89.

49. Monymusk papers, in The Miscellany of the Spalding Club, vol. II (1842), p. 97.

50. Taylor, Fields in the English Landscape (1975), pp. 82-8.

51. The same curve is characteristic in burgh planning, where roods were marked out with a plough, manoeuvred in the usual medieval manner.

52. MA, Stoneyforenoon muniments, ZVSt 77/720/1.

53. Dixon, Puir Labourers and Busy Husbandmen (2002), p. 36.

54. Graham, The Social Life of Scotland in the Eighteenth Century (1950—first published 1899), p. 156.

55. OSA, Elgin, p. 596.

56. Edward Burt, quoted in Scottish Farming (1953), p. 65.

57. Quoted in Scottish Farming (1953), p. 63.

58. Survey of Moray (1798), p. 324.

59. Quoted in Graham, The Social Life of Scotland in the Eighteenth Century (1950—first published 1899), p. 156.

60. Scottish Farming (1953), pp. 66-7.

61. Grant, Highland Folk Ways (1995—first published 1961), pp. 281-3; Allardyce, Scotland and Scotsmen in the Eighteenth Century, vol. II (Edinburgh, 1888), p. 199.

62. OSA, Birnie, p. 462.

63. OSA, p. 473.
64. Grange, GD298/412, baron court (1712).
65. Fife, MS3175/Z/2 (1762).
66. OSA, Dallas, p. 474; Kirkmichael, pp. 281-2, 292; Milliken and Bridgewater, Flora Celtica (2004) pp. 174-9.
67. Whyte, Agriculture and Society in Seventeenth Century Scotland (1979), pp. 69-70.
68. Grange, GD298/412 (1742); Lethen, GD247/63/6 (1658, 1664); Ballindalloch, bundle 800 (1733).
69. Grange, GD298/412.
70. Lethen, GD247/69/30/2 (1831).
71. Henderson and Dickson (eds.) A Naturalist in the Highlands: James Robertson, his life and travels in Scotland 1767–1771 (1994), p. 161, quoted in Smout, Macdonald and Watson, A History of the Native Woodlands of Scotland (2007), p. 109.
72. OSA, Edinkillie, p. 583; Elgin, p. 599.
73. Lethen, GD247/67/19/54, lease (1811).
74. Ballindalloch, bundle 1216, lease (1819).
75. Barrett and Mitchell, Elgin's love-gift (2007), p. 27. The burgh reported the loss of several hundred sheep, but no goats, during the plundering of 1645; Lethen was plundered of 1,800 sheep and goats (p. 52).
76. Smout, 'Goat-keeping in the old highland economy', in Scottish Studies, vol. 9 (1965), p. 2.
77. A single kid was paid among Strathavon rents in 1752–54, see Strathavon (1960), p. 243. Only six goats were listed among beasts stolen from Dallas husbandmen by Grant raiders in 1689—though 359 sheep were lifted: Murray, The Dallas Raid, 1689 (Forres, undated), pp. 6-13.
78. Strathavon (1960), p. 89.
79. OSA, p. 273.
80. Lethen, GD247/67, Monaughty (1807), Kilbuiack (1811).
81. Morris (and others), Field Guide to the Animals of Britain (1984), pp. 104-5. Feral goats also survive in Galloway, the Borders and Western Highlands..
82. Grant, The Farmer's New-Years Gift to His Countrymen (1757), p. 26.
83. Pennant, A Tour in Scotland MDCCLXIX (1776), p. 292.
84. View of Moray (1811), p. 283.
85. Strathavon (1960), p. 89.
86. RHP1795 (1774).
87. Fife, MS3175/RHP31002 (1771).
88. Ballindalloch, bundle 1519, conditions (c. 1800).
89. MA, ZBEl B32/766/121.
90. Strathavon (1960), pp. 82-3
91. Adams, Directory of Former Scottish Commonties (1971), pp. 160-3.
92. Brodie, box 24/4, Hardmuir commonty (1824).
93. Strathavon (1960), pp. 9-24.
94. Surveyof Moray (1798), p. 322.
95. Ibid., p. 170.
96. Fife, MS3175 vol. 1 (3 September 1761).
97. Strathavon (1960), pp. 282-94, 'Cattle grassed in the Forrest of Glenaven' (1750).
98. Gaffney, 'Summer shealings', in The Scottish Historical Review, vol. 38 (1959), pp. 24-7.
99. Gordon, GD44/23/6/2 (c. 1775).
100. Strathavon (1960), pp. 80-93; MA, ZEMm B32/721/5, 724/4, 726/11, 20, 727/16, 738/38, sheriff court processes (1721–38).
101. Bil, The Shieling, 1600–1800 (1990), p. 50; Strathavon (1960), pp. 1, 3.
102. Fenton, Scottish Country Life (1976), pp. 134-51.
103. Bil, The Shieling, 1600–1800 (1990), p. 240.
104. SAS fieldwork.
105. Fife, MS3175/RHP31002, Coxtown (1771).
106. Ballindalloch, bundle 1151.
107. SAS fieldwork; Strathavon (1960), p. 29; RHP2488, Strathavon plans (1762).
108. Strathavon and Glenlivet were held largely by feuars and wadsetters during the 1680s; Strathavon was chiefly possessed by men paying an annual rent in 1708: Strathavon (1960), pp. 193-5, rentals, 1680, 1708.
109. RHP2004, Roseisle plan (1773); Gordon, GD44/51/379/10, granary repairs (1733–4)
110. Brodie, Box 40/4-7, granary repairs (1756).
111. Fife, MS3175, vols 1038 (1764), 1058 (1842).

112. Fife, MS3175/864-875 (1715–37); vol. 1038 (1763); vol. 3 (1768); vol. 4, (1773); vol. 5, p. 82 (1770–73); vol. 1039 (1779).
113. AUL, Duff of Braco, MS3175/2727/1/209 (1756).
114. MA, ZVSt 7/715-723, correspondence (May 1715, May–June 1716, 1720, 3 February 1723).
115. Ballindalloch, bundle 827 (1770).
116. MA, ZVTar 65/653, Tarras rental (1653).
117. MA, ZVBro 65/773, Cloves rental (1773).
118. Strathavon (1960) pp. 223-50, rental (1752–54).
119. Ibid., p. 191, rental.
120. Ibid., pp. 194-5, rentals.
121. Carter, Farmlife in North-east Scotland, 1840–1914 (1979), p. 17.
122. Fife, MS3175/Z/2 (1762).
123. NSA, vol. XIII, p. 137.
124. Gaffney, Tomintoul, Its Glens and Its People (1970), p. 51.
125. MA, ZBEl B32/766/78, process (1766).
126. *Strathavon* (1960), pp. 241, 239 (rental, 1752–54).
127. Quoted in Carter, *Farmlife in North-east Scotland* (1979), p. 16.
128. Ballindalloch, bundle 1216.
129. Fife, MS3175/F/13/3/1 (14 September 1767).
130. Fife, MS3175, vol. 2 (29 March 1763).
131. Gordon, GD44/51/745/3, rental (1755).
132. Fife, MS3175/F12/2.
133. Grange, GD248/443 (1741).
134. MA, ZVSt 7/729/1, letter to factor (22 March 1729).
135. Grange, GD298/406 (1755).
136. Carter, *Farmlife in North-east Scotland* (1979), p. 16.
137. *Strathavon* (1960), pp. 191-275, rentals (1683–1802).
138. Grange, GD298/412 (1727).
139. Grange, GD298/429 (1753).
140. 'By the custom of baronies, house-mills and querns are always broke'—W. M. Morison (editor) *Decisions of the Court of Session* (Edinburgh, 1801) quoted in Gauldie, *The Scottish Country Miller, 1700–1900* (1981), p. 30. The landowner required court sanction to destroy domestic mills and querns, though in practice factors might act without legal authority (ibid., pp. 38-9). An Act of Parliament of 1799 allowed commutation of multures (paid in grain) into money payments—a key stage in the decline of thirlage.
141. Whyte, 'Written leases and their impact on Scottish agriculture in the seventeenth century', in *Agricultural History Review,* vol. 27 (1979), pp. 1-5.
142. *Strathavon* (1960), p. 194, judicial rental.
143. Gordon, GD44/23/2.
144. Ballindalloch, bundle 920.
145. Ballindalloch, bundle 800 (1732–33).
146. Grange, GD298/416.
147. Grange, GD298/430, tack for one half of Craighead and Easter Cotes (1754).
148. Ballindalloch, judicial rentals, bundles 920 (1733), 1142 (1749).
149. Brodie, box 6/7.
150. MA, ZEMm B32/769/7.
151. Brodie, box 41/2.
152. Hay, *Lochnavando No More* (2005), pp. 174-5, rentals (1637–1809).
153. *OSA*, p. 456.
154. *The Ephemera*, XVI (24 March 1823), pp. 186-7.
155. Roy's map (1747-55); *OSA*, Inveravon, p. 239, Kirkmichael, p. 269, Birnie, p. 462, Edinkillie, p. 578-9, Knockando, p. 623; Lindsay, 'The commercial use of woodland coppice management', in Parry and Slater (eds), *The Making of the Scottish Countryside* (1980), p. 272-4.
156. Quoted in Smout, Macdonald and Watson, *A History of the Native Woodlands of Scotland* (2007), p. 66.
157. Roy's map (1747–55).
158. J. Sinclair (ed.) *General Report of the Agricultural State and Political Circumstances of Scotland*, vol. II (1814), p. 324, quoted in Smout, Macdonald and Watson *A History of the Native Woodlands of Scotland* (2007), p. 65.

159. Shaw, *The History of the Province of Moray* (1775), p. 154-5.
160. Murray, *A Companion and Useful Guide to the Beauties of Scotland* (1982—first published 1799), pp. 60-1.
161. RHP2488 (1762).
162. *APS*, vol. II, p. 7 (1424), p. 343 (1535); vol. III, p. 145 (1579); vol. VIII, p. 488 (1685); also 1 George I 'An Act to encourage the planting of timber trees ... and for the better preservation of the same'.
163. Smout and Watson, 'Exploiting Semi-natural woods, 1600–1800', in Smout (ed.), *Scottish Woodland History* (1997), pp. 87-9
164. Stewart, 'Using the woods, 1600–1800', in Smout (ed.) *People and Woods in Scotland* (2003), pp. 100-3.
165. SAS fieldwork; Smout, Macdonald and Watson, *A History of the Native Woodlands of Scotland* (2007), pp. 165-72.
166. Gordon, GD44/51/380/3.
167. Gordon, GD44/39/26/1, GD44/39/27/4, 12, 14, 15.
168. Grange, GD298/412, baron court (1727); Gaffney, *Strathavon* (1960) rental (1752-4), pp. 223-49.
169. *APS*, vol. II, p. 51 (1475). Yard-dyke trees are discussed in Barrett, 'Regular reforestation: woodland resources in Moray 1720–1840', in Mills, *Community, Woodlands and Perceptions of Ownership* (2011), pp. 12-19.
170. *Ibid.*, p. 343 (1535).
171. Brodie, box 13/6.
172. Fife, MS3175/939, 857.
173. Fife, MS3175/943/2.
174. Fife, MS3175941.
175. Fife, MS3175/941.
176. SAS fieldwork.
177. Fife, MS3175/F74/5.
178. SAS Fieldwork; OS, first edition, 1:2500, Banffshire, XXX.3.
179. These have been surveyed and studied (in Strathavon and Speyside) and partly included in the National Monuments Register, by the SAS, whose fieldwork informs all following discussion of township planning and architecture.
180. Edward Burt (1754), quoted in Cameron, *The Ballad and the Plough* (1987), p. 18.
181. Roy's map (1747-55); RHP2004, Roseisle plan (1773).
182. There were fifteen tenants in the 'Survey of Roseisle' by William Anderson (1749), in Barrett, *Roseisle Remembered* (2000); NRS, RHP2004 (1773).
183. Gordon, GD44/51/379/8 (1736); Grange, GD298/406 (1755).
184. Gordon, GD44/151/379/8.
185. Gordon, GD44/51/783/1.
186. Lauder, *The Great Floods of August 1829* (1873—first published 1830) p. 156; NRS RHP1423 (1772–73).
187. Beaton 'The Pattern of Moray building', in Sellar (ed.) *Moray: province and people* (1993), p. 234-5; Walker, *Earth Structures and Construction in Scotland* (1996), p. 67; NRS, RHP1423, plan (1772–73).
188. Fife, MS3175, vol. 8 (16 April 1802).
189. Beaton, 'The Pattern of Moray building', in Sellar (ed.) *Moray: province and people* (1993), p. 237; Walker *Earth Structures and Construction in Scotland* (1996), pp. 67-72.
190. There is no evidence of imported timber in Moray townships, reported in Whyte, *Agriculture and Society in Seventeenth- Century Scotland* (1979), p. 163.
191. Fife, MS3175/831.
192. Grange, GD298/406 (1681).
193. RHP1808, Strathavon (1840); OS, Banffshire, sheet XLIII (1869); SAS fieldwork.
194. Whyte, *The Changing Scottish Landscape, 1500–1800* (1991), pp. 29, 34.
195. Noble, 'Turf-walled houses of the central highlands', in *Folk Life* vol. 22, (1983-4), p. 79; personal comment from Ross Noble and from Scotland's Rural Past staff at the RCAHMS.
196. RHP2487, Glenlivet; RHP2488, Strathavon.
197. Oral information from RCAHMS and from Bob Powell and Ross Noble at Highland Folk Museum, Newtonmore.
198. Iredale and Barrett, *Discovering Your Old House* (2002), pp. 20, 126; Brunskill, *Illustrated Handbook of Vernacular Architecture* (1978), pp. 68-9.
199. Lauder, *The Great Floods of August 1829* (1873—first published 1830), p. 74.
200. MA, ZCMm R2, minutes (30 April 1811).
201. SAS fieldwork; Hunter, *Excavations at Clarkly Hill, Roseisle, 2011, 2012* (2012, 2013).

202. SAS fieldwork. Few townhips have been systematically excavated and published. An example excavated at Eldbotle, East Lothian, comprised buildings of similar size to Moray examples (*viz.* 8.6m × 3.3m internally), though of rather sturdier construction with walls 1m thick. One Eldbotle building was dated to the late thirteenth century, demonstrating the long heritage of stone-found-turf-and-cruck vernacular style. Published in Morrison, Oram and Oliver, 'Ancient Eldbotle unearthed: archaeological evidence for a long-lost early medieval East Lothian village', in *Transactions of the East Lothian Antiquarian and Field Naturalists' Society*, vol. 27 (Haddington, 2008), pp. 21-43. Also excavations by Jeff Oliver at Bennachie, 2013.

203. 'every man made his own house': M. Gray, in Withrington and Grant (eds) *The Statistical Account of Scotland, Vol. XVII, Inverness-shire, Ross and Cromarty* (1981), p. xiii.

204. Stewart, 'Using the woods' (2003) p. 95.

205. Architectural details are largely distilled from SAS fieldwork.

206. SAS fieldwork.

207. Hay, 'The cruck-building at Corrimony, Inverness-shire'. In *Scottish Studies*, vol. 17 (1973), pp. 127-33.

208. When the defendant in a law case could not be 'personally apprehended', the summons was executed 'by placing it in the lockhole of the most patent door, after giving six several knocks'.

209. Walker, 'The hanging chimney in Scottish meat preservation', in *Vernacular Building*, number 9 (1985), pp. 42-50. This, perhaps, was more usual in the laich. Pigs were kept at Gordonstoun in the 1740s: Brereton, *Gordonstoun* (1968), p. 102. Among highlanders 'the swine was reckoned still unclean': *Survey of Moray* (1798), p. 321; an observation repeated in Grant, *Highland Folk Ways* (1961), pp. 7, 87.

210. MA, ZVSt 570/724, comprisings.

211. Grange, GD298/406, comprisings (1717–55); NRS, Gordonstoun, CS96/1341/2, Plewlands comprisings (1708).

212. Grange, GD298/406 (1681).

213. Grange, GD298/406.

214. Boswell, *The Journal of a Tour to the Hebrides with Samuel Johnson* (1955—first published 1785), p. 97.

215. Creelwork dwellings were reported in some highland districts in the 1880s, though they vanished from Moray during the mid-nineteenth century: Smout, Macdonald and Watson, *A History of the Native Woodlands of Scotland* (2007), pp. 94-5.

216. Seventy ells of sailcloth were purchased for this purpose for Fife's fisher houses at Speymouth: Fife, MS3175, vol. 1038 (1763). The arrangement is shown in sketches by Walter Geikie (*c.* 1830), in Carruthers (ed.), *The Scottish Home* (1996), pp. 22, 53.

217. Walker, Macgregor and Little, *Earth Structures and Construction in Scotland* (1996), p. 21.

218. *Survey of Moray* (1798), p. 329.

219. *OSA*, St Andrews-Lhanbryd, p. 642.

220. Milliken and Bridgewater, *Flora Celtica* (2004), p. 177.

221. Grange, GD298/406 (1687).

222. MA, DBL79/1, James Allan's memoirs (1688–91); Barrett, *Mr James Allan* (2004), p. 200: a house for James Allan was erected, finished and furnished within about three weeks in 1690.

223. Fife, MS3175/705, F13/3/2 (1767), vol. 1058 (1771).

224. Dixon, *Puir Labourers and Busy Husbandmen* (2002), pp. 53-4; Hunter, *Excavations at Birnie, Moray, 2008* (Edinburgh, 2009), pp. 42-3, *2009* (2010), pp. 38-9.

225. SAS fieldwork.

226. Grange, GD298/406, comprisings 1717–55; SAS fieldwork.

227. Slade, 'Rothiemay: an 18th century kiln barn', in *Vernacular Building*, no. 4 (1978), p. 21.

228. Walker, Macgregor and Stark, *Scottish Turf Construction* (2006), p. 33.

229. *Survey of Moray* (1798), p. 332.

230. Thomas Morer (1702), quoted in Graham, *The Social Life of Scotland in the Eighteenth Century* (1950—first published 1899), p. 180.

231. *View of Elgin* (1794), p. 23.

232. 'when properly thatched, they were warmer and freer of damp than what was built of stone and clay': Allardyce, *Scotland and Scotsmen in the Eighteenth Century*,vol. II (1888), p. 200.

233. Lauder, *The Great Floods of 1829* (1873—first published 1830), p. 74; NRS, RHP1808 (1840); SAS fieldwork.

234. The turf-walled United Presbyterian manse at Howford Bridge, Nairn, was photographed by George Washington Wilson around 1860, in Walker, Macgregor and Little, *Earth Structures and Construction in Scotland* (1996), p. 15.

235. Quoted in Devine, *Clearance and Improvement* (2006), p. 42.

3 Revolutionary theory

1. Rampini, *A History of Moray and Nairn* (1898), p. 301.
2. Wittington, 'Was there a Scottish agricultural revolution?', in Cole (and others), *Modern Scottish History 1707 to the Present* vol. 3 (1998), p. 79; the question was substantially, and positively, answered by Adams, 'The agricultural revolution in Scotland: contributions to the debate', in *Area*, vol. 10, no. 3 (1978), pp. 198-205.
3. Adams (ed.), *Papers on Peter May Land Surveyor, 1749–1793* (1979) p. xi; Adams, 'Agents of agricultural change', in Parry and Slater *The Making of the Scottish Countryside* (1980), p. 173.
4. Whyte, 'Rural housing in lowland Scotland; the evidence of estate papers', in *Scottish Studies*, vol. 19 (1975), p. 55.
5. Fenton 'How did pre-improvement landscape and society work?', in *Review of Scottish Culture*, number 15 (2002–03), p. 13.
6. Smith, 'The background to planned village formation in north east Scotland', in Smith and Stevenson (eds), *Fermfolk and Fisherfolk* (1989), p. 1.
7. Handley, *The Agricultural Revolution in Scotland* (1963).
8. Devine, *Clearance and Improvement* (2006), p. 46.
9. Ferguson, *Scotland 1689 to the Present* (1978), p. 169.
10. *OSA*, vol. XVI, Introduction, p. xxvi.
11. *OSA*, p. 284.
12. Kinloss is omitted from this analysis because its meagre report contains no useful information.
13. *OSA*, p. 582.
14. *NSA*, vol. XIII, p. 190.
15. *Viewof Elgin* (1794), pp. 15-16.
16. *View of Banff* (1794), pp. 12-13.
17. *View of Moray* (1811); *View of Banff* (1812), p. 101.
18. *View of Moray* (1811), pp. 18-19.
19. Dalrymple, *An Essay on the Husbandry of Scotland with a Proposal for the Improvement Thereof* (1732).
20. Mackintosh, *Essay on Ways and Means for Inclosing, Fallowing, Planting, &c.* (1729).
21. Campbell, 'The Scottish improvers', in Cullen and Smout (eds), *Comparative Aspects of Scottish and Irish Economic and Social History, 1600–1900* (1977), p. 205.
22. Fife, MS3175/921.
23. *Gentleman Farmer* (1776) title page.
24. *Ibid.*, pp. xii-xiii.
25. *Ibid.*, p. xiv.
26. Dalrymple, *An Essay on the Husbandry of Scotland with a proposal for the improvement thereof, by a lover of his* country (1732), p. 5.
27. The first use in print of the term 'gentleman-farmer' is in Henry Fielding's *Tom Jones*, book 8, chapter 11 (first published 1749).
28. *Gentleman Farmer* (1776), p. xv.
29. Boswell, *The Journal of a Tour to the Hebrides with Samuel Johnson* (London, 1955—first published 1785), pp. 62, 81.
30. *Gentleman Farmer* (1776) p. xvii.
31. Alexander Pope 'Essay on Man, epistle iii', in B. Dobree (ed.) *Alexander Pope's Collected Poems* (London, 1956—first published 1733) p. 205.
32. Quoted in Hamilton, *An Economic History of Scotland in the Eighteenth Century* (1963), p. 55.
33. Mackintosh, *An Essay on Ways and Means for Inclosing, Fallowing, Planting, &c.* (1729), p. xxvi.
34. Peters, *The Rational Farmer* (1770), p. 5-6. asserted, 'Agriculture may justly be called a *Science ... next in kindred to philosophy*'.
35. *View of Banff* (1812), p. v.
36. *Ibid.*, pp. 34, 102.
37. P. Graham, *General View of the Agriculture of Stirlingshire* (1812), quoted in McGuire, *Agricultural Improvements in Strathkelvin 1700–1850* (1988), p. 15.
38. Fife, MS3175, vol. 1058, offers (1836).
39. Quoted in Mowat, *Easter Ross 1750–1850* (1981), p. 31.
40. Quoted in *Scottish Farming* (1953), p. 117.

41. Mackintosh, *Ways and Means for Inclosing* (1729), pp. xlvi, xlvii.

42. Gordon, GD44/14/15/40.

43. *Gentleman Farmer* (1776), p. vii.

44. Glass, 'Sugar for the brose', part 1, in *History Scotland*, part 6, number 4 (May/June 2006), p. 43.

45. MA, *A Catalogue of the Singular and Curious Library originally formed between 1610 and 1660 by Sir Robert Gordon of Gordonstoun, which will be sold by auction J. G. Cochrane, Mon 29 March 1816.* The other agricultural titles were J. Crawshey, *The Countryman's Instructor ... containing ... remedies for the diseases befalling to horses, sheep, and other cattle* (London, 1636); *The Countryman's Recreation, or the Art of Planting, Grafting and Gardening* (London 1640); and N. Crew, *Anatomy of Plants* (London, 1682).

46. Ballindalloch, bundle 1002 (*c.* 1797) lists Millar's *Gardener's Dictionary*; *Sylva* and *Pomona* by John Evelyn; James Gorton's *Practical Gardener*; Thomas Mawe's *Every Man's Gardener*; a herbal by Joseph Miller; Thomas Hitts' *Treatise on Fruit Trees*; William Boutcher's *Treatise on Forest Trees*; and *Botanicum Officiale*. Subsequently the library acquired Peter Lawson's 1843 *Treatise on Cultivated Grasses and Other Herbage and Forage Plants*.

47. Towsey, *Reading the Scottish Enlightenment* (2010), p. 48.

48. *Ibid.*, pp. 48-50.

49. Brodie, castle library catalogue lists: Francis Home, *Agriculture and Vegetation* (1776); John Johnstone, *An Account of the Mode of Draining Land* (1801); and Robert Bell, *A Treatise on Leases* (1805); also legal treatises and *Elements of Criticism* by Lord Kames—but not the *Gentleman Farmer* (1776).

50. Gordon, GD44/14/15/40 (1754), GD44/49/14 (1729-1832).

51. Towsey, *Reading the Scottish Enlightenment* (2010), pp. 106-8.

52. Hitchings, *Defining the World: the extraordinary story of Dr Johnson's dictionary* (2005), p. 50.

53. Adams, 'Agents of agricultural change', in Parry and Slater, *The Making of the Scottish Countryside* (1980), p. 172.

54. Grant, 'Agriculture in Banffshire 150 years ago', reprinted from *Banffshire Journal*, 1 January–2 April 1901 (1902), p. 21.

55. *View of Banff* (1812), p. 102.

56. *Practical Farmer* (1766), p. 20.

57. quoted in Holmes, 'The circulation of agricultural books during the eighteenth century', in *Agricultural History Review*, no. 54, vol. I, (2006), p. 78.

58. *Ibid.*, pp. 60-3, 71.

59. *Scots Magazine*, vol. x (April 1848), pp. 187-90.

60. Towsey, *Reading the Scottish Enlightenment* (2010), p. 107.

61. Chambers and Mingay, *The Agricultural Revolution 1750–1880* (1966), pp. 74-5.

62. *The Compact Edition of the Dictionary of National Biography* (1975), vol. II, p. 2352.

63. Quoted in Hamilton, *An Economic History of Scotland in the Eighteenth Century* (1963), p. 60.

64. *Scottish Farming* (1953), p. 159.

65. Mowat, *Easter Ross* (1981), pp. 31-2.

66. *Scottish Farming* (1953), pp. 149-50.

67. *Ibid.*, p. 159.

68. *Ibid.*, p. 147-8.

69. *Gentleman Farmer* (1776), p. xii.

70. Whyte, 'Rural transformation and lowland society', in Cooke (and others) *Modern Scottish History 1707 to the Present* (1998), p. 96.

71. *Scottish Farming* (1953), p. 145; Macmillan, *Letters of Patrick Grant, Lord Elchies* (1927), p. 61; Gordon, GD44/51/24, 74, 75.

72. Whyte, 'Agriculture in Aberdeenshire in the seventeenth and early eighteenth centuries: continuity and change', in Stevenson, *From Lairds to Louns* (1986), p. 18.

73. Roy's map (1747-55).

74. *OSA*, Dyke & Moy, p. 537.

75. Roy's map (1747-55).

76. Macmillan, *Letters of Patrick Grant, Lord Elchies* (1927), pp. 38, 45, 53

77. *Scottish Farming* (1953) pp. 160-1; Hamilton (ed.), *Selections from the Monymusk Papers, 1713–55* (1945); Hamilton, *Life and Labour on an Aberdeenshire Estate, 1735–1750* (1946).

78. *Miscellany of the Spalding Club*, vol. ii (1842), pp. 96-7.

79. Quoted in Grant, 'The social effects of the agricultural reforms and enclosure movement in Aberdeenshire', in *Economic History*, 1926–29 (1929), p. 97.

80. Whyte, *The Changing Scottish Landscape 1500–1800* (1991), p. 147.
81. Roy's map (1747–55).
82. *View of Moray* (1811), p. 199.
83. Grant, 'Agriculture in Banffshire 150 years ago', reprinted from *Banffshire Journal*, 1 January 1901–2 April 1901 (1902), pp. 21-2.
84. MA, ZVCu 60/1, Cullen mains cashbook (1760–67).
85. *Scottish Farming* (1953), p. 165.
86. *View of Moray* (1811), p. 199.
87. Sir Balfour Paul *The Scots Peerage*, vol. 4 (Edinburgh, 1907) pp. 39-40.
88. Gordon, GD44/43/18/64 (16 December 1763).
89. Newte, *Prospects and Observations on a Tour in England and Scotland* (1791), pp. 148-9.
90. Lawson, *A Country Called Stratherrick* (1987), pp. 109-11; Withrington and Grant (eds), *The Statistical Account of Scotland*, vol. XVII, Inverness-shire, Ross and Cromarty (1981), Boleskine & Abertarf, pp. 20-31.
91. Hay, *Lochnavando No More* (2005), p. 140; Ballindalloch, bundles 1093, 1195, correspondence (1816).
92. Adams (ed.), *Papers on Peter May Land Surveyor 1749–93* (Edinburgh, 1979) p. xxii; Adams, 'The agents of agricultural change', in Parry and Slater (eds), *The Making of the Scottish Countryside* (1980), p. 173.
93. Quoted in Youngson, *After the Forty-five* (1973), p. 27.
94. Mowat, *Easter Ross* (1981), pp. 29-30.
95. 'Letters of a young farmer to his father', in *The Farmer's Magazine*, vol. viii (1807), p. 369.
96. Quoted in Patrick, *Scotland: the age of achievement* (1976), p. 33.
97. MA, ZBEl C6/825.
98. Alexander Brodie of Lethen married, in 1754, Henrietta, daughter of William Grant of Ballindalloch; and Lethen was Ballindalloch's superior in respect of Struthers in Kinloss.
99. This sketch is distilled from *A History of the Family of Brodie* (anon, *c*. 1870) and Brodie, *Brodie Country* (1999).
100. Herman, *The Scottish Enlightenment* (2002), pp. 163-4; Daichies, *The Scottish Enlightenment* (1986), pp. 23-9.
101. Adams, 'The agents of agricultural change', in Parry and Slater (eds), *The Making of the Scottish Countryside* (1980), p. 170.
102. Davidson, *The Royal Highland and Agricultural Society of Scotland, 1784–1984* (1984), pp. 1-2.
103. Grant, *The Farmer's New-Years Gift to this Countrymen* (1757), p. 2. Though the group that formed around Boulton, Watt, Priestley, Darwin and Wedgwood about 1775 most famously enjoyed the title of 'The Lunar Society', it had long been usual for gentlemen or clergymen to schedule meetings for nights when a full moon facilitated travel.
104. Smith, *The Gordon's Mill Farming Club, 1758–1764* (1962), p. 36.
105. *Aberdeen Journal*, 10 January 1749.
106. Smith, *Gordon's Mill Farming Club* (1962), pp. 72-3, 27.
107. Davidson, *The Royal Highland and Agricultural Society of Scotland, 1784–1984* (1984), pp. 5-10.
108. *Prize Essays and Transactions of the Highland Society of Scotland*, vol. vi (1824), pp. 221-8.
109. Adams, 'Agents of agricultural change', in Parry and Slater (eds), *The Making of the Scottish Countryside* (1980), p. 171.
110. Fife, MS3175/121.
111. Towsey, *Reading the Scottish Enlightenment* (2010). Forsyth's library certainly stocked improvement tracts.
112. Macandrew, *Memoir of Isaac Forsyth* (1889), pp. 30, 50-1, 68-9.
113. *View of Moray* (1811), p. 444.
114. Mackintosh, *Elgin Past and Present* (1914), p. 193.
115. Fife, MS3175, vol. 9.
116. *View of Moray* (1811), p. 443; Ballindalloch, bundle 729 (1809).
117. Fife, MS3175/421.
118. Bulloch, *The Badenoch & Strathspey Farming Society, (Banff, undated)*.

4 Practical revolutionaries and statutory regulation

1. Patrick, *Scotland, the age of achievement* (1976), p. 30.
2. Glass 'Sugar for the brose: Sir Archibald Grant, Jamaica and agricultural improvements at Monymusk *c*. 1720–1760', in *History Scotland*, vol. 6, no. 4 (March/April 2006), p. 40.

3. Richards, *Patrick Sellar and the Highland Clearances* (1999), p. 19.
4. Landowners' extravagances are discussed in Nenadic, *Lairds and Luxury* (2007).
5. Glass, 'Sugar for the brose', in *History Scotland* vol. 6, no. 3 (March/April 2006), pp. 35-9 and , vol. 6, no. 4 (May/June 2006), pp. 40-5.
6. Dowds, 'The Scots and Slavery', in *History Scotland* vol. 11, no. 2 (March/April 2011), p. 20.
7. Adams, 'The agents of agricultural change', in Parry and Slater, *The Making of the Scottish Countryside* (1980), p. 165-6.
8. Mingay, 'The eighteenth century land steward', in Jones and Mingay (editors) *Land, Labour and Population in the Industrial Revolution* (1967), pp. 10-11.
9. *The Compact Edition of the Dictionary of National Biography* (1975), vol. 1, p. 1124.
10. Cowie, *The Life and Times of William Marshall* (1999), pp. 30-3.
11. Laurence, *The Duty of a Steward to his Lord* (1743), p. 24.
12. Bain, *The Lordship of Petty* (1925), pp. 106-12.
13. Young, *The Parish of Spynie* (1871), pp. 248-9.
14. This story is told at length in Ross, 'Improvement on the Grant estates in Strathspey', in Hoyle (ed.), *Custom, Improvement and the Landscape in Early Modern Britain* (2011), pp. 289-311.
15. *Ibid.*, pp. 291-2.
16. Adams, 'The Agents of agricultural change', in Parry and Slater, *The Making of the Scottish Countryside*(1980), pp. 160-3.
17. Ross, 'Improvement on the Grant estates in Strathspey', in Hoyle (ed.), *Custom, Improvement and the Landscape in Early Modern Britain* (2011), pp. 292-3.
18. *Ibid.*, p. 294.
19. *Ibid.*, p. 295.
20. *Ibid.*, pp. 299-300.
21. *Ibid.*, pp. 301-2.
22. *Ibid.*, p. 306. The debt was reduced to £113,693 in the early 1790s—*ibid.* p. 308.
23. *Ibid.*, pp. 308-10.
24. Fife, MS3175, vol. 1958 (1850).
25. Fife, MS3175, vol. 7, (1800).
26. Gordon, GD44/51/136/1 (1795).
27. Gordon, GD44/51/150 (1803); Hay, *Lochnavando No More* (2005), pp. 139-40.
28. *Strathavon* (1960), pp. 84-94.
29. Gordon, GD44/23/6/2.
30. *OSA*, Kirkmichael, p. 305; *The Ephemera*, VIII (11 November 1822) pp. 93-4.
31. *Strathavon* (1960), pp. 86-93; Gordon, GD44/23/6/2.
32. Ballindalloch, bundle 827, correspondence (1769-70).
33. Hay, *Lochnavando No More*(2005), pp. 139-44.
34. Gordon, GD44/51/129 (1816–24).
35. Grange, GD298/443 (1741).
36. Grange, GD298/384, (1722).
37. Brodie, bundle 41/2.
38. *View of Banff* (1794), pp. 9, 14.
39. Fife, MS3175/F54/4 (1787).
40. For example Fife, MS3175/ M/743 (1768).
41. Fife, MS3175, vol. 10 (1817).
42. Fife, MS3175, vol. 1058 (1850).
43. *APS*, (1424), vol. II, p. 7; (1503), vol. II, pp. 242, 251; (1535), vol. II, p. 343; (1579), vol. III, p. 145; (1617), vol. IV, p. 537; (1655), vol. VI, part ii, p. 834; (1661), vol. VII, p. 308; (1696), vol. X, p. 36. These Acts of Scottish Parliaments were largely superseded by 6 George III, chapter XLVIII 'Act for the better preservation of timber trees, and of woods and underwoods; and for the further preservation of roots, shrubs and plants' (1766), extended by 13 George III, chapter XXXIII '... to poplar, alder, maple, larch and hornbeam' (1773).
44. *Survey of Moray* (1798), p. 341.
45. *APS*, vol. IX, p. 421, Act anent lands lying run-rig (1695).
46. MA, 'Plan of the Lands of Roseisle as they now ly in Runrigs' (1773–75); NRS, RHP2004.
47. Hay, *Lochnavando No More* (2005), p. 143.
48. *View of Moray* (1811), p. 131.
49. Ballindalloch, bundle 1226, correspondence (1800).

50. 'Sketch Plan of the Aughteen Parts', in Cramond, *Records of Elgin* (1903), vol. I, p. 200.
51. Gordon, GD44/32/7/69 offers to Fochabers feuars (1776); GD44/32/7/109, Fochabers feuars, (*c.* 1775).
52. OS, Elginshire, first edition, 1:10,560 , sheet IX (surveyed 1870–71, published 1874).
53. *APS*, vol. VI, part, i, p. 803, 'anent the comounties' (1647); vol. IX, p. 462 'concerning the Dividing of Commonties', (1695).
54. Adams, *Directory of Former Scottish Commonties* (1971), pp. 160-3.
55. *View of Moray* (1811), p. 132.
56. Adams, *Directory of Former Scottish Commonties* (1971), pp. 158-63.
57. *Strathavon* (1960), pp. 9-24; RHP2490, 'plan of the contraverted ground at the Fea Vait' (*c.* 1770–86); Gordon, GD44/39/13/1-3.
58. Brodie, box 19/5, box 24/6 (1824–36).
59. Gordon, GD44/43/41/22.
60. Gordon, GD247/65/15/1; Fife, MS3175/RHP31341, plan of Alves common (1835).
61. Lethen, GD247/65/15/6 (1835).
62. Ballindalloch, bundle 1349 (1842).
63. Devine, *The Transformation of Rural Scotland* (1994), p 65.
64. 'An act to encourage the improvement of lands held under settlements of strict entail in Scotland', 10 George III, chapter 51.
65. Elginshire records are amissing.
66. NRS, SC2/66/1, register of entail improvements, Banffshire.
67. *Ibid.*
68. NRS, SC266/2, register of entail improvements, Banffshire.
69. NRS, SC266/3, register of entail improvements, Banffshire.
70. *APS*, vol. II, p. 494, 'Anent the maner of the warning of tennentis to flit ...' (1555).
71. Hay, *Lochnavando No More* (2005), p. 71; details of procedure are taken from Moray processes, MA, ZBEl B32.
72. NRS, CS1/14, pp. 75r-77r.
73. *OSA*, St Andrews-Lhanbryd, p. 646.
74. Iredale and Barrett, 'The lowland clearances', in *The Scots Magazine* (September 1992), pp. 636-6; Banffshire processes have been destroyed.
75. MA, ZBEl B32/766.
76. MA, ZBEl B32/766/78.
77. MA, ZEMm B32/768/3; 770/11; 771/9; 771/12; 772/5; 773/7; 773/9. All these estates were given up to settle the Brodie debts.
78. MA, calendars, ZBEl B32, ZEMm B32, ZBFo B32.
79. Population estimated from *OSA*.
80. MA, ZEMm/770/14.
81. MA, ZEMm B32/769/2, 3, 14; ZBEL B32/766/82.
82. Fife, MS3175/831.
83. MA, ZEMm B32/769/2.
84. MA, ZEMm B32/769/3.
85. MA, ZBEl B32/766/82.
86. There is a similar mismatch between court records and estate muniments on Grant estates in Strathspey. Here A. Ross refers to 'mass clearance' and 'decreets of removal against hundreds of tenants'. These removals however do not appear as processes among sheriff court papers, suggesting (if the court papers are indeed intact) that removal was accomplished as an administrative procedure that did not come to court: Ross, 'Improvement ... in Strathspey (Farnham, 2011) pp. 308-10.
87. MA, calendars, ZBFo B32, ZBEl B32.

5 Landscape by the Rule

1. *View of Banff* (1812), p. 339.
2. Sinclair, *An Account of the Systems of Husbandry Adopted in the More Improved Districts of Scotland* (1814), pp. 30, 38.
3. Fenton, *Scottish Country Life* (1976), p. 16.

4. Fife, MS3175, vol. 1055, minutes of let (1798–1823).
5. Ballindalloch, bundle 1132.
6. Rampini, *A History of Moray and Nairn* (1897), p. 302.
7. OS, Elginshire sheets VIII, IX, XVII.
8. Adams, *Papers on Peter May Land Surveyor 1749–1793* (1979), p. xvi.
9. Fife, MS3175/703/2.
10. Ballindalloch, bundle, 1013, 1019.
11. Searles, *The Land Steward's and Farmer's Assistant* (1779).
12. Gordon, GD44/14/15/40, Gd44/49/14, inventories and catalogues of books (1754, 1729–1832).
13. Laurence, *The Duty of a Steward to his Lord* (1723), pp. 86-90.
14. Campbell, *The Grampians Desolate* (1804), book 3, p. 55.
15. RHP35982; Adams, *Papers on Peter May Land Surveyor 1749–1793* (1979), p. xx.
16. Fife, MS3175 vol. 3, letter (29 August 1764); vol. 4, letter (13 Nov 1772).
17. Grange, GD298/416, report on drainage (*c.* 1760).
18. Adams, 'The agents of agricultural change', in Parry and Slater (eds), *The Making of the Scottish Countryside* (1980), pp. 161, 170.
19. Gordon, GD44/51/381/15.
20. Peter May's professional descendants are described in Adams, 'Agents of agricultural change', in Parry and Slater (eds) *The Making of the Scottish Countryside* (1980), p. 168. Peter May's career—and the activities of his descendants—are documented in Adams, *Papers on Peter May Land Surveyor 1749–1793* (1979).
21. Fife, MS3175/RHP31002.
22. Fife, MS3175/703/2.
23. Gordon, GD44/27/10 (30 June 1770).
24. Brodie, estate map (1770).
25. Douglas, *The Lord Provosts of Elgin* (1926), pp. 66-8.
26. For example, see McWilliam's plans in Fife, MS3175/RHP31308, Easter Kintrea as subdivided (1834); MS3175/RHP31009, Kintrea (1843); MS3175/RHP31336, Blervie (1841); and NRS, RHP1807, 1808, 1809, 1811, 1815, Strathavon (1840); Fife, MS3175, vol. 1058, includes offers for farms valued by McWilliam down to the late 1830s.
27. Ballindalloch, bundle 1234, plans of Parks of Pitchaish (*c.* 1812).
28. MA, 'Plan of the estate of Balnageith ... surveyed by G. Campbell Smith' (1827).
29. MA, Lethen estate atlas (1746).
30. Lethen, GD247/69/30/1/2.
31. Lethen, GD247/69/30/1/2.
32. RHP1774, 1776, 2487, Glenlivet (1761) 1 inch: 8 Scots chains, 1:7100; RHP2488, Strathavon plans, 1 inch: 8.5 Scots chains—1:7550.
33. SAS fieldwork.
34. RHP2488.
35. Fife, MS3175/RHP31002.
36. RCAHMS, D16476, Easter Elchies, Knockando, plan copied from the archive of The Macallan Distilleries Limited.
37. RHP1746, 1747, 1748, 1749, 1750, 1751 (1773–1822).
38. RHP1807 (*c.* 1840).
39. RHP1808, 1809, 1810, 1811, 1812, 1814, 1815 (*c.* 1840).
40. *Practical Farmer* (1766), p. 4.
41. *View of Banff* (1794), p. 40.
42. *View of Moray* (1811), p. 133.
43. Roy's map (1747–55).
44. *OSA*, Aberlour, p. 4; Rafford, p. 628; Speymouth, p. 656; Urquhart, p. 701.
45. *NSA*, Drainie, p. 155; Inveravon, p. 142; Knockando, p. 74; Elgin, p. 14; Speymouth, pp. 54-5.
46. MA, ZBFo A2, Forres Town Council, minutes (24 August 1835).
47. Fife, MS3175/RHP31336, plan of the farm of Blervie by George McWilliam (1841).
48. Young, *The Parish of Spynie* (1871), pp. 49, 53.
49. Fife, MS3175/942, tacks, (1742–79); Ballindalloch, bundle 1132, tacks (1785-96), bundle 1343, conditions of lease (1819).
50. Fife, MS3175/RHP31055, Mosstowie (*c.* 1820).
51. Fife, MS3175, vol. 9.

52. Lethen, GD247/69/30/1/2 (1792).
53. Fife, MS3175, vol. 3, letter from Archibald Duff, factor (29 August 1764).
54. Fife, MS3175/831.
55. Fife, MS3175/831.
56. Fife, MS3175, vol. 9.
57. Gordon, GD44/23/2, tacks (1692–1738).
58. Ballindalloch, bundle 1132.
59. Ballindalloch, bundle 1343, conditions of lease (1819).
60. Ballindalloch, bundle 1119, vouchers (1821–31).
61. Brodie, box 16/6, tacks (1768–87).
62. Brodie, box 16/8.
63. Brodie, box 13/1, 'General Estimates for the Improvement of Brodie Estates' (1832).
64. Lethen, GD247/30/1/9.
65. MA, ZBFo P8/1, plan of Burdsyards, by W. Cumming (1819).
66. Mackintosh, *An Essay on Ways and Means for Enclosing, Fallowing, Planting, &c. Scotland* (1729), pp. li, 101, 105-11.
67. Anderson, *A Practical Treatise on Draining Bogs and Swampy Grounds* (1797), p. 177.
68. Sinclair, *Systems of Husbandry* (1814), p. 45.
69. *View of Banff* (1794), p. 40.
70. *View of Banff* (1812), p. 139.
71. *NSA*, pp. 47-8.
72. Pearson (ed.), *Flitting the Flakes* (1992).
73. *NSA*, Drainie, p. 156; Dyke & Moy, p. 224; Rafford, p. 253.
74. Gordon, GD44/51/129, outlays at Drumin (1824).
75. NRS, SC2/66/2, register of entail improvements, Banffshire.
76. Fife, MS3175, vol. 1041.
77. MA, ZBFo A2, Forres Town Council, minutes (21 October 1814).
78. MA, DBA A91/2, *Forres Gazette* handbills.
79. The heroic labour involved in manual land clearance in Buchan in the 1830s is documented in Smout and Wood, *Scottish Voices, 1745–1960* (1990), pp. 90-3.
80. SAS fieldwork: Belon, Balcorach, Lyne, Tom Cruim, Bailecnoic, Baluig, Ballintomb, Tombain, Dalbeithachan, Wester Gaulrig.
81. Grange, GD298/437/2.
82. Gordon, GD44/40/10; SAS fieldwork.
83. Gordon, GD44/49/10/1 (*c.* 1800).
84. Fife, MS3175, vol. 9 (1814).
85. Fife, MS3175, bundle 941.
86. Mackintosh, *An Essay on Ways and Means for Inclosing* (1729) p. 71.
87. SAS fieldwork.
88. Roy's map (1747–55).
89. Fife, MS3175, vol. 6.
90. SAS fieldwork.
91. *View of Moray* (1811) p. 133.
92. Macandrew, *Memoir of Isaac Forsyth, bookseller in Elgin, 1768–1859* (1889), p. 30.
93. Gordon, GD44/49/2/3 (late eighteenth century).
94. Lauder, *The Great Moray Floods of August 1829* (1873—first published 1830), p. 76.
95. Young, *The Parish of Spynie* (1871), pp. 77-8.
96. Fife, MS3175/706.
97. Fife, MS3175/F30/3/1.
98. Fife, MS3175, vol. 1041.
99. MA, ZBEl A2, Elgin Town Council, minutes (12 May 1788).
100. Fife, MS3175/RHP31336, plan by George McWilliam (1841).
101. AUL, MS2226/337/31, Tulloch of Tannachy, heritable bond for £300 (1775).
102. NRS, SC2/66/2, register of entail improvements, Gordon estates (1839-40).
103. Young, *The Parish of Spynie* (1871), p. 78.
104. Mackintosh, *Elgin Past and Present* (1891), pp. 140-1.
105. Grant, *The Farmer's New-Years Gift to his Countrymen* (1757), p. 3.

106. During the fifteenth century the planting of broom (*Sarothamnus* Scoparius—which also fixes nitrogen) was encouraged—but not gorse/whin (*Ulex Europaeus*): *APS*, vol. II, p. 51 (1457).
107. AUL, Duff of Braco papers, MS2727/1/226.
108. NRS, SC2/66/2, SC2/66/3, registers of entail improvements, Gordon estates (1840, 1841).
109. Hay and Stell, *Monuments of Industry* (1986) p. 18.
110. A whin mill has been reported in Kellas—though the local informant cannot now remember exactly where it is.
111. *Aberdeen Journal Notes and Queries*, vol. VI (1913), pp. 78-9; Mason, *Rafford in the Past* (1889), p. 12; Fenton and Walker, *The Rural Architecture of Scotland* (1981), pp. 161-3; Milliken and Bridgewater, *Flora Celtica* (2004), pp. 243-5.
112. Gordon, GD44/23/2, tacks: Easter Lettoch (1709); Achavaich, Ruthven, Dell, Delavorar (1710); Corries (1719).
113. Caird, 'The reshaped agricultural landscape', in Parry and Slater, *The Making of the Scottish Countryside* (1980), p. 215.
114. Fife, MS3175/F74/5.
115. Grange, GD298/416.
116. Gordon, GD44/23/4.
117. Gordon, GD44/23/6/2, process of removing against Robert Farquharson (1778).
118. Fife, MS3175, vol. 9.
119. Fife, MS3175/F72/3/1.
120. Ballindalloch, bundle 1135 (1821–37).
121 Gordon, GD44/51/129, Drumin debts (1816–23).
122. Gordon, GD44/23/6/2.
123. Fife, MS3175, vol. 1055.
124. *View of Elgin* (1794) pp. 16, 33.
125. Lethen, GD247/69/30/1.
126. Fife, MS3175/RHP31338, plan of Teindland by P. Macbey (1859); MS3175/RHP31346, plan of Cranloch improvements, by P. Macbey (1857); MS3175/RHP31055, plan of Mosstowie (*c.* 1830).
127. *Practical Farmer* (1766), p. 6.
128. *Gentleman Farmer* (1776), p. 70.
129. Mackintosh, *An Essay on Ways and Means for Inclosing* (1729), pp. 46-7.
130. Birnie, 'Ridge cultivation in Scotland', in *The Scottish Historical Review*, vol. 24, (1927), p. 198.
131. *Gentleman Farmer* (1776), p. 56.
132. Laurence, *The Duty of a Steward to his Lord* (1727), p. 27.
133. Ballindalloch, bundle 965.
134. *NSA*, p. 109.
135. Brodie, box 13/1.
136. Gordon, GD44/51/365/3.
137. Brodie, library catalogue.
138. Gordon, GD44/51/365/2.
139. Harvey, *Fields, Hedges and Ditches* (1987), pp. 21-3.
140. *NSA*, p. 208.
141. Brodie, box 16/8.
142. *NSA*, Inveravon, p. 136.
143. Ballindalloch, bundle 1343.
144. SAS fieldwork.
145. Fife, MS3175/831.
146. *NSA*, Knockando, p. 75.
147. NRS, SC2/66/2, register of entail improvement, Banffshire.
148. Brodie, box 13/1.
149. Grange, GD298/416.
150. Fife, MS3175, vol. 9.
151. Fife, MS3175, vol. 9.
152. Fife, vol.1058.
153. Fife, vol. 1058.
154. Fife, MS3175, vol. 9.
155. Fife, MS3175, vol. 9.

156. Fife, MS3175, vol. 9.
157. Fife, MS3175, vol. 10.
158. Fife, MS3175, vol. 9.
159. 'Plan of ... Mosstowie Hillside and the Greens ... surveyed Nov. 1762', in Cramond, *The Records of Elgin*, vol. I, (1903), p. 384.
160. Fife, MS3175/421.
161. Fife, MS3175, vol. 9.
162. Fife, MS3175, vol. 10.
163. Iredale and Barrett, 'The Lowland Clearances', in *The Scots Magazine* (September 1992), pp. 633-40.
164. *OSA*, St Andrews-Lhanbryd, p. 638.
165. Fife, MS3175, vol. 1038.
166. *Survey of Moray* (1798), p. 116.
167. Fife, MS3175, vol. 6.
168. Fife, MS3175, vol. 7.
169. Fife, MS3175, vol. 1160.
170. *The Farmer's Magazine*, vol. iii, p. 319 (August 1802).
171. Brereton, *Gordonstoun* (1968), p. 112.
172. *Ibid.* The supply of whisky may be regarded, not as a drunken indulgence, but equivalent to the rum ration that was issued to soldiers and sailors—as sustenance, encouragement and reward for arduous service.
173. *View of Elgin*, (1794), p. 36.
174. *Survey of Moray* (1798), p. 115.
175. Roy's map (1747–55).
176. *Survey of Morayy* (1798), pp. 114-5.
177. Watt, *Loch Spynie* (undated), pp. 6-8.
178. Blaeu, *Atlas Novus* (1654).
179. Brereton, *Gordonstoun* (1968), p. 108.
180. Watt, *Loch Spynie* (undated), p. 8.
181. Brodie, box 40/4/7.
182. Brereton, *Gordonstoun* (1968), pp. 108-9.
183. Mackintosh, *An Essay on Ways and Means for Inclosing* (1729), p. xlvi.
184. Watt, *Loch Spynie* (undated), p. 28.
185. Fife, MS3175, vol. 7.
186. Fife, MS3175, vol. 9.
187. Brereton, *Gordonstoun* (1968), p. 110.
188. Watt, *Loch Spynie* (undated), p. 39.
189. Fife, MS3175, vol. 9.
190. Watt, *Loch Spynie* (undated), p. 39.
191. *NSA*, Drainie, p. 146.
192. Brereton, *Gordonstoun* (1968), p. 111; Watt, *Loch Spynie (undated), p. 40.*

6 The Regulated Estate

1. *Gentleman Farmer* (1776) chapter XIII.
2. Sinclair, *An Account of the Systems of Husbandry Adopted in the More Improved Districts of Scotland* (1814), p. 103.
3. *Ibid.*, pp. 137-8.
4. *View of Elgin* (1794), p. 15.
5. *View of Banff* (1794), p. 12.
6. *OSA*, Bellie, p. 82; Duffus, p. 491; Speymouth, p. 659.
7. *Survey of Moray* (1798), pp. 169, 96, 161, 125, 157, 307, 279, 109, 137, 247.
8. *OSA*, p. 633.
9. *NSA*, p. 155.
10. Fife, MS3175, vol. 1056 (1827).
11. Fife, MS3175/1161B, plan by John McKenzie, Aberchirder (1815); MS3175/1161A, verbal survey by George McWilliam (1826).
12. Fife, MS3175, vol. 8 (January 1802).

13. Fife, MS3175/RHP31465.
14. Fife, MS3175/RHP31308, 31009, plans by George McWilliam.
15. Fife, MS3175, vol. 1058, trustees' minutes (1838).
16. Fife, MS3175, vol. 1058, trustees' minutes (1855).
17. Whyte, 'Written leases and their impact on Scottish Agriculture in the seventeenth century', in *The Agricultural History Review*, vol. 27, part 1 (1979), p.3.
18. Ballindalloch, bundle 786.
19. *View of Moray* (1811), pp. 94, 96.
20. Lethen, GD247/69/30 (25 April 1831).
21. *OSA*, Knockando, p. 624.
22. *Gentleman Farmer* (1776), pp. 378-9.
23. *View of Banff* (1812), p. 73.
24. Young, *The Parish of Spynie* (1871), pp. 83-4.
25. Ballindalloch, bundle 920, judicial rental (1733), bundle 1142, judicial rental (1749); nineteen-year leases were general among tacks preserved in bundle 1132—at Knockan (1785), Glenarder (1787–88), Blacksboat (1788), Tomlea (1790), Isle of Pitchaish (1791), Nether Kirdellbeg (1791), Stroangalls (1791), Delnapot (1792), Upper Kirdellbeg (1795), Pitchaish (1796), Knockanshalg (1796); *View of Elgin* (1794), p. 14.
26. Gordon, GD44/23/2.
27. Gordon, GD44/23/6/2.
28. Fife, MS3175/939, 942 and vol. 1038, judicial rental (1753).
29. Fife, MS3175/Z213/1.
30. For example at Bankhead (1725)—Brodie, box 4, drawer 5, 'leases expiring 1815'.
31. Brodie box 6/7.
32. *Strathavon* (1960), p. 258.
33. Fife, MS3175, vols 1075, 1076, 1079, 1084, rentals (1790–1800).
34. Fife, MS3175, vol. 1088, vol. 1089, rentals (1817, 1824).
35. *NSA*, Aberlour, p. 117; Alves, p. 110; Bellie, p. 120; Duffus, p. 39; Forres, p. 170; Elgin, p. 15; Knockando, p. 74; Spynie, p. 98.
36. Gordon, GD44/40/12.
37. Quoted in *Strathavon* (1960), p. 177.
38. Fife, MS3175/943/2.
39. Fife, MS3175/943/2.
40. *APS*, 'Of sornaris' vol. II, p. 3 (1424).
41. Fife, MS3175/F57/1.
42. Lethen, GD247/66/16/1/43 (*c.* 1810).
43. NRS, GD247/66/16/2/26.
44. MA, Blervie baron court, ZVBl B32/766/1.
45. *Strathavon* (1960), pp. 191-3, rentals (1680, 1698).
46. *Ibid.*, pp. 223-48, rentals (1752–54); Gordon, GD44/51/745/3.
47. Gordon, GD44/23/6/2.
48. MA, ZVBro 65/773, Cloves rental (1773).
49. Lethen, GD247/67/23/2, Burgie; GD247/67/26, Asleesk; GD247/67/3x, note on abstract rental.
50. Murray, *The Book of Burgie* (1930), pp. 109-11.
51. Hay, *Lochnavando No More* (2005), pp. 95-6.
52. Ballindalloch, bundle 920, judicial rentals, bundles 920 (1733), 1142 (1749); tacks and leases, bundles 1132 (late eighteenth century), 1200 (1801), 1220 (1803-4); bundle 1342, offers for tacks beginning 1820.
53. Fife MS3175, vols 1075, 1076, 1079, 1084, 1086, 1087, 1088, 1089, rentals, (1790–1827): figures rounded up to the nearest £ or boll.
54. Fife, MS3175, vol. 1058.
55. *OSA*, p. 540.
56. Hay, *Lochnavando No More* (2005), pp. 174-7, rentals; some uncertainty arises from the ubiquity of the surname Barron among Altyre tenants.
57. Murray, *Book of Burgie* (1930), pp. 109-11.
58. Rentals for 1764, 1766, 1767, 1770, 1778, 1785, 1790, in *Strathavon* (1960), pp. 251-71.
59. Ballindalloch, bundle 1342, offers for tacks commencing 1820.
60. Turnock, 'The retreat of settlement in the Grampian uplands', in *Northern Scotland*, vol. 4, nos 1-2, (1981), p. 90.

61. Allan, *The North East Lowlands of Scotland*, (1952), p. 79.
62. Fife, MS3175/831, offers (1768).
63. Fife, MS3175/ M/753.
64. Fife, MS3175/F72/3/1, offers (1763).
65. Fife, MS3175, vol. 1058, offers (1837).
66. *Surveyof Moray* (1798), p. 165.
67. Fife, MS3175, vol. 1160.
68. Fife, MS3175/831, offers (1768).
69. Lethen, GD247/16/19/1.
70. Fife, MS3175, vol. 1056.
71. Fife, MS3175, vol. 10 (20 November 1817).
72. Fife, MS3175, vol. 1058.
73. MA, ZEMm B32/769/7, sheriff court process (1769).
74. *View of Moray* (1811) p. 91.
75. Brodie, box 7/4.
76. Fife, MS3175/M/xvii/C52.
77. Brodie, box 7/4.
78. Fife, MS3175/857.
79. Fife, MS3175/724.
80. Fife, MS3175, vol. 1056.
81. Fife, MS3175, vol. 1058.
82. Fife, MS3175/831, offers (1768).
83. Fife, MS3175, vol. 1058, offers (1837).
84. Fife, MS3175, vol. 1058.
85. Fife, MS3175/831, offers (1768).
86. Fife, MS3175, vol. 10.
87. Fife, MS3175/831.
88. Fife, MS3175, vol. 1056.
89. Fife, MS3175, vol. 1058.
90. Fife, MS3175, vol. 1058.
91. Lethen, GD247/69/30/2, offers (1820–27).
92. Gordon, GD44/23/6/3.
93. Gordon, GD44/23/6/3, offers (1803).
94. Sinclair, *Systems of Husbandry* (1814), p. 184.
95. *Ibid.*, pp. 170-1
96. Gordon, GD44/23/6/2, letter (23 March 1773).
97. Fife, MS3175/831.
98. This sentiment was expressed by C. Smout in Aitchison an. Cassell, *The Lowland Clearances* (2003), pp. 84-5.
99. *Survey of Moray* (1798), p. 341.
100. Hay, *Lochnavando No More* (2005), pp. 159-61.
101. Data gathered from *OSA* and *NSA*.
102. *NSA*, p. 97.
103. *OSA*, p. 635.
104. *OSA*, p. 464.
105. *NSA*, p. 87.
106. *OSA*, p. 620.
107. *OSA*, p. 471.
108. *OSA*, p. 5.
109. *OSA*, p. 493.
110. Harper, *Emigration from North-East Scotland*, vol. 1, *Willing Exiles (1988), p. 4.*

7 Regular Reforestation

1. *Johnson, A Journey to the Western Islands of Scotland* (1924—first published 1775), pp. 12, 13.
2. Boswell, *The Journal of a Tour to the Hebrides with Samuel Johnson* (1955—first published 1785), pp. 223-4.

3. *Ibid.*, p. 81.

4. *Ibid.*, pp. 80-3.

5. Roy's map (1747–55); *Survey of Moray* (1798), p. 169 described woodland extending 'more than 5 miles ... a vast extent of oak, ash, elm, and venerable fir ... weeping birch ... many more than 8 feet in circumference'.

6. Brodie, estate plan (1770). Brodie was said to be 'finely planted' when visited by Bishop Pococke, in Kemp (ed.) *Tours in Scotland, 1747, 1750, 1760 by Richard Pocock, bishop of Meath* (1887), pp. 182-3.

7. Boswell, *The Journal of a Tour to the Hebrides with Samuel Johnson* (1955—first published 1785), p. 80; Johnson, *A Journey to the Western Islands of Scotland* (1924—first published 1775), p. 31.

8. Burt, *Letters from a Gentleman in the North of Scotland*, vol. 1 (1754), p. 8.

9. Mackintosh, *An Essay on Ways and Means for Inclosing, Fallowing, Planting, &c.* (1729), p. 23.

10. *NSA*, pp. 208-9.

11. Smout, Macdonald and Watson, *A History of the Native Woodlands of Scotland, 1500–1920* (2007), pp. 196-201.

12. Smout, 'The history of the Rothiemurchus woodlands', in Smout and Lambert (eds), *Rothiemurchus* (1999), p. 60-1.

13. Anderson, *Kingston-on-Spey* (1957), pp. 96-107.

14. Smout, 'The history of the Rothiemurchus woodlands', in Smout and Lambert (eds), *Rothiemurchus* (1999), pp. 61-3.

15. Gordon, GD44/43/3.

16. Gordon, GD44/51/379/10.

17. Gordon, GD44/51/379/8.

18. Fife, MS3175/F44/3.

19. Tod (ed.), Elizabeth Grant of Rothiemurchus, *The Memoirs of a Highland Lady* (1988), p. 271.

20. Stewart, 'Using the woods, 1600–1800: 2 managing for profit', in Smout (ed.) *People and Woods in Scotland* (2003), p. 114.

21. Smout, Macdonald and Watson, *A History of the Native Woodlands of Scotland, 1500–1800* (2007), p. 129.

22. Smout, 'The history of the Rothiemurchus woodlands', in Smout and Lambert (eds), *Rothiemurchus* (1999), pp. 62-3.

23. Anderson, *Kingston-on-Spey* (1957), pp. 10-11, 35-6.

24. Skelton, *Speybuilt* (1995), p. 21.

25. Ballindalloch, bundle 1215.

26. Skelton, *Speybuilt*, (1995), p. 26.

27. Smout and Watson, 'Exploiting Semi-natural woods, 1600–1800', in Smout (ed.), *Scottish Woodland History* (1997), p. 87.

28. Smout, 'The history of the Rothiemurchus woods in the eighteenth century', in *Northern Scotland* vol. 15 (1995), p. 28-9.

29. *APS*, vol. II. p. 7 (1424)—and subsequent acts.

30. *Survey of Moray* (1798), p. 340-1.

31. *View of Moray* (1811), p. 91.

32. Gordon, GD44/23/2.

33. Brodie, box 16/7.

34. *Gentleman Farmer* (1776), p. 259-60.

35. Mackintosh, *An Essay on Ways and Means for Inclosing Falowing, Planting, &c.* (1729), p. 111.

36. *NSA*, Rafford, p. 244.

37. Grant, 'Description of ... Monymusk', in *Miscellany of the Spalding Club*, vol. 2 (1842), p. 93.

38. Defoe, *Tour through the Whole Island of Britain* (1974—first published 1724-6), p. 367.

39. Boswell, *The Journal of a Tour to the Hebrides with Samuel Johnson* (1955—first published 1785), p. 81.

40. House and Dingwell, 'A nation of planters', in Smout (ed.) *People and Woods in Scotland* (2003), p. 130-40.

41. Shaw, *The History of the Province of Moray* (1775), p. 173.

42. Ballindalloch, bundle 824.

43. Fife, MS3175/F39/5; Military Survey (1747–55).

44. Brodie, estate plan (1770).

45. Fife, MS3175, vol. 1038.

46. *View of Moray* (1811), p. 245.

47. The quotation crystallises the aims of Perth town council in planting trees on the burgh muir in 1714, quoted in Macdonald, 'Both profitable and pleasant', in *Scottish Economic and Social History*, vol. 17, part 2 (1997), p. 111.

48. House and Dingwell, 'A nation of planters', in Smout (ed.), *People and Woods in Scotland* (2003), p. 135.
49. *Ibid.,* p. 137.
50. *OSA,* p. 4.
51. *OSA,* p. 239.
52. *OSA,* pp. 269, 290.
53. *OSA,* p. 631.
54. *OSA,* p. 472; *Survey of Moray* (1798), p. 165.
55. *OSA,* vol. XVI, p. 688.
56. *OSA,* pp. 536-7.
57. Roy's map (1747-55); *Survey of Moray* (1798), p. 144.
58. *NSA,* pp. 29-32. The report was 'Drawn up from notes furnished by Mr Leslie', its meagre content perhaps reflecting the declining powers of the elderly minister.
59. *NSA,* Speymouth, pp. 57-8.
60. *NSA,* p. 3.
61. *NSA,* p. 163.
62. *NSA,* p. 303.
63. Bain, *The Lordship of Petty* (1925), pp. 107-8.
64. *View of Moray* (1811), pp. 242-3, 51.
65. Hay, *Lochnavando No More* (2005), pp. 98-9.
66. *View of Elgin* (1794), pp. 42-3.
67. Ballindalloch, bundle 1343, offers and conditions of lease (1819).
68. OS, 1:10,560 maps.
69. Ross, *The Culbin Sands* (1992), pp. 73, 75.
70. Young, *The Parish of Spynie* (1871), p. 53.
71. Ballindalloch, bundle 402.
72. Ballindalloch, bundle 1300, records a planting density of 2,500 trees per acre; Fife planted only around 1,200 trees to the acre—Anderson, *History of Scottish Forestry*, vol. I (1967), p. 614.
73. Fife, MS3175, vol. 1056, offers and tacks (1815).
74. Fife, MS3175/706.
75. Fife, MS3175/703/2.
76. *The Ephemera*, no. XIV (24 June 1822), p. 158.
77. Fife, MS3175/703/2.
78. MA, ZBEl A71/810, Elgin burgh correspondence; Barrett, 'Moray murder', in *Leopard* (December 2000), pp. 6-9.
79. MA, ZBFo A2, Forres town council minutes.
80. Ballindalloch, bundle 824.
81. Ballindalloch, bundle 965.
82. Ballindalloch, bundle 1519, conditions of lease (*c.* 1790, revised 1842); bundle 1343, Morinsh leases (1820).
83. NRS, SC2/66/1, register of entail improvements, Banffshire.
84. Ballindalloch, bundle 1315.
85. Fife, MS3175/706.
86. Anderson, *A History of Scottish Forestry*, vol. I (1967), p. 614.
87. MA, DBA Mf, Moray Firth and London Steam Packet Company (1834-8).
88. Anderson, *Kingston-on-Spey* (1957), p. 57; Skelton, *Speybuilt* (1995), p. 34.
89. Gordon, GD44/51/180/3.
90. Milliken and Bridgewater, *Flora Celtica* (2004), p. 95.
91. Rackam, *The History of the Countryside* (1986), p. 57.
92. Ballindalloch, bundle 965.
93. *View of Moray* (1811), p. 91; 'cycamore' was noted as a timber tree in 1716, in Grant, 'Description of ... Monymusk', in *Miscellany of the Spalding Club*, vol. 2 (1842), p. 96.
94. Anderson, *History of Scottish Forestry*, vol. I (1967), pp. 579-80.
95. *View of Moray* (1811), p. 247.
96. *Practical Farmer* (1766), p. 13.
97. Fife, MS3175, vol. 10.
98. Fife, MS3175/F30/3/1.
99. Gordon, GD44/51/383/1.
100. *View of Moray* (1811), p. 248.

101. Anderson, *History of Scottish Forestry*, vol. I (1967), pp. 598-60.
102. Fife, MS3175/706.
103. Anderson, *History of Scottish Forestry*, vol. I (1967), p. 598-9.
104. Gordon, GD44/49/2/3.
105. AUL, Duff of Braco papers, MS2727/1/226.
106. Fife, MS3175/Z21.
107. Hay, *Lochnavando No More* (2005), p. 99.
108. Ballindalloch, bundles 1075, 1168.
109. Fife, MS3175/1039.
110. Fife, MS3175, vol. 10.
111. Ballindalloch, bundle 965.
112. Ballindalloch, bundle 1234.
113. Fife, MS3175/1426/1.
114. Fife, MS3175, vol. 10. It is unclear how—or whether—the different Dickson nurseries were connected.
115. Newte, *Prospects and Observations on a Tour in England and Scotland* (1791), p. 150.
116. *OSA*, pp. 536-7.
117. *Survey of Moray* (1798), p. 151.
118. Fife, MS3175/Z106/3.
119. MA, DBA A91/2, *Forres Gazette* handbills.
120. Fife, MS3175 vol. 1938.
121. Fife, MS3175, vol. 1160.
122. Fife, MS3175, vol. 1041.
123. Fife, vol. 9, vol. 1160.
124. Fife, MS3175/Z106/3.
125. Lindsay, 'The commercial use of woodland and coppice management', in Parry and Slater (eds), *The Making of the Scottish Countryside* (1980), p. 276.
126. *NSA*, Drainie, p. 156.
127. Boswell, *The Journal of a Tour to the Hebrides with Samuel Johnsons* (1785), p. 82.
128. *OSA*, p. 490.
129. Arthur Johnstoun (1587–1641), *Poemata Omnia* (Middelburg, Zeeland, 1642)—translated by John Barclay, minister of Cruden, published in Alexander Skene, *Memorialls for the Government of Royall-Burghs in Scotland* (1685).
130. Gordon castle library catalogue and inventories, GD44/14/15/40 (1754), GD44/49/14 (1729–1832).
131. Fife, MS3175/F30/3/1.
132. MA, ZBEL A2, Elgin Town Council minutes.
133. *View of Moray* (1811), pp. 54-5.
134. *Survey of Moray* (1798), p. 79.
135. Fife, MS3175, vol. 9.
136. Fife, MS3175/979.
137. Ballindalloch, bundle 1105, 1106.
138. NRS, CS2/66/1, register of entail improvements, Banffshire; Ballindalloch, bundle 1348.
139. *Survey of Moray* (1798), p. 168.
140. Anderson, *A History of Scottish Forestry*, vol. I (1967), p. 618.
141. Hay, *Lochnavando No More* (2005), pp. 152-4.
142. NRS, SC2/66/1, register of entail improvements, Banffshire.
143. Fife, MS3175, vol. 10.
144. Fife, MS3175, vol. 9.
145. Ballindalloch, bundle 1234.
146. MA, DBA A97/2, 'The Planting' a new song composed by Donald Ross, Dallas, printed at the *Gazette Office, Forres*.

8 Farming by New Rules

1. *Home, The Principles of Agriculture and Vegetation* (1776) connected agriculture and 'chymistry', though most of Home's assertions are erroneous.
2. *OSA*, p. 535.

3. *Survey of Moray* (1798), p. 343.
4. *View of Moray* (1811), pp. 290-1.
5. Grange, GD298/437/2.
6. *Prize Essays and Transactions*, vol. VI (1824), pp. 221-8.
7. Ballindalloch, bundle 1237.
8. Gordon, GD44/51/365/3.
9. Hall, *Travels in Scotland* (1807), p. 458.
10. *Practical Farmer* (1766), pp. 7-8.
11. *Gentleman Farmer* (1776), chapter VII.
12. Fife, MS3175/Z145.
13. Fife, MS3175/F57/1, MS3175/943/2.
14. Brodie, box 10/6.
15. Brodie, box 6/1.
16. *View of Elgin* (1794), pp. 16-17.
17. *View of Banff* (1794), p. 17.
18. *View of Elgin* (1794), pp. 17, 20.
19. Ballindalloch, bundle 1519.
20. Lethen, GD247/67/19/68.
21. *NSA*, Alves, p. 109; Bellie, p. 120; Birnie, p. 89; Elgin, p. 13; Kinloss, p. 208; Rafford, p. 253; Speymouth, p. 54; Duffus, p.39.
22. *NSA*, Kirkmichael, p. 304.
23. *NSA*. Knockando, p. 76; Inveravon, p. 135; Drainie, p. 155.
24. *NSA*, Drainie, p. 155; Forres, p. 171.
25. *Survey of Moray* (1798), pp. 328-9.
26. Ballindalloch, bundle 1519, new regulations for Tullochcarron, Kilmaichlie and Kirdells (1842), bundle 1348, regulations for Corshellach model farm (1858); Lethen, GD247/66/16/2/26, regulations (1848); Fife, MS3175/Z145, Asleesk, Buinach and Woodside regulations (1858).
27. MA, DBA A91/2, *Forres Gazette* handbills.
28. *View of Banff* (1794), p. 17.
29. *View of Elgin* (1794), p. 19.
30. *View of Moray* (1811), p. 169.
31. *OSA*, Alves, p. 455; Birnie, p. 463; Drainie, p. 482; Dyke & Moy, pp. 542-3; Duffus, p. 488; Spynie, p. 690.
32. *Survey of Moray* (1798), pp. 124, 148, 329.
33. *View of Elgin* (1794), p. 18.
34. *NSA*, Birnie, p. 88; Dyke & Moy, p. 224; Elgin, p. 14; Kinloss, p. 208; Bellie, p. 121; Speymouth, p. 54; Urquhart, p. 48.
35. *NSA*, Edinkillie, p. 189; Inveavon, p. 136.
36. Higgs, *The Land* (1965), illustrations 28-30.
37. *OSA*, Speymouth, p. 655; Drainie, p. 482; Dyke & Moy, p. 542; Birnie, p. 463.
38. *OSA*, Aberlour, p. 4; Inveravon, p. 239; Edinkillie, p. 582; Knockando, p. 623.
39. Grange, GD298/437.
40. *OSA*, p. 654-5.
41. *View of Moray* (1811), p. 164.
42. Gordon, GD44/51/180/4.
43. *View of Banff* (1794), p. 18.
44. *View of Elgin* (1794), pp. 19-20.
45. *NSA*, Edinkillie, p. 189; Kinloss, p. 208; Drainie, p. 155.
46. Chambers and Mingay, *The Agricultural Revolution, 1750–1880* (1966), p. 55-6.
47. *Scottish Farming* (1953), pp. 149-50.
48. *View of Moray* (1811), p. 198.
49. MA, ZBEl A2, Elgin Town Council, minutes.
50   *Gentleman Farmer* (1776), p. 101.
51. *View of Banff* (1794), p. 19.
52. *View of Moray* (1811), p. 199.
53. MA, ZVCu 60/1, Cullen mains cash book (1760–67).
54. Fife, MS3175/943/2, regulations (1772); MS3175/941, tacks (1743–87).
55. Grange, GD298/437/2.

56. Ballindalloch, bundle 1287.
57. *OSA*, Aberlour, p. 4; Bellie, p. 82; Dallas, p. 472; Dyke & Moy, pp. 541-2; Speymouth, p. 654.
58. Ballindalloch, bundle 1519.
59. Higgs, *The Land* (1965) pp. 30-1; Chambers and Mingay, *The Agricultural Revolution, 1750–1880* (1966) p. 56.
60. Lethen, GD247/70/32/1.
61. 'Letters from a young farmer', in *Farmer's Magazine*, vol. viii (August 1807), pp. 368-9.
62. Fife, MS3175/F57/1 contains *An Account of the Culture and use of the Mangel Wurzel ... translated 'from the French of the Abbe de Commerell* (3rd ed.) (London, 1787).
63. Mason, *Rafford in the Past* (1889), p. 13.
64. MA, ZBEl A2, Elgin Town Council minutes, petty customs (24 August 1742).
65. *View of Elgin* (1794), p. 20.
66. Ballindalloch, vouchers, bundle 827 (1769); bundle 822 (1770); bundle 965 (1776).
67. Ballindalloch, bundle 1075.
68. Gordon, GD44/51/365/3.
69. *Gentleman Farmer* (1776), p. 107.
70. *Survey of Moray* (1798), p. 330.
71. Gordon, GD44/51/180/2.
72. *Survey of Moray* (1798), p. 330.
73. *View of Moray* (1811), p. 218.
74. *OSA*, pp. 482-3.
75. Mason, *Rafford in the Past* (1889), p. 13.
76. *View of Moray* (1811), p. 220.
77. *OSA*, pp. 540-2.
78. Mackintosh, *An Essay on Ways and Means for Inclosing, Fallowing, Planting, &c.* (1729), p. 41.
79. *View of Elgin* (1794), p. 21: 'sown grass was introduced many years ago'.
80. *Practical Farmer* (1766), p. 9.
81. Grange, GD289/129.
82. Brodie, box 16/8.
83. Brodie, box 6/1, tacks (1801–12).
84. Gordon, GD44/51/180/3.
85. Fife, MS3175/700/2.
86. Ballindalloch, bundles 1153, 1286-7.
87. Ballindalloch, bundle 1024 (20 February 1786).
88. Gordon GD44/51/180/3.
89. *OSA*, Alves, p. 455; Bellie, p. 82; Elgin, p. 595.
90. *OSA*, Speymouth, p. 654; Inveravon, p. 239; St Andrews-Lhanbryd p. 641; Edinkillie, p. 582; Spynie, p. 689.
91. *OSA*, St Andrews-Lhanbryd, p. 641.
92. *Survey of Moray*, (1798), p. 330.
93. *View of Moray* (1811), p. 218.
94. Gordon, GD44/55/136/1.
95. *View of Elgin* (1794), p. 21.
96. *Survey of Moray*, (1798), p. 330.
97. Fife, MS3175, vol. 1038.
98. Fife, MS3175/Z164/2.
99. *Gentleman Farmer* (1776), p. 240.
100. 'Letters from a young farmer', in *Farmer's Magazine*, vol. viii (August 1807), p. 375.
101. Mackintosh, *An Essay on Ways and Means for Inclosing, Fallowing, Planting, &c.* (1729), p. 63.
102. Grant, *The Farmer's New-Years gift to his Countrymen* (1757), p. 23.
103. *Practical Farmer* (1766), p. 7.
104. *NSA*, Bellie, p. 121; Drainie, p. 155.
105. Laurence, *The Duty and Office of a Land Steward* (1763), pp. xi.
106. Lethen, GD247/67/19/54.
107. Lethen, GD247/67/19/68.
108. Grange, GD298/406.
109. Brodie, box 16/8.
110. Fife, MS3175/MI/A3.

111. Lethen, GD247/67/19/54.
112. Whyte, *Agriculture and Society in Seventeenth Century Scotland* (Edinburgh, 1979) pp. 199-204.
113. Whyte, 'Agriculture in Aberdeenshire in the Seventeenth and Early Eighteenth Centuries', in Stevenson, *From Lairds to Louns* (1986), p. 15.
114. Brodie, box 13/4.
115. Fife, MS3175/939.
116. *View of Banff (1794), pp. 41-2.*
117. *Fife, MS3175/1011/1.*
118. *Fife, MS3175/705.*
119. *Fife, MS3175/F53/1.*
120. *Fife, MS3175/705.*
121. Fife, MS3175, vol. 1058.
122. *Survey of Morayy* (1798), p. 149.
123. *OSA*, Speymouth, p. 656; Dyke & Moy, p. 562; Kirkmichael, p. 271.
124. *View of Elgin* (1794), p. 17.
125. SAS fieldwork.
126. Gordon, GD44/43/101.
127. McPherson (ed.), *Hopeman 1805-2005* (2008), p. 37.
128. Ballindalloch, bundle 1200.
129. Ballindalloch, bundle 1153.
130. Ballindalloch: bundle 965.
131. Ballindalloch, bundle 1132.
132. Ballindalloch, bundle 1343.
133. *NSA*, Knockando, p. 74; Aberlour, p. 114; Edinkillie, p. 190; Inveravon, p. 127.
134. Brodie, box 6/3, box 41/3.
135. *OSA*, Kirkmichael, p. 239; NSA, p. 128.
136. *View of Moray* (1811), p. 280.
137. Fife, MS3175, vol. 9.
138. *NSA*, Birnie, p. 89; Speymouth, p. 54.
139. Gordon, GD44/51/365/2.
140. Fife, MS3175, vol. 1158, manure register, 1830–39.
141. *NSA*, Dyke & Moy, p. 224; Urquhart, p. 48.
142. *NSA*, p. 121.
143. MA, DBA A91/1, *Forres Gazette* handbills (4 May 1840).
144. Gordon, GD44/51/365/3.
145. *OSA*, pp. 273, 473.
146. Grant, *Highland Folk Ways* (1995—first published 1961) pp. 87; *Survey of Moray* (1798), pp. 343-4.
147. *View of Moray* (1811) p. 330.
148. Ballindalloch, bundle 729.
149. *NSA*, Knockando, p. 74; Elgin, p. 13.
150. *View of Moray* (1811), pp. 333-4.
151. *Ibid.*, p. 335.
152. MA, DBA A91/1, *Forres Gazette* handbills (*c*. 1835).
153. *View of Moray* (1811), p. 334.
154. Ballindalloch, bundle 1010.
155. Ballindalloch, bundle 1278.
156. Brodie, box 6/1, box 10/6.
157. Lethen, GD247/65/15/18/11.
158. *OSA*, Edinkillie, p. 583.
159. *OSA*, Elgin, p. 599.
160. *OSA*, Duffus, p. 483; Alves, p. 456.
161. *OSA*, Alves, p. 456; St Andrews-Lhanbryd, p. 641; Bellie, p. 83; Dallas, p. 473; Edinkillie, p. 582; Inveravon, p. 240; Speymouth, p. 658.
162. Ballindalloch, bundle 1229.
163. Fife, MS3175, vol. 10.
164. *Scottish Farming* (1953), p. 228.
165. Fife, MS3175/943/2.

166. Lethen, GD247/16/2/26.
167. *OSA*, Inveravon, p. 240; Knockando, p. 623; Kirkmichael, p. 273.
168. *NSA*, Rafford, p. 252; Speymouth, p. 55; Edinkillie, p. 189; Aberlour, p. 117; Birnie, p. 89; Kirkmichael, p. 304.
169. Gordon, GD44/51/365/2.
170. Ballindalloch, letter from Reverend J. Anderson (24 January 1806).
171. Gordon, GD44/23/6/2.
172. Lethen, GD247/66/16/2.
173. Fife, MS3175, vol. 10.
174. *Gentleman Farmer* (1776), pp. 27-31.
175. Sinclair, *An Account of the Systems of Husbandry Adopted in the More Improved Districts of Scotland* (1814) pp. 121-2.
176. *OSA*, p. 547.
177. *OSA*, Knockando, p. 623; Kirkmichael, p. 273.
178. *Survey of Moray* (1798), p. 167.
179. *OSA*, Kirkmichael, p. 270; Bellie, p. 83.
180. *Survey of Moray* (1798), p. 331.
181. Hamilton, *An Economic History of Scotland in the Eighteenth Century* (1963), pp. 92-3.
182. Fife, MS3175/F23/5/1.
183. MA, ZVBro 638/817/1.
184. Ballindalloch, bundle 1616, cattle (1808–11); bundle 1096, (11 October 1819).
185. Ballindalloch, bundle 1388.
186. 'Sir George Macpherson Grant (1839–1907)', in *Oxford Dictionary of National Biography*, online edition (2004–10).
187. Ballindalloch, bundle 1184.
188. *NSA*, p. 55.
189. *OSA*, pp. 252-3.
190. Gordon, GD44/51/365/3.
191. *OSA*, Dyke & Moy, p. 543; Edinkillie, p. 582; Duffus, p. 492.
192. *NSA*, p. 89.
193. *View of Moray* (1811), p. 311.
194. *Aberdeen Journal* (November 1837).
195. Gordon, GD44/51/365/2.
196. Gordon, GD44/51/365/2.
197. MA, DBA A91/1-2, *Forres Gazette* handbills (23 March 1840, 2 April 1840, April 1841, 1842).
198. MA, DBA A91/1, *Forres Gazette* handbills.
199. *NSA*, Elgin, p. 13.
200. Ballindalloch, bundle 1193.
201. Tull, *Horse-hoeing husbandry* (1733).
202. *Scots Magazine* vol. X (1748), p. 187-90; *Scottish Farming* (1953), p. 167-8.
203. *Gentleman Farmer* (1776), p. 103.
204. Powell, *Scottish Agricultural Implements* (1988), p. 25.
205. Higgs, *The Land* (1965), p. 31.
206. Cameron, *The Ballad and the Plough* (1987), p. 174.
207. *Gentleman Farmer* (1766), pp. 57-8.
208. Sinclair, *Systems of Husbandry* (1814) p. 72.
209. Powell, *Scottish Agricultural Implements* (1988), pp. 4-6.
210. Cameron, *The Ballad and the Plough* (1987), p. 174.
211. Fife, MS3175, RHP31002.
212. *OSA*, Speymouth, pp. 658-9; Urquhart, p. 699, Rafford, p. 628, Knockando, p. 623.
213. *View of Elgin* (1794), pp. 21-2.
214. *NSA*, pp. 74-5.
215. *OSA*, pp. 540, 542.
216. Fife, MS3175, vol. 1 (13 November 1761).
217. *OSA*, p. 474.
218. *Scottish Farming* (1953), pp. 217-8.
219. *Ibid.*, p. 219.

220. *Survey of Moray* (1798), p. 326.
221. *NSA*, Forres, p. 171; Rafford, p. 253.
222. See, for example surviving machines at Balcorach, Scalan, Lyne, Knock (Kirkmichael).
223. Fenton and Walker, *The Rural Architecture of Scotland* (1981) pp. 160-82; Hay and Stell, *Monuments of Industry* (1986), pp. 11-14.
224. See, for example, surviving gear at Balcorach, Lyne, Scalan (Kirkmichael); Badiemichael (Dallas); Balliemore (Glenrinnes).
225. SAS fieldwork.
226. Ballindalloch, bundles, 1348, 1349.
227. There are well-preserved wheels, dams and lades at Lyne and Knock (Kirkmichael).
228. Fife, MS3175, vol. 1058.
229. NRS, SC2/66/2, register of entail improvements, Banffshire.
230. Sinclair, *Systems of Husbandry* (1814), pp. 87-8.
231. Described with fulsome praise for an ideal modern grieve in 'Letters from a young farmer', in *Farmer's Magazine*, vol. viii (1807), pp. 369-75.
232. Cameron, *The Ballad and the Plough* (1987), p. 173.
233. Fenton, *Scottish Country Life* (1976), pp. 53-60.
234. *Ibid.*, p. 207.
235. Morgan, 'Agricultural wage rates in late eighteenth-century Scotland', in *The Economic History Review*, second series, vol. XXXII, no. 3 (1979) pp. 181-201; Devine, 'Temporary migration and the Scottish highlands in the nineteenth century' in *The Economic History Review*, second series, vol. XXIV, no. 3, (1971), pp. 344-59. Fenton, *The Shape of the Past*, vol. 1 (1985), pp. 114-35 describes harvest practices. MA, DBA A91/3, *Forres Gazette* handbills, 'The Manbean shearin'', by Danie Ross, poet, Dallas (*c.* 1840) immortalises a mixed harvest crew of highlanders and locals. Harvest on the idealised laichland farm, described in 'Letters from a young farmer', in *Farmer's Magazine, vol. viii (1807), p. 369-70, gave work to 144 shearers and twenty-four bandsters.*

9 Building Regulation

1. 'The Choice', in D. N. Smith (ed.), *The Oxford Book of Eighteenth Century Verse* (Oxford, 1926), p. 1.
2. Grant, 'Description of ... Monymusk', in *Miscellany of the Spalding* Club, vol. 2 (1842).
3. *Survey of Moray* (1798), pp. 103-4; McKean, 'The architectural evolution of Innes House', in *Proceedings of the Society of Antiquaries of Scotland*, vol. 133 (2003).
4. Leslie *A Manual of the Antiquities ... of Moray* (1823), p. 13.
5. Tranter, *The Fortified House in Scotland*, vol. 5 (1977), pp. 45-6, 133-4.
6. *Ibid.*, pp. 61-2; RCAHMS, D16476, 'Improvement of Easter Elchies', plan by Thomas White (1789).
7. Nenadic, *Lairds and Luxury* (2007), p. 171.
8. *Ibid.*, p. 160.
9. *View of Moray* (1811), pp. 48-9.
10. West, *Discovering Scottish Architecture* (1985), pp. 99-102; Walker and Ritchie, *Discovering Scotland's Heritage: Fife and Tayside* (1987), p. 75; Baldwin, *Exploring Scotland's Heritage: Lothian and the Borders* (1985), pp. 63-4.
11. *Vitruvius Scoticus* (1812), plate 91.
12. *Survey of Moray* (1798), p. 289.
13. MacIvor, *Fort George* (1970), p. 11; Gifford, *Highlands and Islands* (1992), pp. 174-9.
14. Boswell, *The Journal of a Tour to the Hebrides with Samuel Johnson* (1955—first published 1775), pp. 82-3; Rhind, *Sketches of ... Moray* (1839), pp. 56, 116; McKean (and others), *Central Glasgow* (1989), p. 24 describes similar arcades in Glasgow.
15. *Survey of Moray* (1798), p. 124.
16. *District of Moray* (1987), pp. 95-9.
17. Tait, *Duff House* (1985), pp. 7-13; Shepherd, *Exploring Scotland's Heritage: Aberdeen and North-East Scotland* (1996), pp. 78-9.
18. GD44/49/14 (1734), GD44/14/15/40 (1754): Gordon castle library catalogues list eight architectural publications dated between 1686 and 1752.
19. Mays, 'Middle-sized detached houses', in Stell (and others), *Scottish Life and Society: Scotland's buildings* (2003), pp. 70-1.

20. *The Rudiments of Architecture or the Young Workman's Instructor* (Edinburgh, 1778) pp. 35, 49-51.
21. MA, ZBEl C6/825, rental.
22. Oliver, *Archiestown as it was* (2010), pp. 19-20.
23. Beaton, *William Robertson, 1786–1841, 'Architect in Elgin'* (1984).
24. NRS, SC2/66/2, register of entail improvements, Banffshire, 1840-41.
25. MA, ZVSt A570/725/1, Stoneyfornoon estate, valuation, 1725; Leslie, *Manual of the Antiquities ... of Moray* (1823) p. 67; *Survey of Moray* (1798), p. 173; RCAHMS, MOD/34/2-15, Soane Museum and SRO, RHP38227.
26. *Survey of Moray* (1798), p. 173; Hay, *Lochnavando No More* (2005), p. 84.
27. *District of Moray* (1987), pp. 54, 59, 58.
28. *Ibid.*, p. 31.
29. *View of Moray* (1811), p. 52-3.
30. *District of Moray* (1987), pp. 106, 152, 124.
31. *Ibid.*, p. 156.
32. Whyte, *The Changing Scottish Landscape, 1500–1800* (1991), p. 100.
33. Gifford, *Highland and Islands* (1992), p. 277.
34. *District ofMoray* (1987), pp. 95-7; Roy's map (1747–55).
35. Nenadic, *Lairds and Luxury* (2007), pp. 161-2.
36. Tod (ed.), *Memoirs of a Highland Lady* (2006—first published 1898), p. 120.
37. *View of Moray* (1811), pp. 53-4.
38. Cruft, 'Country houses, mansions and large villas' (2003).
39. *District of Moray* (1987), p. 115.
40. Quoted in Gibson, *The Scottish Countryside* (2007), p. 21.
41. *District of Moray* (1987), pp. 114-5, 117; Leslie, *Manual of the Antiquities ... of Moray* (1823), p. 5; *Survey of Moray* (1798), pp. 312-3; Cordiner, *Antiquities and Scenery of the North of Scotland* (1780), p. 56; Watson, *Morayshire Described* (1868), pp. 82-3.
42. *District of Moray* (1987), pp. 51-3; Watson, *Morayshire Described* (1868), p. 65.
43. Campbell, *The Grampians Desolate*, book 3 (1804), p. 45.
44. *District of Moray* (1987), p. 52; Watson, *Morayshire Described* (1868), pp. 125-6; Fife, MS3175/RHP31011, 'Sketch of ... Westerton', 1845.
45. R. Southey, *Journal of a Tour of Scotland in 1819*, quoted in Shepherd, *Aberdeen and North-east Scotland* (1996), pp. 87-8.
46. Brunskill, *Traditional Buildings of Britain* (1988), p. 24.
47. Statutory list, St Andrews-Lhanbryd, no. 15.
48. Roy's map (1747–55); Historic Scotland, *Measured Survey and Building Recording* (2003) p. 107; Beaton, *Ross & Cromarty* (1992), p. 91.
49. *District of Moray* (1987) p. 167.
50. Ballindalloch, bundle 1142. The walls of the house stood barely shoulder height.
51. Gordon, GD44/23/3.
52. Gordon, GD44/23/4.
53. Gordon, GD44/24/33/3/6.
54. Brodie, box 6/1.
55. Ballindalloch, bundle 1519.
56. Fife, MS3175, vol. 1055.
57. This trend, established in Moray by 1800, was noted by Sir John Sinclair in the most improved districts in the south of Scotland. Sinclair recommended 'the landlord, who has a permanent interest in the soil, should be at the expence of all substantial improvements': Sinclair, *Systems of Husbandry* (1814), p. 28.
58. Lethen, GD247/66/16/1.
59. Lethen, GD247/66/16/2.
60. *OSA*, Duffus, p. 492, Rafford, pp. 628, 631, Spynie, p. 692.
61. *Survey of Moray* (1798), p. 330.
62. *View of Moray* (1811), pp. 60-1. The painted chimneys were presumably hanging lums rather than masonry gable-wall flues.
63. Sinclair, *Systems of Husbandry* (1814), p. 15.
64. Brodie, box 13/1 (1832).
65. Lethen, GD247/66/16/2, leases (1833).
66. Lethen, GD247/66/16/2.

67. *NSA*, Alves, p. 109, Drainie, p. 105, Duffus, pp. 42-3, Knockando, p. 74, Inveravon, p. 137.
68. RHP1752 (1774).
69. SAS fieldwork.
70. Black, *Report on the Cottage Accommodation in the District of Buchan* (1851), pp. 21-3.
71. *Ibid.*, houses of this type, occupied by settlers on the Bennachie commonty in Aberdeenshire were excavated by Jeff Oliver in 2013.
72. Fife, MS3175, RHP31002.
73. SAS fieldwork; NRS, SC2/66/2, register of entail improvements, Banffshire, Glenavon forester's house (1839).
74. Lauder, *The Great Floods of August 1829*, (1873—first published 1830), plate xlv, p. 123 illustrates the gable-end lean-to as an early feature of an improved houses.
75. Maudlin 'The Legend of Brigadoon', in *Traditional Dwellings and Settlements Review*, vol. XX, number 11 (2009), pp. 1, 5.
76. MA, ZBEl A37/3/10; the specification was changed during the building of these houses which were completed with masonry gable-end fireplaces.
77. Brodie, box 14/4-7.
78. Emerton, *The Pattern of Scottish Roofing* (2000), p. 19.
79. Iredale and Barrett, 'Building royal burghs', in *The Scots Magazine*, vol. 142, number 1 (January 1995), p. 16.
80. *District of Moray* (1987), pp. 73-5; Braeriach datestone, 1821; otherwise dating is by style and Statutory Lists; MA, lithograph prospect of 'Forres from Breakback' shows suburban housing generally in regular style (*c.* 1825).
81. RHP1423, plan by George Taylor.
82. Lauder, *The Great Floods* (1830) p. 156.
83. Ballindalloch, bundle 1283.
84. Fife, MS3175/XVII/C53, plan by John Home (1790).
85. *NSA*, Edinkillie (erected 1823) p. 192, Duffus (1830) p. 41, Urquhart (1822) p. 49, Kirkmichael (1825) p. 307.
86. *NSA*, p. 200.
87. *NSA*, p. 212.
88. *District of Moray* (1987), p. 162.
89. Fife, MS3175/F44/3.
90. *OSA*, Alves, p. 102, Drainie, p. 149, Duffus, p. 40, Spynie, p. 98-9; *NSA*, vol. XIII, Alves, p. 457 Drainie, p. 477, 484, Duffus, p. 493, Spynie, p. 688.
91. Gordon, GD44/43/3.
92. Brodie, box 13/6.
93. Gordon, GD44/151/379/8 (1735).
94. *District of Moray* (1987), pp. 61, 83.
95. Young, *The Parish of Spynie* (1871), p. 116.
96. Moray District Libraries, *The Planned Villages of Moray* (*c.* 1980).
97. *NSA*, Alves, p. 103.
98. Ballindalloch, bundle 1142, baron court (1749); bundle 1220, tacks (1804).
99. Emerton, *The Pattern of Scottish Roofing* (2000), pp. 22-5; Rhind, *Sketches of ... Moray* (1839), p. 52.
100. Beaton, 'The Pattern of Moray building', in Sellar, *Moray: province and people* (1993), pp. 243-5.
101. Gordon, GD44/23/4.
102. Gordon, GD44/23/6/3.
103. *Ibid.*
104. Emerton, *The Pattern of Scottish Roofing* (2000), pp. 52-62.
105. Beaton, 'Sources of slate in Banffshire and Aberdeenshire', in Riches and Stell, *Materials and Traditions in Scottish Building* (1992).
106. *NSA*, Rafford, p. 242.
107. *View of Moray* (1811), p. 65; *NSA*, Kinloss, p. 210.
108. Fenton, 'Traditional buildings', in Omand (ed.), *The Grampian Book* (1987), p. 262; Fenton and Walker, *The Rural Architecture of Scotland* (1981), pp. 63-4, 67-8; Fenton, *Country Life in Scotland* (1987), p. 76.
109. Fenton, *Country Life in Scotland* (1967), pp. 71-2.
110. *View of Banff* (1794), p. 22.
111. Presumably Monauchty—*View of Elgin* (1794), p. 23.
112. Fife, MS3175/XVII/C53, plan by John Home (1790).
113. *View of Moray* (1811) p. 61.

114. *Ibid.*, pp. 48-9, 51-4.
115. Miller, *Archibald Simpson* (2006), pp. 135-6; NRS, RHP2394; Glendinning and Martins, *Buildings of the Land* (2008); NSA, Bellie, p. 119.
116. *Survey of Moray* (1798), p. 332.
117. Brodie, box 10/6.
118. Brodie, box 6/1.
119. Ballindalloch, bundles 1231, 1348.
120. SAS fieldwork.
121. T. Devine, speaking on BBC Radio 4 (November 2011).
122. Lockhart, 'Migration to planned villages in Scotland between 1725 and 1850', in *Scottish Geographical Magazine* (April 1986), p. 165, estimated 450—revised to 490, in 'Lotted lands and planned villages in north-east Scotland', in *The Agricultural History Review*, vol. 49, part 1 (2001), p. 17.
123. Youngson, *After the Forty-five* (1973), p. 36.
124. Smith and Stevenson (eds), *Fermfolk and Fisherfolk* (1989), p. 2.
125. Quoted in Withrington, 'The 18th and 19th centuries', in Omand (ed.), *The Moray Book* (1987), p. 158. The earl of Fife responded to Findlater's gambit—and trumped it—with new villages at Newmill, a mile from Keith and another, named Fife-Keith, above the old kirktown.
126. MA, ZBLo P1-2, Lossiemouth plans (1784).
127. Heron, *Scotland Delineated*, second edition, (1799), p. 92; RHP2004, Roseisle plan (1773).
128. RHP2312/3, Fochabers plan (1764); Pennant, *A Tour in Scotland* (1776), p. 160.
129. RHP2004, Roseisle plan (1773); Brodie, estate plan (1770); Fife, MS3175/RHP31339, Urquhart plan (1800).
130. Smout 'The landowner and the planned village in Scotland, 1730–1830', in Phillipson and Mitchison, *Scotland in the Age of Improvement* (1970), pp. 73-5.
131. Houston, 'Village planning in Scotland, 1745–1845', in *The Advancement of Science*, vol. V, number 17 (1948), p. 130.
132. *Ibid.*
133. Millman, *The Making of the Scottish Landscape* (1975), p. 155.
134. W. Aiton, *General View of the Agriculture of the County of Ayr* (London, 1812) p. 129, quoted in Lockhart, *Scottish Planned Villages* (2012), p. 20.
135. Moray District Libraries, *Planned Villages of Moray*, (c. 1980); Watson, *Morayshire Described* (1868); *District of Moray* (1987).
136. McPherson, *Hopeman, 1805–2005* (2008), p. 5; Moray District Libraries, *Planned Villages of Moray* (c. 1980).
137. Gordon, GD44/43/18/64.
138. MA, ZBLo P1, plan (1784); *Registers of Seisins: Elgin & Forres* (1781–1860).
139. *NSA*, Duffus, P. 40.
140. *Strathavon* (1960), pp. 42-3.
141. Census, 1841.
142. Fife, MS3175/RHP31339 (1793); MS3175, vol. 1160 (1800).
143. RHP2312-3, plan (1764); Gordon, GD44/32/7/40, 109 (1775-6).
144. Gordon, GD44/32/7/69, GD44/52/40.
145. Quoted in *District of Moray* (1987), p. 117.
146. Census, 1841.
147. Muir, *The Lost Villages of Britain* (1985).
148. Oliver Goldsmith, 'The deserted village'
149. RHP31757-9 (1775–78).
150. *Strathavon* (1960), pp. 42-3.
151. Gordon, GD44/23/33/4 (1777).
152. *Strathavon* (1960), p. 56.
153. *OSA*, Kirkmichael, p. 279.
154. *OSA*, Kirkmichael, p. 279; census, 1841; *Strathavon* (1960), p. 55; *NSA*, p. 303-5.
155. Quoted in Smith and Stevenson (eds), *Fermfolk and Fisherfolk* (1989), p. 8.
156. *Aberdeen Journal* (1771 and 1773), quoted in Oliver, *Archiestown as it was* (2010), pp. 10-12.
157. Lockhart 'The construction and planning of new urban settlements in Scotland in the eighteenth century', in *Wolfenbutteler Forschungen Sonderdruck*, Band 47.
158. *Survey of Moray* (1798), p. 284.
159. Census, 1841.

160. *Ibid.*
161. *Inverness Journal* (30 September 1808), quoted in Lockhart, *Scottish Planned Villages* (2012), p. 83.
162. Moray District Libraries, *Planned Villages of Moray* (*c.* 1980); Census, 1841.
163. RHP2436 (*c.* 1810); RHP2511 (1833).
164. Census, 1841.
165. *Aberdeen Journal* (15 October 1808).
166. McPherson, *Hopeman* (2008), pp. 6, 17, 21.
167. Watson, *Morayshire Described* (1868), p. 293.
168. Census, 1841.
169. Moray District Libraries, *Planned Villages of Moray* (*c.* 1980); RHP2004, Telford harbour (1801); RHP2001, Burghead, 1808; NRS, GD248/623/1/2, memorial by promoters (1806).
170. John Wood's plans (1822–23); OS, first edition, 1:500 (*c.* 1870); Iredale and Barrett, 'Building royal burghs', (1995); Barrett, *Forres 500* (1996), pp. 34-6.
171. *Gentleman's Magazine* (March 1803) p. 26; John Wood's plan (1822); Robert Ray's plan (1838).
172. MA, Elgin kirk papers, ZBEl X37/1.
173. OS, 1:500, town plans (*c.* 1870); MA, Elgin town plan (*c.* 1850).
174. MA, ZBEl UG1/1, will of Alexander Gray, 18 July 1807; *District of Moray* (1987), p. 46; Watson, *Morayshire Described* (1968), p. 136.
175. Wills, *A History of General Anderson, 1745–1824* (2009), p. 45; Miller, *Archibald Simpson* (2006), pp. 140-7.
176. MA, DAW P, courthouse plans; Watson, *Morayshire Described* (1868), p. 166.
177. *District of Moray* (1987), p. 20; Rhind, *Sketches of … Moray* (1839), p. 52-4.
178. Watson, *Morayshire Described* (1868), p. 142; inscription added when a statue of the duke was added in 1855—with financial assistance from the Morayshire Farmer Club.
179. *District of Moray* (1987), p. 74; Watson, *Morayshire Described* (1868), pp. 263-4.
180. Miller, *Archibald Simpson* (2006), p. 147.
181. MA, ZCMm B2/2, Elginshire Commissioners of Supply, minute, 17 July 1822.
182. MA, ZBFo V3, Forres tolbooth (*c.* 1800); DAW P359, tolbooth plans (1837–40); DBA A91/2, memorial on the new public buildings (10 December, 1838); Iredale and Barrett 'Building royal burghs' (1995), pp. 21-2.
183. MA, ZBFo P19/1-3.
184. Hunter, *Excavations at Birnie, 2008* (2009), pp. 44-51; *District of Moray* (1987), p. 64; Shepherd, *Exploring Scotland's Heritage: Aberdeen and North-East Scotland* (1996), p. 128.
185. *Survey of Moray* (1798), p. 166.
186. *OSA*, p. 662; Howat and Seton, *Churches of Moray* (1981), p. 47.
187. *Survey of Moray* (1798), p. 130; *OSA*, vol. XVI, Spynie, p. 695.
188. *District of Moray* (1987) ,p. 91; Howat and Seton, *Churches of Moray* (1981), p. 16; Shepherd,, *Exploring Scotland's Heritage: Aberdeen and North-East Scotland* (1996), p. 124.
189. *Survey of Moray* (1798), p. 166; *District of Moray* (1987), p. 60; Howat and Seton, *Churches of Moray* (1981), p. 14.
190. Howat and Seton, *Churches of Moray* (1981), p. 44.
191. *District ofMoray* (1987), p. 159; *Survey of Moray* (1798), p. 287; Beaton, *William Robertson* (1984), p. 21.
192. *District of Moray* (1987), p. 117; Howat and Seton, *Churches of Moray* (1981), p. 4.
193. Rhind, *Sketches of … Moray* (1839).
194. Miller, *Archibald Simpson* (2006), p. 109; MA, ZBEl P9, St Giles plans, 1826–28.
195. Leslie, *A Manual of the Antiquities … of Moray* (1823), pp. 14-15.
196. *District of Moray* (1987), p. 40; Beaton, *William Robertson* (1984), p. 26.
197. *District of Moray* (1987), pp. 117-8. Howat and Seton, *Churches of Moray* (1981), p. 26.
198. *District of Moray* (1987), p. 166.
199. *NSA*, p. 254; Howat and Seton, *Churches of Moray* (1981), p. 42.
200. Howat and Seton, *Churches of Moray (1981), p. 50.*

10 Conclusions

1. *Fife, MS3175/RHP31002.*
2. *Smout, quoted in Aitchison and Cassell, The Lowland Clearances* (2003), p. 19.
3. NRS, CS1/14, pp. 75r-77r.
4. Aitchison and Cassell, *The Lowland Clearances* (2003), p. 84-5.

5. Cameron, *The Ballad and the Plough* (1978), p. 175; Devine, *Clearance and Improvement* (2006), p.146, further asserts 'there was no hidden agrarian revolt ... yet to be discovered'.

6. Devine, *The Scottish Nation* (1999), p. 147.

7. Aitchison and Cassell, *The Lowland Clearances* (2003), p. 150.

8. Lauder, *The Great Floods of August 1829*, third edition (1873—first published 1830), p. 74.

9. RHP1808, Strathavon plan (1840); OS, Banffshire, sheets XXIX, XXXV, XL, XLIII, XLVI, surveyed 1868–68 (1872).

10. Ballindalloch, bundle 1179.

11. Fife, MS3175, vol. 1058.

12. See, for instance, description of mid-nineteenth century improvements at Westfield, in *Elgin Courant* (24 June 1864).

13. 'Sir George Macpherson Grant (1839–1907)', in *Oxford Dictionary of National Biography* (online edition, 2010).

14. Franklin, *A History of Scottish Farming* (1952), p. 127.

15. Ballindalloch, bundle 1349.

16 MA, DBA A91/2, *Forres Gazette* handbill.

17. *The Compact Edition of the Dictionary of National Biography* (1975), p. 2438.

18. Franklin, *A History of Scottish Farming* (1952), p. 127.

19. Birnie, 'Ridge cultivation in Scotland', in *The Scottish Historical Review*, vol. 24, (1927), p. 201.

20. Powell, *Scottish Agricultural Implements* (1988), pp. 20-3; Fenton, *The shape of the Past*, vol. 1 (1985), pp. 125-31. McCormick's design was developed from a reaping machine invented by Patrick Bell during the 1820s, which won a £50 premium from the Highland and Agricultural Society.

21. *NSA*, Forres, p. 171.

22. Rampini, *A History of Moray and Nairn (1898), p. 301*.

BIBLIOGRAPHY

1. Archives and Manuscripts

1a. Primary sources in private hands

Ballindalloch Castle muniments—National Register of Archives (Scotland) NRAS 771.
The archive is held at Ballindalloch Castle, Moray. The references cited in notes refer to the catalogue in use at Ballindalloch Castle, which differs somewhat from the current NRAS listing.

Brodie Castle muniments—National Register of Archives (Scotland) NRAS 770.
The archive is held by the National Trust for Scotland at Brodie Castle, Moray. The references cited in footnotes refer to the catalogue in use at Brodie Castle, which differs somewhat from the current NRAS listing.

1b. Primary sources in public repositories

Aberdeen University Library, Special Libraries and Archives
MS2226/337/31 (Duff family of Duff House and William Rose of Montcoffer, their factor)—Tannachy and Brodie correspondence, 1775–92
MS2727—Duff of Braco papers
MS3175—papers of Duff House/Montcoffer—earls of Fife

Moray Council Archives
Includes resources variously of The Moray District Record Office, Moray Archives, Moray District Local Studies Library, and The Moray Council Local Heritage Service
Official records
ZBEl—Elgin town council archives
ZBEl B32/755-830—Elgin sheriff court processes, 1755–1830
ZBFo—Forres town council archives
ZBLo P1-2—Lossiemouth feuing plans, 1784
ZCMm B2—Elginshire Commissioners of Supply, minutes, 1793–1840
ZEMm A52/1—register of seisins, Elgin & Forres, 1781–1860
ZEMm B32/583-855—Forres sheriff court processes, 1583–1855
Miscellaneous Moray archives
DAW P—William Robertson architectural plans: Elgin courthouse, 1841; Forres courthouse and jail, 1837–45
DBA A91/1-3—*Forres Gazette* handbills and other printer-work, *c.* 1838–52
DBA Mf—Moray Firth and London Steam Packet Company, 1834–38
DBL 79/1—memoirs of Mr James Allan, 1689–91
ZVBl B32/766/1—Blervie estate baron court, 1766
ZVBro 638/817/1—Layhill and Darklass roup roll, 1817

ZVBro 65—Brodie estate rentals: Pennick, 1771; Cloves and Monaughty, 1773
ZVCu 60/1—Cullen Mains cashbook, 1760–80
ZVSt—Stoneyfornoon estate muniments, 1720–25
ZVTar 65/653—Tarras rental, 1653
Unclassified Moray archives
Lochinver farm plan, 1830
Lethen estate atlas (temporary deposit), 1746

National Records of Scotland

GD44—Gordon castle muniments—dukes of Gordon
GD247—Lethen estate muniments
GD248/623/1/2—Seafield muniments: memoir by the proposers of Burghead harbour, 27 May 1806
GD298—Grange estate muniments
Miscellaneous public records
CS1/14, pp75r-77r—Act of Sederunt of Court of Session, 14 December 1756
CS96/1341/ 2—valuation of buildings at Gordonstoun, 1713
SC26/2/10—Elgin sheriff court diet books
SC2/66/1-3—registers of entail improvements, Banffshire, 1815–40
Register House plans
RHP287—Speymouth and Fochabers, 1760
RHP1423—lands of Garmouth, 1772–73
RHP1746—Strathavon, *c.* 1773
RHP1749—Strathavon, *c.* 1773
RHP1752—Drumin and Alltglander, 1774
RHP1795—Tomdow, Glenlivet, 1774
RHP1808—Strathavon, *c.* 1840
RHP1809—Strathavon, *c.* 1840
RHP1815—Strathavon, *c.* 1840
RHP1819—Tomintoul, 1825
RHP2001—Burghead, 1808
RHP2004—Roseisle, 1773
RHP2016—Roseisle, 1749
RHP2312/3—Gordon Castle policies and Fochabers, 1764
RHP2351—Fochabers, *c.* 1770
RHP2356—Fochabers, 1773
RHP2358—Fochabers, *c.* 1770
RHP2359—Fochabers, 1783
RHP2430—Inchberry, *c.* 1775
RHP2434—Garmouth, 1781
RHP2436—Kingston-on-Spey, 1810
RHP2487—daugh of Deskie, 1761
RHP2488—'A Short Description of Strath Avin', 1762
RHP2490—Faevait, 1762
RHP2393—Gordon Castle home farm, 1828–29
RHP2511—Kingston-on-Spey, 1833
RHP4156—Faevait, 1766
RHP9024—Rothes, 1769
RHP9025—Rothes, 1790
RHP11614—Burghead harbour, 1801
RHP11816/2—Birnie, 1769
RHP11817—Linkwood estate, 1818
RHP11822—Bishopmill, 1823
RHP14305—Clunie, Shade, Hill-head, Ferney Lee, Black Hallock, 1840
RHP31167/1-2—Blervie, 1852
RHP31757—Tomintoul, 1775
RHP31758—Tomintoul, 1777
RHP31759—Tomintoul, 1778

Royal Commission on the Ancient and Historical Monuments of Scotland
D16476—plan of Easter Elchies, 1789
MO/1246-7, 1253—Orton House, photographs
MOD/34—Moy House plans, *c.* 1762
MO/86—Dunphail House plans, 1820
Westerton House photographs

Miscellaneous primary sources
Census, 1841—microfilm at Moray Archives
Military survey (Roy's map—1747-55) <http://www.scran.ac.uk>
Timothy Pont's map, *c.* 1590 with additions by Robert Gordon, *c.* 1650—at National Library of Scotland
Robert Gordon, *Map of Moravia*, 1654.

1c. Printed primary sources

Allardyce, A. (ed.), *Scotland and Scotsmen in the Eighteenth Century, from the MSS. of John Ramsay, Esq. of Ochtertyre* (Edinburgh, 1888)

Barrett, J. R. (ed.), *Mr James Allan: the journey of lifetime* (Kinloss, 2004)

Blaeu, J., *Atlas Novus* (1654); <http://maps.nls.uk/atlas/blaeu>

Boswell, J., *The Journal of a Tour to the Hebrides with Samuel Johnson* (London, 1955—first published, 1785)

Burt, E. *Letters from the North of Scotland*, second edition, (Edinburgh, 1876)

Campbell, A., *The Grampians Desolate* (Edinburgh, 1804)

A Catalogue of the Singular and Curious Library Originally Formed between 1610 and 1660 by Sir Robert Gordon of Gordonstoun, which will be sold by auction by J. G. Cochrane, Mon 29 March 1816 at 1 Catherine-Street, Strand (1816)

The Compleat Housewife; or Accomplish'd Gentlewoman's Companion (15th ed.) (London, 1753)

Cordiner, C., *Antiquities & Scenery of the North of Scotland, in a Series of Letters to Thomas Pennant, Esquire* (London, 1780)

Cramond, W. (ed.), *The Records of Elgin* (Aberdeen, 1903)

Dalrymple, J., *An Essay on the Husbandry of Scotland with a Proposal for the Improvement Thereof, by a lover of his country* (Edinburgh, 1732)

Cruden, J., *Convenient and Ornamental Architecture* (London, 1770)

Defoe, D., *A Tour Through the Whole Island of Great Britain* (London, 1962—first published 1725-26)

Donaldson, J., *General View of the Agriculture of the County of Banff* (Edinburgh, 1794)

Donaldson, J., *General View of the Agriculture of the County of Elgin or Moray* (Edinburgh, 1794)

The Ephemera (1822-23)

Francis, W., *The Gentleman's, Farmer's, and Husbandman's most Useful Assistant in Measuring and Expeditiously Computing of Any Quantity of Land* (London, 1818)

The Gentleman's Magazine (March 1803)

Gibbs, J., *A Book of Architecture* (London, 1739)

Gordon, R., map of *Moravia* (1654), in Joan Blaeu *Atlas Novus* (1654)

Grant, A., 'Description of the present state of [Monymusk], and what hath been done to make it what it is', in *The Miscellany of the Spalding Club*, vol. 2 (Aberdeen, 1842)

Grant, A., *The Farmer's New-Years Gift to his Countrymen, Heritors, and Farmers, for the Year 1757* (Aberdeen, 1757)

Grant, A., 'Memoires of the state of the country in the early part of the eighteenth century', in *The Miscellany of the Spalding Club*, vol. 2 (Aberdeen, 1842)

Grant, A., *The Practical Farmer's Pocket-Companion* (Aberdeen, 1766)

Grant, Mrs A. M., *Essays on the Superstitions of the Highlanders of Scotland* (London, 1811)

Gray, A., *Explanation of the Engravings of the Most Important Implements of Husbandry Used in Scotland* (Edinburgh, 1814)

Gray, A., *The Plough-Wright's Assistant, or a practical treatise on various implements employed in agriculture* (Edinburgh, 1808)

Hall, J., *Travels in Scotland by an Unusual Route: with a trip to the Orkneys and Hebrides, containing hints for improvements in agriculture and commerce* (London, 1807)

Hamilton, H. (ed.), *Life and Labour on an Aberdeenshire Estate, 1735–1750* (London, 1946)

Hamilton, H. (ed.), *Selections from theMonymusk Papers, 1713–55* (Edinburgh, 1945)

Heron, R., *Scotland Delineated, or a geographical description of every shire in Scotland* (Edinburgh, 1799)

Highland and Agricultural Society of Scotland, *Prize Essays and Transactions*, vols 1–6 (Edinburgh, 1799–1824)

Home, F., *The Principles of Agriculture and Vegetation* (Edinburgh, 1776)

Home, H., *The Gentleman Farmer* (Edinburgh, 1776)

Hoppus, E., *The Gentleman's and Builder's Repository: or architecture displayed* (London, 1737)

Hume, P. Brown, *Early Travellers in Scotland* (Edinburgh, 1973)

Hutcheon, T. S., *Plan of the Burgh of Elgin, in the County of Moray: new survey together with illustrations of the principal buildings &c. chiefly from Daguerrotypes* (1855)

James, W., *The Gentlemen's or Builders' Companion* (1739)

Jameson, G., *The Rudiments of Architecture, or the young workman's instructor* (Edinburgh, 1772)

Jameson, G., *Thirty-three Designs: with orders of architecture according to Palladio* (Edinburgh, 1765)

Johnson, A., *Poemata Omnia* (Middelburg, Zeeland, 1642), translated by John Barclay, minister of Cruden, in A. Skene, *Memorialls for the Government of Royall-Burghs in Scotland* (Aberdeen, 1685)

Johnson, S., *A Journey to the Western Islands of Scotland* (London, 1924—first published, 1775)

Johnstone, J., *An Account of the Most Approved Mode of Draining Land: according to the system practised by Mr Joseph Elkington, late of Princethory in the County of Warwick* (Dublin, 1800)

Kemp, D. W. (ed.) *Tours in Scotland, 1747, 1750, 1760 by Richard Pococke, bishop of Meath* (Edinburgh, 1887)

Kirk, J., *The Books of Assumption of the Thirds of Benefices: Scottish ecclesiastical rentals at the Reformation* (Oxford, 1995)

Lauder, T. Dick., *The Great Floods of August 1829*, 3rd edition (Elgin, 1873—first published 1830)

Laurence, E., *The Duty of a Steward to his Lord* (London, 1727)

Lawrence, J., *The Modern Land Steward: in which the duties and functions of stewardship are considered and explained ... by the author of the new farmer's calendar* (London, 1801)

Lawson, J., 'Comparative experiments in the sowing of wheat', in *Prize Essays and Transactions of the Highland and Agricultural Society*, vol. VI (Edinburgh, 1824) pp. 221-8

Leslie, W., *General View of the Agriculture in the Counties of Nairn and Moray* (London, 1811)

Leslie, W., *A Manual of the Antiquities, Distinguished Buildings and Natural Curiosities of Moray in its Ancient Prelatic Extent; with an outline of the geology and mineralogy of the county and an itinerary of the province for the information of inquisitive travellers and others* (Elgin, 1823)

Leslie, W., *A Survey of the Province of Moray; historical, geographical, and political* (Aberdeen, 1798)

'Letters from a young farmer to his father', in *The Farmer's Magazine*, vol. viii (1807)

Ley, C., *The Nobleman, Gentleman, Land Steward, and Surveyor's compleat guide.in which is described every particular instance relative to the proper management of estates* (London, 1786)

Mackintosh, W., *An Essay on Ways and Means for Inclosing, Fallowing, Planting, &c. Scotland* (Edinburgh, 1729)

Merson, D., Wallace, M. and N. Wallace, N. (eds), *Grange 1694–1702* [kirk session minutes] (Aberdeen, 1995)

Millar, W., map of *The Province of Moray* (*c*. 1790)

Morris, R. and Lightoler, T., *The Modern Builder's Assistant* (London, 1757)

Murray, S., *A Companion and Useful Guide to the Beauties of Scotland* (Hawick, 1982—first published 1799)

The New Statistical Account of Scotland,vol. XIII, Banff—Elgin—Nairn (Edinburgh, 1845)

Newte, T., *Proposals and Observations on a Tour in England and Scotland* (London, 1791)

Ordnance Survey, Banffshire, 1:10560, first edition, sheets XXIX, XXXV, XLIII, XLVI, XLVIII, surveyed 1869 (Southampton, 1871–72)

Ordnance Survey, Banffshire, 1:10,560, second edition, sheets XXIX NE, XXIX NW, XXIX SE, XXIX, SW, XXXIV SE, XXXV NE, XXXV SE, XXXV SW, XL, XVIII, XLVI, revised 1900-2 (Southampton, 1902–05)

Ordnance Survey, Elginshire, 1:2500 and 1:10,560, first edition, surveyed 1866–71 (Southampton, 1868–72)

Ordnance Survey, Elginshire, 1:2500 and 1:10,560, second edition, revised *c*. 1904 (Southampton, 1905)

Pearson, M., *Flitting the Flakes: the diary of J. Badenoch a Stonehaven farmer, 1789–97* (Edinburgh, 1992)

Pennant, T., *A Tour in Scotland, MDCCLXIX* (London, 1776)

Peters, M., *The Rational Farmer* (Newport, 1770)

Ray, R., *Plan of the burgh of Elgin* (1838)

Rhind, W., *Sketches of the Past and Present State of Moray* (Edinburgh, 1839)

Searles, M., *The Land Steward's and Farmer's Assistant* (London, 1779)

Shaw, L., *The History of the Province of Moray* (Edinburgh, 1775)

Sinclair, J., *An Account of the Systems of Husbandry adopted in the more Improved Districts of Scotland* (Edinburgh, 1814)

Skene, A., *Memorials of the Government of Royall-Burghs in Scotland (Aberdeen, 1685)*

Slezer, J., Theatrum Scotiae (London, 1693)

Small, J., A Treatise on Ploughs and Wheel Carriages (Edinburgh, 1784)

Smith, G. Campbell, *Plan of the Estate of Balnageith lying in the parish of Forres and County of Elgin; the property of The Revd. Wm. Leslie* (Banff, 1827)

Souter, D., *General View of the Agriculture of the County of Banff* (Edinburgh, 1812)

Statutes at Large (13 vols) (1769–1780)

Stephens, H., *The Book of the Farm* (Edinburgh, 1844)

Stone, J. C., The*Pont Manuscript Maps of Scotland* (Tring, 1989)

Stone, J., *Illustrated Maps of Scotland, from Blaeu's Atlas Novus of the 17th Century* (London, 1991—Blaeu's *Atlas* was first published 1654)

Thomson, T. and Innes, C., *The Acts of the Parliaments of Scotland* (Edinburgh, 1814-75); <http://rps.ac.uk>

Tod, A., (ed.) *Elizabeth Grant of Rothiemurchus: Memoirs of a Highland Lady* (Edinburgh, 1988—first published, 1898)

Tull, J., *Horse-hoeing Husbandry: or an essay on the principles of tillage and vegetation. Wherein is shewn a method of inducing a sort of vineyard-culture into the corn-fields ... by the use of instruments described in cuts* (Dublin, 1733)

Vitruvius Scoticus: being a collection of plans, elevations and sections of public buildings, noblemen's and gentlemen's houses in Scotland, from the designs of the late William Adam, esq., architect (Edinburgh, 1812)

Watson, J. and W., *Morayshire Described: being a guide to visitors* (Elgin, 1868)

Withrington, D. J. and Grant, I. R. (eds), *The Statistical Account of Scotland, 1791–1799, edited by Sir John Sinclair*, vol. XVI, Banffshire, Moray & Nairnshire (Wakefield, 1982); vol. XVII, Inverness-shire, Ross and Cromarty (Wakefield, 1981)

Wood, J., Plan of the royal burgh of *Forres* (1823)

Wood, J., Plan of the royal burgh of *Elgin* (1823)

2. Secondary sources

2a. Books

Adams, I. H., *Descriptive List of Plans in the Scottish Record Office* vols 1–3 (Edinburgh 1966, 1970, 1974)

Adams, I. H., *Directory of Former Scottish Commonties* (Edinburgh, 1971)

Adams, I. H., *Papers on Peter May, Land Surveyor, 1749–1793* (Edinburgh, 1979)

Adams, I. H. and Timperley, L. R., *Descriptive List of Plans in the Scottish Record Office* vol. 4 (Edinburgh, 1988)

Aitchison, P. and Cassell, A., *The Lowland Clearances: Scotland's silent revolution, 1766–1830* (East Linton, 2003)

Alcock, N. W. (ed.), *Cruck Construction, an introduction and catalogue* (London, 1981)

Alexander, W., *Notes and Sketches Illustrative of Northern Rural Life in the Eighteenth Century* (Finzean, 1981)

Allan, J. R., *The North East Lowlands of Scotland* (London, 1952)

Anderson, G., *Kingston-on-Spey* (Edinburgh, 1957)

Anderson, M. H., *A History of Scottish Forestry*, vol. 1, edited by C. J. Taylor (London, 1967)

Aston, M. and Rowley, T., *Landscape Archaeology: an introduction to fieldwork techniques on post-Roman landscapes* (London, 1974)

Bailey, R. M., *Scottish Architects' Papers: a source book* (Edinburgh, 1996)

Bain, G., *The Lordship of Petty* (Nairn, 1925)

Baldwin, J. R., *Exploring Scotland's Heritage: Lothian and the Borders* (Edinburgh, 1985)

Barrett, J., *Forres 500* (Forres, 1996)

Barrett, J. R. and Mitchell, A., *Elgin's Love-gift: civil war in Scotland and the depositions of 1646* (Chichester, 2007)

Beaton, E., *Ross & Cromarty: an illustrated architectural guide* (Edinburgh, 1992)

Beaton, E., *William Robertson, 1786–1841, 'architect in Elgin'* (Inverness, 1984)

Bil, A., *The Shieling, 1600–1840* (Edinburgh, 2003)

Bingham, C., *Beyond the Highland Line* (London, 1991)

Bishop, B. B., *The Lands and People of Moray* (Miltonduff, published episodically from 2000 onwards)

Branigan, K., *The Last of the Clan: General Roderick Macneil of Barra, 41st chief of clan Macneil* (Stroud, 2010)

Brereton, H., *Gordonstoun: ancient estate and modern school* (Edinburgh, 1968)

British Geological Survey, Scotland, 1:50,000, sheet 75W, *Glenlivet*, surveyed 1895–1987 (Nottingham, 1996)

British Geological Survey, Scotland, 1:50,000, sheet 85W, *Knockando*, surveyed 1878–1991 (Nottingham, 1997)

British Geological Survey, Scotland, 1:50,000, sheet 85E, *Glenfiddich*, surveyed 1884–1993 (Nottingham, 1996)

Brodie, J., *Brodie Country* (Birmingham, 1999)

Brunskill, R. W., *Illustrated Handbook of Vernacular Architecture*, second edition (London, 1978)

Brunskill, R. W., *Traditional Buildings of Britain* (London, 1988)

Bulloch, J. M., *The Badenoch & Strathspey Farming Society* (Banff, no date)

Bumsted, J. M., *The People's Clearance, 1770–1815* (Edinburgh, 1982)

Buxbaum, T., *Scottish Garden Buildings* (Edinburgh, 1989)

Cameron, D. K., *The Ballad and the Plough: a folk history of the Scottish farmtouns* (London, 1987)

Campbell, R. H., *Scotland Since 1707: the rise of an industrial society* (Oxford, 1965)

Carruthers, A. (ed.), *The Scottish Home* (Edinburgh 1996)

Carter, I., *Farmlife in North-east Scotland, 1840–1914: the poor man's country* (Edinburgh, 1979)

Cassilis, Earl of, *The Rulers of Strathspey: a history of the lords of Grant and earls of Seafield* (Inverness, 1911)

Chambers, J. D. and Mingay, G. E., *The Agricultural Revolution 1750–1880* (London, 1966)

Cheape, H. and Sprott, G., *Angus Country Life* (Edinburgh, 1980)

The Compact Edition of the Dictionary of National Biography (London, 1975)

Cooke, A., Donnachie, I., MacSween, A. and Whatley, C. A., *Modern Scottish History 1707 to the Present*, vol. 1, *The Transformation of Scotland 1707–1850* (Dundee, 1998)

Cowie, M., *The Life and Times of William Marshall, composer of Scottish traditional music and clock maker* (1999)

Cramond, W., *The Church of Lhanbryd* (1900)

Crossley, D., *Post-medieval Archaeology in Britain* Leicester, 1990)

Cunningham, R. J. H., *The Geognosy of Banffshire* (1842)

Daichies, D., *The Scottish Enlightenment* (Edinburgh, 1986)

Dallas, R., *Measured Survey and Building Recording* (Edinburgh, 2003)

Davidson, J. D. G., *The Royal Highland and Agricultural Society: a short history 1784–1984* (Edinburgh, 1984)

Devine, T. M., *Clearance and Improvement: land, power and people in Scotland, 1700–1900* (Edinburgh, 2006)

Devine, T. M., (ed.) *Conflict and Stability in Scottish Society, 1700–1850* (Edinburgh, 1990)

Devine, T. M. (ed.), *Lairds and Improvement in Scotland of the Enlightenment* (Glasgow, 1979)

Devine, T. M., *The Scottish Nation, 1700–2000* (Harmondsworth, 1999)

Devine, T., *To the Ends of the Earth: Scotland's global diaspora, 1750–2010* (London, 2011)

Devine, T. M., *The Transformation of Rural Scotland: social change and the agrarian economy, 1660–1815* (Edinburgh, 1994)

Dixon, P., *Puir Labourers and Busy Husbandmen: the countryside of lowland Scotland in the middle ages* (Edinburgh, 2002)

Dodgshon, R. A., *Land and Society in Early Scotland* (Oxford, 1981)

Dodgshon, R. A., *The Origins of British Field Systems* (London, 1980)

Douglas, R., *Annals of the Royal Burgh of Forres* (Elgin, 1934)

Douglas, R., *The Lord Provosts of Elgin* (Elgin, 1926)

Douglas, R., *Sons of Moray* (Elgin, 1930)

Duff, P., *Sketch of the Geology of Moray* (Elgin, 1842)

Dunbar, E. Dunbar-, *Social Life in Former Days, chiefly in the Province of Moray* (Edinburgh, 1865)

Dunnett, H., *Inveraan: a Strathspey parish* (Paisley, 1919)

Emerton, G., *The Pattern of Scottish Roofing* (Edinburgh, 2000)

Fenton, A., *Clay Building and Clay Thatch in Scotland* (Ulster, 1970)

Fenton, A., *Country Life in Scotland: our rural past* (Edinburgh, 1987)

Fenton, A., *Scottish Country Life* (East Linton, 1999)

Fenton, A., *The Shape of the Past: essays in Scottish ethnology*, vols 1–2 (Edinburgh, 1985-6)

Fenton, A. & Walker, B., *The Rural Architecture of Scotland* (Edinburgh, 1981)

Ferguson, W., *Scotland, 1689 to the present* (Edinburgh, 1968)

Finberg, H. P. R. and Skipton, V. H. T., *Local History: objective and pursuit* (Newton Abbot, 1967)

Franklin, T. B., *A History of Scottish Farming* (London, 1952)

Fry, M., *Wild Scots: four hundred years of highland history* (London, 2005)

Gaffney, V., *The Lordship of Strathavon: Tomintoul under the Gordons* (Aberdeen, 1960)

Gaffney, V., *Tomintoul: its glens and people* (Golspie, 1970)

Gauldie, E., *The Scottish Country Miller, 1700–1900* (Edinburgh, 1981)

Garner, L., *Dry Stone Walls* (Princes Risborough, 1984)

Geological Survey, *"Ten Mile" Map*, 1:625,000 (Chessington, 1957)

Gibson, R., *The Scottish Countryside: its changing face, 1700 -2000* (Edinburgh, 2007)

Gifford, J., *The Buildings of Scotland: Highlands and Islands* (Edinburgh, 1992)

Glendinning, M, and others, *A History of Scottish Architecture from the Renaissance to the Present Day* (Edinburgh, 1996)

Glendinning, M., and Martins, S. W., *Buildings of the Land: Scotland's farms, 1750-2000* (Edinburgh, 2008)

Gordon, G., *The Last Dukes of Gordon and their Consorts, 1743-1864* (Aberdeen, 1980)

Gordon, J. F. S., *The History of the Province of Moray* (Glasgow, 1882)

Graham, H. G., *The Social Life of Scotland in the Eighteenth Century* (London, 1950)

Grant, D. P. T., *A History of Clan Grant* (Chichester, 1983)

Grant, I. F., *Highland Folk Ways* (Edinburgh, 1995)

Grant, J., *Agriculture in Banffshire 150 Years Ago* (Banff, 1902)

Gray, M., *The Highland Economy, 1750-1880* (Edinburgh, 1957)

Groome, F. H., *Ordnance Gazetteer of Scotland: a survey of Scottish topography, statistical, biographical, and historical* (Edinburgh, 1882)

Haldane, A. R. B., *The Drove Roads of Scotland* (Edinburgh, 1952)

Hamilton, H., *Life and Labour on an Aberdeenshire Estate, 1735-1750* (Aberdeen, 1946)

Hamilton, H., *An Economic History of Scotland in the Eighteenth Century* (Oxford, 1963)

Hammond, J. L. and Hammond, B., *The Village Labourer, 1780-1830* (Stroud, 1987—first published 1911)

Handley, J. E., *The Agricultural Revolution in Scotland* (Glasgow, 1963)

Handley, J. E., *Scottish Farming in the Eighteenth Century* (London, 1953)

Harper, M., *Adventurers and Exiles: the great Scottish exodus* (London, 2003)

Harper, M., *Emigration from North-East Scotland*, vol. 1, *Willing Exiles* (Aberdeen, 1988)

Harvey, N., *Fields, Hedges and Ditches* (Princes Risborough, 1987)

Hay, G. and Stell, G., *Monuments of Industry* (Edinburgh, 1986)

Hay, R., *Lochnavando No More: the life and death of a Moray farming community* (Edinburgh, 2005)

Herman, A., *The Scottish Enlightenment: the Scots' invention of the modern world* (London, 2002)

Higgs, J., *The Land* (London, 1965)

Hinxman, L. W. (and others), The *Geology of Mid-Strathspey and Strathdearn* (Edinburgh, 1915)

Hinxman, L. W. and Wilson, J. S. Grant, *The Geology of Lower Strathspey* (Glasgow, 1902)

Historic Scotland, *Thatch and Thatching Techniques* (Edinburgh, 1996)

A History of the Family of Brodie of Brodie [and] Brodie of Lethen (no date)

Hoskins, W. G., *The Making of the English Landscape* (Harmondsworth, 1970)

Hoskins, W. G., *The Midland Peasant: economic and social history of a Leicestershire village* (Chichester, 2008—first published 1957)

Howat, A. J. and Seton, M., *Churches of Moray* (Elgin, 1981)

Hunter, F., *Excavations at Birnie, 2004, 2008, 2009* (Edinburgh, 2005, 2009, 2010)

Institute of Geological Sciences Scotland, *Elgin, sheet 95*, solid edition (1:63,360), surveyed 1886-1964 (Southampton, 1969)

Iredale, D. and Barrett, J., *Discovering Your Old House* (Princes Risborough, 1991)

Keay, J. and Keay, J. (eds), *Collins Encyclopaedia of Scotland* (London, 1994)

Keith, A., *The Parish of Drainie and Lossiemouth* (1975)

Knox, S. A., *The Making of the Shetland Landscape* (Edinburgh, 1985)

Kyd, J. G., *Scottish Population Statistics* (Edinburgh, 1975)

Lawson, A. B., *A Country Called Stratherrick* (1987)

Lenman, B. P., *Integration and Enlightenment: Scotland, 1746-1832* (Edinburgh, 1981)

Lindsay, M., *The Castles of Scotland* (London, 1986)

Lockhart, D. G. (ed.) *Scottish Planned Villages* (Edinburgh, 2012)

Logue, K. J., *Popular Disturbances in Scotland, 1780-1815* (Edinburgh, 1979)

Lynch, M., *Scotland: a new history* (London, 1991)

Macaulay Institute for Soil Research, *Soil Survey of Scotland, Land Capability for Agriculture: sheet 5, Eastern Scotland*—1:250,000 map (Aberdeen 1981)

Macgregor, A. A., *The Buried Barony* (London, 1949)

McGregor, R. E., *The Story of Gregor Willox MacGregor, Willox the warlock* (Aberdeen, 1994)

McGuire, D. E., *Agricultural Improvements in Strathkelvin, 1700-1850* (Glasgow, 1988)

McKean, C., *Banff & Buchan: an illustrated architectural guide* (Edinburgh, 1990)

McKean, C., *The District of Moray: an illustrated architectural guide* (Edinburgh, 1987)

McKean, C., Walker, D. and Walker, F., *Central Glasgow: an illustrated architectural guide* (Edinburgh, 1989)

Mackenzie, A., *The History of the Highland Clearances: containing a reprint of Donald Macleod's 'Gloomy Memories'* (Inverness, 1986—first published 1883)

Mackie, J. D., *A History of Scotland* (Harmondsworth, 1969—first published 1964)

Macmillan, H. D., *Letters of Patrick Grant Lord Elchies* (Aberdeen, 1927)

McPherson, J. (ed.), *Hopeman, 1805–2005* (Hopeman, 2008)

Mason, T. L., *Rafford in the Past* (Elgin, 1889)

Miller, D. G., *Archibald Simpson, Architect: his life and times, 1790–1847* (Kinloss, 2006)

Milliken, S. and Bridgewater, S., *Flora Celtica: plants and people in Scotland* (Edinburgh, 2004)

Millman, R. N., *The Making of the Scottish Countryside* (London, 1975)

Mitchell, J. B., *Historical Geography* (London, 1954)

Mitchell, S., *Pittyvaich: the history of an old Mortlach farm* (Aberdeen, 1997)

Moray District Libraries, *Planned Villages of Moray* (Elgin, c. 1980)

Morris, P., (and others) *Field Guide to the Animals of Britain* (London, 1984)

Mowat, I. R. M., *Easter Ross, 1750–1850: the double frontier* (Edinburgh, 1981)

Muir, R., *The Lost Villages of Britain* (London, 1985)

Muir, R., *The Shell Guide to Reading the Celtic Landscapes* (London, 1985)

Murray, J. G., *The Book of Burgie* (Edinburgh, 1930)

Murray, J. G., *The Dallas Raid* (Forres, no date)

Naismith, R. J., *Buildings of the Scottish Countryside* (London, 1985)

O'Dell, A. C. and Walton, K., *The Highlands & Islands of Scotland* (Edinburgh, 1962)

Oliver, A., *Archiestown: the way it was* (2006)

Omand, D., *The Grampian Book* (Golspie, 1987)

Omand, D. (ed.), *The Moray Book* (Edinburgh, 1976)

Oxford Dictionary of National Biography (Oxford, 2004); <http://www.oxforddnb.com>

Parry, M. L. and Slater, T. R. (eds), *The Making of the Scottish Countryside* (London, 1980)

Patrick, J., *Scotland: the age of achievement* (London, 1976)

Peacock, J. D. (and others), *The Geology of the Elgin District* (Edinburgh, 1968)

Peck, E. H., *Avonside Explored* (Tomintoul, 1983)

Powell, B., *Scottish Agricultural Implements* (Princes Risborough, 1988)

Prebble, J., *The Highland Clearances* (Harmondsworth, 1969)

Rackham, O., *The History of the Countryside* (London, 1986)

Rackham, O., *Trees and Woodland in the British Landscape* (London, 1976)

Rampini, C., *A History of Moray and Nairn* (Edinburgh, 1897)

Richards, E., *Debating the Highland Clearances* (Edinburgh, 2007)

Richards, E., *The Highland Clearances: people, landlords and rural turmoil* (Edinburgh, 2008)

Richards, E., *Patrick Sellar and the Highland Clearances: homicide, eviction and the price of progress* (Edinburgh, 1999)

Richardson, D., *The Curse on Patrick Sellar* (Stockbridge, 1999)

Royal Commission on the Ancient and Historical Monuments of Scotland, *Mar Lodge Estate, Grampian: an archaeological survey* (Edinburgh, 1995)

RCAHMS, *A Practical Guide to Recording Archaeological Sites* (Edinburgh, 2011)

RCAHMS, *Scotland's Rural Past: community archaeology in action* (Edinburgh, 2011).

RCAHMS, *'Well sheltered & Watered': Menstrie Glen, a farming landscape near Stirling* (Edinburgh, 2008)

Ross, S., *The Culbin Sands—fact and fiction* (Aberdeen, 1992)

Sanderson, M. H. B., *Scottish Rural Society in the Sixteenth Century* (Edinburgh, 1982)

Sellar, W. D. H., *Moray: province and people* (Edinburgh, 1993)

Shepherd, I., *Aberdeen and North-East Scotland* (2nd ed.) (Edinburgh, 1996)

Simmons, I. G., *An Environmental History of Great Britain from 10,000 years ago to the present* (Edinburgh, 2001)

Skelton, J., *Speybuilt: the story of a forgotten industry* (Garmouth, 1994)

Slimon, C., *Stells, Stools, Strupay* (Laggan, 2007)

Smith, J. S. and Stevenson, D., *Fermfolk and Fisherfolk: rural life in northern Scotland in the eighteenth and nineteenth centuries* (Aberdeen, 1989)

Smout, T. C., *A History of the Scottish People, 1560–1830* (London, 1969)

Smout, T. C. (ed.) *People and Woods in Scotland: a history* (Edinburgh, 2003)

Smout, T. C. (ed.), *Scottish Woodland History* (Dalkeith, 1997)

Smout, T. C. and Lambert, R. A., *Rothiemurchus: nature and people on a highland Estate, 1500–2000* (Dalkeith, 1999)

Smout, T. C., Macdonald, A. R. and Watson, F., *A History of the Native Woodlands of Scotland, 1500–1920* (Edinburgh, 2007)

Smout, T. C. and Wood, S., *Scottish Voices, 1745–1960* (London, 1990)

Stell, G., Shaw, J., and Storrier, S. (eds), *Scotland's Buildings* (Edinburgh, 2003)

Storrier, S. (ed.), *Furniture and Fittings in the Traditional Scottish Home* (Edinburgh, 2006)

Tait, A. A., *The Landscape Garden in Scotland, 1735–1835* (Edinburgh, 1980)

Taylor, C., *Fields in the English Landscape* (London, 1975)

Taylor, C., *Fieldwork in Medieval Archaeology* (London, 1974)

Taylor, W., *The Military Roads in Scotland* (Newton Abbot, 1976)

Towsey, M. R. M., *Reading the Scottish Enlightenment: books and their readers in provincial Scotland 1750–1820* (Boston, 2010)

Tranter, N., *The Fortified House in Scotland*, vol. 5, *northwest Scotland and miscellaneous* (Edinburgh, 1977)

Turnock, D., *The Historical Geography of Scotland Since 1707* (Cambridge, 1982)

Turnock, D., *The Making of the Scottish Rural Landscape* (Aldershot, 1995)

Walker, B., McGregor, C. and Little, R., *Earth Structures and Construction in Scotland* (Edinburgh, 1996)

Walker, B., McGregor, C., and Stark, G., *Scottish Turf Construction* (Edinburgh, 2006)

Walker, B., McGregor, C. and Stark, G., *Thatch and Thatching Techniques* (Edinburgh, 1996)

Walker, A. D. (and others), *Land Capability for Agriculture: Eastern Scotland* (Aberdeen, 1982)

Walker, B. and Ritchie, G., *Exploring Scotland's Heritage: Fife and Tayside* (Edinburgh, 1987)

Watt, S. G., *The History of the Loch of Spynie and the Laich o' Moray* (no date)

West, T. W., *Discovering Scottish Architecture* (Princes Risborough, 1985)

Whatley, C., *Scottish Society, 1707–1850* (Manchester, 2000)

Whittington, G. and Whyte, I. D., *An Historical Geography of Scotland* (London, 1983)

Whittington, G. and Gibson, A. J. S., *The Military Survey of Scotland, 1747–1755* (Leicester, 1986)

Whyte, I. D., *Agriculture and Society in Seventeenth-Century Scotland* (Edinburgh, 1979)

Whyte, I. and K., *The Changing Scottish Landscape, 1500–1800* (London, 1991)

Whyte, I. and K., *Exploring Scotland's Historic Landscapes* (Edinburgh, 1987)

Whyte, I. D., *Scotland Before the Industrial Revolution* (London, 1995)

Williams, R., *Limekilns and Limeburning* (Princes Risborough, 1989)

Wood, S., *The Shaping of 19th Century Aberdeenshire* (Stevanage, 1985)

Wood, S. and Patrick, J., *History in the Grampian Landscape* (Finzean, 1982)

Young, R., *The Parish of Spynie* (Elgin, 1871)

Youngson, A. J., *After the Forty-Five* (Edinburgh, 1973)

2b. Articles

Adams, I. H., 'The agricultural revolution in Scotland: contributions to the debate', in *Area*, vol. 10, no. 3 (1978)

Allen, N. G., 'Walling materials in the eighteenth century highlands', in *Vernacular Buildings* (1979)

Barrett, J., 'Moray murder', in *Leopard* (Dyce, September 2000)

Barrett, J. R., 'Regular reforestation: woodland resources in Moray 1720–1840', in C. M. Mills (ed.), *Community, Woodlands and Perspectives of Ownership: historical perspectives*—Native Woodlands Discussion Group, Woodlands History Conference, notes XVI (St Andrews, 2011)

Barrow, G. W. S., 'Rural settlement in central and eastern Scotland', in *Scottish Studies* (1962)

Beaton, E., 'The pattern of Moray building', in W. D. H. Sellar, *Moray: province and people* (Edinburgh, 1993)

Beaton, E., 'Sources of Slate in Banffshire and Aberdeenshire', in A. Riches and G. Stell, *Materials and Traditions in Scottish Building* (Edinburgh, 1992)

Beaton, E. and Moran, M., 'A cottar house with a hinging-lum', in *Vernacular Architecture*, no. 8, (1977)

Birnie, A., 'Ridge cultivation in Scotland', in *Scottish Historical Review*, vol. XXIV, no. 95 (April 1927)

Britnell, W. (and others), 'A 15th century corn drying kiln from Collfryn, Llansantffraid Deuddwr, Powys', in *Medieval Archaeology*, no. 28 (1984)

Campbell, R. H., 'Scottish improvers and the course of agrarian change in the eighteenth century', in Cullen, L. M. and Smout, T. C., *Comparative Aspects of Scottish and Irish Economic and Social History, 1600–1900* (Edinburgh, 1977)

Clark, G., 'Yields per acre in English agriculture, 1250–1860', in *The Economic History Review*, vol. XLIV, no. 3 (August 1991)

Coull, J. R., 'Fisheries in the north-east of Scotland before 1800', in *Scottish Studies* vol. 13 (Edinburgh, 1969)

Denoon, J., 'Queer folk in Knockando', in *Old Morayshire Characters* (Elgin, 1931)

Devine, T. M., 'Temporary migration and the Scottish highlands in the nineteenth century', in *The Economic History Review*, second series, vol. XXXII, no. 3, (August 1979)

Dodgshon, R. A., 'Scandinavian solskifte and the sunwise division of land in eastern Scotland', in *Scottish Studies*, vol. 19, (Edinburgh, 1975)

Dodgshon, R. A., 'The nature and development of infield-outfield in Scotland', in *Transactions of the Institute of British Geographers*, no. 59 (July 1973)

Dodgshon, R. A., 'Towards an understanding and definition of runrig: the evidence for Roxburghshire and Berwickshire', in *Transactions of the Institute of British Geographers*, no. 64 (March 1975)

Dodgshon, R. A., Gilbertson, D. D. and Gratton, J. D., 'Endemic Stress, farming communities and the influence of Icelandic Volcanic Eruptions in the Scottish Highlands', Geological Society Special Publications, vol. 171, pp. 267-80 (London, 2000)

Dowds, T., 'The Scots and slavery', in *History Scotland*, vol. 11, no. 2 (March/April 2011)

Eyre, S. R., 'The curving plough-strip and its historical implications' in *The Agricultural History Review*, vol. III, part II, (1955)

Fenton, A., 'The housing of agricultural workers in the nineteenth century', in T. M. Devine (ed.) *Farm Servants and Labour in Lowland Scotland, 1780–1914* (Edinburgh, 1984)

Fenton, A., 'How did the pre-improvement landscape and society work?', in *Review of Scottish Culture*, no. 15, (Edinburgh, 2002)

Gaffney, V., 'Summer shealings', in *The Scottish Historical Review*, vol. XXXVIII (1959)

Glass, J. 'Sugar for the brose: Sir Archibald Grant, Jamaica and agricultural improvements at Monymusk, c. 1720–1760', in *History Scotland* vol. 6, nos. 2–3 (March/April–May/June 2006)

Grant, I. F., 'The social effects of the agricultural reforms and enclosure movement in Aberdeenshire', in *Economic History*, vol. I, (January 1926)

Gray, M., 'Farm workers in north-east Scotland', in T. M. Devine (ed.) *Farm Servants and Labour in Lowland Scotland, 1780–1914* (Edinburgh, 1982)

Gray, M., 'The social impact of agrarian change in the rural lowlands', in T. M. Devine and R. Mitchison (eds) *People and Society in Scotland, 1760–1830* (Edinburgh, 1988)

Green, F. H. W., 'Rural and coastal settlement in the Moray Firth lowlands', in *Scottish Geographical Magazine*, vol. 52, no. 5, (March 1936)

Hamilton, A. and Davies, A., 'Written in the hills: an environmental history project in the southern uplands', in *History Scotland*, vol. 7 no. 3 (May/June 2007)

Hay, J. D., 'The cruck building at Corimony, Inverness-shire', in *Scottish Studies*, no. 17 (1973)

Historic Buildings and Monuments Scotland, *Buildings of Special Architectural or Historic Interest: combined statutory and descriptive list, Moray District*, second amendment (Edinburgh, 3 August 1989)

Hodd, A. N. L., 'Runrig on the eve of the agricultural revolution in Scotland', in *Scottish Geographical Magazine*, vol. 90, issue 2 (1974)

Holmes, H., 'The circulation of Scottish agricultural books during the eighteenth century', in *Agricultural History Review*, no. 54, vol. I (2006)

Houston, J. M., 'Village planning in Scotland', in *The Advancement of Science* (1948)

Howatson, W., 'Grain harvesting and harvesters', in T. M. Devine (ed.) *Farm Servants and Labour in Lowland Scotland 1780-1914* (Edinburgh, 1984)

House, S. and Dingwell, C., 'A nation of planters: introducing new trees, 1650–1900', in T. C. Smout (ed.) *People and Woods in Scotland: a history* (Edinburgh, 2003)

Imrie, H. B., 'Sheriff court files', in *Scottish Local History* no. 54 (2002)

Iredale, D. and Barrett, J., 'Building royal burghs', in *The Scots Magazine*, new series, vol. 142, no. 1 (January 1995)

Iredale, D and Barrett, J., 'The lowland clearances', in *The Scots Magazine*, new series, vol. 137, no. 6 (September 1992)

Lockhart, D. G., 'The construction and planning of new urban settlements in Scotland in the eighteenth century', in *Wolfenbutteler Forschungen Sonderdruck*, band 47 (no date)

Lockhart, D. G., 'Lotted lands and planned villages in north-east Scotland', in *The Agricultural History Review*, vol. 49, part 1 (2001)

Lockhart, D. G., 'Migration to planned villages in Scotland between 1725 and 1850', in *Scottish Geographical Magazine* (April 1986)

Logan, A., 'Moray personality of yesteryear', in *The Northern Scot* (December 1954)

McKean, C., 'The architectural evolution of Innes House, Moray', in *Proceedings of the Society of Antiquaries of Scotland*, vol. 133 (2003)

Maudlin, D. 'The legend of Brigadoon', in *Traditional Dwellings and Settlements Review*, vol. XX, no. 11 (2009)

Mingay, G. E., 'The eighteenth-century land steward', in E. L. Jones and G. E. Mingay *Land, Labour and Population in the Industrial Revolution* (London, 1967)

Noble, R. Ross, 'Turf-walled houses of the central highlands: an experiment in reconstruction', in *Folk Life*, vol. 22 (1983-4)

Robertson, U., 'Pigeons as a source of food in eighteenth-century Scotland ', in *Review of Scottish Culture*, no. 4, (Edinburgh, 1998)

Ross, A., 'Assessing the impact of past grazing regimes: transhumance in the forest of Stratha'an, Banffshire', AHRC Research Centre for Environmental History, University of Stirling, short report 3 (*c.* 2005)

Ross, A., 'The dabhach in Moray', in A. Woolf, *Landscape and Environment in Dark Age Scotland* (St Andrews, 2006)

Ross, A., 'Improvement on the Grant estates in Strathspey in the later eighteenth century: theory, practice, and failure?', in R. W. Hoyle, *Custom, Improvement and thre Landscape in Early Modern Britain* (Farnham, 2011)

Slade, H. Gordon, 'Rothiemay: an 18th century kiln barn', in *Vernacular Building*, no. 4, (1978)

Smith, J. S., 'Deserted farms and shealings in the Braemar area of Deeside', in *Proceedings of the Society of Antiquaries of Scotland*, no. 116 (1986)

Smout, T. C., 'Goat keeping in the old highland economy', in *Scottish Studies*, no. 9 (1965)

Smout, T. C., 'Highland land-use before 1800', in T. C. Smout (ed.) *Scottish Woodland History* (Dalkeith, 1997)

Smout, T. C., 'The history of the Rothiemurchus woods in the eighteenth century', in *Northern Scotland*, vol. 15 (1995)

Smout, T. C. and Watson, F., 'Exploiting semi-natural woods, 1600–1800', in T. C. Smout (ed.), *Scottish Woodland History* (Dalkeith, 1997)

Smout, T. C., 'The landowner and the planned village in Scotland, 1730–1830', in N. T. Phillipson and R. Mitchison, *Scotland in the Age of Improvement* (Edinburgh, 1970)

Stewart, M., 'Using the woods, 1600–1850', in T. C. Smout (ed.) *People and Woods in Scotland: a history* (Edinburgh, 2003)

Thomson, S., 'Agricultural improvement on the Cromarty estate', in *History Scotland*, vol. 11, no. 2 (March/April, 2011)

Turnock, D., 'The retreat of settlement in the Grampian uplands', in *Northern Scotland*, vol. 4, no. 1–2 (1980)

Walker, B., 'The hanging chimney in Scottish meat preservation', in *Vernacular Building*, no. 9, (1985)

Walton, J., 'Cruck-framed buildings in Scotland', in *Gwerin*, vol. 1 (1956–57)

Warde, P., 'The idea of improvement, *c.* 1520–1700', in R. W. Hoyle (ed.) *Custom, Improvement and the Landscape in Early Modern Britain* (Farnham, 2011)

Whatley, C., 'How tame were the Scottish lowlanders during the eighteenth century?', in T. Devine, *Conflict and Stability in Scottish Society, 1700–1850* (Edinburgh, 1990)

'The whin mill', in *Aberdeen Journal Notes and Queries*, vol. VI, no. 261 (Aberdeen, 18 April 1913)

Whitaker, I., 'Two Hebridean corn-kilns', in *Gwerin*, vol. I (1956–57)

Whittington, G., 'Was there a Scottish agricultural revolution?', in *Area*, vol. VII (1975)

Whyte, I., 'Agriculture in Aberdeenshire in the seventeenth and early eighteenth centuries', in D. Stevenson, *From Lairds to Louns* (Aberdeen, 1986)

Whyte, I., 'Rural transformation and lowland society', in A. Cooke (and others) *Modern Scottish History, 1707 to the present* (Dundee, 1998)

Whyte, I. D., 'Rural housing in lowland Scotland in the seventeenth century', in *Scottish Studies*, vol. 19 (1975)

Whyte, I. D., 'Written leases and their impact on Scottish agriculture in the 17th century', in *Agricultural History Review*, vol. 27, part 1 (1979)

Withrington, D., 'The 18th and 19th centuries', in D. Omand (ed.) *The Moray Book* (Edinburgh, 1976)

Woolmer, H., 'Grantown-on-Spey: an eighteenth-century new town', in *Town Planning Review*, vol. 41, no 3 (July 1970)

INDEX